Architectural Drawing and Design

Principles and Practices

Joseph D. Falcone, A.I.A.

Prentice Hall, Englewood Cliffs, NJ 07632

Library of Congress Cataloging-in-Publication Data

Falcone, Joseph D.
    Architectural drawing and design : principles and practices /
  Joseph D. Falcone.
        p.   cm.
    ISBN 0-13-044132-5
    1. Architectural drawing. 2. Architectural design.   I. Title.
  NA2700.F25 1989
  720'.28'4--dc20   89-16240
                                                         CIP

Editorial/production supervision
  and interior design: **Kathryn Pavelec**
Cover design: **20/20 Services, Inc.**
Manufacturing buyer: **David Dickey**

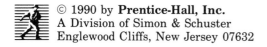 © 1990 by **Prentice-Hall, Inc.**
A Division of Simon & Schuster
Englewood Cliffs, New Jersey 07632

Note: The material in this book may be subject to local
codes and regulations. Check with local building
officials when planning your project.

Printed in the United States of America

10 9 8 7 6 5 4 3 2 1

ISBN   0-13-044132-5

Prentice-Hall International (UK) Limited, *London*
Prentice-Hall of Australia Pty. Limited, *Sydney*
Prentice-Hall Canada Inc., *Toronto*
Prentice-Hall Hispanoamericana, S.A., *Mexico*
Prentice-Hall of India Private Limited, *New Delhi*
Prentice-Hall of Japan, Inc., *Tokyo*
Simon & Schuster Asia Pte. Ltd., *Singapore*
Editora Prentice-Hall do Brasil, Ltda., *Rio de Janeiro*

*This book is dedicated to my daughter Nancy
for her relentless hours of labor,
and without whom this book would not be possible.*

Contents

3 Linework   48

4 Lettering   60

5 Freehand Drawing   83

6 Perspective Drawing   94

7 Residential Plan Development   106

8 Mechanical System   143

9 Construction Details   173

10   Nonresidential Building   264

Preface

Drafting is a means of communication between the designer, draftsperson, or architect, and the builder or contractor. It is a graphic language consisting of lines, symbols, and dimensions. If there is any doubt about the intent of the drawing then the line of communication has been broken and confusion, misunderstanding, and chaos will result.

This book was written for the student of drafting who has little or no experience. It was written for the purpose of teaching drafting students the language of drafting and building and, like all books written on this subject, cannot be complete because of the complex and vast amount of material and study required on this (or any) subject.

It was written to introduce the student to the technique of drafting, and to encourage further study in more advanced books or construction techniques.

This book is written in sequential order, first giving an overview of the construction industry. Chapter 1 describes the many jobs available to the student in addition to, or instead of, a drafting career.

Chapter 2 introduces the student to the tools and equipment required in drafting. Many illustrations show the proper use of these tools and equipment.

Once the student becomes familiar with the tools and how to use them, drafting instruction begins with exercises in line work and the different meanings of lines.

One subject which most students find boring is the technique of lettering. This book eliminates the drudgery and monotony, and encourages the student to learn the different styles of lettering. In order to improve communication skills in drafting an entire chapter is devoted to free-hand drawing, from the simplest figures to the most complex, for those students who wish to broaden their horizon.

The third dimension of perspective drawing begins with its terminology, taking the student each step of the way (including shade and shadow).

Once the basics of different kinds of drawings are learned an entire chapter is devoted to a simple residential plan development, enabling the student to use the lessons learned in previous chapters.

An education in drawing would be incomplete without the student becoming familiar with the mechanical system of a building. Chapter 8 teaches the student an overview of plumbing, heating, electrical systems, and ventilation and air conditioning of a building.

Chapter 9, Construction Details, is the most intensive and longest chapter in the book, and advances the student beyond basic drawing knowledge.

Because residential drawing is but a small part of the vast knowledge required in drafting, advanced study in commercial buildings is offered in a technique that is easy to understand and apply.

Chapter 11 is devoted to the writing and meaning of specifications, without which no building is complete.

For the advanced student who wishes a wider means of communication in the field of construction, Chapter 12, on model building, is offered in easy-to-understand language and examples.

This book is not intended for the student to read it and immediately become proficient in drafting; only time and practice will achieve that goal. This book *is* intended to introduce the fundamental techniques of drafting to the student and to enable the student to seek further study knowledgeably. The amount learned or gained from this book can correspond only to the effort, time, and study put into it.

JOSEPH D. FALCONE, A.I.A.

1

The Construction Industry

Introduction

By providing houses for people, the construction industry contributes to human security, comfort, and relaxation. There are many jobs in construction that are open to beginners, ranging from laborer to company owner. The financial rewards are satisfying, and the sense of creativity and accomplishment is not equaled in any other job. The construction worker can choose either inside or outside work, and the opportunity of constantly moving about provides an ongoing, built-in physical exercise routine.

Construction workers are offered the opportunity to work with many people and learn to get along with co-workers. Not only does the industry offer a chance for gainful employment, but it also provides the opportunity and "know-how" to perform the many jobs required around the construction worker's own home. With this background, construction workers can perform small jobs for other people, thus obtaining additional income. As long as there are people there will be a need for construction workers.

Overview of Timber

The sixteenth-century Spanish explorers Ponce de León and de Soto were the first non-natives to penetrate the forests of North America. Little did they realize the great value and future economic importance of the vast areas of virgin timber. From early colonial days, the history of the United States has been closely associated with our forest wealth. To some pioneers, the forest was an enemy, to be fought and conquered to make room for the planting of crops. To all, it offered a fine, versatile building material with which to build homes, forts, stockades, boats, and ships.

The development of the English colonies in the seventeenth century marked the beginning of the commercial use of timber. There is on record a sawmill at Jamestown, Virginia, as early as 1625, believed to be the first commercial sawmill in the United States. Early mills were powered by water and often doubled as gristmills. Such a mill was operated by George Washington at his Mount Vernon estate. The sawmill soon became an essential factor in almost every colony, supplying the colony's lumber requirements and often providing a surplus for export.

In 1803, in New Orleans, a man built a new type of mill. This new mill had a circular saw and was operated by steam power. The rapid increase in the population of the country toward the end of the nineteenth century resulted in a tremendous demand for construction lumber. The pioneers quickly learned of the unusual strength and versatility of wood, and as the century developed, numerous buildings, many of which are still standing today and some of which are historically famous, were constructed of wood.

Not long ago, many people believed that the lumber industry could not continue without eventually exhausting the forests. But lumber persons, in cooperation with federal and state forestry agencies, have adopted forestry practices involving fire prevention and control, selective logging, and reforestation. More and more manufacturers of lumber are placing their operations on a sustained-yield basis, which means planting a tree for every one cut. Such a practice will make the forest industry permanent.

Woodworking

The facets of woodworking and construction are vast and varied, providing an opportunity for many types of jobs. In addition, woodworking is one of the most popular leisure-time activities in the United States. Millions of people earn their living by working in some facet of a wood-related industry. There are unlimited opportunities for skilled, semiskilled, limited-skilled, and unskilled woodworking trade occupations. In addition, there are many other jobs related to or associated directly with the industry.

Unskilled and limited-skilled people begin as helpers in the industry and progress to higher-paying jobs as their skill increases. This is usually done through on-the-job training. Most employers prefer their workers to have at least a high school education. Those who wish to enter the industry without a high school education can attend classes in the evening while working during the day.

Generally, a limited-skilled worker or helper will go through several steps to become a master craftsperson or skilled worker. Aside from on-the-job training, a good source of training is education in a public or private trade, vocational, or technical school, with concentration in a particular work area. The major subjects needed for advancement are: reading of plans, mathematics (including shop math and geometry), and English.

The order of advancement begins with the helper or apprentice, advances to the semiskilled, and ends at the master craftsperson or skilled level. The time required to advance depends on the individual, but generally it will take about three years to reach a craftsperson level of proficiency (Figs. 1–1 and 1–2).

No. _____

APPLICATION FOR APPRENTICESHIP IN CARPENTRY

Desiring to become an apprentice in the Carpentry Trade, I hereby make application for an Apprenticeship to the

_____ Date _____
        (Indenturing Agent)

Name (Please Print) _____ _____ _____
                (Last Name)   (First Name)   (Middle Name)

Address _____ City _____ Soc. Sec. No. _____

Phone _____

Date of Birth _____ Age last Birthday _____
           (Month)   (Day)   (Year)

Height _____ Weight _____

Grade completed in school _____ Date _____ Married ( )   Single ( )
                                   (Year)

General physical condition _____

Note any physical handicaps _____

_____

Father or Guardian's Name _____

Address _____

His occupation _____

Were you in the Armed Forces _____ How Long? _____

Have you ever worked at the Carpentry Trade? _____ If so, what type of construction? _____

_____

Do you understand that you will be on _____ days trial, if your application is approved? _____

Are you willing to work for the established wage scale for Carpenter Apprentices throughtout your indenture-

ship? _____

Have you read and do you understand the Apprenticeship Standards?_____

Will you obey all rules and instructions of the Apprentice Committee? _____

Are you willing to serve an apprenticeship of four years? _____

Will you place yourself under the jurisdiction of the Apprentice Committee? _____

Do you understand that it is compulsory for you to attend the apprentice school during the hours designated

by the apprentice committee, and that you will be accountable to the school during that time? _____

REFERENCE OTHER THAN RELATIVES

I have known _____ for two years or more,
and certify that he is of good character and habits.

Personal Signatures of Vouchers

Name	Address	Business
_____	_____	_____
_____	_____	_____
_____	_____	_____

FIGURE 1–1 *Application for apprenticeship in carpentry (courtesy Carpenters' District Council).*

ADDITIONAL INFORMATION CONCERNING YOUR FITNESS FOR AN APPRENTICESHIP _____

_____

_____

_____

_____

CASE HISTORY

_____

_____

_____

_____

_____

RECOMMENDATIONS OF APPRENTICESHIP COMMITTEE

On Probation Period, From_____ To_____

Qualifying Examination given_____, 19_____. Grade_____.
                                    (date)

We have investigated the qualifications of this applicant and recommend:

                                                        Date_____

Approved for apprenticeship_____Place on waiting list_____

Not approved for apprenticeship_____

Remarks: _____

_____

| | Trade Experience Period and Wage Rate | | |
	Period	Rate	Starting Date
	1st 6 months	_____	_____
	2nd 6 months	_____	_____
_____	3rd 6 months	_____	_____
_____	4th 6 months	_____	_____
_____	5th 6 months	_____	_____
_____	6th 6 months	_____	_____
	7th 6 months	_____	_____
	8th 6 months	_____	_____

FIGURE 1-1   (cont'd)

RATING FORM FOR APPRENTICESHIP ENTRY
RECOMMENDED BY
NATIONAL JOINT CARPENTRY APPRENTICESHIP AND
TRAINING COMMITTEE

_____ Joint Apprentice Committee

Name _____ Social Security No. _____

Address _____ Phone No. _____

City _____ State _____ Zip _____

	Yes	No
1. Minimal age requirement reflective of local standards and state statutes_____	_____	_____
2. Minimal formal education requirement reflective of local standards_____	_____	_____
3. A score of 70% correct response on the "Qualifying Test for Apprenticeship and Trainee Applicant" _____	_____	_____
4. Physical qualifications, reflective of local standards and/or state statutes_____	_____	_____

NOTE: All of the above criteria must be answered in the affirmative for an applicant to be accepted into training.

Applicant has validated experience as follows: *Points*

1. Carpentry craft experience, civilian or military, _____ years, 5 points per year, 3 year maximum__ _____

2. Construction work experience (non-Carpentry), 2 points per year, 3 year maximum_____ _____

3. Approved pre-apprenticeship experience, 5 points °_____ _____

4. Approved vocational-education experience, 5 points °°_____ _____

5. Work experience (non-construction), 1 point per year, 3 year maximum_____ _____

6. Experience in the regular military establishment, with honorable discharge, 2 points per year, 3 year maximum_____ _____

                                                                                   Total_____ _____

FIGURE 1–2 *Rating form for apprenticeship (courtesy Carpenters' District Council).*

Optional personal interview may be given with point credit from 0 - 4 points.

Four (4) points are the maximum number of points allowed for the personal interview. Each of the criteria is valenced at five-tenths (½) of a point value.

The interview should be conducted to draw from the applicant evidence of:

Points

1. Interest in the carpentry craft, .5 maximum_____ _____

2. Positive attitude towards physical labor, .5 maximum_____ _____

3. Ability to accept direction/supervision, .5 maximum_____ _____

4. Ability to work with others, .5 maximum_____ _____

5. Knowledge of the trade, .5 maximum_____ _____

6. Positive attitude towards related instruction, .5 maximum _____ _____

7. Understanding of the obligations of an apprenticeship, .5 maximum_____ _____

8. Maturation, .5 maximum_____ _____

Total_____ _____

Total from page one_____ _____

Grand Total_____ _____

---

*Approved pre-apprenticeship experiences are those structured and implemented by member organizations of the National Joint Carpentry Apprenticeship and Training Committee such as, but not limited to, Project Transition and Job Corps.

**Approved vocational-education experiences are those institutionalized vocational carpentry programs utilizing the local joint carpentry apprenticeship and training committee as the technical committee advisory to the program.

FIGURE 1–2   (cont'd)

Carpentry

The craft or skill of shaping, cutting, fitting, and assembling wood is called carpentry and is performed by a carpenter. The carpenter is the backbone of the construction industry, and the position is considered one of importance and prominence. The carpenter is involved in most of the construction of a building. He or she builds foundation forms, floors, walls, ceilings, roofs, and interior finishes. He or she knows how different woods will react and what tool to use for a specific job. The carpenter must know the various construction techniques and must be able to read and interpret plans. There are many levels of carpenter, from carpenter's helper to skilled carpenter.

Job Satisfaction

People in construction must be all-around workers with many skills and a thorough knowledge of building construction. They are important craftspeople on the construction team. The income earned by construction workers is above average and provides a good living. The satisfaction and pride that results in good craftsmanship is an experience that is not enjoyed in many other occupations. The successful worker must have the ability to cooperate and get along with other workers, and to show courtesy, respect, loyalty, and honesty.

Gross National Product

The goods and services required in the field of construction are greater in number and variety than in any other occupation. More people are employed directly in the construction industry or related fields than in any other field of employment. Generally, there is no season of employment; construction workers are needed at all times of the year. Job selection in the construction field is almost unlimited. Construction has become more than a job requiring working with tools. It cannot be defined that simply; it would take many books to describe all construction-related jobs. For those who have the abilities or are willing to learn, the field of construction is one of enormous opportunity.

Labor Unions

A *closed-shop* company is one in which the workers are represented by a labor union. An *open-shop* firm is nonunion. In a closed-shop company, all workers must be members of the same union. All members must pay union dues, which are generally deducted from wages. These dues are used for administration costs and to pay benefits to union members. Closed-shop companies must pay the workers a wage arbitrated with the union. Open-shop companies pay their workers at rates agreeable to both workers and owners, with or without benefits.

Equipment

Construction companies supply their workers with material and special tools or heavy equipment, but each worker must have personal general-purpose hand tools.

Careers

Following are some of the positions available in the construction industry.

Apprentice

This is the beginning of all trades. The construction industry is in the forefront in apprentice activities. Apprentices, who are paid while learning their trade, start producing almost immediately, and each job they do is carefully supervised and inspected. The quality of their work is tested as they advance from one stage of training to another. In addition, the care with which applicants are selected, and the entrance tests required, assure, to a large extent, that the apprentice will make a good craftsperson. In 1937, Congress passed the National Apprenticeship Law, better known as the Fitzgerald Act, "to promote the furtherance of labor standards of apprenticeship. . . ." As a result of this act, the Bureau of Apprenticeship and Training was established as the national administrative agency in the Labor Department to carry out the law's objectives. Employers and vocational schools have set up and conducted apprenticeship programs throughout the country.

Following are the basic standards of apprenticeship:

1. To provide the most efficient way to train craftspeople to meet present and future needs.
2. To assure an adequate supply of skilled tradespeople in relation to employment opportunities.
3. To assure the community of a supply of competent craftspeople, skilled in all branches of their trades.
4. To assure the consuming public of the high-quaity products and services that only trained hands and minds can produce.
5. To increase the individual worker's productivity.
6. To give the individual worker a greater sense of security.
7. To improve employer–employee relations.
8. To eliminate close supervision; craftspeople are trained to use initiative, imagination, and ability in planning and performing their work.
9. To provide a source of future supervisors.
10. To provide the versatility to meet changing conditions.
11. To attract capable young people into the industry.
12. To raise general skill levels in the industry.

For the young worker entering employment, apprenticeship holds these important values:

- The opportunity to develop skills, creating greater economic security and a higher standard of living.
- Further training and education, with pay.
- Assurance of a wage, with regular increases, while serving the apprenticeship.
- Opportunities for employment and advancement.
- Recognition as a skilled craftsperson in a chosen trade.

Rough Carpenter

The work of a rough carpenter is generally restricted to the wood framework of a building, which includes foundation forms, floor framing, wall framing, ceiling framing, and roof framing. The rough carpenter must learn the skill required to joint the component parts of a frame building together to form a tight fit. Being a rough carpenter does not mean doing work that is a rough fit or that is less than acceptable. Careful cutting of each member is vital to the safety of the building because each member depends on the other in framing a building, and all work must be joined together properly. If the fitting or joining is not done properly, the building may suffer or fail in one or more areas. The rough carpenter works mostly outdoors (Fig. 1–3).

FIGURE 1–3   *Rough carpentry (courtesy National Forest Products Association).*

Finish Carpenter

Once the rough carpenter has completed the framework of the building, the finish carpenter is required to install the finish work, such as doors, siding, windows, and floors. This phase of industry is extremely important because the joints must be tight and carefully assembled. No hammer marks are tolerated on the finish wood. This job requires a little more skill than that of the rough carpenter.

Carpenter-in-Charge

When carpenters become good at their jobs, they can be promoted to the position of carpenter-in-charge. The carpenter-in-charge, who may have several carpenters working for him or her, is responsible for progress, scheduling, and quality of the work and for all people working under his or her supervision. The carpenter-in-charge may or may not have the responsibility for any mistakes made by carpenters working under him or her.

Superintendent

The superintendent occupies a position of responsibility second only to that of the owner. The superintendent is responsible for the entire project, including all workers, even the carpenter-in-charge. Generally, the superintendent does not work with tools, but acts as an administrator and may be responsible for more than one project at a time. The superintendent will assign projects to the carpenter-in-charge, maintain close supervision over all workers, and be responsible for the entire project. Part of the job is to make sure that material is available when needed, to avoid delays in the progress of the building. As a rule, the superintendent will have the responsibility to hire and fire.

Cabinetmaker

Of all the wood-related jobs, that of cabinetmaker requires the greatest amount of skill. Cabinetmakers construct and build furniture, cabinets, office equipment, and so on, using electric and hand tools. Generally, they work from a set of design drawings made by architects. The cabinetmaker must be skilled in being able to identify different wood species, often choosing wood for color, matching of grain, texture, and general appearance of the finished product. The cabinetmaker-in-charge is responsible for the finished product.

Patternmaker

The job of the patternmaker, building models of machinery and other objects from wood to be used for production into metal, requires great skill. The skill required in reading plans is high because of the complicated product being worked on. Patternmakers must not only be skilled in woodworking, but must have knowledge of metals and alloys which will be made into molds from the wooden pattern. The model being worked on must account for the expansion and contraction of metals and must allow for how the various parts of the wooden model will be cast from metal by the foundry. An exact pattern or model must be made from wood before any casting is done.

Millworker

Basically, a millworker is a "jack of all trades" and may be called on to repair furniture; set up furniture; do general maintenance; work with wood, metals, paints, and stains; install hardware; and even repair electrical work, plumbing, or roofing leaks.

Millwright

The person who keeps machinery in working order and sharpens knives, blades, and other cutting tools is called a millwright. Millwrights must have a thorough knowledge of the various machines used in the woodworking industry. Some mathematics is required to work with the angles and pitches of various cutting tools. The work must be accurate and exact.

Modelmaker

Similar to the patternmaker, the modelmaker builds models of automobiles, airplanes, buildings, and furniture and of scenes and settings used in stage plays, moviemaking, and television. Modelmakers must be highly skilled at their trade and have a thorough knowledge of the woodworking trade. They may build scaled-down or full-size models.

Forester

There are a variety of jobs related to the forest industry, including the following:

> *Lumberjacks:* cut the tops off tall trees
> *Faller:* cuts down the trees (Fig. 1–4)
> *Swamper or limber:* trims off the branches of trees
> *Log bucker:* cuts the trees into standard lengths
> *Equipment operator:* operates various pieces of motorized equipment in forest or mill
> *Scaler:* measures logs to determine the number of board feet
> *Grader:* selects the quality of lumber after milling
> *Cruiser:* selects trees for cutting (Fig. 1–5)
> *Research scientist:* studies tree growth characteristics (Fig. 1–6)
> *Tree farmer:* grows trees for profit (Fig. 1–7)

FIGURE 1–4 Tree fallers (courtesy National Forest Products Association).

FIGURE 1–5 Tree cruiser (courtesy National Forest Products Association).

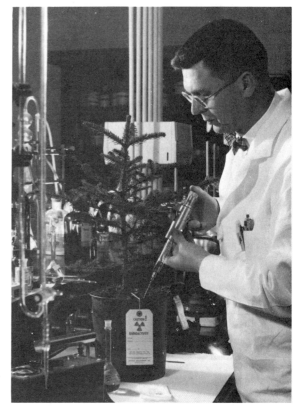

FIGURE 1–6 Research (courtesy American Forest Council).

(a)

(b)

FIGURE 1-7 Tree farming [(a) and (b) courtesy American Forest Council].

Professional and Semiprofessional Personnel

There are many people who may not work with wood but who are associated with the wood industry. Some are employed in creative activities, designing but not producing wood products. Others sell, manage, own, teach, or do research in the wood industry.

QUESTIONS

1-1. What type of training is used to teach unskilled people? _____
_____

1-2. **(a)** What is a closed shop? _____
_____

   (b) What is an open shop? _____
_____

1-3. Most construction workers are union workers.
True or False

1-4. "Rough" carpentry means which of the following?
   (a) Measurements need not be exact
   (b) Building framework
   (c) Semiskilled worker

1-5. "Finish carpentry" means which of the following?
   (a) Fired carpenter
   (b) Doors, windows, trim
   (c) Formwork

1-6. A patternmaker makes clothes.
True or False

1-7. Define *millworker*. _____

1-8. Construction companies supply workers with all necessary tools.
True or False

1-9. Name two jobs related to forestry.
   1. _____
   2. _____

1-10. A superintendent can hire and fire.
True or False

2

Tools and Equipment

Introduction

To the beginning drafter, selecting the proper tools and equipment can be confusing and bewildering. Many models and quality of tools and equipment are available. The easiest way to decide what to purchase is to make a list of the tools and equipment required and purchase from a reputable dealer the best quality affordable (Fig. 2–1). The feel of any tools may seem awkward at first,

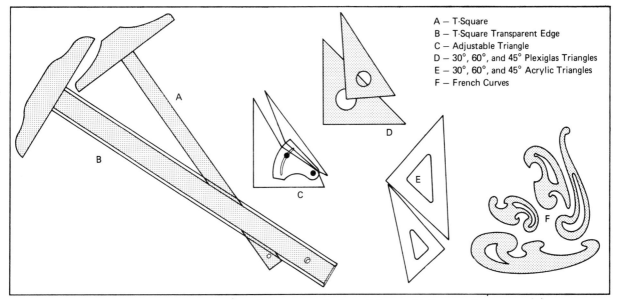

A — T-Square
B — T-Square Transparent Edge
C — Adjustable Triangle
D — 30°, 60°, and 45° Plexiglas Triangles
E — 30°, 60°, and 45° Acrylic Triangles
F — French Curves

FIGURE 2–1   *(Adapted from Fidelity Products Co.)*

but with time, patience, and practice, skill, accuracy, and ease will be achieved. With proper care, tools should serve for many years.

Even with limited artistic ability, serious, dedicated students can produce close to professional-quality drawings from the start. Tools are designed to help the drafter produce good-quality drawing with a minimum of time and effort. Only through practice will skill be developed.

Basic Drafting Equipment

Drafting Board

There are many sizes and types of drafting boards from 12 × 17 in. to 31 × 42 in. The most popular for a beginning student is the 20 × 26 in. drafting board. Most drafting boards are manufactured from basswood or clear white pine, which is light in weight and strong. The edge of the board should be protected from damage because this is the working edge of the board or the edge where the T-square is used. There are no distinctions in drafting boards for left- or right-handed drafters. Right-handed people use the left edge of the board and left-handed people use the right-hand edge in using the T-square. That is called the working edge because the T-square head slides against it. Some drafting boards have metal edges for more accuracy in drawing and smoothness in sliding the T-square. The metal edges are permanent true edges.

An economy lightweight drafting board is also made from hardboard or pressed wood fiber. Thumbtacks should not be used on these boards for holding paper because thumbtacks will punch holes in the drafting board, which will affect line quality when the pencil is drawn over the thumbtack hole. Drafting tape should be used. Unlike drafting tables, drafting boards are portable (Fig. 2–2). This makes it possible to carry a drafting board to class and to do field-work and study.

(a)

FIGURE 2–2(a)   Portable drafting board (courtesy Charrette Corporation).

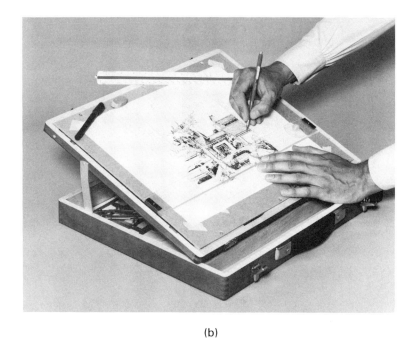

(b)

FIGURE 2–2(b)   Portable drafting machine (courtesy Olson Manufacturing and Distribution, Inc.).

Drafting Table

The difference between a drafting table and a drafting board is mostly in size. A drafting table has a base, can be tilted to an angle, and cannot be carried around (Fig. 2–3). Tables are usually 30 in. wide in lengths up to 6 ft. The base is wood or metal. Most drafting tables have one or a combination of drawers for storing drawings flat and for storing tools and supplies. A very economical drafting table is a flush hollow-core door supported by two wooden sawhorses.

(a)

(b)

FIGURE 2–3   Drafting tables [(a) and (b) courtesy Fidelity Products Co.]

(c)

(d)

(e)

FIGURE 2–3 *Drafting tables [(c) courtesy Charrette Corporation; (d) and (e) courtesy Hamilton Industries Inc.].*

Covering and Surface

The wooden surface on a drafting board or table is generally not used for drafting unless it has a cover. Wooden tops may be accidentally damaged, the joining of the wood may open up, and a hard pencil will sometimes leave a groove in the board. Such circumstances will affect lines drawn on paper. To prevent this from happening, a cover is placed over the board or table. A cover is typically a vinyl laminate, for a smooth drafting surface (Fig. 2–4). It is nonglare with a restful green color on one side and soft ivory on the other. The surface will not chip, crack, or peel and will wipe clean with a damp cloth. It will "recover" from pinholes, compass punctures, and minor razor cuts. The cover is held to the surface by double-sided tape. Another type of covering is a heavy green-surfaced paper laminated with strong acetate film for a smooth, easy-to-clean finish.

FIGURE 2–4 Post board covering (courtesy Teledyne Post).

Drafting Stool

Body comfort is an important part of successful drafting. Chairs and stools vary in quality, cost, and comfort, ranging from upholstered posture stools to swivel stools to stationary steel stools (Fig. 2–5). The posture stool has a forward tilt support, back protective bumpers, a fingertip-control seat height adjustment, and a footrest. All stools can be had with or without casters. The less expensive stools are made of wood or steel with a heavy Masonite seat panel and are stationary with no back support.

(a)   (b)   (c)   (d)

FIGURE 2–5 Drafting stools [(a) and (b) courtesy Charrette Corporation].

T-Square

Horizontal lines are drawn with a T-square, so called because it is shaped like the letter "T." T-squares are manufactured from wood, metal, plastic, or a combination of these materials (Fig. 2–6). The length of a T-square varies from

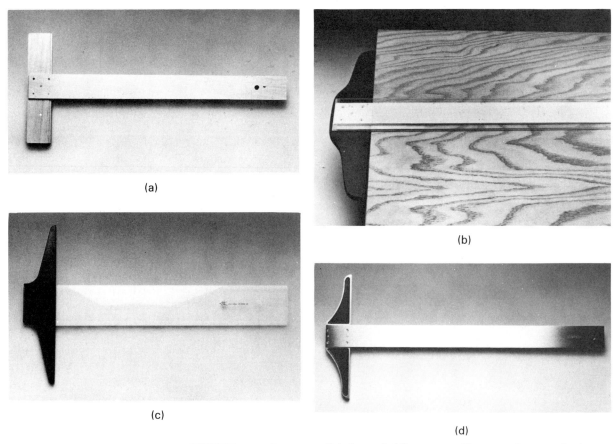

(a)

(b)

(c)

(d)

FIGURE 2–6 *T-squares [(a) through (d) courtesy Charrette Corporation].*

12 to 60 in. The short leg of a T-square, called the *head*, is grasped to slide the T-square along the drawing board or table edge. The long leg, called the *blade*, has a plastic edge used for drawing straight, horizontal lines. The plastic transparent edge along the blade is to enable the drafter to see the lines of the drawing, to line up the drawing, and to line up or position the T-square before drawing lines.

The T-square is held with the left hand while it is being drawn along the blade edge with the right hand. The hands are reversed for left-handed people. The T-square is also used as a guiding edge for the triangle used for drawing vertical lines. Some T-squares have an adjustable head for drawing lines at an angle (Fig. 2–7).

Care must be exercised in use and storage of the T-square. If nicks develop in the edge of the blade, it will affect the quality of lines. The blade is glued and screwed to the head of the T-square. If it becomes loose by dropping the T-square or applying undue pressure on the blade, the quality of lines will be adversely affected.

While drawing a line along the top edge of a T-square, pressure or holding power should remain constant while the pencil is drawn along the top edge.

FIGURE 2–7 *Adjustable T-square (James H. Earle,* Drafting Technology, *© 1982, Addison-Wesley Publishing Co., Inc., Reading, Massachusetts. Fig. on page 12. Reprinted with permission.).*

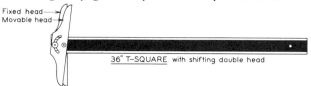

Fixed head
Movable head

36" T–SQUARE with shifting double head

The edge of the T-square must be straight and true. This can be checked by drawing a line full length on top of the T-square. When the T-square is turned upside down, the line should be in alignment with the other edge of the blade. If it is not, the T-square is bowed and should not be used.

A right-handed drafter should hold the head of the T-square firmly against the left edge of the board with the left hand. A left-handed drafter should reverse the T-square and hold it firmly on the right side of the board with the right hand. To draw a horizontal line, the right-handed drafter should position the T-square with the left hand on the T-square and then slide the left hand over on the top surface of the blade and hold with a slight pressure so that the T-square will not move until the line is drawn. It is best to keep the pencil point against the top edge of the blade and lean it slightly in the direction the line is being drawn. The pencil should maintain the same slope and pressure in relation to the T-square throughout the entire length of the line. By slightly changing the angle of the pencil against the blade edge, several parallel lines can be drawn along the blade of a T-square without moving the T-square.

Do not use the T-square to drive tacks into a drafting board or for any rough purpose. Never cut paper along the working edge or blade because the plastic edge is easily cut and even a slight nick will destroy the T-square.

Parallel Rule

Sometimes a parallel rule is called a parallel bar. It is used in place of a T-square and is fastened to the drawing board. The parallel rule slides up and down the drafting board on cables attached to the board (Fig. 2–8). Its use is similar to that of a T-square for drawing horizontal lines, and in conjunction with triangles, it is used for drawing vertical lines. The greatest advantage of the parallel rule is accuracy in drawing long lines. The T-square becomes unsteady when drawing long lines and considerable inaccuracy may result from the give or swing of the blade.

FIGURE 2–8 *Parallel rules (courtesy Charrette Corporation).*

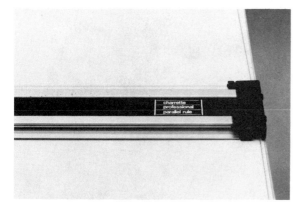
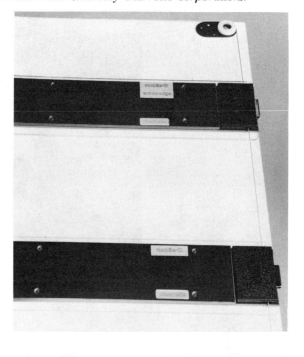

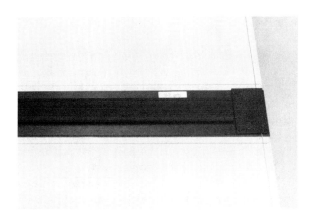

FIGURE 2-8 *(cont'd)*

The parallel rule can be mounted to a drawing board or drafting table. It is available in many lengths, including 42, 48, 54, 60, 72, 84, and 96 in. Hardwood or hard plastic parallel rules with edges of clear plastic are considered best. Some have small roller bearings underneath to prevent the rule from sliding directly onto the paper. On long drafting tables, the parallel rule should not be the full table length. Some space must be reserved for reference material and equipment.

Drafting Machine

Another useful tool for drafting is the drafting machine (Fig. 2-9). This machine is used in place of a T-square or parallel rule. It is attached to the drafting table. A drafting machine eliminates the need for triangles and scales because it has two arms which rotate at any desired angle. The two plastic arms have a scale of choice and are interchangeable. Horizontal and vertical lines are drawn with the arms, which eliminates the need for triangles and a T-square. Any desired angle is achieved with the arms by the central control button. These adjustments will also eliminate the need for a protractor.

FIGURE 2-9 *Drafting machines [(a) courtesy Vemco Corp.].*

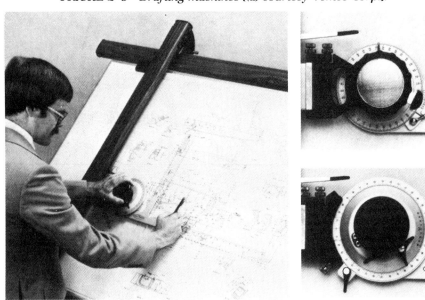

(a)

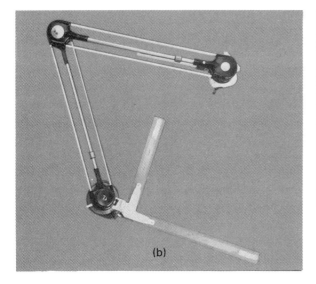

(b)

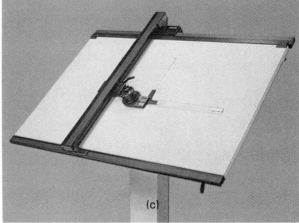

(c)

FIGURE 2–9   Drafting machines [(b) and (c) courtesy Mutoh America, Inc.].

The drafting machine, then, will replace triangles, T-square, protractor, and scale all in one tool. The control head is graduated in degrees, which allows the straight edges or scales to be set and locked at any angle desired. There are automatic stops at the angles used most frequently, such as 15, 30, 45, 60, 75, and 90°.

The advantage of the drafting machine is speed in drawing and a cleaner drawing. The control head is graduated in degrees with a vernier to set the desired angle. The horizontal scale or blade performs the function of a T-square, and the vertical blade or scale performs the function of a triangle. The head is rotated so that either scale or blade can be used to draw lines at any angle. By depressing the head, the machine will rotate into any desired position; releasing the head will lock the machine in place.

Pencils

All drawing begins with a pencil. The selection of pencils must be based on comfort and convenience. Pencils may be of wood or of the mechanical type.

Wood Pencils

Drafters seldom use wooden pencils (Fig. 2–10) because they waste valuable time in sharpening, waste lead, and may be uncomfortable to use when they get short, although there is a wooden pencil extension, called a pencil holder, that may be used when a pencil gets too short as a result of sharpening. Sharpening a wooden pencil requires a knife or some type of wooden pencil sharpener to cut the wood. Once the lead of a wooden pencil is exposed, it is pointed with one of several types of lead pointers.

Wooden pencils are hexagonal so that they will not roll off a drafting board or table. In sharpening a wooden pencil, remove the wood opposite the lead-grade symbol end with a razor knife, penknife, or drafter's pencil sharpener.

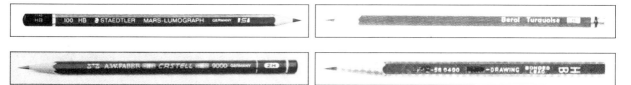

FIGURE 2–10 Drawing pencils (courtesy B.L. Makepeace, Inc.).

Mechanical Pencils

A pencil that requires a separate lead is called a mechanical pencil. The lead is manually inserted into the pencil and held in place by spring clamp jaws. Pressing the end of the pencil will release the jaws to advance the lead about ¼ in. for sharpening (Fig. 2–11). Mechanical pencils are made of plastic or metal.

FIGURE 2–11 Lead holders (courtesy Saga, Division of DADE, Inc.).

Automatic Pencils

The only difference between a mechanical pencil and an automatic pencil is in the diameter of the lead. Lead for the automatic pencil is thin and does not require sharpening. This is a great timesaver and prevents the spread of graphite dust, which will produce a cleaner drawing. The lead for a mechanical pencil is larger in diameter and requires frequent sharpening to produce clear, clean, sharp lines (Fig. 2–12).

FIGURE 2–12 Fine line pencils (courtesy Saga, Division of DADE Inc.).

Leads and Grades

All pencils and leads for drafting are rated as soft, medium, and hard by a number and a letter as follows (Fig. 2–13):

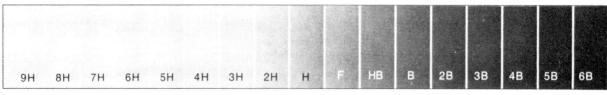

| 9H | 8H | 7H | 6H | 5H | 4H | 3H | 2H | H | F | HB | B | 2B | 3B | 4B | 5B | 6B |

FIGURE 2–13 Lead grades (courtesy Charrette Corporation).

Soft	Medium	Hard
2B	3H	4H
3B	2H	5H
4B	H	6H
5B	F	7H
6B	HB	8H
7B	B	9H
8B		

The hard leads are smaller in diameter than the soft leads. This is to give the soft leads greater strength against breakage. In the hard group, the higher the number, the harder the lead. In the medium group, B is the softest, with HB, F, and H in order of hardness. 2H is softer than 3H. In the soft group, the higher the number, the softer the lead. The B leads are usually used for free-hand sketching. Several factors will dictate which lead grade to use for drafting. Some leads work best on certain types of drafting media. Mylar film will accept lead more easily, making a darker or blacker line using a hard lead such as 4H or 6H. Rag-content paper may require a softer lead, such as H or 2H. A good overall pencil is 2H, which works well on most drafting media.

Lead has clay as well as graphite in its manufacture, and sometimes the clay causes a dry spot. Such spots will not produce a line and may in fact score the medium. When this happens it is best to resharpen the lead to remove the bad spot.

Pencil grades are not standardized. An F lead in one brand may not be of the same softness as an F in another brand. The best solution is to experiment with various leads to determine which is best for the drafting medium being used. The amount of pressure applied to the lead will also determine which grade is best.

Another type of lead, known as plastic lead, is made from polyester. This lead is best suited for drawing on the plastic medium called Mylar. The grades of these leads are the same as those of graphite leads except that the letter H is substituted for the letter S. Drawing with a plastic lead feels somewhat like drawing with a crayon.

Pencil Sharpeners

There are many types of pencil sharpeners, including manual and electric. All will do an acceptable job; it is mostly a matter of cost and preference.

The rotary lead pointer contains a sandpaper insert. The pencil lead is inserted into the sharpener and the exposed lead is sharpened as it rotates against the sandpaper. The sandpaper insert must be replaced periodically (Fig. 2–14a).

Another rotary-type pencil sharpener has case-hardened tool steel cutting wheels which never need to be replaced. Both types of pointers are designed for use on a desk or drafting table. A small hand-held rotating sharpener or pocket model has steel cutting edges. The lead holder and lead are placed between the thumb and forefinger and rotated (Fig. 2–14b).

A sanding block is the simplest of all lead sharpeners. It consists of small layers of sandpaper stapled on a wood base or handle. When the sandpaper sheet is no longer cutting or sharpening, the sandpaper sheet is simply re-

(a)

FIGURE 2–14a Rotary sharpener (courtesy Teledyne Post).

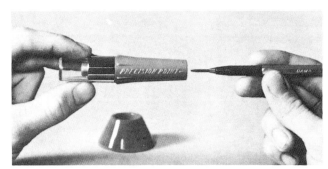

FIGURE 2–14b   Hand-held sharpener (courtesy Teledyne Post).

moved and discarded, exposing a fresh strip of sandpaper (Fig. 2–15). Care should be used when using the sanding block to prevent graphite dust from falling onto the drawing. Sharpening should be done away from the drawing board, preferably over a piece of paper, to collect the graphite for easy disposal.

Hand-crank sharpeners are used for wooden pencils (Fig. 2–16). There is little difference between a drafting model and the regular pencil model except that the drafting model does not sharpen the lead; it only cuts away the wood, exposing the lead for sharpening on a pencil pointer. An electric lead pointer

FIGURE 2–15   Sandpaper pencil pointer (courtesy Charrette Corporation).

FIGURE 2–16   Manual pencil sharpeners (courtesy Teledyne Post).

differs from the mechanical type only in that the device for sharpening is driven by an electric motor. The motors are quiet and maintenance free. Most models have gauges for proper lead extension and will sharpen points to a perfect taper in a matter of seconds (Fig. 2–17).

All pencil pointers except the sanding block have a storage area to collect graphite dust. This area needs to be emptied periodically. Great care must be used in disposing of graphite dust. It should be collected in an envelope and sealed before discarding; otherwise, the graphite dust will spread, making it difficult to remove or clean.

Pencils and leads should be kept sharp at all times. A dull pencil will produce fuzzy, sloppy, indefinite lines. A sharp pencil will produce a clean-cut line with clarity. Never sharpen pencils or leads over drawings or equipment, and after the point is sharpened, it should be wiped clean with paper tissue to remove loose particles of graphite. Keep the pencil sharpener close by for convenience.

FIGURE 2–17   Electric Pencil sharpener (courtesy Teledyne Post).

Pencil Points

A pointed lead should not be needle sharp but rather, should be slightly rounded. After a lead is sharpened, it will have a needle point, but a few rotary motions on a piece of paper will wear the point down slightly to the desired shape.

Three types of lead sharpening are used: *chisel* point, *cone* or wedge point, and *elliptical* point (Fig. 2–18). The chisel point or wedge point and the ellipti-

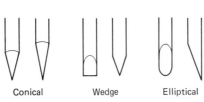

Conical   Wedge   Elliptical

FIGURE 2–18 *Types of drafting points.*

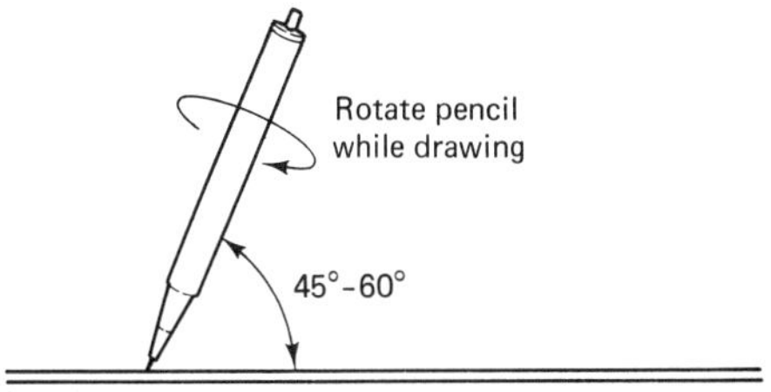

Rotate pencil while drawing

45°–60°

FIGURE 2–19 *Rotating the pencil.*

cal can be sharpened only on a sanding block. The cone point is sharpened with a mechanical pointer. The elliptical point is generally used in a compass, but some drafters use it for all straight lines. The chisel point or wedge point will wear longer than the cone point, but it is time consuming to sharpen the lead frequently.

The conical point should be rotated when drawing to wear the point down evenly; otherwise, the line will be wider on one end than the other (Fig. 2–19). The conical point is preferred by most drafters. Pencils should not be rotated when using a wedge or elliptical point. When sharpening a conical point on a sandpaper block the lead must be rotated as the lead is drawn back and forth across the sandpaper (Fig. 2–20).

If sandpaper is used to sharpen leads, slant it at a low angle to achieve the correct taper

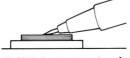

FIGURE 2–20 *Sandpaper sharpening.*

Additional Drafting Equipment

Triangles

The two most commonly used triangles are the 45° triangle and 30°–60° triangles (Fig. 2–21). Both come in a variety of lengths, ranging from 4 in. to 18 in. Most drawings require an 8- or 10-in. triangle. The 30°–60° triangle has three angles: 30°, 60°, and 90°. The 45° triangle has two angles: 45° and 90°.

FIGURE 2–21 *30°–60°, and 45° triangles (courtesy Teledyne Post).*

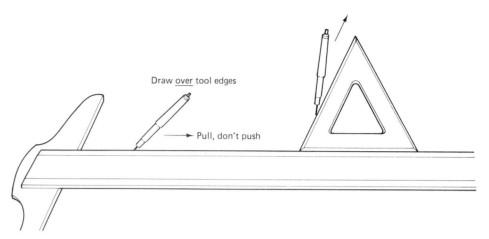

Draw <u>over</u> tool edges

Pull, don't push

FIGURE 2–22 *Triangle T-square use.*

The 45°–45° and 30°–60° triangles can be used
in combination to produce increments of 15°.

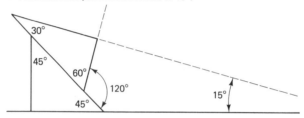

30°

45°

60°

120°

45°

15°

FIGURE 2–23 *Triangle combination use.*

Triangles should be of heavy transparent acrylic plastic about $\frac{1}{16}$ in. thick. The thinner inexpensive triangles are difficult to pick up and they often warp and become useless. The edges of the triangles should be true and accurate without nicks or dents. The edges of the triangles should never be damaged, because if damaged, the lines drawn will not be straight and true.

Triangles also come in tinted fluorescent colors to transmit the light above out through their edges, reducing shadows near the triangle drawing edge. Triangles are used primarily to draw vertical or angled lines, not horizontal lines. Triangles are used in conjunction with a T-square (Fig. 2–22). In addition to 30°, 60°, 45°, and 90° angles, triangles can be used in combination to draw 15° and 75° angles (Fig. 2–23).

The adjustable triangle is convenient for drawing lines other than by standard triangles. It has a protractor scale from 0° to 90° which is adjustable by a thin thumbscrew. The adjustable triangle can take the place of standard triangles (Fig. 2–24). To use a triangle, the base of the triangle should be placed squarely against the T-square blade and held in place with fingertips. Pass the pencil along the edge of the triangle to the line length desired.

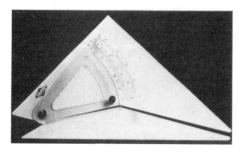

FIGURE 2–24 *Adjustble triangle (courtesy Teledyne Post).*

Triangles are sometimes warped, even when new, so they should be tested. To test triangles for straightness, place the triangle on the T-square and draw a vertical line, then turn the triangle over and draw the line again along the same edge. If the lines are in perfect alignment, the triangles are square. If the lines are not in perfect alignment, the triangles are not square.

Templates

Commonly used drafting symbols cut out of a sheet of plastic called a template are commonly used for plumbing fixtures, door swings, circles, square, door, windows, landscape features, roof pitch, stair design, north arrow, electric symbols, furniture, structural steel, lettering, ellipse, rectangles, and many more. The cutout selected is placed over the drawing and the pencil follows the outline. Templates are available in several scales. The procedure eliminates the need to draw symbols each time they are required, thereby saving a great deal of time (Fig. 2–25).

In using a template, the outline must be drawn with the correct line weight on the first setting. It is difficult, if not almost impossible, to reset the template. It may be easier to erase the symbol and start over. The template must be held down firmly to avoid its slipping out of position. Allowance must be made for the line width in the opening or cutout of the template. Hold the pencil perpendicular to the template cutout for accurate tracing.

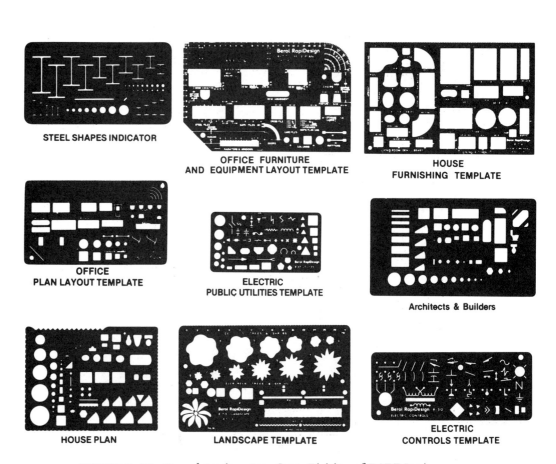

STEEL SHAPES INDICATOR

OFFICE FURNITURE
AND EQUIPMENT LAYOUT TEMPLATE

HOUSE
FURNISHING TEMPLATE

OFFICE
PLAN LAYOUT TEMPLATE

ELECTRIC
PUBLIC UTILITIES TEMPLATE

Architects & Builders

HOUSE PLAN

LANDSCAPE TEMPLATE

ELECTRIC
CONTROLS TEMPLATE

FIGURE 2–25   *Templates (courtesy Saga, Division of DADE Inc.).*

SQUARE FOOTAGE

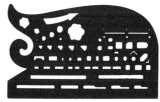

ARCHITECTS TEMPLATE

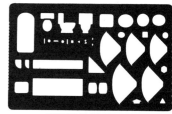

SCALE MODENIZER

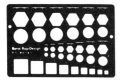

BOLTS & NUTS TEMPLATE

ARCHITECTS TEMPLATE

40 ACRE LAND LOCATOR

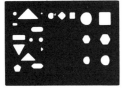

ARCHITECTS TEMPLATE

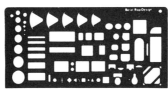

HOUSE TEMPLATE

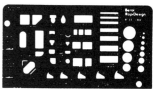

HOUSE TEMPLATE

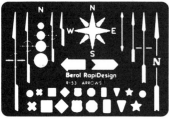

ARROW TEMPLATE

RADIUS GUIDE

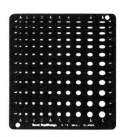

SMALL ELLIPSE TEMPLATE

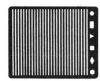

QUICK LINER

SQUARE TEMPLATE

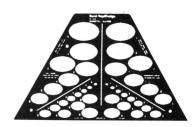

ISOMETRIC ELLIPSES

No. R-960

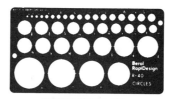

CIRCLE TEMPLATE

SET OF THREE
ARC LETTERING SLOTS

FIGURE 2–25 *(cont'd)*

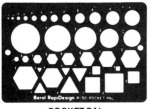

POCKET PAL

LARGE ISOMETRIC ELLIPSES

FLOW TEMPLATE

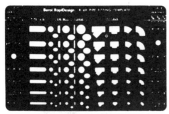

PIPE FITTING TEMPLATE

LARGE CIRCLE TEMPLATE

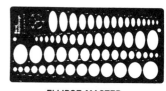

ELLIPSE MASTER

ISOMETRIC PIPING

DECIMAL CIRCLE TEMPLATE

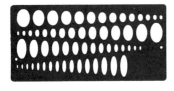

ELLIPSE MASTER

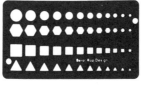

SKETCH MATE

**TRIANGLE
AND DIAMOND TEMPLATE**

FIGURE 2–25 *(cont'd)*

Erasers

Selection of erasers varies according to the type of line to be erased and the quality of the drafting paper. The selection includes electric, hand, pencil, plastic, and ink erasers (Fig. 2–26). It has been stated that an eraser is the secret to drafting success. No one is prone to making errors, but excessive erasures indicate poor planning and lack of concentration. Erasers should be chosen so as not to damage or discolor the paper. Erasing a line is as important as drawing a line.

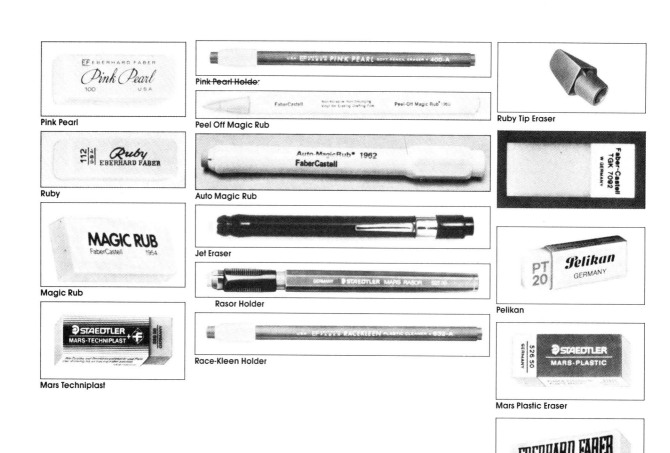

FIGURE 2–26 *Erasers (courtesy Charrette Corporation).*

A very popular eraser is the Pink Pearl, available in various shapes and sizes. A paper-wrapped pencil-shaped Pink Pearl eraser is sharpened by peeling the paper off the eraser's pointed end. Another is a pencil-type eraser holder, much like a lead pencil holder, which can be let out as needed. A Pink Pearl eraser is used mostly on paper rather than on plastic media. Vinyl, tracing paper, vellum, and film are best erased with a plastic eraser. These media usually work best with plastic leads. An Artgum eraser and cleaning powder are used for cleaning a drawing. Avoid rubbing the Artgum eraser over pencil lines, as it will weaken or lighten the lines (Fig. 2–27).

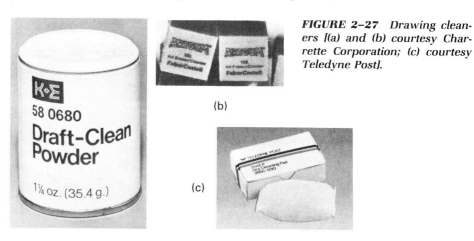

FIGURE 2–27 *Drawing cleaners [(a) and (b) courtesy Charrette Corporation; (c) courtesy Teledyne Post].*

FIGURE 2–28   Electric eraser (courtesy Charrette Corporation).

An electric erasing machine saves time. The eraser, called a plug, is inserted in the holder and held in place with a screw-type holder or a wedged pressure holder. Only the tip of the eraser is visible. As the eraser wears down, more of the plug is released (Fig. 2–28). The electric eraser should be lightweight and well balanced. Some electric erasers have turn-on switches and some have a mercury switch. If too much pressure is applied to the paper when erasing, the electric eraser could wear a hole through the paper. The machine must be kept moving.

When erasing with any type of eraser, it should be done thoroughly and completely, without ghost lines. Ghost lines, caused by indentations or grooves in the paper caused by drawing the line, may be reproduced when the drawing is printed.

Erasers must be chosen according to the type of drafting paper or film used and whether the line is pencil or ink. Soft pink or soft green pencil erasers can be used on the most sensitive papers without damage to the paper surface. There is no pumice in these erasers. The color has no effect on eraser quality.

White erasers have a little pumice and can be used as a general-purpose eraser for pencil lines without damaging the paper surface. Grey ink erasers contain a large amount of pumice, which is an abrasive material and is used to erase ink lines. They must be used with care or the paper may be torn. These erasers are firm to the touch.

Pink Pearl erasers contain less pumice than is in a white pencil eraser. They are used as general-purpose erasers and are perhaps the most widely used of all erasers for pencil lines. Red erasers are the firmest of all pencil erasers and contain the greatest amount of pumice. They may leave a red residue on the paper if too much pressure is applied. The residue may be removed by using a softer eraser. Sometimes the red residue will permanently stain the paper. These erasers are used primarily to erase pencil lines drawn with a hard lead such as 6H. Care must be used with these erasers or the paper will be torn.

Kneaded erasers are soft, pliable, stretchable, nonabrasive pencil erasers. They can be formed to any shape or size. They are used for soft pencils and charcoal work. The Artgum eraser is very soft and is used primarily to clean smudges from the surface of paper. The pressure should be very light; otherwise, the pencil or ink lines will become lighter.

Vinyl or plastic erasers contain no abrasive material or pumice. They are used to erase lines drawn with plastic lead on film media. Care must be used to avoid damaging the surface of the film. If damaged, it will affect the quality of the lines redrawn on the erased surface.

Erasing Shield

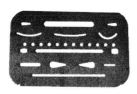

FIGURE 2–29 Erasing shield (courtesy Charrette Corporation).

There must be some control of lines being erased so as not to erase lines that need not be erased. This is done with an erasing shield (Fig. 2–29). The shield is made of thin metal or plastic with various shapes of cutouts that are placed over the lines to be erased. The shield protects the lines that are to remain in the surrounding area. To erase with a shield, select the cutout or opening that best fits the line to be erased and hold the shield firmly over that line. Rub the eraser over the opening and that line alone will be erased.

Dusting Brush

When erasing, eraser shavings are deposited on the paper surface. If the shavings are not removed, line quality will be affected because when a pencil is drawn over a speck of eraser shaving, a void or break in the line will occur. Eraser shavings should be removed with a dusting brush (Fig. 2–30). Use of the brush does not smudge the linework because the brush bristles are soft. The brush needs to be washed periodically with soap and water to remove the graphite dust. Do not use sweeps of the hand to remove eraser shavings because lines will become smudged.

FIGURE 2–30   Dusting brush (courtesy Charrette Corporation).

Drawing Cleaner

Two types of drawing cleaners are used (Fig. 2–27). One is in powder form and the other is in pad form. The powder type is sprinkled over the drawing to pick up and loosen dirt or lead dust that might interfere with the quality of the drawing. The powder remains on the drawing and is spread around by the movement of the T-square and triangle. As it spreads it will lighten the lines because it will pick up graphite in the lines. After some use and after it gets soiled with dirt, it is brushed off the drawing and a new sprinkle is applied. It also acts as a glide for the T-square and triangles, keeping the paper cleaner. The pad type is like a stuffed sock filled with eraser-like dust. The pad is gently swept across the paper picking up graphite dirt, dust, and grit.

Curves

Not all lines are straight. Curved lines other than arc or circles are drawn with a french curve or irregular curve (Fig. 2–31). The curve is made of the

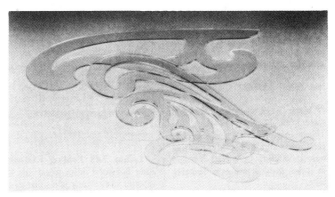

FIGURE 2–31   French curves (courtesy Charrette Corporation).

same material as triangles—transparent plastic—and has many irregular curved edges. The curve shape that best fits the curved line to be drawn is positioned on the drawing and the pencil is drawn along the curved edge to produce a curved line. The french curve may need to be repositioned to continue the curved line and should overlap the drawn line to achieve a smooth, even, unbroken curved line. French curves are available in a variety of shapes and sizes.

Another type of curve is a flexible curve that has a lead core covered with plastic (Fig. 2–32). They can be formed to any shape and are especially well adapted to long curved lines. Once the flexible curve is shaped, it will remain in that shape until reshaped. The pencil is drawn along the curved edge to draw the line. All curves have no constant radii.

FIGURE 2–32   Flexible curve (courtesy Teledyne Post).

Protractor

Straight angular lines that cannot be drawn with triangles require a protractor. An adjustable triangle set by degrees is one type of protractor. Such an instrument has a fixed base with angles imprinted and an adjustable arm for setting degrees. Other types of protractors are semicircular and circular (Fig. 2–33). Protractors can measure angles to within $\frac{1}{2}°$.

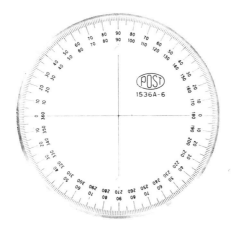

FIGURE 2–33   Transparent protractor (courtesy Teledyne Post).

Scales

It is impracticable to draft or draw buildings at full size. That is the purpose of a scale, to reduce the building drawing size to a convenient size (Fig. 2–34). Scales are separated into two groups: architect's scales and engineer's scales. The most popular sizes are as follows:

ENGINEER'S SCALE	ARCHITECT'S SCALE
$1'' = 10'$	$\frac{3}{32}'' = 1'\text{-}0''$
$1'' = 20'$	$\frac{1}{8}'' = 1'\text{-}0''$
$1'' = 30'$	$\frac{3}{16}'' = 1'\text{-}0''$
$1'' = 40'$	$\frac{1}{4}'' = 1'\text{-}0''$
$1'' = 50'$	$\frac{3}{8}'' = 1'\text{-}0''$
$1'' = 60'$	$\frac{1}{2}'' = 1'\text{-}0''$
$1'' = 100'$	$\frac{3}{4}'' = 1'\text{-}0''$
$1'' = 200'$	$1'' = 1'\text{-}0''$
$1'' = 500'$	$1\frac{1}{2}'' = 1'\text{-}0''$
Full size	$3'' = 1'\text{-}0''$
	$\frac{1}{2}$ full size

The choice of scale is dependent on the object or detail to be drawn and the size of paper drawn on. Scales are manufactured from boxwood and plastic in a triangular or flat shape and in lengths of 6 or 12 in. Scales are also subdivided in metric units.

Architect's Scale. An architect's scale is used to reduce drawings to a convenient size to fit the paper. It allows the drafter to relate the actual size of a building to a smaller scale for the purpose of illustration. The selection of scale is determined by what is to be drawn or detailed and the size of the building.

Care must be exercised in use of a scale. Pencil points must be sharp and the scale marking must be accurate. Distances should not be accumulated on the scale; each unit should be measured separately. This will reduce the margin of error. An architect's scale has different markings on both ends of the same edge. For example, a $\frac{1}{8}$-in. scale is on the left end and is read left to right, and a $\frac{1}{4}$-in. scale is on the right end of the same edge reading right to left. The two scales overlap like a double-exposure negative. Care must be used in reading the correct numbers of the selected scale. The combined scales are read singly, but one is larger than the other and the two points are on opposite ends of the scale.

In marking drawings, the scale must be read accurately. To use the scale accurately and correctly, select the proper scale edge and place it on the drawing with the end away from the body. The numbers can be read easily. The scale must be parallel to the measured line.

Count from zero the full dimension in feet and make a small mark on the paper at the proper unit of measurement. If the dimension has inches, add the inches to the feet dimension. Any fractional part of an inch will refine interpolation or estimate between inches. The pencil must be kept sharp to get an accurate dimension. A group of dimensions should be marked separately to avoid accumulative errors without moving the scale. Do not move the scale to a new position for each measurement in a series. This could result in errors.

Four Bevel: Four faces have plenty of room for multiple scales.

Regular Triangle: Has full face contact with drawing surface.

Concave (Relieved Facet) Triangle: Only edges of bottom scales are in contact with drawing.

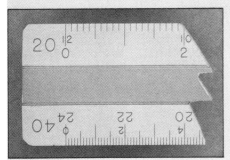

Fully Divided: Each main unit on the scale is fully subdivided throughout the scale.

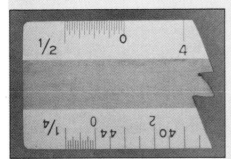

Open Divided: Only the main units of the scale are graduated, though there is a fully-subdivided extra unit at each end.

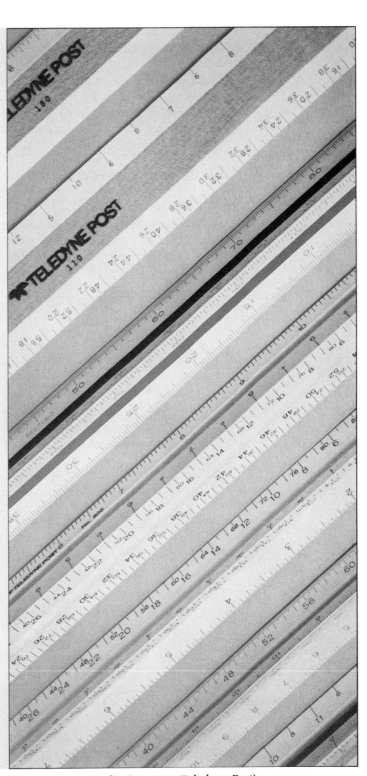

FIGURE 2–34 *Scales (courtesy Teledyne Post).*

Scale shapes vary. Triangular scales have 11 different readings and must be turned to find the desired scale. Flat scales have four readings. Beveled scales have eight scales, four on each side. Scales are made of boxwood with laminated plastic faces or all plastic or all wood, including the faces. Scale lengths are 6, 12, and 18 in.

Engineer's Scale. In addition to the architect's scale, an engineer's scale is necessary. These scales are used in drawing plot plans, land measurement, and stress diagrams. They have the same shape and length as the architect's scale and are read in decimal parts of a foot instead of inches.

Drafting Instruments

Most drafting instruments are sold in sets stored in fabric-lined cases (Fig. 2–35). The usual set includes a compass, dividers, a bow pen and pencil, bow dividers, ruling pens, and accessory parts. In drafting, accuracy, neatness, and speed are important. These can be accomplished only by using good-quality drafting instruments.

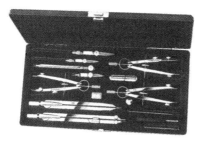

Contents:
6½″ Friction Head Compass with
lengthening bar and pen handle
6″ Plain Dividers
4½″ Bow Pen
4½″ Bow Pencil
4½″ Bow Dividers
5½″ Cross-Hinge Ruling Pen
Center Tack, 1cm diameter
Lead Box
Repair Box
Screwdriver

FIGURE 2–35   *Drawing set (courtesy Charrette Corporation).*

Compass

FIGURE 2–36   Compass (courtesy Teledyne Post).

There are many types of compasses. The most popular is the bow compass. This compass has a center wheel to adjust the compass for drawing arcs or circles (Fig. 2–36). The compass is adjusted simply by turning the center wheel left or right to increase or decrease the spacing between the compass legs. The compass has two legs, one holding the needle point and the other holding the lead, both of which are secured to the leg by a holding screw. Such screws are also used to adjust the lead and point. The point of the compass should be slightly longer than the lead so that when the point pierces the paper, the lead touches the paper. The bow compass can be adjusted to draw an arc or circle from 0 in. to about 6 in. in diameter.

The beam compass is another type of compass. It is used for drawing circles larger than 6 in. in diameter. In the beam compass the lead and point legs slide on a bar of adjustable length (Fig. 2–37).

A third compass, which usually is part of an instrument set, is a smaller compass with an outside adjusting screw attached to spring-type legs. The thumbscrew holds the desired spacing that has been set on the compass. This compass is not as accurate as the center thumbscrew compass or bow compass.

FIGURE 2-37   Beam compass (courtesy Teledyne Post).

Another type of compass is the drop bow compass, used for drawing small circles. The center rod contains the fixed needle and the lead revolves around the needle point (Fig. 2–38).

Compass Use.   To use a compass, adjust the legs to the required radius, place the needle point at the exact center or mark, lean the compass forward to place the lead in contact with the paper, and rotate the handle between the thumb and forefinger to complete the line. The points are removable for sharpening or replacing.

FIGURE   2–38   Drop   compass
(courtesy Charrette Corporation).

Compass Lead Sharpening.   Several points can be sharpened on the compass lead: conical point, chisel point, or side cuts that resemble a screwdriver. These points are formed by a sandpaper pad.

Dividers

One type of dividers is the proportional dividers. This is an instrument used to transfer drawings from one scale to another and to reduce or enlarge drawings. Proportional dividers are calibrated to obtain ratios up to 10 times larger or smaller. Proportional dividers are also used to divide a distance into a number of equal parts (Fig. 2–39). A second type of dividers is used to transfer measurements and to divide lines into a number of parts. It is also used to transfer measurements from one drawing to another (Fig. 2–40).

FIGURE 2–39   Proportional divider (courtesy Teledyne Post).

FIGURE 2–40   Divider (courtesy Teledyne Post).

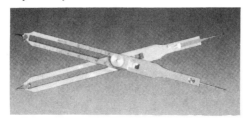

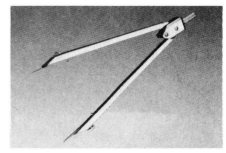

Drafting Media (Fig. 2–41)

Rag Paper

There are many types and qualities of drafting paper. The better papers have up to 100% pure rag stock, which means stronger fibers, superior erasing quality, and superior toughness. These papers do not discolor or become brittle with age. A good paper should also have a fine grain which will pick up the graphite from the pencil and produce a clean, dense, black line. If the grain of the paper is too rough, it will wear the pencil down excessively and produce a ragged, grainy line. Good paper should also have a hard surface so that it will not groove or leave a ghost line when erasing.

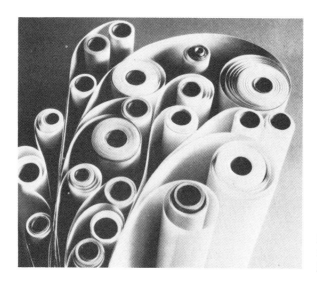

FIGURE 2–41 Drafting media (courtesy Charrette Corporation).

Vellum

A thin transparent paper treated with oils, waxes, or similar substances is called vellum. Some vellum paper may deteriorate with age and become brittle. Vellum is also affected by humidity and other atmospheric conditions which make the paper unstable.

Tracing Cloth

A thin transparent muslin fabric, usually cotton, is commonly called tracing cloth. It is covered with a starch compound or plastic to provide a good working surface. Tracing cloth is much more expensive than tracing paper. There is a difference in the quality of tracing cloth depending on whether starch or plastic was used in its manufacture. The lines produced on tracing cloth are dense black, do not smudge easily, and stand up well under handling.

Polyester Film

A superior drafting surface is made by bonding a matte surface to one or both sides of a clear Mylar sheet. The result is excellent transparency and printing quality. The matte surface will take pencil or ink, and erasers leave no ghost marks. The film is dimensionally stable; it will not crack, bend, or tear and is virtually indestructible.

Selection of Drafting Media

The following are qualities to look for in selecting a drafting surface:

1. Transparency for good reproduction
2. Suitable smoothness for pencil lines
3. Good erasing qualities
4. Nonyellowing
5. Resistance to wear and tearing
6. Resistance to brittleness and shrinking
7. Grooves free of pencil lines and erasures

A white surface will show linework best, but off-white and buff are easier on the eyes. If a drawing will have heavy use, good durability should be a factor in the selection of a drawing medium. Transparency is important because in most reproduction systems a light shines through the medium and the more transparent it is, the better the copies that will be produced. The cost of drafting media is important because if the best reproduction, durability, dimensional stability, smoothness, and erasability are important, there is little cost difference. If these qualities are not very important, a less expensive medium can be used. The smoothness of paper relates to line quality. A smooth paper should produce a dark and sharp image.

When erasing, no ghost lines should remain, as these lines may appear in a reproduction of the drawing. With a good-quality medium, it is easy to erase a line cleanly. A less expensive paper will expand and contract due to atmospheric conditions such as moisture, humidity, heat, or cold.

Drafting Tape

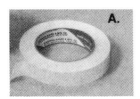

FIGURE 2–42a
*Drafting tape
(courtesy Teledyne
Post).*

Thumbtacks should never be used to fasten drafting paper to a drafting table. The paper will be weakened by the tack holes and the drafting surface will be disfigured. Poor line quality results when a pencil is drawn over a tack hole.

Drafting tape is sold in rolls ⅝ in. or ¾ in. wide. It is torn from the roll in small pieces and secured to the four corners of the drafting paper. Precut tape is also available and is used by peeling off the backing paper. Drafting tape should be removed from the drafting paper by pulling it back slowly toward the outside corners or outside edge of the paper. If the tape is not removed carefully, it may tear the corner of the paper (Fig. 2–42A). When taping drafting paper to a drafting board, line up the edge with the T-square blade.

Mending Tape

FIGURE 2–42b
Transparent mending tape (courtesy Teledyne Post).

Occasionally, accidents will cause paper to tear or excessive erasures will wear a hold through paper. Repairs can be made with mending tape, a transparent stick-on tape that is almost invisible when drawings are reproduced (Fig. 2–42B).

Media and Paper Size and Cutting

Drafting media can be purchased by the roll or in single sheets. Roll widths vary from 18 to 48 in., with various lengths. Precut paper and film media are approved by the American Standards Association in the following sizes:

PAPER SIZE (in.)	TYPE	FILM SIZE (in.)
$8\frac{1}{2} \times 11$	A	9×12
11×17	B	12×18
17×22	C	18×24
22×34	D	24×36
34×44	E	36×48

Roll paper can be cut with scissors or by folding to crease the paper and sliding the triangle along the folded crease to cut the paper.

Drawing Reproduction

Most finished drawings are copied or reproduced. There are many ways of reproducing drawings. The primary objective or reproduction is to make a number of copies of an original drawing with the best possible fidelity, but no reproduction will better the clarity of the original. The quality of reproduction depends on the drafting medium used for the original drawing. The best reproduction is from black opaque lines or images on best-quality drafting media. The highest quality is obtained from inked lines on Mylar.

"Blueprint" is an archaic term that derives from reproducing drawings using the sun. The original drawing was laid over chemically treated paper and left in the sun. The sun turned the chemically treated paper blue except for the lines on the original drawing. They remained white because the sun did not penetrate through them. Later the same process was done by machine with a strong light acting as the sun and a chemical on the surface of the paper acting to speed up the process.

More modern, faster, and better quality methods of reproducing original drawings are now available. One of these is diazo reproduction (Fig. 2–43). This process results in ozalid dry prints or blueline prints on a white background. The printing process uses an ultraviolet light passing through a trans-

(a)

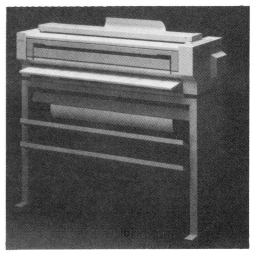

FIGURE 2-43 Reproduction machine diazo [(a) courtesy Teledyne Post; (b) courtesy Charrette Corporation].

lucent original drawing, exposing a chemically coated paper or print material. The light will not penetrate the lines on the drawings, which does not expose the chemical coating on the paper. After passing through the ultraviolet light the paper is exposed to ammonia vapors, which activate the chemical coating to produce a blue, black, or brown line on a white background. Print quality is controlled by the speed of the machine, which can be adjusted. Prolonged exposure to natural light will cause the chemical to overexpose, which will result in reduced print quality. Diazo prints should not be exposed to light for too long.

Sepia is another way of reproducing original drawings (Fig. 2–44). A sepia print is a reproducible copy of the original. Copies can be made from a sepia print. Sepia prints are very useful when the originals are required at more than one location. Changes can be made on sepia prints while keeping the original intact. Sometimes sepias are produced or printed in reverse. This means that the drawing is on the back side of the sheet, which makes it easier to make changes in the copy.

FIGURE 2-44 Sepia, blue line/black line printing (courtesy Teledyne Post).

Photocopy is another means of reproduction. In this photographic method of reproduction from the original, the copy can be increased or decreased in size. This is an excellent way of storing many drawings without taking up much room. This drawing can later be developed or copied to any desired size (Fig. 2–45).

FIGURE 2–45 Electronic vertical camera (courtesy nuArc Co. Inc.).

Another means of reproduction is by microfilm. This is a system of photography that reduces the drawings to 16, 35, or 70 mm. These become a permanent record of the drawings with little storage space required.

When scale is not critical, xerography offers the advantages of photographic quality. Material can be enlarged or reduced on bond, vellum, or Mylar in sizes ranging from $8\frac{1}{2} \times 11$ in. up to 36 in. wide by any reasonable length. Quality is generally excellent. Redrawing of originals can be eliminated by using cut-and-paste drafting, then making a new original on vellum or Mylar.

Following are some of the common terms used in discussing drawing reproduction.

Negative   4- or 7-mil film negatives may ensure excellent final reproduction; 12×18 in. negatives may ensure quality and ease for touch-up.

Mylar wash-off   A wet, erasable 4-mil double-matte film; image may be reduced or enlarged; 42×60 in. maximum; negative required.

Fixed-line Mylar   A 4-mil double-matte film; image is eradicable and may be reduced or enlarged; 24×36 in. maximum finished size; negative required.

Photo print   A dense black image on snow-white heavy photographic paper; image is permanent and will not discolor; may be colored without bleeding; image may be reduced or enlarged, and a negative is required.

Clear film positive   A 4-mil clear film used for overlay, silk screen, and printed-circuit work; negative required; 24×36 in. maximum finished copy.

Direct positive Mylar   A 4-mil double-matte film that requires a good original for best results; image is eradicable; 24×36 in. maximum size; no negative required.

Blueprints   Still the best and least expensive method of large-document copying. When the original is of good quality, the resulting prints have good line definition and are easily readable.

Blackline prints   Not quite as good a line or as readable as blueline.

Mylar   A 3-mil translucent blackline Mylar with a drafting surface on both sides; again, usually made with a reverse image; this product also has an erasable image for ease of changes. A very dense, black image on a 27-lb opaque white photographic-quality paper. It may be colored, as the material will not bleed. Great for presentations or special jobs.

Cloth prints   For maps, charts, recording purposes, or where prints are subject to a lot of handling.

Diazochrome   Used primarily to make high-quality transparencies for overhead projection; also used for overlays and back-lighted displays; very vivid colors.

A very important point to remember when reproducing drawings: Take care in the preparation of originals. The more dense the linework, the better the reproduction.

Lighting

General lighting is not enough light for performing drafting. In addition to general lighting, drafting table lighting is recommended (Fig. 2–46). This is generally provided by a lamp, with incandescent or fluorescent lighting, attached to the drafting board by clamps or screws. Most lamps swivel to provide maximum lighting where needed. Sometimes the concentrated lighting causes an annoying glare. This can be eliminated by slightly changing the position of the lamp. In the fluorescent type the usual arrangement is two tubes 12 or 16 in. long giving off a concentrated light of about 40 to 60 watts. Incandescent lamps usually have a single 50-watt bulb. General lighting usually comes from the ceiling and provides illumination for general purposes.

(a)

FIGURE 2–46   *Lighting: (a) fluorescent light; (b) incandescent light; (c) illuminated magnifier (courtesy Charrette Corporation).*

(b)

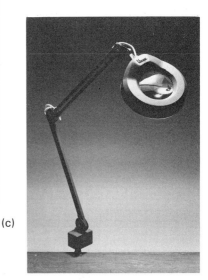

(c)

QUESTIONS

2–1. A left-handed draftsperson must use a right-handed drafting board or table.
True or False

2–2. What is the difference between a drafting table and a drafting board?
_____
_____

2–3. The best covering for a drafting surface is:
(a) Wood
(b) Heavy paper
(c) Vinyl laminate

2–4. The best drafting stools contain the following features:
1. _____
2. _____
3. _____

2–5. What drafting instrument is used to draw horizontal lines? _____

2–6. There is no method of checking the accuracy of a T-square.
True or False

2–7. Name the parts of a T-square.
1. _____
2. _____

2–8. What instrument can be used in place of a T-square? _____

2–9. Define *parallel rule*. _____
_____

2–10. Drafting machines require the use of triangles and compasses.
True or False

2–11. Name the ways in which scaling is done by use of a drafting machine.
_____
_____

2–12. A drafting machine is limited in adjusting the angle that can be set.
True or False

2–13. Name three types of drafting pencils:
1. _____
2. _____
3. _____

2–14. A dark heavy drafting line is accomplished with a 9H lead.
True or False

2–15. Name at least three types or grades of drafting leads.
1. _____
2. _____
3. _____

2–16. Drafting pencils and leads are generally sharpened at the factory and cannot be resharpened.
True or False

2–17. Describe a sandpaper block. _____
_____

2–18. Name three ways of sharpening a drafting pencil or lead.
1. _____
2. _____
3. _____

2-19. The two most commonly used triangles are the 35° and 75° triangles.
True or False

2-20. Discuss the purpose and use of an adjustable triangle. _____
_____

2-21. The purpose of a drafting template is to _____
_____

2-22. The best eraser for use on vellum is _____

2-23. What is the purpose of an erasing shield? _____
_____

2-24. Erasing dust helps keep drawings clean.
True or False

2-25. What drafting instrument is used to draw curves? _____

2-26. A protractor is used to track the direction of a line.
True or False

2-27. Name two types of scales used for drafting.
1. _____
2. _____

2-28. Name at least two drafting instruments usually found in a set of instruments.
1. _____
2. _____

2-29. Discuss the use of a compass. _____
_____

2-30. Dividers separate more than one line.
True or False

2-31. Name two types of drafting media.
1. _____
2. _____

2-32. Thumbtacks are used to fasten paper to drawing boards.
True or False

2-33. What are some of the standard sizes of drafting media? _____
_____

2-34. Name two ways of reproducing drawings.
1. _____
2. _____

2-35. What is the best type of artificial lighting to use for drafting? ____
_____

3

Line Work

Introduction

It would be difficult to read a building plan if all lines were the same. Difficulty in reading building plans can result in misunderstanding, lack of communication, and chaos. Lines drawn in building plans have different forms, different widths, different weights, and different meanings. Drafting is a language of graphics, a means of communicating through lines, notes, and symbols which describe in detail a building to be built. It is a means of communication between the architect and the builder.

All lines must be clear, crisp, sharp, and clean because they will be reproduced, and quality and intent should not be lost in the reproduction process. A given line should not vary in thickness or variation. Every line has significance and meaning according to its weight and width. Dark lines are reserved for the building lines; lighter lines are used to interpret and back up the building lines with dimension lines and a variety of other meanings.

Types of Lines

Border Lines

The first line is drawn on any drafting medium is the border line, indicating the inner limits for the drawing. The purpose of the border is to frame the paper and to allow or plan enough space or room within the border lines to complete the drawing and not run out of space. There are no set rules, but common practice is to draw the border line $\frac{1}{2}$ in. from the paper edge on all sides except the left side. Because the sheets will be stapled together, the left border line is generally $\frac{3}{4}$ in., to allow space for stapling and not conceal any of the drawing (Fig. 3–1).

Centerline

It is most helpful for greater accuracy in drafting to draw a centerline which indicates the center of the object or form to be drawn. Both sides of the centerline have the same dimensions. The centerline is usually drawn as a dash–dot line to avoid misreading the line for an object line. The centerline is a useful line for drawing elevations of doors, windows, and fireplaces and to locate the ridge of the roof (Fig. 3–1).

Cutting Line

When the plan drawings of a building are nearing completion, additional information is required to illustrate how the building is to be assembled. This is referred to as a cutting line, a line drawn through the building plan representing cutting of the building at that line and drawing the building section from that line. The line is a heavy, wide line with arrows pointing in the direction of viewing the cut or section, as it is called (Fig. 3–1).

Object Line

The purpose of a drawing is to illustrate the object to be built, such as a building or parts of a building. The object line is used to illustrate or draw that object. It is the main line or lines of the drawing. These are solid lines of medium weight illustrating the entire unit or object to be built (Fig. 3–1).

Hidden Line

When a building is completed and viewed from the exterior, the foundation below the ground is not visible but must be shown on the drawing. This is called a hidden line and is drawn as a series of dashed lines. This line is used for any part of a building that is not visible, yet must be shown to complete the building (Fig. 3–1).

Dimension Line

All drawings require objects or plans to be dimensioned. Dimension lines connect two points on a drawing with an arrowhead, slash, or dot. This denotes the dimension from point A to point B, and the actual figures of the dimensions are written above or below the dimension lines. These lines are solid, lighter

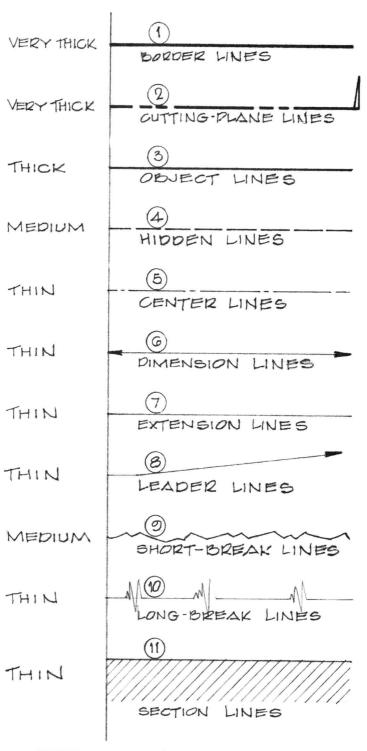

VERY THICK — ① BORDER LINES

VERY THICK — ② CUTTING-PLANE LINES

THICK — ③ OBJECT LINES

MEDIUM — ④ HIDDEN LINES

THIN — ⑤ CENTER LINES

THIN — ⑥ DIMENSION LINES

THIN — ⑦ EXTENSION LINES

THIN — ⑧ LEADER LINES

MEDIUM — ⑨ SHORT-BREAK LINES

THIN — ⑩ LONG-BREAK LINES

THIN — ⑪ SECTION LINES

FIGURE 3–1   *Types of lines (Edward J. Muller, Architectural Drawing and Light Construction, 3/E, © 1985, Prentice-Hall, Inc. Englewood, Cliffs, N.J. Fig. 1-24 on p. 17. Reprinted by permission of Prentice-Hall, Inc., Englewood Cliffs, N.J.).*

than the object line but not so light that they will not reproduce when copying. Dimension lines should be spaced a uniform distance apart (Fig. 3–1).

Lead Line

Often, a part of a drawing needs focal attention supplmented by a note. A leader line connects the two. It is an irregular curved solid line with an arrow at the end pointing to the focal point of the drawing. Leader lines should never cross each other and should be placed carefully. Sometimes straight lines are drawn for leader lines. This may not be good practice because straight lines may be misread as object lines or a line of other meaning. Curved leader lines are usually drawn freehand (Fig. 3–1).

Break Line

When a drawing or part of a drawing has been clearly defined, a break line is used. This line is a solid line broken by one or more irregular lines that break the solid line. It means that if the entire drawing were shown or drawn, it would not add to the information or message intended. The break line saves drawing time and space on the paper (Fig. 3–1).

Use of Pencil or Lead

Good line technique necessitates a sharp pencil point. The choice of pencil is a personal decision based on preference and on the quality and type of drafting medium used. Dark and light lines are controlled by pressure applied at the wrist. The pencil is drawn in one motion along the top edge of a T-square and the edge of a triangle (Fig. 3–2). Do not stop before the entire line length is complete. Stopping on a partially drawn line may result in misalignment when the line is continued. Hold the lead at a slight angle away from the T-square edge. This will enable you to see the line and will also help to reduce graphite deposit on the T-square edge and triangle.

Every line drawn has a meaning, and the weight of that line will define the importance relative to the drawing. All lines are important and the totality of the lines will convey the message intended. More important lines are drawn darker and less important lines are drawn lighter. This is controlled by wrist pressure. There is no need to change lead from hard to soft or soft to hard every time the line quality changes.

Generally, the outline of a drawing is made with very light lines, called construction lines. This is to assure clean erasing and to leave no ghost marks on the paper. When the drawing is well advanced these light lines are redrawn in final form, which will result in a clean, well-defined drawing. All defined lines must be the same weight from beginning to end. While drawing a pencil along a T-square edge, rotate the pencil to afford the lead to wear evenly, assuring an even line width from beginning to end. Lines are drawn from left to

FIGURE 3–2 Use of triangle and T-square: (a) drawing vertical lines with triangle; (b) placing T-square in position on board; (c) holding T-square with slight pressure; (d) drawing horizontal line (Edward J. Muller, Architectural Drawing and Light Construction, *3/E, © 1985, Prentice-Hall, Inc. Englewood Cliffs, N.J. Fig. 1–6 on p. 5, and Fig. 1–11 on p. 8. Reprinted by permission of Prentice-Hall, Inc., Englewood Cliffs, N.J.).*

right. Allow lines to touch or run past each other slightly at their insection. Never allow a space at the intersection of lines.

If the line to be drawn is longer than the triangle, first draw the entire length of the triangle. Reposition the T-square and triangle, place the pencil point on the end of the line already drawn, and slide the triangle up to the pencil point. This will assure an even, unbroken, continuous line.

Symbols

Drafting is a universal language composed of lines, dimensions, and symbols. These are means of communication between the drafter and the builder. Symbols have been devised and accepted as having a specific meaning and are used to save time in drafting (Fig. 3–3). There are symbols for most every shape,

ARCHITECTURAL SYMBOLS

EARTH	COMMON BRICK	STRUCTURAL IRON
GRAVEL	FACE BRICK	CERAMIC TILE
PLASTER	FIRE BRICK	INSULATION
WOOD-FINISH	CONC. BLOCK	MARBLE
WOOD-ROUGH	POURED CONCRETE	ROCK
SOLID INSULATN	STONE-RUBBLE	GLASS

APPLICATIONS

STONE VENEER-W/WOOD FRAME	STONE VENEER W/MASONRY	BRICK VENEER W/BLOCK WALL
CONC. FURRED	CONC. BLOCK-FURRED	SOLID PLASTER
BRICK VENEER-W/WOOD FRAME	BRICK-FURRED	PLYWOOD
8" BRICK CAVITY WALL	STUD	BRICK-PLASTER
TILE FLOOR	WOOD FLOOR	BRICK FLOOR
MARBLE FL.	CONCRETE FL.	FLASHING

MECHANICAL SYMBOLS

ELECTRICAL

CEILING OUTLET	SPECIAL PURPOSE OUTLET
FAN OUTLET	SINGLE POLE SWITCH
DROP CORD	DOUBLE POLE SWITCH
EXIT LIGHT OUTLET	THREE WAY SWITCH
WALL OUTLET	FOUR WAY SWITCH
TELEPHONE EXTENSION	WATERPROOF SWITCH
WATERPROOF OUTLET	FLUORESCENT LIGHT
DUPLEX OUTLET	OUTSIDE TELEPHONE
SWITCH & DUPLEX OUTLET	PUSH BUTTON
TRIPLEX OUTLET	BELL
RANGE OUTLET	LIGHTING PANEL

4 WAY SWITCH   **3 WAY SWITCH**   **DUPLEX OUTLET**   **FLOOD LIGHT**

FIGURE 3-3 Symbols.

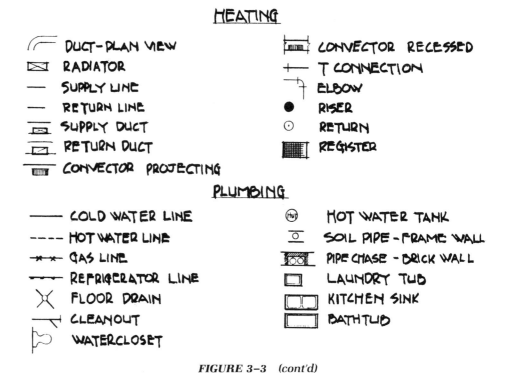

HEATING

⌐ DUCT-PLAN VIEW   CONVECTOR RECESSED
⊠ RADIATOR   ⊢ T CONNECTION
— SUPPLY LINE   ⌐ ELBOW
— RETURN LINE   ● RISER
▭ SUPPLY DUCT   ⊙ RETURN
▭ RETURN DUCT   ▦ REGISTER
▭ CONVECTOR PROJECTING

PLUMBING

—— COLD WATER LINE   (HW) HOT WATER TANK
- - - - HOT WATER LINE   ⊙ SOIL PIPE - FRAME WALL
—×—×— GAS LINE   ▦ PIPE CHASE - BRICK WALL
—·—·— REFRIGERATOR LINE   ▭ LAUNDRY TUB
╳ FLOOR DRAIN   ⊞ KITCHEN SINK
—⊣ CLEANOUT   ▭ BATHTUB
⊳ WATERCLOSET

FIGURE 3–3   *(cont'd)*

purpose, or subject. They are categorized into architectural, structural, plumbing, electrical, landscaping, heating, and a variety of other shapes.

Smudging of Drawings

When a T-square and triangle are sliding across a drawing medium, the graphite dust from the pencil is spread across the drawing, which causes smudging. This will make the drawing difficult to read, and cleaning may present a problem. The solution is to avoid smudging by lifting the T-square and triangle in place instead of sliding them in place. Should the drawing smudge, there are several methods of cleaning the drawing. One is to sprinkle clean powder over the drawing (Fig. 2–27), which cleans as it spreads. Another way is to dust it with cleaning powder (Fig. 2–27), which is used by rubbing it across the drawing. Another is to use an Artgum eraser (Fig. 2–27), by rubbing lightly across the drawing. Any cleaning method used will also remove graphite from the lines, causing them to become lighter. Care must be exercised in using all cleaners.

Compass Bearing

All drawings should show the direction of north. Usually, this is shown on the site plan or plot plan. It is important to know the points of the compass because the sun and weather play an important part in the orientation of a building

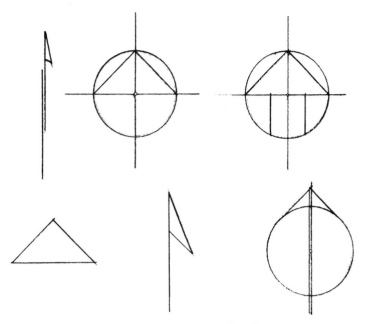

FIGURE 3–4 *Arrowheads.*

on the property. When north is known, south, east, and west are also known. Because the sun rises in the east and sets in the west, the southern exposure is sunny all day. Some homeowners prefer a sunny kitchen, which means that the kitchen should face south. As most winter storms originate from the north, a buffer such as a garage is best placed on the northern exposure. The best natural light comes from the north. Where natural light is preferred by the owner (Fig. 3–4), certain rooms should be located with respect to this exposure.

Use of Scales

Since all drawings are drawn to scale, extreme care must be used in reading the scale while executing a drawing. Plans and elevations are usually drawn at $\frac{1}{8}$- or $\frac{1}{4}$-in. scale. Details and sections are drawn at larger scales. Reading the scale is not difficult but takes a little practice and patience. To a beginner, reading may be confusing because two different scales are stamped on the same face of a scale much like a photographic double exposure (Fig. 3–5). Looking carefully at a 12-in.-long scale of $\frac{1}{8}$ in. and $\frac{1}{4}$ in., the $\frac{1}{8}$-in. scale is on one face of the scale and the $\frac{1}{4}$-in. scale is on the opposite face. The numbers on the face of the $\frac{1}{8}$-in. scale are 4, 8, 12, and so on. From point zero on the scale, these represent 4 ft, 8 ft, 12 ft, and so on. Although the 1, 2, and 3 are not marked, there are division lines representing the 1-ft intervals. The scale would be too crowded with numbers to list all the 1-ft intervals. The $\frac{1}{8}$-in. scale numbers are on the outer edge of the scale. The inner edge has another set of numbers, which relate to the $\frac{1}{4}$-in. scale read from the opposite or right side of the scale. These numbers are 46, 44, 42, and so on. This is where the confusion lies. Reading the numbers in numerical order beginning with zero on the scale selected will take the mystery out of reading architectural scales.

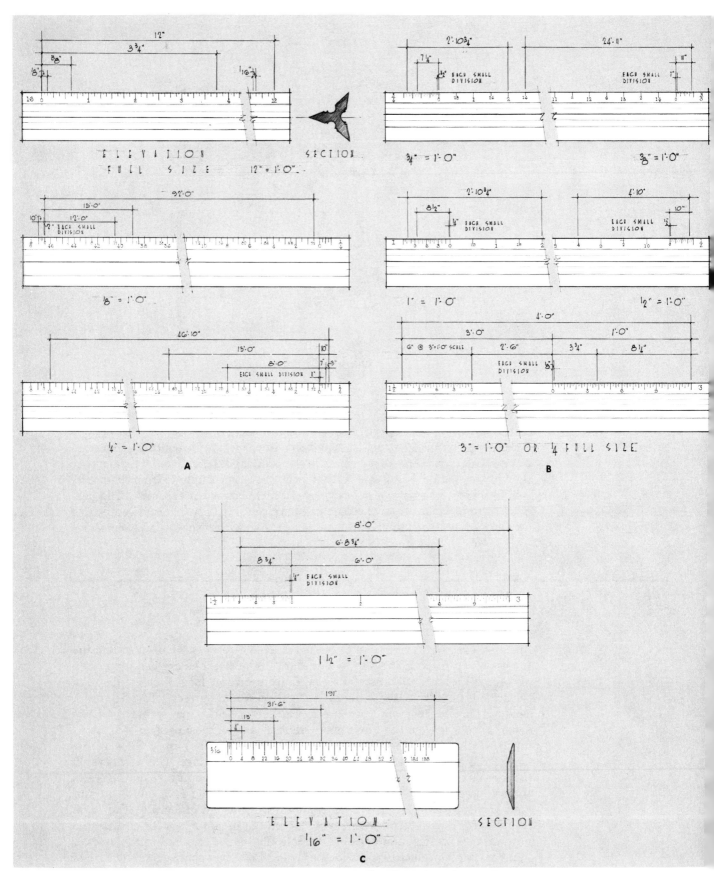

FIGURE 3–5 *Use of scales (Edward J. Muller,* Architectural Drawing and Light Construction, *3/E, © 1985, Prentice-Hall, Inc. Englewood Cliffs, N.J. Fig. 1–18 on p. 12. Reprinted by permission of Prentice-Hall, Inc., Englewood Cliffs, N.J.).*

At the very beginning of the scale are many lines spaced closely together. The $\frac{1}{8}$-in. scale has six lines. This is 1 foot of the $\frac{1}{8}$-in. scale divided into inches; each line represents 2 in. If the dimension scale is 5 ft 2 in. on the $\frac{1}{8}$-in. scale, the line after the number 4 is 5 and the first division or line of the inch-divided foot is 2 in. The $\frac{1}{4}$-in. scale has 12-in. lines dividing the 1 foot, which means that each represents 1 in. The larger the scale, the more inch subdivisions because the scale is larger.

Engineer's scales are read in the same manner as architectural scales, except that each scale takes the entire side. There is no double exposure and there are no inch subdivisions; all the lines are divisions at 1-ft intervals (Fig. 3–6).

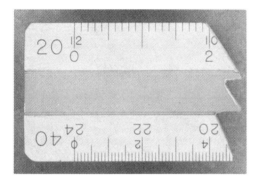

FIGURE 3–6   Engineer's scale (courtesy Teledyne Post).

Arrowheads

Every line that is drawn representing a distance or dimension has a beginning and an end. These must be very clear and unambiguous. There are several ways of showing these points on a drawing. It does not matter which style the drafter selects; what is important is that the dimension line have a beginning and an end. Some drafters use arrowheads, some use a slash, and some use a large dart. Whichever style is used must be used consistently throughout a project (Fig. 3–7).

Drawing Protector

It is not unusual with large buildings that large sheets of media are required for drawing. Sometimes it is difficult for the drafter to reach the top of the drawing to letter or draw. It is more comfortable to move the drawing down to the bottom of the drawing table and let the drawing hang down in front of the table. Although this is more comfortable for working, leaning over the edge of the drafting table could crease the drafting medium, making a permanent fold which will show up as a line in reproduction. To prevent this from happening, a Speroll Drawing Protector may be fastened to the bottom edge of the drafting table. The paper is then rolled into the spiral to protect it while the drafter is working on the upper half (Fig. 3–8).

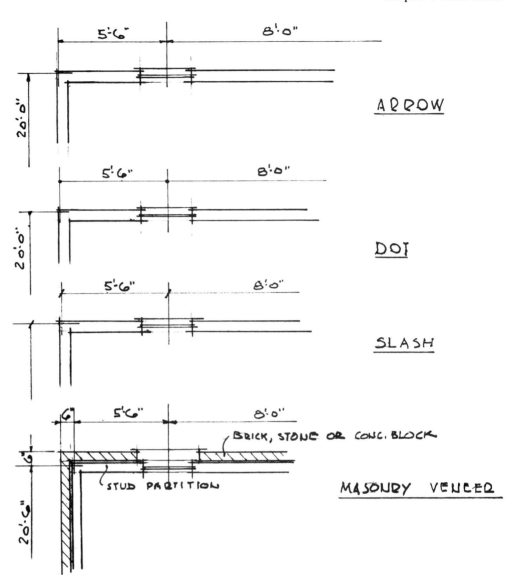

FIGURE 3–7 *Dimension lines.*

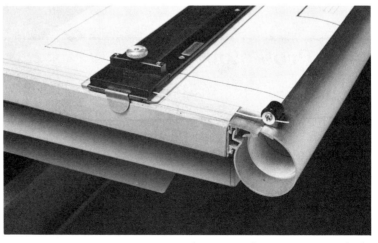

FIGURE 3–8 *Drawing protector (courtesy Charrette Corporation).*

QUESTIONS

3–1. What type of line frames a drawing?
 (a) Border line
 (b) Cutting line
 (c) Object line

3–2. What is the purpose of a centerline? _____
_____

3–3. When only a portion of a drawing is shown, what line cuts up or terminates the drawing? _____
_____

3–4. The darkest line on a drawing is the object line.
 True or False

3–5. How are hidden lines drawn? _____
_____

3–6. A dimension line is:
 (a) A light line
 (b) A dark line
 (c) A medium-weight line

3–7. Describe a lead line. _____
_____

3–8. A break line is used for _____
_____

3–9. What controls the weight of a drafting line? _____
_____

3–10. Drafting symbols are sometimes used in the form of templets.
 True or False

3–11. What causes a drawing to smudge? _____
_____

3–12. Define *compass bearing.* _____
_____

3–13. What is the purpose of a scale? _____
_____

3–14. Show three ways of starting and ending a dimension line.
_____
_____
_____

3–15. What can be used to prevent drafting media from creasing while hanging over the bottom of a drafting table? _____
_____

4

Lettering

Introduction

The reputation of the drafter is most often formed by the appearance of a finished drawing. The size, style, and shape of lettering will enhance or detract from the appearance of the drawing. Good lettering is more important than good line work. Only time and practice will improve good lettering technique, and individual style is self-developed once the lettering technique and basics are learned. Lettering can be accomplished freehand or by mechanical means, including stick-on and typewriter.

All drawings are collections of bits of information, each of which is necessary and relates to the finished drawing. Drawings are made up of words and lines. It is impossible to complete a project with lines only. This is why good lettering is very important.

Classification

Lettering style, called classification, consists of Roman, Gothic, script, and text (Fig. 4–1). One of these classifications of lettering is used for almost all modern commercial lettering.

Roman lettering was perfected by the Greeks and Romans and was modernized during the eighteenth century by typefounders. There is grace and dignity in Roman lettering, considered to be one of the most beautiful styles. The distinguishing feature of Roman lettering is the "serif," a spur or boot forming the end of a stroke. There are many modifications of Roman lettering, but the basic form is always present.

ABCDEFGHIJK
0123456789

abcdefghijkl

ROMAN

ABCDEFGHIJ
0123456789

GOTHIC

ABCDEFGHIJ
abcdefghijklm
1234567890

SCRIPT

ABCDEFG
0123456789

TEXT

FIGURE 4-1   Lettering style (courtesy Charrette Corporation).

Gothic lettering is a block style that is easy to execute and read. It is distinguished by the uniformity and width of the strokes. It can be modified by such means as adding serifs, rounding, or squaring. Modern single-stroke lettering is derived from Gothic-style lettering.

Script lettering is completely different from other styles of lettering. It is almost like writing by hand. Most of the letters in a word are connected in lowercase style except the first word of a sentence or phrase, which has a capital letter. It is a free-flowing style with a delicate personal touch. This style of lettering can also be modified.

Text lettering is sometimes called "Old English." This style was used by central European monks before the invention of the printing press. A flat quill pen was used in lettering, which made the strokes of letters of different widths. Because of the origin of this lettering style, it is used primarily for religious, testimonial, and fraternal writing. Much as with script, a lowercase style is used, with a capital letter for the first word. This style of lettering is difficult to read and draw.

Vertical or Slanted

It does not matter if vertical or slanted (sometimes called inclined) lettering is used (Fig. 4-2). What is important is that the same style of lettering be used throughout all drawings in a series. Each drafter will find a comfortable style of lettering, but both vertical and slanted styles should be learned because

ABCDEFGHIJKL·
ABCDEFGHIJKL·
0123456789·
0123456789·

FIGURE 4-2   Vertical slant lettering (courtesy Charrette Corporation).

often more than one person will work on a project and all lettering should be the same, or a different person may finish a drawing started by someone else.

The American National Standards Institute (ANSI) recommends single-stroke Gothic-style lettering because it is easier to read and letter. All letters are uppercase or capitals. The letters are simple and all line widths are the same.

Good lettering includes the use of guidelines, which will assure uniform lettering size and height, good form (well-shaped letters), good stability (having each letter stand on its own and not become top heavy or larger or smaller than adjacent letters), and good proportions (the letter shape determines the spacing between letters). Round letters such as O and Q require more space than do letters such as I and L. Another factor in good lettering is density. All letters should have the same weight and should be black enough to stand out so that the lettering will be easy to read.

Lettering Size

The size of letters is determined by the subject. Letters for drawing titles are larger than letters for notes. Once the letter sizes are determined, they should be uniform throughout the drawings. The largest letters are used for the job title, which is usually the owner's name and location of the project. This is called a title block and is put on all drawings that make up a complete set or project. Next in size is the drawing title, such as Floor Plan, Elevation, or Section or Detail. The smallest lettering, used for notes, should be in proportion to the scale of the drawing. The smaller the scale drawing, the smaller the lettering, but not so small as to make it illegible. A drawing of $\frac{1}{8}$-in. scale will have smaller lettering than will a drawing of $\frac{1}{4}$-in. scale. The letter size should not overpower the drawing. The lettering should not stand out above the drawing. The lettering and the drawing should complement each other. When lettering notes, the lettering is not allowed to touch the linework but should be placed close to the subject matter to relate to the drawing. A good note letter height for $\frac{1}{4}$-in. scale drawings is $\frac{1}{8}$-in. high.

Guidelines

To achieve the straight, uniform height required in lettering, horizontal guidelines should be used. Guidelines are parallel lines with letters placed between the lines. Once the height of the letters has been determined, guidelines are drawn for every line of lettering. Guidelines should all be the same height as the lettering. There are mechanical helpers to achieve uniform height in drawing guidelines. The guidelines should be drawn very lightly with no more than the weight of the pencil on the paper. If drawn lightly, the lines will not show in reproduction. Guidelines always remain on the drawing. Without guidelines, it is almost impossible to maintain straight lettering. Whether straight or inclined lettering is selected, it may be necessary to use vertical guidelines until skill is attained. Vertical guidelines are drawn with a triangle.

One of the most useful tools used in drawing guidelines is a lettering guide (Fig. 4–3). With a lettering guide it is possible to draw guidelines and sloped lines for lettering from $\frac{1}{16}$ to 2 in. high. Disk numbers from 10 to 2 denote the letter height. Letter height is determined by rotating the disk to the desired setting. After the height has been selected, place a sharp-pointed pencil in the top hole and lightly slide the guide along the T-square, keeping the guide edge along the T-square edge until the guideline length is reached. After the first guideline is drawn, repeat the second guideline by inserting the pencil into the other hole and repeat the process. Some triangles have holes punched through for drawing guidelines.

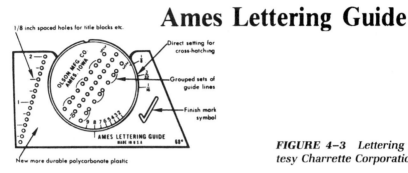

Ames Lettering Guide

FIGURE 4–3   Lettering guide (courtesy Charrette Corporation).

Freehand or Mechanical

Freehand Lettering

No mechanical aids are required in freehand lettering. Freehand lettering should not be attempted until lettering feels comfortable. It requires a great deal of practice and skill to letter freehand. Guidelines are still required for freehand lettering. Freehand lettering is much faster than the use of mechanical aids. In addition, freehand lettering is considered the ultimate skill in drafting and lends a personal touch to the finished product.

Mechanical Lettering

There are many mechanical devices available for lettering, as described below.

The *Leroy lettering instrument* (Figs. 4–4 and 4–5) is a device used for mechanical lettering by means of which a guide pin follows pregrooved letters

FIGURE 4–4   Leroy lettering instrument (courtesy Charrette Corporation).

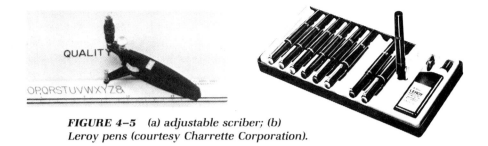

FIGURE 4–5 *(a) adjustable scriber; (b) Leroy pens (courtesy Charrette Corporation).*

in a template. The guide pin shapes the letters with an inky point attached. The arm is adjustable for vertical or inclined letters. Several templates afford a selection of lettering sizes. The pens are adjustable for width or style of letters. Each pen has a cleaning pin used to keep the small ink tube open to prevent clogging. The pens must be cleaned after each use.

The *Wrico* is a lettering pen (Fig. 4–6) that moves along the edges of a guide which forms the letters.

A *Varigraph* is a more elaborate mechanical lettering device for making a wide variety of single-stroke letters or built-up letters. A guide pen moves along the grooves of a template and the pin forms the letters.

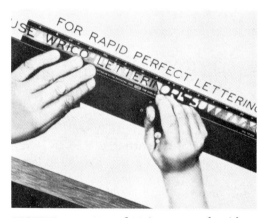

FIGURE 4–6 *Use of Wrico pen and guide.*

The *Letter Guide Scriber* is a much simpler mechanical instrument which makes a large variety of styles and sizes of letters. It operates with a guide pin moving in the grooved letters of a template. The adjustable armed pen forms the letter.

Dry-transfer lettering consists of letters arranged on a transparent sheet which are transferred to the finished drawing by rubbing over the letter with a smooth instrument. The transparent sheet is then lifted away, leaving the letter on the drawing. A clear acrylic spray will preserve the letters when the drawing will be handled frequently.

Adhesive lettering is similar to pressure-sensitive type lettering in appearance. The letter is cut out, placed in position, and rubbed with a smooth instrument. The plastic sheet has an adhesive material on the reverse side which holds the letter to the drawing surface.

Templates have openings in which the pencil is placed and moved along the edge of the letter selected. It may be the simplest of all mechanical letter devices. Templates come in different sizes and styles of letter.

A *lettering typewriter* (Figs. 4–7 and 4–8) is a useful and unique mechanical lettering device. The keyboard of the lettering typewriter is not the standard typewriter keyboard but is, instead, arranged in alphabetical and numerical order.

Underlays are similar to templates. Drawn or printed symbols are placed under the drawing and traced. The underlays are symbols most often used, such as trees, brick, and stone.

Overlays are printed on a transparent film and are attached directly to the drawing face by an adhesive backing. They remain a permanent part of the drawing.

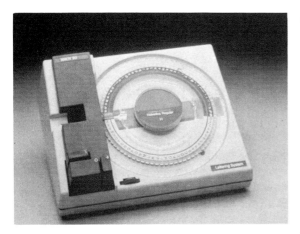

FIGURE 4–7   *Lettering machine (courtesy Teledyne Post).*

FIGURE 4–8   *Lettering machine (courtesy Teledyne Post).*

Skill and Style

All drawings require notes and dimensions, which must be lettered. The ability to construct legible freehand letters is very important to avoid misunderstanding in communication. There are many styles of lettering and only after some time and practice will the drafter develop a style, much like a developed style of handwriting.

A measure of professionalism of drafters is the style and technique of their lettering. Good lettering is a skilled talent. Only through practice can a drafter develop talent and skill. The reason lettering is so distinctive is because this is one of few creative areas where one leaves his or her mark. This is why lettering does not have a standard single stroke or style. In any style of lettering, uniformity is important. To ensure a pleasing drawing, all lines, spacing of words and letters, and strength of lines must be uniform. To attain uniform letter height, guidelines must be used.

Practice alone will not improve lettering. Practice must be accompanied by continuous effort to improve. Lettering is not writing; it is freehand drawing. The three most important skills and steps in learning to letter are:

1. Proportion and forming the letters
2. Spacing of letters and words
3. Continuous effort to improve

Letter Formation

The correct position of the hand in lettering is to use vertical strokes downward or toward the bottom of the paper using a finger movement, drawing horizontal strokes from left to right using a wrist movement—all without turning the paper. The forearm should be about a right angle to the line of lettering, and the forearm should rest on the board. Do not suspend the forearm in midair. It does not matter if the left or right hand is used; skill can be developed by either. The hooked-wrist left-hander will adopt a system that seems comfortable for the drafter's particular habits.

Even pressure must be used on the pencil and the pencil should be rotated to achieve uniform lettering lines. All lettering is uppercase or capital letters. Seldom is lowercase lettering used in architectural drafting. The size of lettering will vary with the scale of drawing. The smaller the scale of drawing, the smaller the lettering. The lettering size should not overpower the drawing. Once a lettering size is established, it should be uniform throughout the drawing. Main titles take the largest lettering, with subtitles next in size, and finally, notes, the smallest lettering on a drawing. On $\frac{1}{4}$-in. scale drawings a lettering size of good proportion is about $\frac{1}{8}$ in. high on main titles, $\frac{3}{32}$ in. on subtitles, and $\frac{1}{16}$ in. on notes. Do not allow lettering to touch any linework. The lettering for notes should be as close to the subject drawing as possible, using several lines of notes if necessary. All spaces between lines should be uniform and may be spaced the height of the letters.

Letter Spacing and Numbers

Most lettering styles are of single stroke with all lines and curves of the character having the same line weight and thickness (Fig. 4–9). The single stroke is similar to Gothic-style lettering. In architectural lettering, the letters of the alphabet are not spaced mechanically. The letters have variations in their forms, creating a pleasant style. The spacing of the letters is done by visual distance. Some letters—I and N, for example—do not have the same spacing as letters such as W and M, which are wider and require more space (Fig. 4–10). Spacing of words is as important as spacing of letters. Words should not be run together, nor should there be too much space between words. A common rule of thumb is to allow the same space between words as the height of the letters.

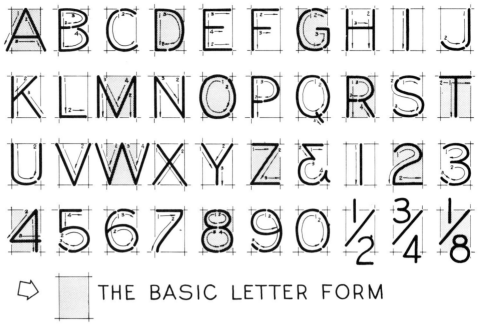

⇨ ▨ THE BASIC LETTER FORM

FIGURE 4–9 *Letter form.*

LETTER SPACING
VISUAL — *Good*

LETTER SPACING
MECHANICAL — *Poor*

FIGURE 4–10 *Letter spacing.*

Following are basic rules that if used and practiced will improve lettering.

1. Use guidelines.
2. Chose one style of lettering.
3. Execute bold and clear strokes in forming letters.
4. Do not draw letters; print letters with a quick, sure stroke.
5. Start practice with large letters, gradually working down to smaller letters.
6. Practice visually spacing the distance between letters and words.
7. Use only capital letters.
8. Work slowly at first; speed will come naturally.
9. Practice both slanted and vertical lettering.
10. Make the letter size relate to the drawing size—do not overpower the drawing with letters.

As with letters, some numbers require more space than others. The number 0 requires more space than the number 1. The rules for spacing between numbers are no different from the rules for spacing letters. Visual spacing is the key to good numbering.

Drafting Exercises (pages 68–81)

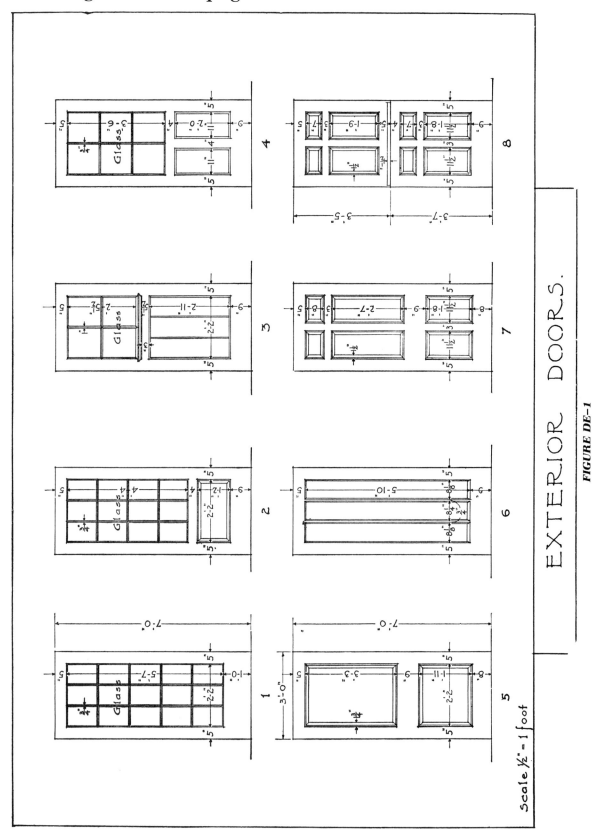

EXTERIOR DOORS.

FIGURE DE-1

Scale ½" = 1 foot

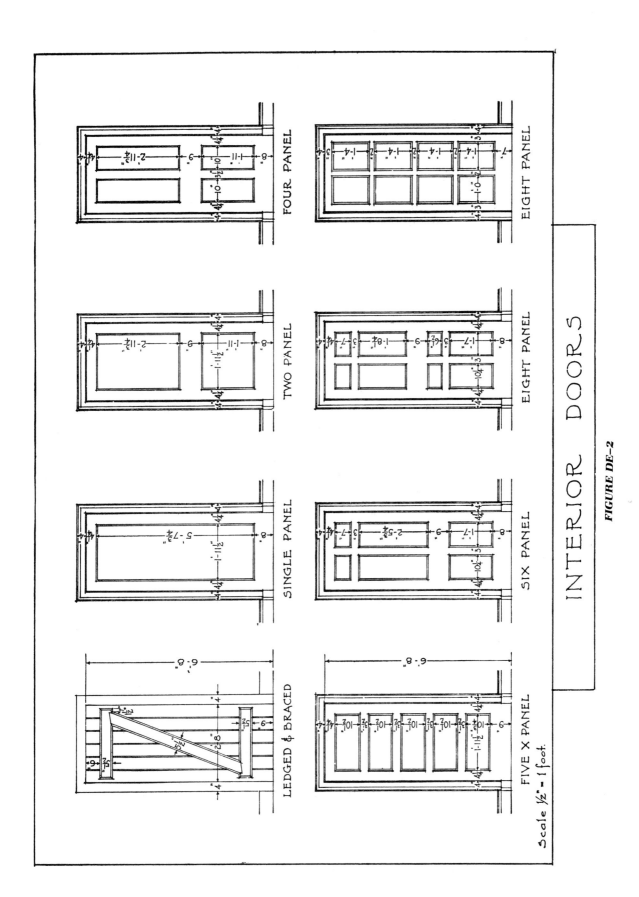

FIGURE DE–2

INTERIOR DOORS

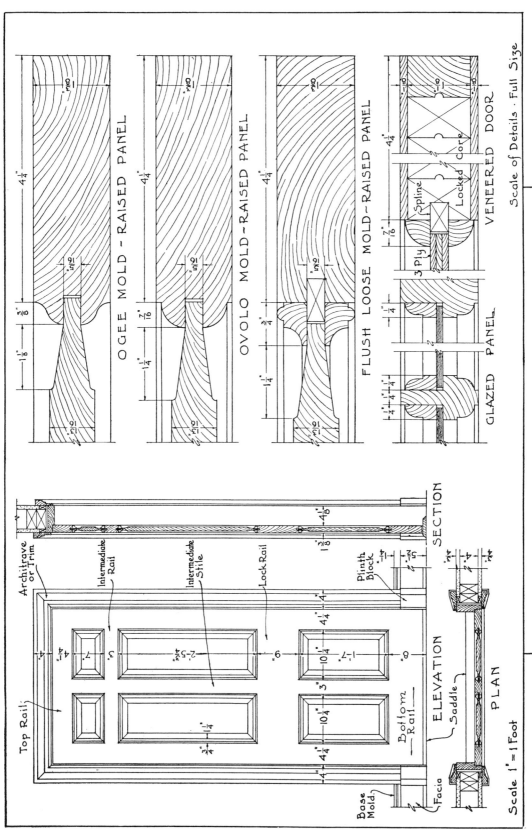

OGEE MOLD ~ RAISED PANEL

OVOLO MOLD ~ RAISED PANEL

FLUSH LOOSE MOLD ~ RAISED PANEL

VENEERED DOOR

GLAZED PANEL

3 Ply   Spline   Locked Core

Scale of Details · Full Size

DOOR AND PANEL DETAILS

FIGURE DE-3

Architrave or Trim

Intermediate Rail

Intermediate Stile

Lock Rail

Plinth Block

Top Rail

Bottom Rail

Saddle

Facia

Base Mold.

SECTION

ELEVATION

PLAN

Scale 1" = 1 Foot

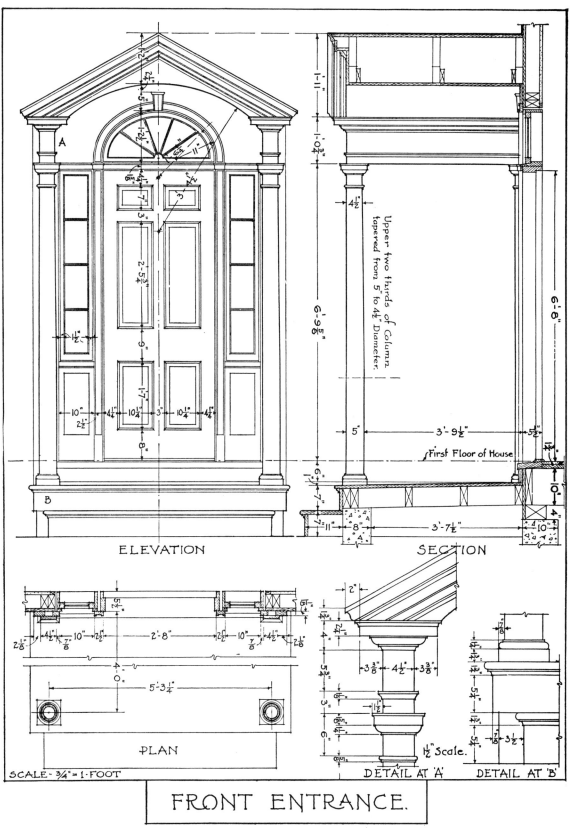

ELEVATION

SECTION

PLAN

DETAIL AT 'A'   DETAIL AT 'B'

SCALE - 3/4" = 1·FOOT

FRONT ENTRANCE.

FIGURE DE–4

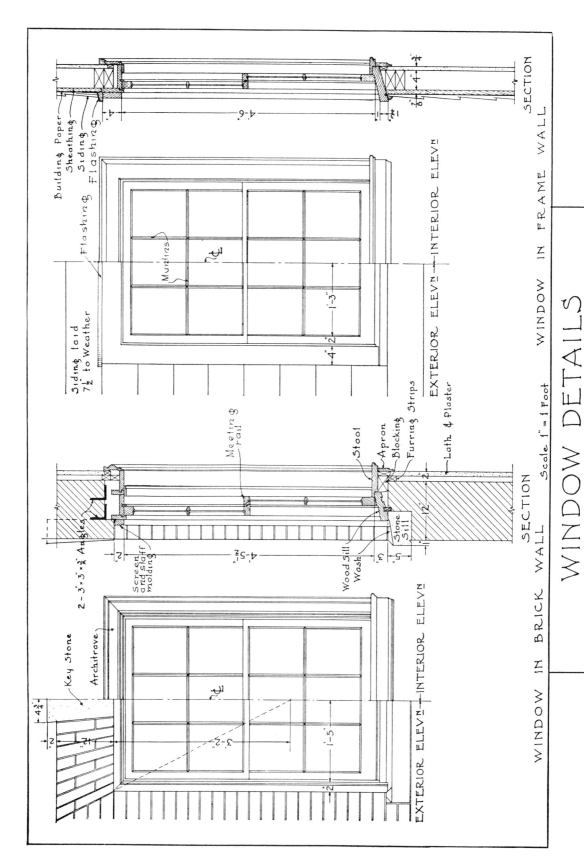

Building Paper
Sheathing
Siding
Flashing
Flashing

Muntins

₵

Siding laid 7½" to Weather

EXTERIOR ELEV.—INTERIOR ELEV.

Flashing

4'-6"

7/8" 4" ¾"

1'-3"

4'-2"

SECTION   WINDOW IN FRAME WALL

Lath & Plaster

Furring Strips

Blocking

Apron

Stool

Meeting rail

Screen and staff molding

2 - 3"×3"×3/8" Angles

Key Stone

Architrave

2"

1"

4'-5½"

Wood Sill Wash

Stone Sill

5"

11"

12"

2"

EXTERIOR ELEV.—INTERIOR ELEV.   SECTION   WINDOW IN BRICK WALL   Scale 1" = 1 Foot

4¾"

2"

1"

3'-2"

1'-5"

2"

₵

WINDOW DETAILS

FIGURE DE-5

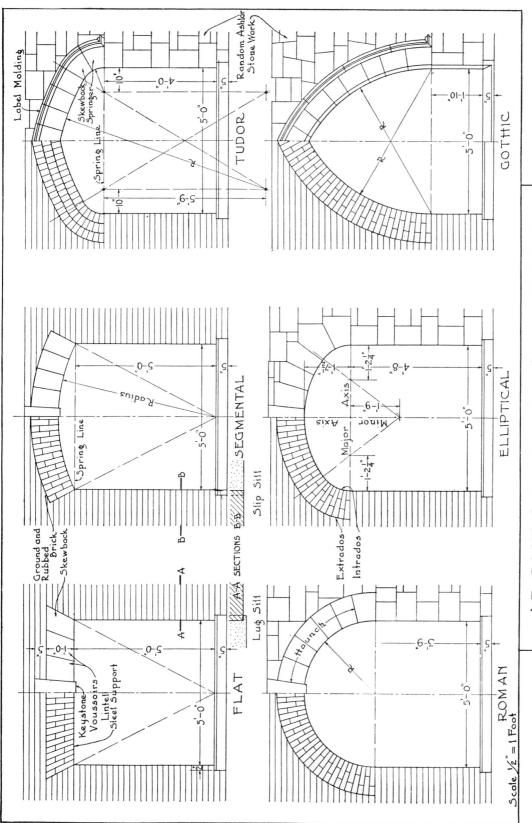

ARCHES IN BRICK AND STONE

FIGURE DE-6

73

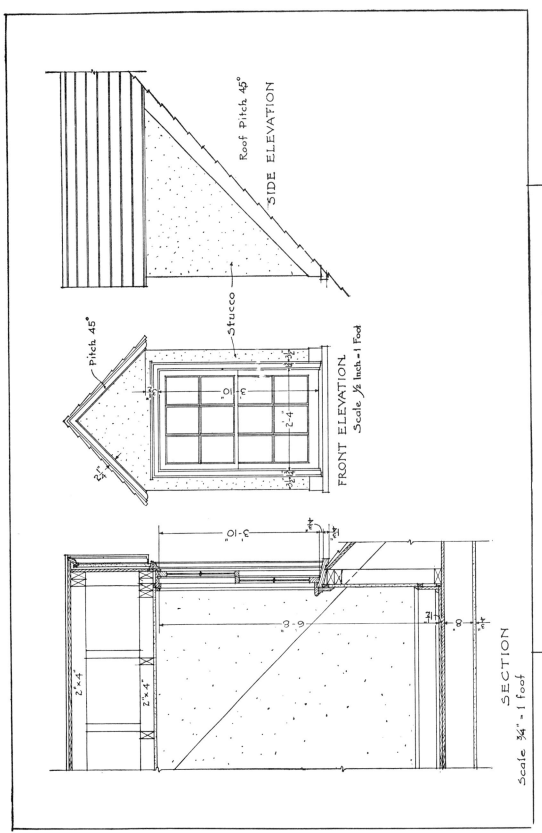

Roof Pitch 45°

SIDE ELEVATION

Pitch 45°

Stucco

FRONT ELEVATION
Scale ½ Inch – 1 Foot

SECTION
Scale ¾" = 1 foot

DORMER WINDOW

FIGURE DE-7

74

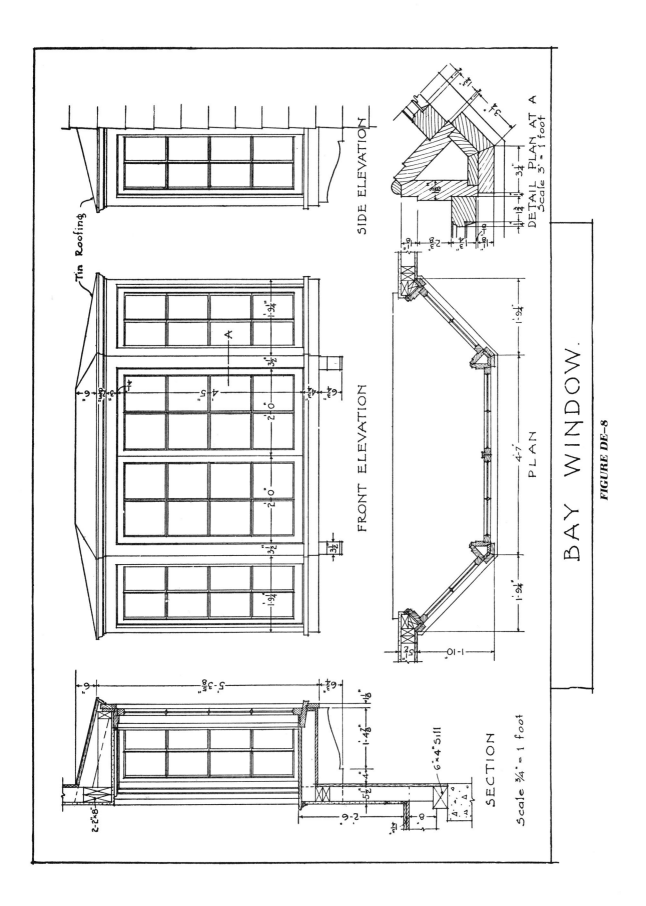

SIDE ELEVATION

Tin Roofing

FRONT ELEVATION

DETAIL PLAN AT A
Scale 3" = 1 foot

PLAN

SECTION
Scale ¾" = 1 foot

BAY WINDOW.

FIGURE DE-8

75

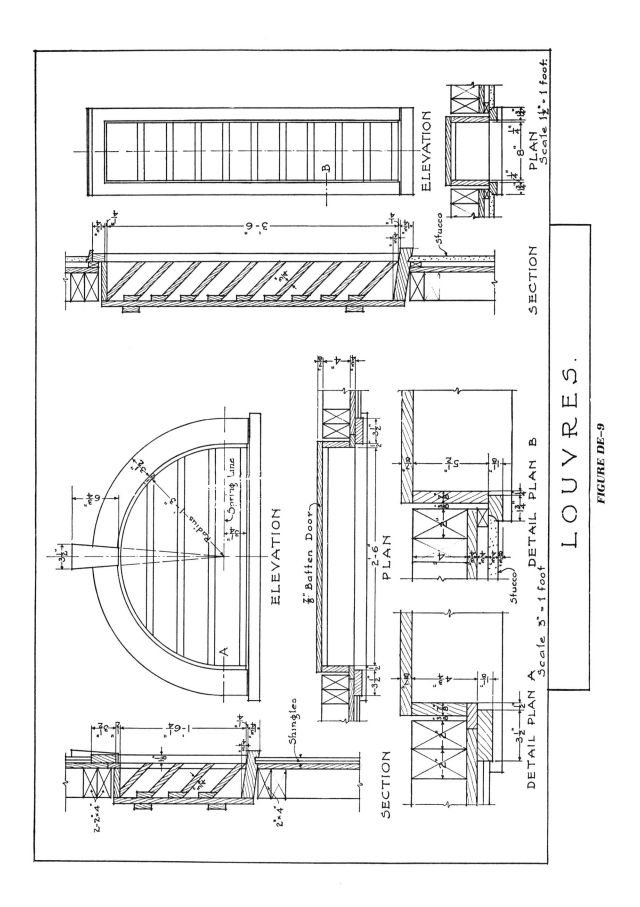

L O U V R E S.

FIGURE DE-9

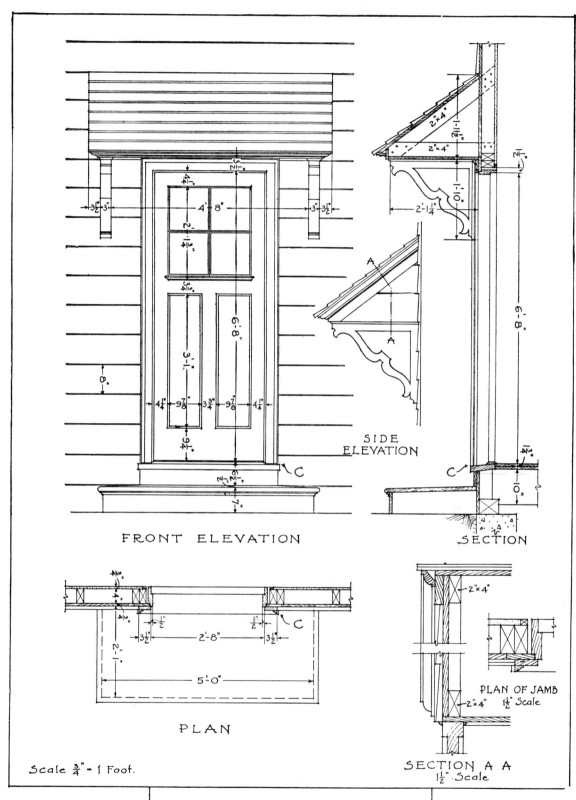

FRONT ELEVATION

SIDE ELEVATION

SECTION

PLAN

PLAN OF JAMB
1½" Scale

SECTION A A
1½" Scale

Scale ¾" = 1 Foot.

ENTRANCE DOOR.

FIGURE DE–10

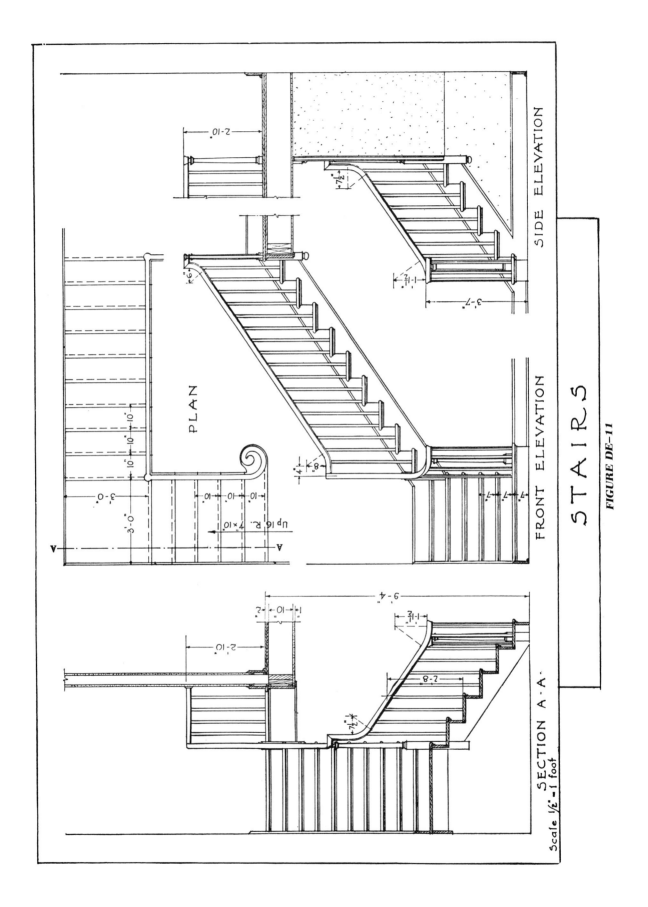

PLAN

Up 16 R. 7"×10"

SECTION A-A

Scale 1/2' = 1 foot

FRONT ELEVATION

SIDE ELEVATION

STAIRS

FIGURE DE-11

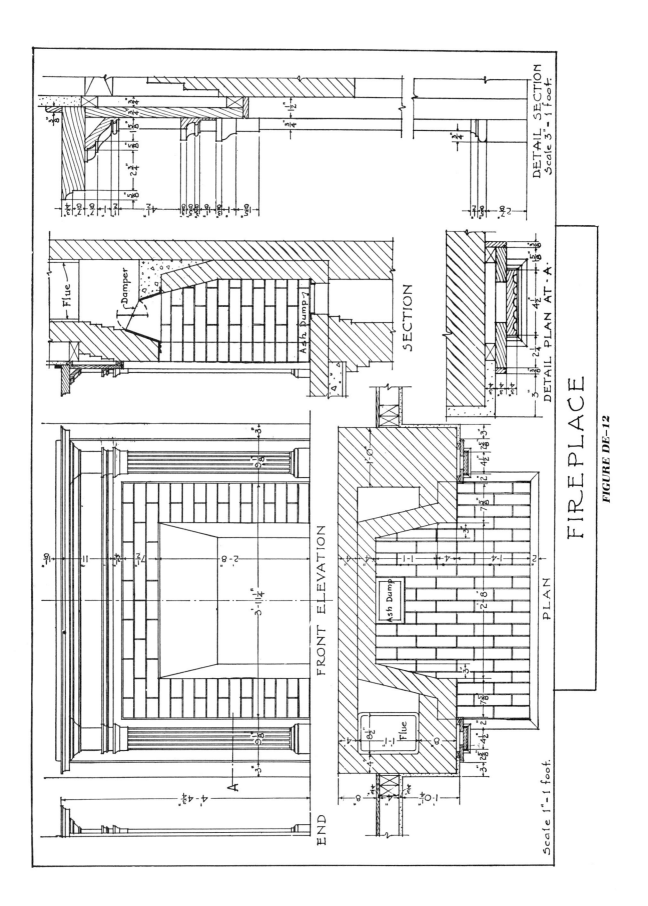

FIREPLACE

FIGURE DE-12

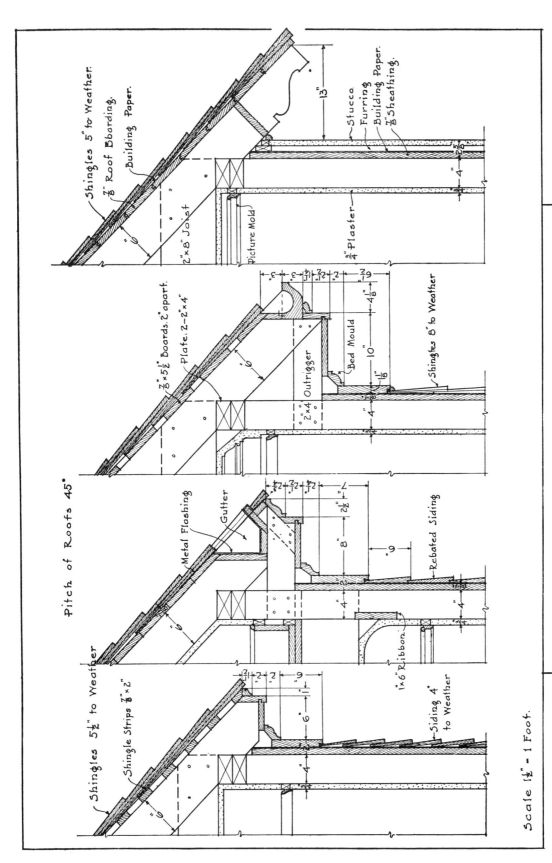

Shingles 5" to Weather.
⅞ Roof Boarding.
Building Paper.

Stucco
Furring
Building Paper.
⅞ Sheathing.

13"

2"×8" Joist

Picture Mold

¾" Plaster

Pitch of Roofs 45°

⅞×5½ Boards. 2" apart.
Plate. 2-2×4"

2"×4" Outrigger

Bed Mould

10"

Shingles 8" to Weather

Metal Flashing
Gutter

Rebated Siding

8"

1×6 Ribbon

Shingles 5½" to Weather

Shingle Strips ⅞ × 2"

Siding 4"
to Weather

Scale 1½" = 1 Foot.

CORNICE DETAILS.

FIGURE DE–13

80

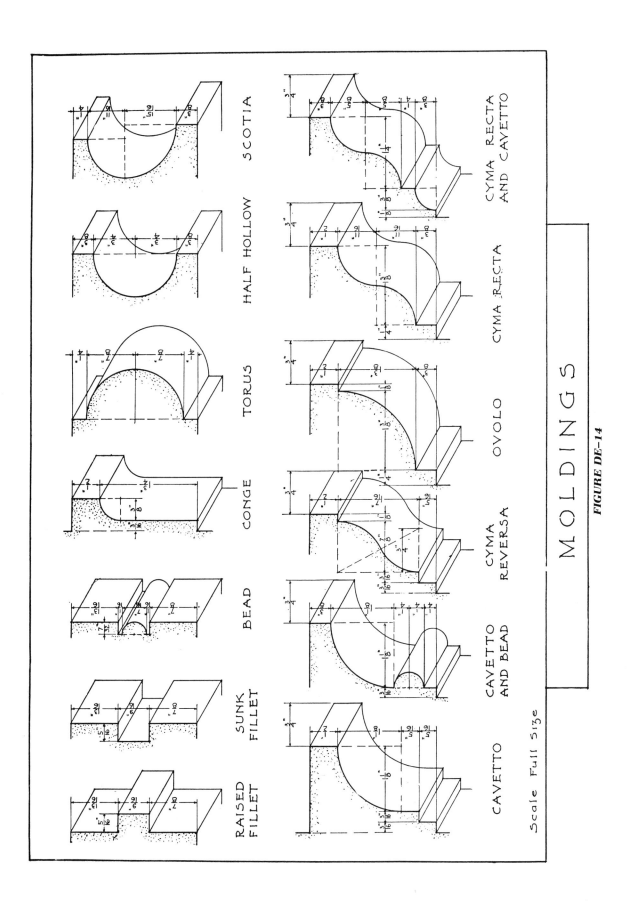

MOLDINGS

FIGURE DE-14

Scale Full Size

QUESTIONS

4–1. Name two classifications of lettering:
1. _____
2. _____

4–2. What are serifs? _____

4–3. Vertical and slanted lettering may be used on the same drawing.
True or false

4–4. What will assure uniform lettering size? _____
_____

4–5. Name the order of letter size on a drawing, starting with the largest size.
1. _____
2. _____
3. _____

4–6. What tool is used to draw guidelines? _____

4–7. Name six ways of lettering using mechanical means.
1. _____
2. _____
3. _____
4. _____
5. _____
6. _____

4–8. What is a Varigraph? _____

4–9. A template is a device used to control temperature.
True or False

4–10. What constitutes good lettering? _____
_____

4–11. On a ¼-in. scale drawing, approximately how high should the letters for notes be? _____
_____

4–12. All letters are equally spaced.
True or False

4–13. What is the most common style of lettering used in drawing? _____
_____

4–14. Name four basic rules to improve lettering.
1. _____
2. _____
3. _____
4. _____

4–15. The spacing of numbers has different rules from those of the spacing of letters.
True or False

5

Freehand Drawing

Introduction

One of the very first means of communication was freehand drawing. Unlike architectural drawing, which requires the use of tools and instruments, freehand drawing requires only pencil, eraser, and paper. It is a fast, simple, and convenient way of translating thoughts into visual representation.

Freehand drawing is essentially a thinking process that will lead to a solution. Even if not a complete drawing, expressing ideas on paper quickly and efficiently generally leads to a complete drawing. The freehand technique is not difficult to learn. All that is required is an understanding of what is and is not required of the finished product. The hand controls the pencil; the pencil does not control the hand.

Tools and Equipment

Most freehand drawing or sketching requires a soft pencil, such as F grade or softer, and an eraser. An Artgum eraser works well, in addition to a soft pink pearl eraser. Do not use a hard eraser because it may tear the paper. Any paper, clear or lined, can be used for sketching. An opaque transparent paper is best for overlay sketching. Graph paper is sometimes used for guidelines in sketching.

Lead Grades

It does not matter if the pencil is encased in wood or in a mechanical lead holder. What does matter is the grade or hardness of lead (Fig. 5–1). The lead should flow freely by action of one sweep of the wrist. Once a line is drawn, it should not be necessary to go over it to make it darker. To accomplish a one-sweep line, a semisoft lead should be used. The range of semisoft leads are H, HB, 2B, and 3B. Any lead harder than H is too hard for freehand drawing, resulting in lines being too light; any lead softer than 3B will result in smudging the drawing because the wrist is in contact with the paper and sliding the wrist on the paper will spread the graphite, smudging the paper.

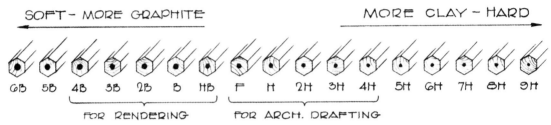

FIGURE 5–1 Pencil hardness chart (Edward J. Muller, Architectural Drawing and Light Construction, *3/E, © 1985, Prentice-Hall, Inc. Englewood Cliffs, N.J. Fig. 1–7 on p. 6. Reprinted by permission of Prentice-Hall, Inc., Englewood Cliffs, N.J.).*

A pen should be used in sketching except for drawing over pencil lines to make them permanent. Pencil is easy to erase, ink is not. Sometimes colored pencils are used for freehand sketching, but most often, color is not necessary. Color may be used to clarify various parts of a drawing. Colors are also available in felt-tip pens.

Pen Sketching

Freehand sketching with pen is not unusual (Fig. 5–2). Felt-tip pens are more convenient because they are easy to work with and many colors are available. Before a freehand drawing is inked, it must be drawn in pencil. Pencil lines can be erased, ink lines cannot. When the pencil drawing is complete, ink over the pencil lines for a final, longer-lasting drawing.

Felt tips are available in both cone point and chisel point. The cone point produces a fine line used for detail. The chisel point is used for a variety of line weights. By using the pen's corner, fine lines can be drawn, and by using the flat edge of the chisel, wide lines can be drawn. If felt-tip pens are not tightly capped when not in use, they will dry out. Felt tips become blunt from repeated use and can be redressed with razor blade.

FIGURE 5–2 Felt-tip pens (Edward J. Muller, Architectural Drawing and Light Construction, *3/E, © 1985, Prentice-Hall, Inc. Englewood Cliffs, N.J. Fig. 5–41 on pg. 96. Reprinted by permission of Prentice-Hall, Inc., Englewood Cliffs, N.J.).*

Paper

Any paper can be used for freehand sketching. Inexpensive transparent tracing paper or drafting paper is more convenient because it can be placed over previously drawn sketches or drafting for study. Graph or ruled paper can also be used for freehand drawing and has the advantage of graph lines to keep as guidelines for vertical and horizontal lines. Lined or grid rulings may be 4, 5, 8 or 10 to the inch. Some drafters feel restricted when using lined or graph paper, which may be a psychological factor (Fig. 5–3).

The graph lines on some graph paper will not show when printed. Called fade-out grids, they are made of a special ink that will not reproduce when printed. The better paper has a slight "tooth," or roughness. Such a paper will take pencil better than will a hard, slick, shiny-surface paper.

Ruled Papers

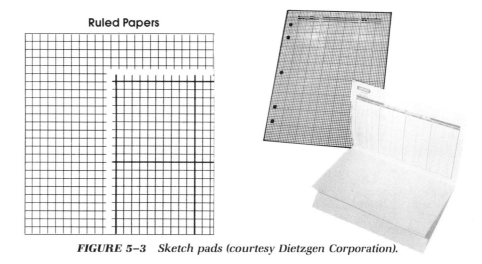

FIGURE 5–3   Sketch pads (courtesy Dietzgen Corporation).

Eraser

Mistakes that need to be corrected by erasing cannot be avoided. The type of eraser used is important. The eraser should be soft and pliable. If a hard eraser is used, it may tear the paper. If the pencil used in sketching is too soft, erasing will spread the graphite and smudge the paper (Fig. 5–4). The best erasers to use are the vinyl, Pink Pearl, kneaded, or Artgum. All are soft erasers and will erase cleanly. Apply no more pressure when erasing than is needed to remove the line to be erased. Excessive erasing may crease or tear the paper.

FIGURE 5–4   Erasers (courtesy Dietzgen Corporation).

Pencil Points

In freehand drawing the shape of a line is controlled by the shape of the pencil point (Fig. 5–5). A general-purpose pencil point is slightly rounded. This will result in a sharp line. In using a slightly rounded pencil point, rotate the pencil while using. This will result in even wear on the point and the lines will be uniform. In addition, less sharpening will be required. If the pencil is not rotated, the lead will wear in one spot, resulting in a wider line each time a line is drawn. A sharp point will produce a very fine line, but if pressure is applied for a darker line, the point may break. A bell-shaped point will give a fuzzy line. A chisel point will give a wide line.

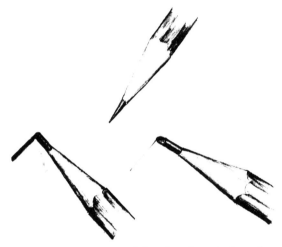

FIGURE 5–5   Pencil points used for sketching (Edward J. Muller, Architectural Drawing and Light Construction, 3/E, © 1985, Prentice-Hall, Inc. Englewood Cliffs, N.J. Fig. 5–1 on p. 78. Reprinted by permission of Prentice-Hall, Inc., Englewood Cliffs, N.J.).

Use care when sharpening pencils. Sharpen away from the drafting board; otherwise, the graphite dust will fall on the drawing, resulting in a smudgy, dirty drawing and a dirty T-square and triangles. Sharpen the lead over a wastebasket or on a piece of waste paper.

Beginning Exercise

Any object to be sketched should be outlined very lightly. The lines should be short and made in one continuous movement; otherwise, a line that should be long and straight may curve (Fig. 5–6). Lines should be light to make them easier to erase. In fact, if the line is light enough, it may not need to be erased.

Lines in freehand drawing should not be rigidly straight or exactly uniform as in a mechanical line. The line should show freedom and variety. Since most lines are straight lines, it is necessary to make them well. The pencil should be held about $1\frac{1}{2}$ in. back from the pencil point and at a right angle to the line to be drawn (Fig. 5–7). Draw horizontal lines left to right with a free-and-easy wrist and arm movement. Vertical lines should be drawn in a downward movement with the fingers and wrist in an easy relaxed motion. The

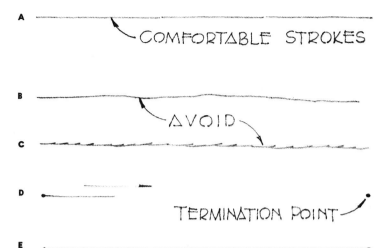

FIGURE 5–6 Sketching long lines freehand (Edward J. Muller, Architectural Drawing and Light Construction, 3/E, © 1985, Prentice-Hall, Inc. Englewood Cliffs, N.J. Fig. 5–5 on p. 79. Reprinted by permission of Prentice-Hall, Inc., Englewood Cliffs, N.J.).

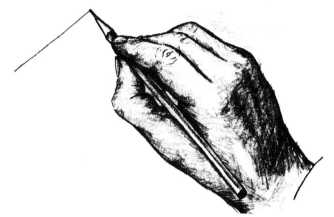

FIGURE 5–7 Holding a pencil (Edward J. Muller, Architectural Drawing and Light Construction, 3/E, © 1985, Prentice-Hall, Inc. Englewood Cliffs, N.J. Fig. 5–2 on p. 78. Reprinted by permission of Prentice-Hall, Inc., Englewood Cliffs, N.J.).

pencil should be drawn, not pushed. Angled or slanted lines are easy to draw by shifting the position of the paper in the direction of horizontal or vertical lines (Fig. 5–8, page 88). Do not strive for true straight-line work. One of the characteristics of freehand drawing is the slightly irregular appearance of lines as compared to the sharp straightness of a mechanical line.

Proportioning and Dividing

One of the most important aspects of freehand drawing is correct proportions. All lines drawn must relate by size and direction to the objects being drawn. The size of a drawing is not as important as correct proportions. Scale is not used in freehand drawing, so the correct proportions must relate to the object drawn. The first line drawn, called the *measurement line*, determines the proportion of the drawing. The rest of the lines drawn will relate to the measurement line for proportion.

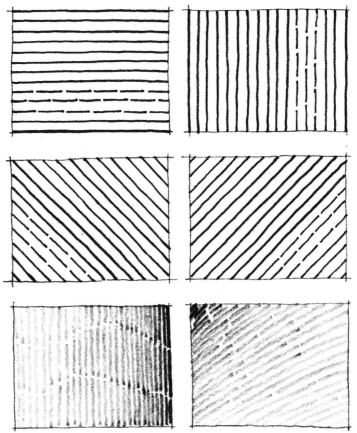

FIGURE 5–8   Practice exercises (Edward J. Muller, Architectural
Drawing and Light Construction, 3/E, © 1985, Prentice-Hall, Inc.
Englewood Cliffs, N.J. Fig. 5–4 on p. 78. Reprinted by permission of
Prentice-Hall, Inc., Englewood Cliffs, N.J.).

The second important fact to learn about freehand drawing concerns the relationship between the lines. What is the line direction and position in relation to other lines in the drawing? Are the lines parallel? Do they touch each other? Are they perpendicular or are they at some other angle to each other? The answers to these questions should result in a clear, concise, well-proportioned drawing.

This concept can also relate to space, such as a table in a room (Fig. 5–9). The proportion and direction of lines in relation to each other will convey the feeling of space between the table and the room. The lines will communicate how large the room is in relation to the table, and vice versa.

Quite often areas need to be divided into equal parts, such as halves and quarters. This is easily done with squares or rectangles (Fig. 5–10). Sketch two intersecting diagonals through the area to be divided. Sketching a vertical line through the point of intersection will divide the area into two equal halves. Sketching a vertical and a horizontal line through the intersection will divide the area into four equal parts.

The basic elements in learning to draw freehand are the square and the rectangle. These are considered the foundations of freehand sketching. Unless the simple shapes are mastered, freehand drawing is difficult, if not impossible.

There are many ways of drawing a square, but the simplest is to draw two intersecting lines, one horizontal and one vertical. Use the pencil as a

FIGURE 5–9 *Freehand sketching (Edward J. Muller, Architectural Drawing and Light Construction, 3/E, © 1985, Prentice-Hall, Inc. Englewood Cliffs, N.J. Fig. 5–37 on p. 94. Reprinted by permission of Prentice-Hall, Inc., Englewood Cliffs, N.J.).*

FIGURE 5–10 *Dividing an area into equal parts (Edward J. Muller, Architectural Drawing and Light Construction, 3/E, © 1985, Prentice-Hall, Inc. Englewood Cliffs, N.J. Fig. 5–23, 5–24 on p. 84; Fig. 5–46 on p. 98. Reprinted by permission of Prentice-Hall, Inc., Englewood Cliffs, N.J.).*

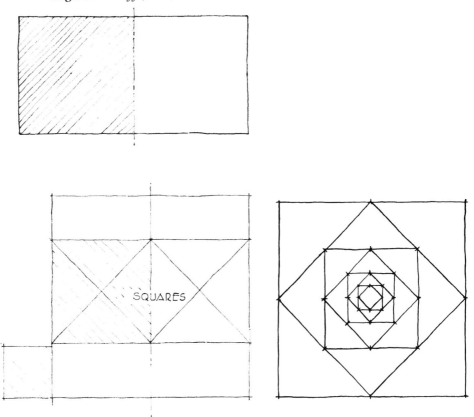

marking gauge and tick off each intersecting line an equal distance from the center. Drawing a parallel line to the axis lines at the tick mark will complete the square. A rectangle is drawn in a similar manner except that the tick marks are farther apart on one axis line.

Angles, Circles, and Curves

Drawing nonstraight lines is not as difficult as it may seem. Circles can be drawn by layout first, which consists of a square. Mark the midpoints of all sides of the square, draw tangents to the sides of the square, and the circle is completed (Fig. 5–11).

Another method of drawing circles is to draw horizontal and vertical cross lines. Then draw 45° diagonals through the centerline. From the center, mark off equal distances on all lines and that will outline the circle. An easy method of drawing large circles is to mark the radius and center on a piece of scrap paper or card. Lay the scrap paper over the drawing paper and from the center of the horizontal and vertical cross lines, make as many marks as needed as the scrap paper is rotated from the center point.

Another easy method of drawing a circle is to use the little finger as a center. Place the pencil between the forefinger and thumb. On the paper main-

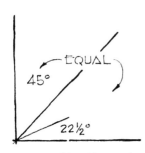
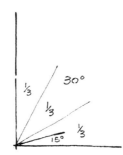

Sketching angles by convenient divisions.

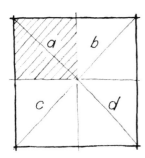

Sketch an accurate square by starting with center lines.

FIGURE 5–11 *Freehand sketching: angles, squares, and circles (Edward J. Muller,* Architectural Drawing and Light Construction, *3/E, © 1985, Prentice-Hall, Inc. Englewood Cliffs, N.J. Fig. 5–10, 5–11, 5–12, 5–13 on p. 80. Reprinted by permission of Prentice-Hall, Inc., Englewood Cliffs, N.J.).*

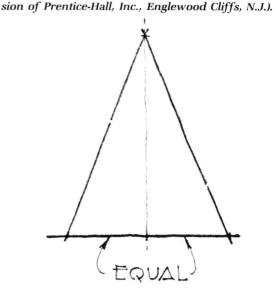

Using a center line for symmetry.

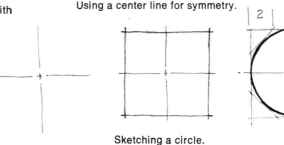

Sketching a circle.

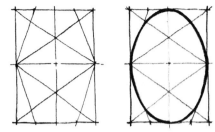

FIGURE 5–12 Sketching an ellipse (Edward J. Muller, Architectural Drawing and Light Construction, *3/E, © 1985, Prentice-Hall, Inc. Englewood Cliffs, N.J. Fig. 5–17 on p. 81. Reprinted by permission of Prentice-Hall, Inc., Englewood Cliffs, N.J.).*

tain the position of the little finger as the center and rotate the paper full circle.

An ellipse has the appearance of a circle viewed from an angle (Fig. 5–12). Drawing an ellipse is as simple as drawing a circle and the same techniques can be used. The parallelogram method of drawing an ellipse is easy (Fig. 5–13). Draw intersecting horizontal and vertical lines. Let the horizontal line be longer than the vertical line and call that the major axis or line AB. Call the vertical line DE; that becomes the minor axis. From both axis lines, draw a rectangle or parallelogram with sides equal to both axis. Divide AO and AC into an equal number of parts. Draw light lines from point D through the AO divisions and from point D through the AC divisions. Intersections of similar numbered lines will create points along the ellipse. Complete the remaining three quadrants by the same procedure and draw the ellipse as an irregular curve.

A 90° angle is seldom missing from a freehand sketch. It is important to be able to sketch such angles. One easy way to draw angles is to use the edge of the paper as a guide. A 45° angle is drawn by dividing a 90° angle equally (Fig. 5–11).

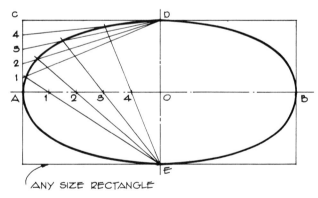

FIGURE 5–13 Sketching a parallelogram ellipse (Edward J. Muller, Architectural Drawing and Light Construction, *3/E, © 1985, Prentice-Hall, Inc. Englewood Cliffs, N.J. Fig. 3–13 on p. 46. Reprinted by permission of Prentice-Hall, Inc., Englewood Cliffs, N. J.).*

Isometric Drawing

The eye sees objects in three dimensions. Drawing objects in three dimensions is called isometric drawing. These drawings are fairly realistic images of objects (Fig. 5–14, page 92). Since the eye sees in three dimensions, laying out an isometric drawing is easy once the blocking out or outline is drawn. To

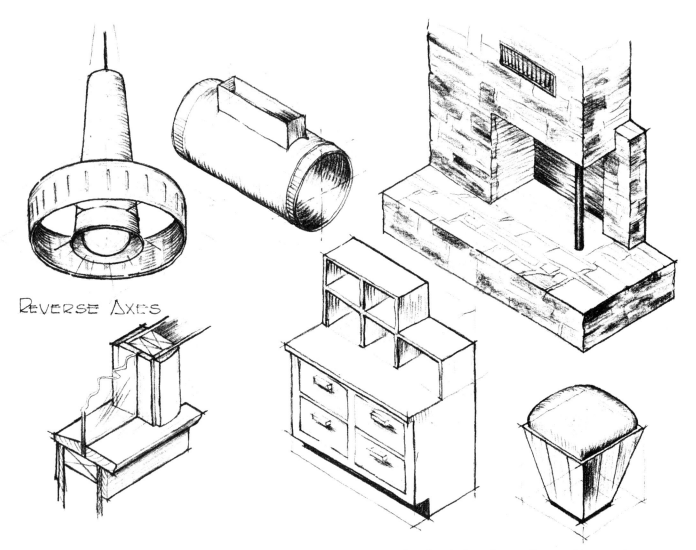

REVERSE AXES

FIGURE 5–14 *Isometric sketches (Edward J. Muller,* Architectural Drawing and Light Construction, *3/E, © 1985, Prentice-Hall, Inc. Englewood Cliffs, N.J. Fig. 5–31 on p. 90. Reprinted by permission of Prentice-Hall, Inc., Englewood Cliffs, N.J.).*

draw the outline, draw a horizontal line and let that be the ground level. Draw a vertical line from the horizontal line and that will be the line for measuring the heights of the object to be drawn. From the point where the horizontal line and the vertical line meet, draw a 30° angle line on both sides of the point. This blocking out becomes the corner of the object to be drawn.

Select a view of the object and determine the best position to view. Begin by sketching a box using the blocking-out lines as a guide. Stay within the box and sketch the features that will outline the object. All lines within the box will be parallel to the outline lines, such as roof pitch lines. Simply connect the nonisometric lines to connect their end points.

In isometric drawings, circles and arcs appear as ellipses. To sketch circles and arcs, start again with a box, which is the beginning of all isometric sketching. Draw diagonals on each face of the box. Divide each face into four equal parts. Points drawn midway between each segment become the outline points for the ellipse.

QUESTIONS

5–1. What grade of lead is recommended for freehand drawing? _____

_____

5–2. A pencil should be used for freehand drawing.
True or False

5–3. Light lines are obtained by using a harder pencil lead.
True or False

5–4. What must be done before a freehand sketch can be inked? _____

_____

5–5. What type of paper will make it easier to draw freehand? _____

_____

5–6. Any eraser can be used in freehand drawing.
True or False

5–7. What happens to a line if the lead is not rotated? _____

_____

5–8. Before any object is drawn freehand, what must be done? _____

_____

5–9. A measuring line is used for correct proportions in freehand drawing.
True or False

5–10. Describe one way of drawing a square freehand. _____

_____

6

Perspective Drawing

Introduction

The truest kind of drawing is called perspective. It is drawing as the eye sees an object. The basic rules of perspective drawing are not difficult, but skill in the finished product requires time, patience, and practice. A perspective drawing is a three-dimensional drawing—an effective way of communicating with people who have difficulty reading plans.

There is a built-in limit to perspective drawing. Even when accurate projections and rules have been followed, a distorted drawing will sometimes result. Slight line modifications may have to be made to make the drawing pleasing to the eye.

There are two different ways of drawing a perspective, called a one-point perspective and a two-point perspective. A *one-point perspective* is usually reserved for, but not limited to, an interior room perspective (Fig. 6–1). A *two-point perspective* is generally used for an outside perspective of an object or building.

Perspective

The language of perspective drawing must be understood before it can be mastered. Following is a discussion of some important terms.

Picture Plane

The picture plane represents a horizontal line that is used as a reference line on which a floor plan is placed. It is the plane onto which the view of the object is projected (Fig. 6–2, page 96). The picture plane also controls the height of a

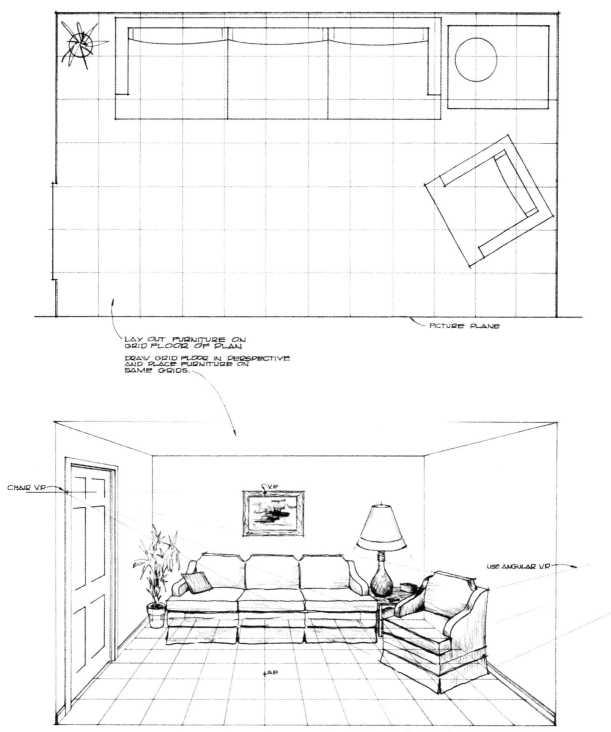

LAY OUT FURNITURE ON
GRID FLOOR OF PLAN

DRAW GRID FLOOR IN PERSPECTIVE
AND PLACE FURNITURE ON
SAME GRIDS.

PICTURE PLANE

CHAIR V.P.

V.P.

USE ANGULAR V.P.

S.P.

FIGURE 6–1 *One-point perspective (Edward J. Muller,* Architectural Drawing and Light Construction, *3/E, © 1985, Prentice-Hall, Inc. Englewood Cliffs, N.J. Fig. 13–20 on p. 381. Reprinted by permission of Prentice-Hall, Inc., Englewood Cliffs, N.J.).*

structure and the amount of surface that will be exposed. The structure to be drawn can be placed at an angle of 15°, 30°, 45°, or 60° to the picture plane. The angle should be selected on the basis of the effect of the side of the structure it is desired to show. The most attractive wall or side should be the angle which shows that wall.

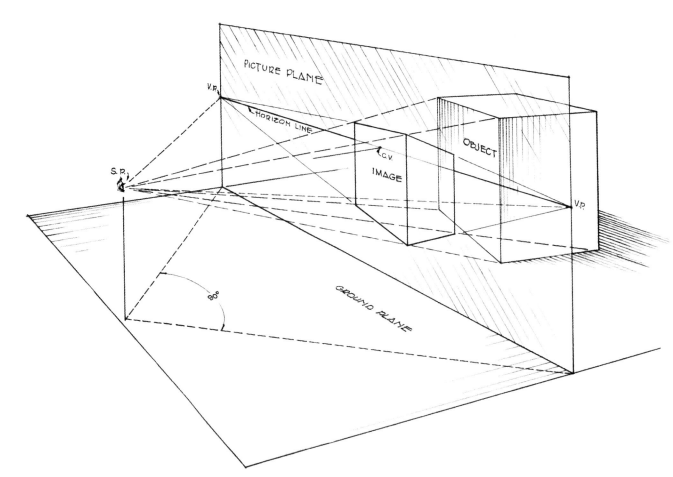

FIGURE 6–2 *Picture plane (Edward J. Muller,* Architectural Drawing and Light Construction, *3/E,* © *1985, Prentice-Hall, Inc. Englewood Cliffs, N.J. Fig. 13–1 on p. 362. Reprinted by permission of Prentice-Hall, Inc., Englewood Cliffs, N.J.).*

Ground Plane

The ground plane or ground line is the horizontal surface at the bottom of the perspective. It is a point that gives the true height of the structure from which one judges. The ground line is also used as a base when marking vertical dimensions on a drawing.

Station Point

The observer's eye represents the station point. The location of the station point in relation to the picture plane will affect the size of the drawing (Fig. 6–3). The greater the distance between the two points, the larger the picture. The station point can be placed anywhere on a drawing, but a good rule is to place it to form a 30° angle from the corners of the plane. Another good rule is to place the station point twice the length of the building from the picture plane (Fig. 6–4).

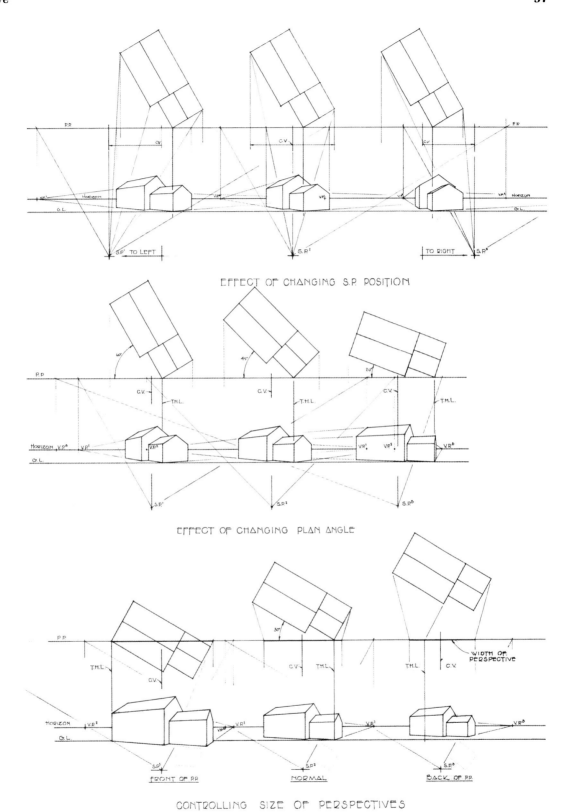

EFFECT OF CHANGING S.P. POSITION

EFFECT OF CHANGING PLAN ANGLE

CONTROLLING SIZE OF PERSPECTIVES

FIGURE 6–3 Size of perspective (Edward J. Muller, Architectural Drawing and Light Construction, *3/E, © 1985, Prentice-Hall, Inc. Englewood Cliffs, N.J. Fig. 13–7 on p. 366. Reprinted by permission of Prentice-Hall, Inc., Englewood Cliffs, N.J.).*

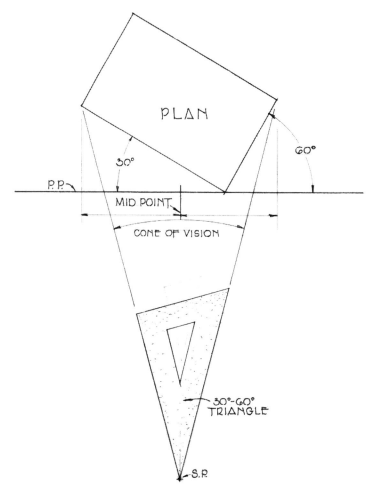

FIGURE 6–4 Station point (Edward J. Muller, Architectural Drawing and Light Construction, *3/E, © 1985, Prentice-Hall, Inc. Englewood Cliffs, N.J. Fig. 13–4 on p. 363. Reprinted by permission of Prentice-Hall, Inc., Englewood Cliffs, N.J.).*

Horizon Line

The line that intersects the sky and the ground is called the horizon line. The distance above the ground line where the horizon is placed will determine the area of the structure. The placement of the horizon line will tell if the drawing has a bird's-eye look, a worm's-eye look, or is at eye level. The higher the horizon line above eye level, the more rooftop will be visible (Fig. 6–5).

Vanishing Point

When looking at railroad tracks, they seem to converge far in the distance. The point of convergence is called a vanishing point. In a two-point perspective ("point" meaning "vanishing point"), there are two vanishing points. There is a vanishing point to the left of the station point and one to the right of the station point. From the station point line, all lines of a building on the right

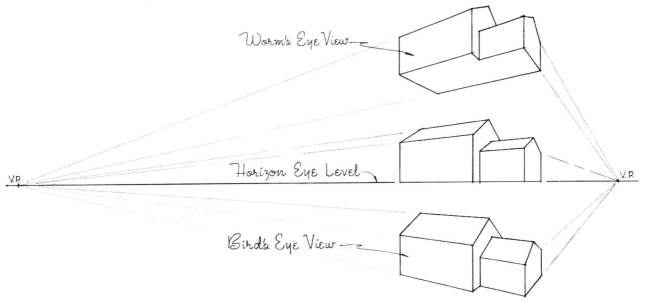

FIGURE 6–5 *Horizon line (Edward J. Muller, Architectural Draw-ing and Light Construction, 3/E, © 1985, Prentice-Hall, Inc. Englewood Cliffs, N.J. Fig. 13–8 on p. 367. Reprinted by permission of Prentice-Hall, Inc., Englewood Cliffs, N.J.).*

of the station point will converge to the right vanishing point, and all lines to the left of the station point will converge to the left vanishing point.

The vanishing points will always be on the horizon line. To locate the vanishing points, from the station point, draw lines parallel to the wall of the building in plan. Where these lines intersect with the picture plane, draw a perpendicular line down to the horizontal line and these points become the vanishing points (Fig. 6–6).

FIGURE 6–6 *Vanishing point (Edward J. Muller, Architectural Drawing and Light Construction, 3/E, © 1985, Prentice-Hall, Inc. Englewood Cliffs, N.J. Fig. 13–6 on p. 365. Reprinted by permission of Prentice-Hall, Inc., Englewood Cliffs, N.J.).*

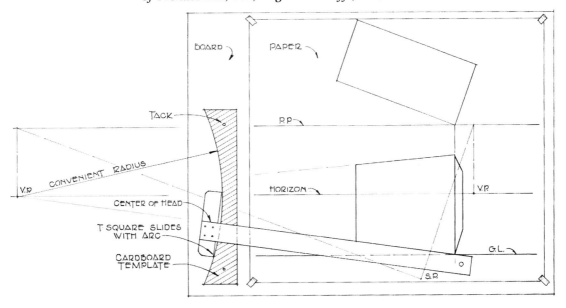

True Height Line

In a two-point perspective, one corner of an object touches the picture plane. This is the line where all the vertical heights are shown. This line is called the true height line. All other lines have their heights projected to the vanishing points.

For a step-by-step perspective drawing, see Fig. 6–7a through 6–7d.

FIGURE 6–7a (Edward J. Muller, Architectural Drawing and Light Construction, *3/E, © 1985, Prentice-Hall, Inc. Englewood Cliffs, N.J. pp. 368 and 372. Reprinted by permission of Prentice-Hall, Inc., Englewood Cliffs, N.J.).*

How to Draw a Two-Point Angular Perspective of an Exterior

Step A

1. Draw the floor plan, or roof plan as shown, on a 30°–60° relationship with the horizontal. Or a separate plan can be taped down in a similar position.

2. Draw the horizontal picture-plane line touching the lower corner of the plan. (Other relationships can be used later, if desired.)

3. Locate the center of vision (C.V.) midway on the horizontal width of the inclined plan.

4. Establish the station point on the center of vision, far enough from the picture plane to produce a 30° cone of vision (refer to Fig. 6–4).

5. From the station point, draw perpendicular projectors, parallel to the sides of the plan, to the picture plane. These points are the vanishing points in plan, and are often called distance points.

6. Draw a horizontal ground-plane line a convenient distance below the picture plane. It will need to be placed only far enough below the picture plane to allow sufficient space for the perspective layout.

Step B

7. Draw the elevation view on the ground-line. Place it off to the side of the perspective area; even if projection lines run through the elevation view, no harm will result. This view supplies the heights; therefore it must be drawn to the same scale as the plan. Usually the end elevation is sufficient if the major heights are shown (If a perspective is being drawn from a separate set of plans, the elevation, like the plan, can merely be taped on the ground plane in a convenient position.)

8. Draw the horizon line as shown. The heights of the elevation view will aid in determining the most effective eye-level height. Usually if a level view is desired, the horizon line is scaled 6′-0″ above the ground-plane line. This distance is optional.

9. Drop vertical projectors from the picture-plane distance points (projectors originating at the station point) to the horizon. These points on the horizon line are the vanishing points of the perspective and should be made prominent to avoid mistaken identity.

10. Draw vertical true-height lines from the corner of the plan touching the picture plane and the extension of the two ridges as they intersect the picture plane. Unless they are "boxed in," ridgelines of gable roofs should be brought to the picture plane, where a true-height line can be established. Usually this is the simplest method of plotting their heights; from the true-height line, the ridge height is vanished to the proper vanishing point.

11. Now we are ready to start the perspec-

FIGURE 6–7a (cont'd)

tive itself. From the intersection of the main true-height line at the corner of the building and the ground plane, construct the bottom of the building by projecting the point toward both vanishing points. All perspectives should start at this point.

Step C

12. Next, continue developing the main blockmass of the building. Take the height of the basic block from the elevation view and project it to the true-height line. This gives us the height of the block on the perspective. Again, project this point on the true-height line to both vanishing points.

13. To find the width of the basic block, we must go to the plan. With a straight-edge, project both extreme corners of the plan toward the station point. Where these projectors pierce the picture plane, drop verticals to the perspective. This establishes the basic-block width; the back corner can be located, if desired, by vanishing the outer corners to the correct vanishing points.

14. Next, plot the main ridge so that the roof shape can be completed. Project the height of the ridge from the elevation view to the main ridge true-height line. Vanish this point to the left vanishing

point. The ends of the ridge must be taken again from the plan view. Project both ends of the ridge on the plan toward the station point; where the projectors pierce the picture plane, drop verticals to the vanished ridgeline. This defines the main ridge, and the edges of the roof can then be drawn to the corners of the main block.

15. The small ridge of the front gable roof can be established by the same method as above. Because this ridge is perpendicular to the main ridge, the small ridge is vanished to the right vanishing point. The remaining corners and features of the gable extension in front of the main block can be taken from the plan by the method previously mentioned and vanished to the correct vanishing point.

16. Continue plotting the remaining lines and features on the perspective by locating each from the plan as usual and projecting their heights from the elevation view. After heights are brought to the true-height line, they must usually be projected around the walls of the building to bring them to their position. Remember that true heights are first established on the picture plane and then vanished along the walls of the building to where they are needed.

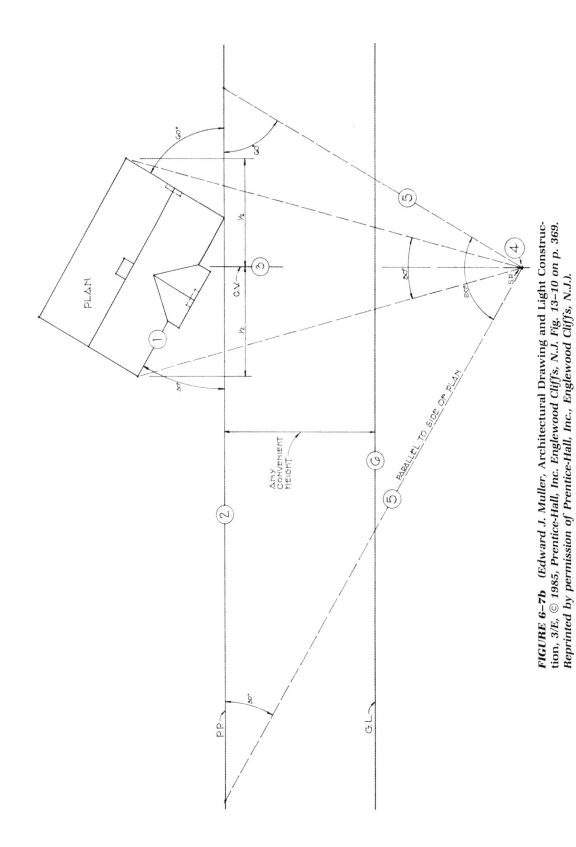

FIGURE 6–7b *(Edward J. Muller, Architectural Drawing and Light Construction, 3/E, © 1985, Prentice-Hall, Inc. Englewood Cliffs, N.J. Fig. 13–10 on p. 369. Reprinted by permission of Prentice-Hall, Inc., Englewood Cliffs, N.J.).*

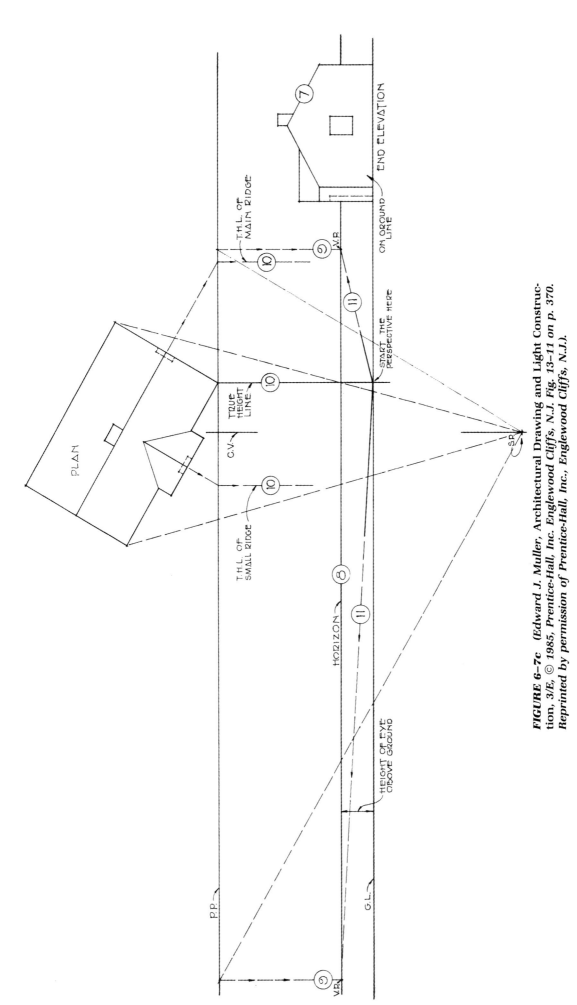

FIGURE 6–7c *(Edward J. Muller, Architectural Drawing and Light Construction, 3/E, © 1985, Prentice-Hall, Inc. Englewood Cliffs, N.J. Fig. 13–11 on p. 370. Reprinted by permission of Prentice-Hall, Inc., Englewood Cliffs, N.J.).*

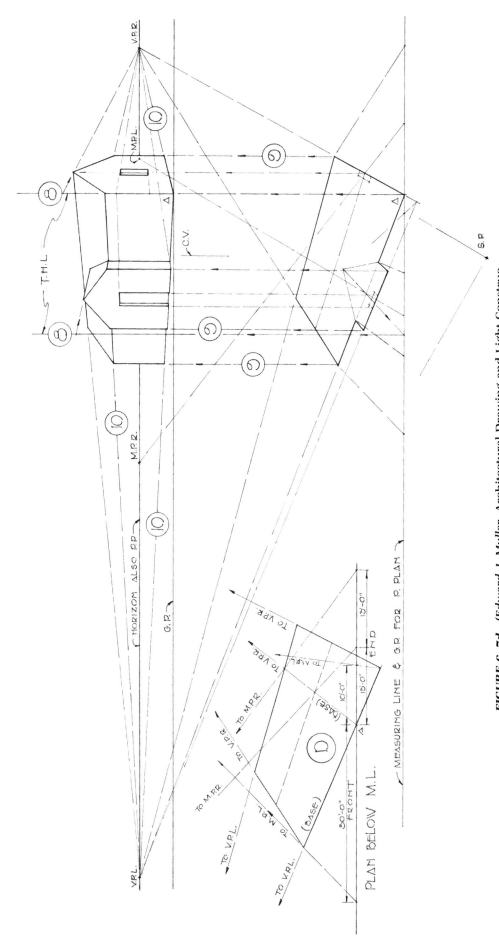

FIGURE 6-7d (Edward J. Muller, *Architectural Drawing and Light Construction, 3/E,* © 1985, Prentice-Hall, Inc. Englewood Cliffs, N.J. Fig. 13–16 on p. 376. Reprinted by permission of Prentice-Hall, Inc., Englewood Cliffs, N.J.).

QUESTIONS

6-1. Name the six most important terms relating to perspective drawing.

1. _____
2. _____
3. _____
4. _____
5. _____
6. _____

6-2. The two principal types of perspective drawing are the one-point and the three-point.
True or False

6-3. Define *picture plane*. _____
_____

6-4. On what line are true heights measured? _____

6-5. How many vanishing points are required for perspective drawing?
_____

6-6. Perspective drawing is used only for exterior views.
True or False

6-7. How many dimensions does perspective drawing show? _____
_____

6-8. The best angle for placing a picture plane is 22°.
True or False

6-9. Where is the picture plane placed on a drawing? _____

6-10. A building can be drawn in perspective from any angle of view.
True or False

Residential Plan Development

Introduction

There are many types of building use planning. Residential is one; others include commercial, educational, professional, and manufacturing. Each building use requires a different type of planning. Residential planning includes the needs of the owner, the budget, the condition of the land, the laws of the area, the aesthetics of the building, and the size of building. Planning thus involves many hours of study and many hours of meetings. It may involve many hours of restudy and changes before the final plans can be completed.

Before study can begin on the outside of a building, the inside must be finished because the inside shape, or plan, will affect the outside or elevations of the building. The entire building will come together in a study of all parts of the building. This phase must be completed and approved before the next phase can be started.

Owner's Requirements

Before planning can begin, many questions must be asked and answered. The number of people in the household and their sex must be known to determine the number of bedrooms required. The living habits of the owner will determine the type of structure to be built. If frequent formal entertaining is done in the household, a formal dining room may be required. If the principals of the household frequently work at home, an office may be necessary. If there are small children in the household, a family room may be a requirement. Are there one, two, or more cars in the family? This will determine the size of the garage. Is the property large enough for all the rooms to be on one floor, or are two floors necessary? The number of household members will determine the number of baths needed.

The family may have a home-type business that must be planned for. If the family are outdoor lovers, patios, decks, porches, and gardens may be included. If music is a hobby in the family, a music room may be included.

The list must go on and on to plan a building properly to meet the requirements of the occupants. Also included are the laws of the area governing construction. If any household member is physically handicapped, the house must be made accessible to that person.

Schematic Studies

Once all requirements have been compiled, the information is incorporated into a schematic study, a freehand one-line plan drawn to scale, showing all the requirements of the owner and complying with the laws of the area (Fig. 7–1, page 108). Several studies will probably be made before a conclusion is reached. The schematic study is a rough draft of a plan; it is polished and refined after approval by the owner. Before further development at this stage, the study must be functional, workable, and comply with the building and zoning laws (Fig. 7–2, page 109).

Building and Zoning Laws

There is no freedom of design in complying with building and zoning laws. These laws have been established to protect the people who live, work, play, and pray in buildings. Building laws control the design of buildings and zoning laws control the use of land (Fig. 7–3). These laws are established by local, state, and federal agencies. Before a building permit is issued, the plans must conform to the laws of the area in which the building is to be built. These laws are continually being changed and differ from area to area.

Building laws also help to reduce maintenance costs and insurance premiums. They control design, construction, materials, maintenance, location of building, use of building, and quality and use of materials; they also reduce loss of life and property from earthquakes, storms, and fires.

Most local building codes are adapted from four national building codes: the Uniform Building Code (UBC), the Basic National Building Code (BNBC), the Building Officials and Code Administrators (BOCA) code, and the Standard Building Code (SBC). There are many variations of these building codes and they have a major influence on construction technique. The codes also affect the plumbing, heating, electrical, ventilation, and air-conditioning systems of buildings.

Most codes are divided into several major categories relating to building classifications, which deal with the type of occupancy of the building. There are eight common classifications of building occupancy (see page 109).

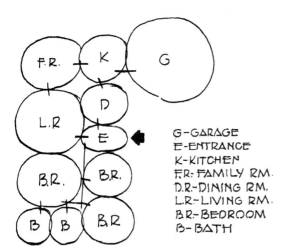

A schematic sketch for starting a floor plan.

Plan   development
sketch and relating elevations.

G–GARAGE
E–ENTRANCE
K–KITCHEN
F.R.–FAMILY RM.
D.R.–DINING RM.
L.R–LIVING RM.
B.R–BEDROOM
B–BATH

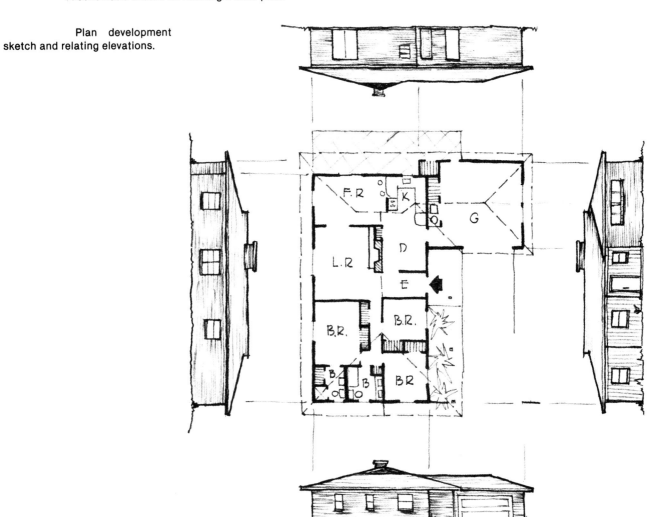

FIGURE 7–1   Schematic sketching (Edward J. Muller, Architectural Drawing and Light Construction, 3/E, © 1985, Prentice-Hall, Inc. Englewood Cliffs, N.J. Fig. 5–27, 5–28 on p. 87. Reprinted by permission of Prentice-Hall, Inc., Englewood Cliffs, N.J.).

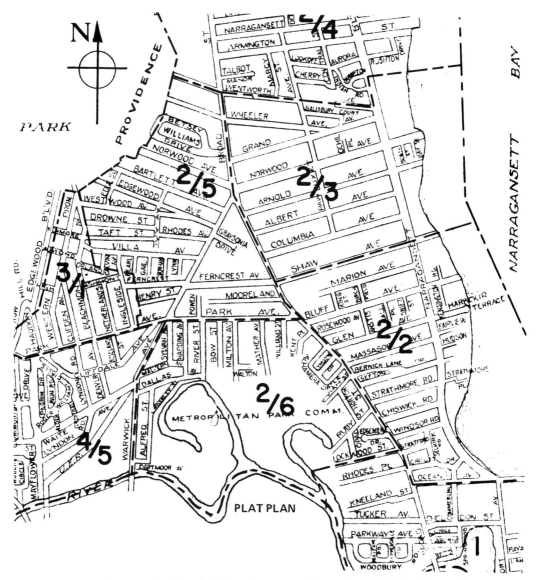

FIGURE 7-2 Plat plan. All properties are divided into Plats and Lots indexed by letters or numbers. Each Lot has a Plat and Lot No. which is recorded at the Town or City Hall. These in turn are separated by Zones reserving certain areas as residential, business, manufacturing, industrial, and so on. Residential zones are again separated into single-family, two-family, and multi-family units. It is important to know what each lot is zoned for. Each zone must comply with specific building requirements to receive a building permit.

Common Classifications of Building Occupancy

1. Assembly
   a. Theaters
   b. Restaurants
   c. Museums
2. Educational
   a. Schools
   b. Colleges
   c. Universities
3. Institutional

   a. Hospitals
   b. Prisons
   c. Nursing homes
4. Residential
   a. Hotels
   b. Apartments
   c. Condomiums
   d. Dwellings
5. Mercantile

   a. Shopping malls
   b. Retail stores
6. Offices
7. Industrial
   a. Factories
   b. Manufacturing facilities
8. Storage
   a. Warehouses

LAND USE

• = special permit X = Permitted — = prohibited Principal Use	Districts											
	A-80	A-20 A-12 A-8 A-6	B-1	B-2	C-1	C-2	C-3	C-4	C-5	M-1	M-2	S-1
Food stores, delicatessen	—	—	—	—	—	X	X	X	—	—	—	—
Bakery, provided all baked goods sold on premises	—	—	—	—	—	X	X	X	—	—	—	—
Drug store, newstand, variety and notice stores	—	—	—	—	—	X	X	X	—	—	—	—
Book, stationery, and gift shops	—	—	—	—	—	X	X	X	—	—	—	—
Florist shops 1. excluding greenhouse 2. including greenhouse	— —	— —	— —	— —	— —	X —	X —	— X	— X	— —	— —	— —
Hardware stores	—	—	—	—	—	X	X	X	X	—	—	—
Banks and financial institutions	—	—	—	—	X	X	X	X	X	•	•	—
Barber shops and beauty parlors; tailor and custom dressmaking shops	—	—	—	—	—	X	X	X	—	—	—	—
Laundry, dry cleaning, and pressing establishments 1. 5 employees or less working at any one time within the establishment	—	—	—	—	—	X	X	X	X	—	—	—
2. 6 employees or more working at any one time within the establishment	—	—	—	—	—	—	—	—	X	X	X	—

INTENSITY REGULATIONS

District	Minimum Lot Area (sq. ft.)	Minimum Lot Width and Frontage (ft.)	Minimum Yards (ft.)			Maximum Lot Coverage (%)	Maximum Building Height (ft.)
			Front	Rear	Side		
S-1, A-80	20,000	200	40	100	20	10	35
A-20	20,000	125	30	30	15	20	35
A-12	12,000	100	25	20	10	30	35
A-8	8,000	80	25	20	10	30	35
A-6	6,000	60	25	20	8	30	35
B-1	6,000	60	25	20	8	35	35
B-2	6,000	60	25	20	8	50	- -
C-1	6,000	60	25	20	8	60	- -
C-2	6,000	60	25	20	8	60	30
C-3	6,000	60	0	20	0	100	35
C-4	12,000	120	60	20	8	50	35
C-5	10,000	80	30	20	8	60	35
M-1	30,000	150	40	30	20	60	- -
M-2	60,000	200	40	30	25	60	- -

FIGURE 7–3 *Land use and intensity regulations.*

Another major category is classification of construction type. This deals with the type of material used in construction.

- ■ Type 1: Fire-resistant construction
- ■ Type 2: Heavy timber construction
- ■ Type 3: Noncombustible construction
- ■ Type 4: Ordinary construction
- ■ Type 5: Wood frame construction

Contour Profile

Part of the process of a schematic study deals with the shape of the surface of the ground on which a building is to be built. This is called a *contour elevation* or *topographic survey* (Fig. 7–4). This information is usually compiled by a land surveyor. The shape of the ground must be known in order to plan the building on the property to determine if any change is required in the shape of the land. Sometimes it may be necessary to alter the ground to suit the design. For example, sloping land may afford a basement floor at ground level or a garage in the basement. There may be holes that need to be filled in the ground, or there may be hills that need to be cut down. The plan must state how deep in the ground the house is to be built. If there is plumbing in the basement, the

FIGURE 7–4   *Plot plan.*

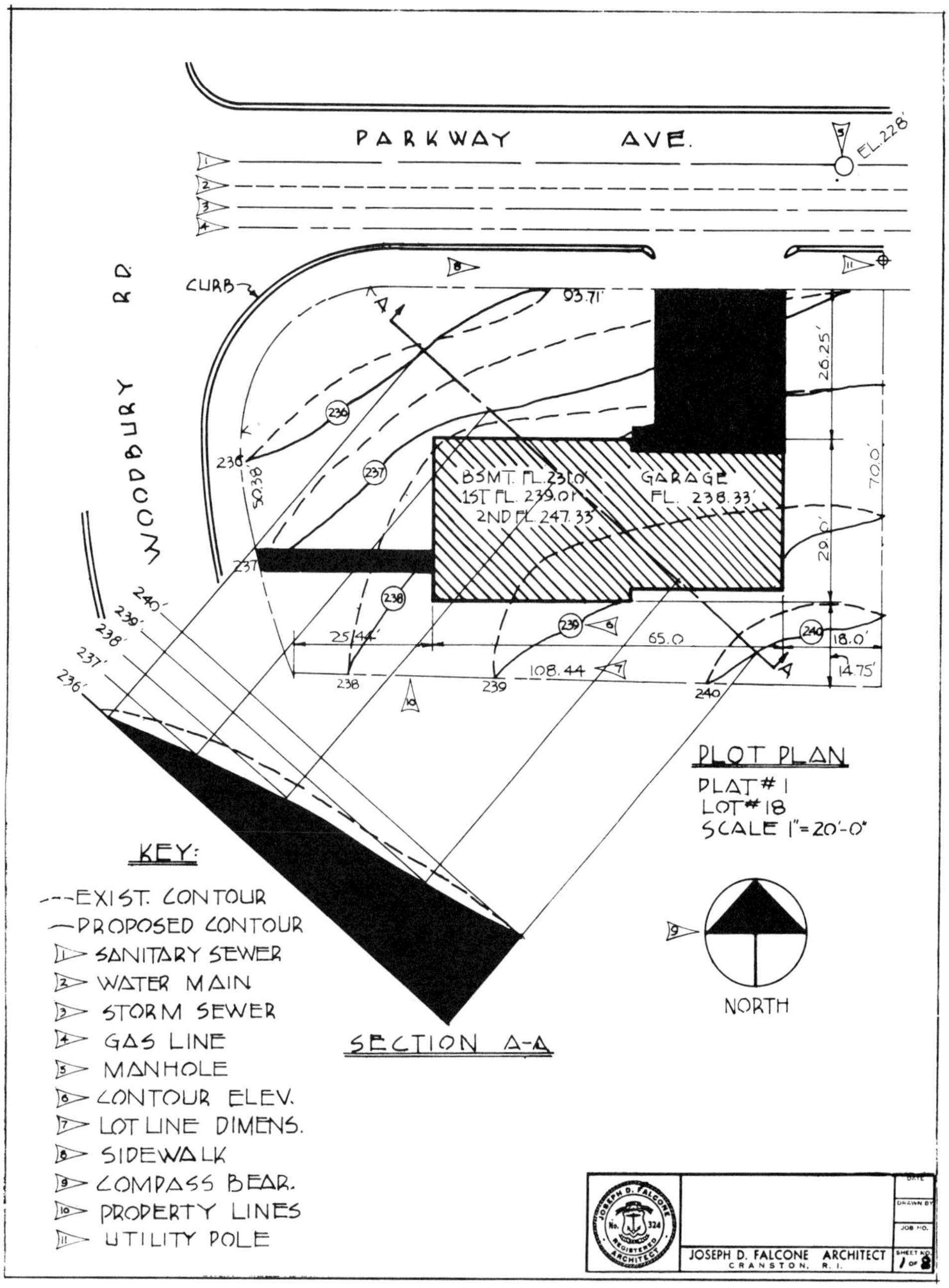

basement floor level must not be below the sewer level in the street. The height of the first floor above the ground will determine how many steps are required to reach the first floor from the ground.

Another consideration in the shape of the land is to drain the surface properly to avoid water puddling, yet not cause surface water to drain onto adjacent property. The property survey will also show the location and size of trees on the land. Trees that interfere with the building location must be removed.

Compass Bearing

The position of the sun relates to compass bearings. The sun rises in the east and sets in the west, which means that little sun is exposed in the north. The sun shines all day in the south. The compass bearing should be considered in orienting the building on the land. Usually, the cold winds and storms of winter comes from the north, which may cause the northern exposure of a building to be a little colder. A good buffer for cold north winds is to landscape by planting or restoring trees or by placing an accessory building such as a garage on the north side. On the other hand, the best natural light comes from the north, so this is the best exposure for displaying art, painting, and sculpture. It is also the best exposure for an art studio. The southern exposure is the warm side because it is exposed to the sun most of the day. This is the exposure for rooms where sunlight is preferred and is also in the best exposure for solar energy.

Budget

The cost of a building must be known before any work on plans is started. The plans are tailored to this budget for obvious reasons. If after the plans are completed, the cost of the construction is more than the owner can afford, all the work put into preparing the plans will have been wasted. The cost need not be exact at this stage, but it must at least be realistic and reasonable. It takes more time to change the plans because of cost overrun than it takes to prepare the original documents because what has already been done needs to be erased and the changes redrawn. The building cost can be approximated on a square-foot basis.

Approval

Before any work is done on the final drawings, the preliminary drawings must be approved. The approval will include not only function and aesthetic design, but also cost of construction. By this time preliminary approval must also be obtained from the various building officials to be certain that no major changes are required to comply with the local building and zoning laws.

Final Drawings

After approval of the preliminary drawings, work may begin on the final plans, being careful not to make any major changes from the preliminary drawings. The final drawings will consist of the following drawings:

1. Plot plan
2. Basement plan or foundation plan (the basement plan is also used as the foundation plan)
3. Floor plan: one plan for each floor
4. Elevations (the outside of the building)
5. Section
6. Details
7. Schedules: include finish, door, and window schedules

The success or failure of a building under construction depends on the completeness and understanding of the building plans. If the plans are not clear or complete, the chain of communication is broken, resulting in chaos, confusion, and misunderstanding. A complete knowledge and understanding of the local building laws and zoning laws is necessary if the plans are to comply with the laws. If the plans fail to follow the building and zoning laws, a building permit may not be issued, and if issued through an oversight, the building may pose a danger to the inhabitants and require rebuilding to conform with the laws at the risk of removing all that does not comply.

Specifications are also a part of building plans. There are generally several $8\frac{1}{2} \times 11$ in. sheets explaining specifically the quality of material to be included in the building. For example, there are many models of kitchen sinks based on style, material, size, and color. The specification will be specific as to the name of the sink manufacturer, model number, color, number of compartments, and size. The same detail is specified for all parts of the building. Together the plans and specifications constitute a complete set of building documents (Fig. 7–5, pp. 114–126).

When a set of drawings and specifications has been completed, there is to be no doubt or question as to the intent of the job. But if all that is available is an incomplete or unfinished set of plans and specifications, it will be almost impossible for a builder to construct the building, and even more difficult to estimate the cost of the building. The document, which consists of plans and specifications, constitutes a legal contract, which means that the builder will build according to the document and the owner will pay the builder for work and material that he or she has performed. The owner should expect no more than what is contained in the plans and specifications.

Laws Governing Construction

Two different types of laws are involved in the construction of a residence: building laws and zoning laws.

FIGURE 7–5   Home specifications (courtesy Home Plan Book Co.).

SPECIFICATIONS

The contractor shall provide all necessary labor and materials and perform all work of every nature whatsoever to be done in the erection of a residence for

_____

as owner, in accordance with these specifications and accompanying drawings. The location of the residence will be as follows:

_____

_____

_____

GENERAL CONDITIONS

All blank spaces in these specifications that apply to this building are to be filled in. Items that do not apply are to be crossed out.
The general conditions herein set forth shall apply to any contract given under these specifications and shall be binding upon every sub-contractor as well as General contractor.
The plans, elevations, sections and detail drawings, together with these specifications, are to form the basis of the contract and are to be of equal force. Should anything be mentioned in these specifications and not shown in the drawings, or vice versa, the same shall be followed as if set forth in both, as it is the intent of these specifications and accompanying drawings to correspond and to embody every item and part necessary for the completion of the structure. The contractor shall comply with all health and building ordinances that are applicable.

EXCAVATION AND GRADING

The contractor shall do all necessary excavating and rough grading. The excavation shall be large enough to permit inspection of footings after the foundation has been completed. All excess dirt shall be hauled away by the contractor. Black surface loam to be piled where directed by owner for use in grading. Grade level shall be established by the owner who will also furnish a survey of the lot showing the location of the building. The finish grading, seeding, sodding and landscaping shall be done by the owner unless specified as follows: _____

_____

INSURANCE

The contractor will provide liability insurance and workmen's compensation insurance in full until completion of the building. Fire and windstorm insurance during construction to be provided by the owner.

EXTRAS OR CREDITS

Any deviation from these specifications or plans involving an extra charge or a credit must be agreed upon in writing between the contracting parties before the change is made. The contractor shall not take advantage of any discrepancies in the drawing and specifications. If any discrepancies are found they shall be referred to the owner or architect and be corrected before any contract is entered into. Dimensions shown in figures, on the drawing, shall take precedence over scaled dimensions.

.1.

Published by Home Plan Book Co. (all rights reserved), 1596 Selby Ave., St. Paul 4, Minn.   Printed in U. S. A.

FIGURE 7-5 (cont'd)
CONCRETE FOOTINGS

Concrete footings for walls and piers shall be mixed in the proportion of one part cement,_____

parts sand and_____ parts gravel. Pit run gravel may be used if its proportions of sand and gravel are as called for. All aggregate shall be clean and sharp and free from organic matter. Coarse aggregate to pass 1¼-inch screen and to be retained upon a ¼-inch screen.

Footings for walls shall be_____ inches thick and_____ inches wider than wall on each

side; pier footings shall be not less than_____ inches square and_____ inches thick._____

BASEMENT WALLS

Shall be of_____ construction, straight, plumb and level, and as shown on plans. All joints shall be struck flush on both sides. Beam fill as shown on plans. Basement

walls *will or will not* be waterproofed with_____ coats of_____

BASEMENT FLOOR

Shall be 4 inches thick, laid with sufficient slope to drain. If made in one pour, the mixture shall be the same as for the footings, troweled level and smooth. If made in two pours, the finish coat shall be one inch thick and shall be of a mixture of one part of cement to two parts of sand.

CEMENT WALKS AND STEPS

Cement walk from street curb line to front steps shall be_____ feet wide and_____ inches

thick. Walk from front steps to rear door step shall be_____ feet wide and_____ inches thick. The steps at the front and rear entrances shall be of wood, cement or brick construction as indicated on the plan. Concrete splash blocks *shall or shall not* be furnished.

CHIMNEYS

Chimneys shall be constructed of common brick with face brick top unless otherwise shown. The footings shall be concrete. The size of the flues shall be as shown. All mortar drippings shall be cleaned from flues leaving them uniform in size from top to bottom. All flues shall be properly lined with vitrified flue lining extending from the footing. Thimbles shall be placed as directed and cast-iron clean-out door shall be provided. If gas heating unit is used, the flue shall be circular vitrified

tile with bell top, or_____
Fireplace, if any, shall be lined with fire brick and provided with a flue with an area not less than 1/10 of the area of the fireplace opening. Damper, ash dump and clean-out doors shall be provided.

Circulating type fireplace, if any, shall be _____

Concrete hearth support to be fireproof, hearth floor to be _____

Face of fireplace opening if masonry, shall be _____

Mantel shelf if masonry, shall be _____ Incinerator if any, shall be _____

BRICK WORK AND STONE WORK

All brick work shall be laid in cement and lime mortar, with all bricks well bedded and shoved into place, with both vertical and horizontal joints on straight lines. Joints to be of color selected by owner.

The price allowed for face brick, if any, is $_____ per 1,000. Any cost in excess of that amount shall be borne by the owner and any cost lower than this amount shall be credited to the owner. Lintels to be properly placed above all openings where masonry is shown above. Exterior stone

work, if any, shall be_____

.2.

FIGURE 7–5 (cont'd)

TILE WORK

The contractor shall furnish and set all tile, if any, in a neat and workmanlike manner. The tile

shall be as follows: _____

_____

Towel bars, grab bar, paper holder, soap dish or other fixtures, if furnished by tile contractor,

shall be _____

_____

_____

_____

CARPENTER WORK

The contractor shall and will provide all necessary labor and perform all carpenter work of every nature whatsoever to be done. He shall lay out all work and be responsible for all measurements, and keep a competent foreman in charge. All work shall be done in substantial conformity with the plans and specifications or any variations, changes or amendments thereof that have been approved in writing by the contracting parties.

GIRDERS

Girders or supporting beams shall be as required by the size of building, and as shown on plans, all

to be _____ . Columns to be _____ of size shown on plans.

JOISTS

First floor joists to be 2″ x _____ ″, placed _____ ″ on centers, Grade _____

Second floor joists to be 2″ x _____ ″, placed _____ ″ on centers, Grade _____

Ceiling joists to be   2″ x _____ ″, placed _____ ″ on centers, Grade _____

Rafters to be   2″ x _____ ″, placed _____ ″ on centers, Grade _____

Collar ties to be   2″ x _____ ″, placed _____ ″ on centers, Grade _____

Valley and hip rafters to be 2″ x _____ ″,   Grade _____

STUDDINGS

Studdings shall be sized 2x4's, spaced 16″ on centers, single plate on bottom and double plate on top of each wall or partition, 2x4's shall be doubled around all openings. Outside studdings shall be

_____ Inside studdings shall be _____

BRIDGING

First and second floor joists shall have one row of 1x3ʹ beveled bridging for all 14ʹ spans or less. All spans over 14ʹ shall have two rows, all nailed securely to joists at each end.

SUB-FLOORING

Sub-flooring shall be laid diagonally with _____ , securely nailed. All joints shall be made on joists.

FIGURE 7–5   (cont'd)
SHEATHING

Outside wall sheathing shall be _____ Roof sheathing shall be _____

_____

WALL SIDING

Siding, if any, to be _____

ROOF SHINGLES

Shingles for roof to be _____

laid _____ inches to weather using galvanized nails. _____

SIDEWALL SHINGLES

Sidewall shingles, if any, to be _____

INSULATION AND PAPER

Sidewall insulation to be _____ Top floor ceiling insulation to be _____

Building paper under shingles to be _____

Building paper over sheathing to be _____

Building paper between sub-floor and finish floor to be_____

OUTSIDE FINISH

All lumber required for outside finish shall be _____

WINDOW AND DOOR FRAMES

All window and outside door frames as shown on plans shall be of sound clear pine, free from ob-

jectionable defects. Outside casing _____ thick. Door sills shall be _____

_____

Assembled basement sash units, if any, shall be _____

Assembled window units, if any, shall be _____

Assembled door units, if any, shall be _____

WEATHER STRIPPING

Shall be _____

WINDOWS, STORM SASH AND SCREENS

All windows and sash shall be_____thick of pine, as shown on plans. All check rail windows *shall or shall not* be grooved for sash cord and properly fitted with weights. All check rail windows *shall or shall not* be grooved and properly fitted with sash balancers. Storm sash and screens 1⅛″ thick fitted with hangers and fasteners *shall or shall not* be furnished for all windows and hinged sash.

Screen cloth shall be _____ mesh _____ wire. Glass to be _____

Combination storm sash and screen units, if any, shall be _____

FIGURE 7–5 (cont'd)
FINISH FLOORS

Finished floors in Living Room and Dining Room to be _____

Finished floor in Vestibule to be _____

Finished floors in Bedrooms to be _____

Finished floor in _____ to be _____

Finished floor in Kitchen to be _____

Finished floor in Rear Entry to be _____ Porch fl. to be _____

Finished floor in Bathroom to be _____ Fin. fl. in Toilet to be _____

Linoleum sub-floor lining to be _____

Flooring in Attic of house to be _____ Flooring in Attic of Garage to be _____

All hardwood floors shall be properly nailed and machine-sanded to a smooth, even surface. Floors under linoleum shall be securely nailed with coated nails and machine sanded.

INSIDE FINISH

Trim in the Living Room, Dining Room and Vestibule shall be _____

Trim in _____ shall be _____

Trim in the Kitchen and Rear Entry shall be _____

Trim in the Bedrooms, Bathroom and Hall shall be _____

_____

All trim shall be freshly cut and sanded at the mill. Chair rail *shall or shall not* be provided in kitchen and bath. Picture moulding *shall or shall not* be provided in all main rooms. Ceiling cove *shall or shall not* be provided in living and dining rooms.

Base to be _____

DOORS

All of the inside doors shall be 1⅜" thick as follows: _____

_____

The front door shall be 1¾" thick of _____

The remaining outside doors shall be 1¾" thick of _____

Provide scuttle door to attic and plumbing access door.

Provide combination storm and screen doors for all outside doors.

FIGURE 7–5 (cont'd)
JAMBS AND CASINGS

All inside jambs shall be ¾" thick, and of kinds specified above. Casings shall be_____" thick

of _____ design. _____

STAIRWORK

Stairs leading from first to second floor shall be as shown on plan with _____ risers and

_____ treads and _____ wall rail. Basement stairs shall have _____

risers and_____ treads and_____ wall rail. _____

Three stair horses shall be provided for each stair and shall be_____" x _____".
Wall stringers *shall or shall not* be housed.

CABINET WORK

Built-in Medicine Cabinet in bathroom, size _____

Kitchen cabinets shall be of_____ placed as shown on plan. Same *shall or shall not* have

_____ backing and doors shall be_____ inches thick, *shall be panel doors, shall be flush doors,*
and *shall or shall not* be rabetted. Cabinet drawers and doors *shall or shall not* have lips. If **catalog**

design is selected by owner, same shall be _____

_____

Kitchen counter tops to be_____ Splash back to be _____

Mantel shelf (if shelf only), shall be _____ Design No._____ Kind of wood _____

Mantel shelf and facing for fireplace opening, if wood, shall be Design No.____ Kind of wood ____

_____

Other cabinet work, if any, shall be as follows: _____

_____

_____

Clothes Chute, if any, shall be _____

CLOSETS

All closets shall have the necessary hook strips with hooks and one shelf and one clothes rod.

STORAGE ROOMS

Provide a _____ 'x _____ ' coal bin in the basement, using _____

Provide one _____ 'x _____ ' storage room in basement, using _____

with _____ shelves 18 inches wide. _____

FIGURE 7–5 (cont'd)

LATHING PLASTERING AND GROUNDS

Plaster base shall be gypsum lath, structural insulating lath, or metal lath and shall be applied in accordance with the manufacturer's directions. Wood lath, if used, shall be _____

All plastering to be two coat work with _____

All corners and angles must be finished plumb, straight and true, and all surfaces smooth and flush with grounds. The plasterer is to point up and finish all defects after carpenters are through if necessary and remove from premises all rubbish pertaining to his work and leave the building broom clean. Keene's cement *will or will not* be used in bathroom up to height of chair rail. All exposed plaster corners to be provided with metal corner beads, inside corners to be reinforced. Ceiling cove with one break at ceiling or wall *shall or shall not* be furnished. Plaster grounds around all inside door openings are to be _____ . Temporary heat, if necessary, shall be furnished by____ ____.

Plastering in the basement shall consist of the following: _____

_____ Plastering in garage shall consist of the following: _____

DRY WALL

Dry-Wall, if any, shall consist of _____

All exposed corners *shall or shall not* be reinforced with _____

Ceiling cove, if any, shall be_____

Joints shall be finished by _____

INTERIOR PAINTING

All woodwork to be carefully cleaned of finger marks, stains and other defects before any oil, filling, paint or varnish is applied, and all rough spots to be sand-papered smooth before being filled or finished, and all nails and brad holes to be filled with colored putty to match color desired. Finish to consist of the following:

Living Room _____   Dining Room _____

Kitchen _____   Rear Entry_____

Bedrooms and Halls _____   Vestibule _____

Bathroom _____   Basement _____

Radiators _____   Floors _____

DECORATING

Interior wall decorating shall be as follows: _____

EXTERIOR PAINTING

All exterior woodwork shall have _____ coats of pure lead and oil paint of colors to be selected by owner. All sash and trim to be neatly traced. All knots and other defective work to be shellacked, and all nail holes to be puttied before applying last coat. Roof to have a brush coat of creosote stain if unstained wood shingles are used. All exposed sheet metal shall have_____

.7.

FIGURE 7–5 (cont'd)

STUCCO

All stucco, if any, shall be three coat work over _____ gauge _____ metal lath. The dash coat shall be selected as to color and kind by the owner. Put waterproof paper on sheathing under the metal lath. All work to be done in a neat and workmanlike manner.

HARDWARE

The contractor shall furnish all rough hardware, such as nails, window weights or sash balancers, sash cord, coal chute, mail box, and garage door hardware if garage is included. The amount to be

allowed for finish hardware is $ _____. Any cost in excess of that amount shall be paid by owner and any cost lower than this amount shall be credited owner. Stop screws and washers *shall or shall not* be furnished for all windows.

SHEET METAL

Contractor shall and will provide all necessary labor and materials and perform all sheet metal work of every nature whatsoever to be done, including gutters under all eaves with suitable conductors. All joints to be well soldered and securely fastened, and all work to be done in a neat and

workmanlike manner. Gutters to be _____ gauge _____ metal _____ type. Down

spouts to be _____. Proper _____ flashing shall be provided wherever necessary. Valley

flashing, if any, shall be _____ metal _____ inches wide. Clothes chute, if shown on plan, shall

be lined with _____

HEATING

Contractor shall and will provide all necessary labor and material and perform all heating work of every nature whatsoever to be done, including all plumbing and electrical connections, in the installation of a heating plant of sufficient size to properly heat all parts of the house in the coldest weather, and to put same in full operating condition.

WARM AIR SYSTEM: If gravity type or blower type of hot air heating is to be used, same shall be installed according to the code of the National Society of Heating and Ventilating Engineers, and in all cases shall conform to local ordinance. The heating plant shall consist of the following:

_____

_____

AIR-CONDITIONING SYSTEM: If any, shall be _____

_____

_____

OTHER HEATING SYSTEM: If hot water, steam, or any other heating system is to be used, such

installation shall consist of the following: _____

_____

GAS or OIL: If an oil or gas burner is to be used, such installation shall include the following:

_____

_____

_____

FIGURE 7–5 (cont'd)

PLUMBING

Contractor shall provide all labor and material and perform all plumbing work of every nature whatsoever to be done including items under "Built-Ins" if specified.

All plumbing shall be properly installed and all connections thoroughly tested and shall be installed according to local ordinance. Hot and cold water connections shall be made with bath tub, shower, lavatory, kitchen sink and laundry tray. Water connections shall be made with water main in the street, sewer connection shall be made with sewer in the street, gas connections shall be made with gas main in the street, all to be paid for by the plumbing contractor. Equipment under this plumbing contract requiring electrical connections shall be furnished and put into working operation by the plumbing contractor. All meters shall be paid for by owner. All piping to be according to local ordinance.

Plumbing fixtures shall be as follows: _____

____ Bath Tub _____ Color _____

____ Shower over Tub, if any, *shall or shall not* have curtain rod but no curtain _____

_____

_____

____ Water Closet _____ Color _____

_____

____ Lavatory _____ Color _____

_____

____ Kitchen Sink _____ Color _____

_____

_____

_____

_____ Water heater with _____ gal. storage tank.   Laundry tray _____

____ Rain leaders *shall or shall not* be connected to sewer. _____

_____ Lawn faucets, _____ Gas openings, _____ Floor drain, _____ Gas vent, Towel bars, grab bar, paper holder, soap dish or other fixtures, if furnished by the plumbing contractor, shall be _____

BUILT-INS

Contractor shall provide all labor and material for the installation of the built-in equipment herein specified.

Subcontractor shall connect with water, gas or electric supply the equipment he installs and shall put it into working operation. The incinerator, if any, and the fans, if any, shall be vented.

Garbage Disposer _____   Incinerator _____

Built-in Oven _____   Counter-top Range _____

Hood and Fan _____   Bathroom Fans _____

Shower Door _____   Tub Enclosure _____

Bath Heaters _____   Room Air Cond. _____

Refrigerator _____   Freezer _____

Dishwasher _____   Clothes Washer _____

Clothes Dryer _____   Comb. Washer-Dryer _____

Television _____   Radio-controlled Gar. Dr. Operator _____

. 9 .

FIGURE 7–5   (cont'd)

ELECTRICAL WORK

Contractor shall provide all necessary labor and material and perform all electric work of every nature whatsoever to be done. All work to comply with local ordinances. Provide wiring outlets as per following schedule. All outlets to be placed as directed by owner and shall consist of the following:

WIRING SCHEDULE

SYMBOLS	ROOMS / OUTLETS AND SWITCHES	LIVING	DINING	KITCHEN	DINETTE	HALL	STAIRWAYS	BEDROOM	BEDROOM	BEDROOM	CLOSETS	BATHROOM	LAVATORY	SHOWER	BASEMENT	LAUNDRY	UTILITIES	ENTRANCES	REC' ROOM	GARAGE	YARD	PORCHES	ATTIC	TOTAL
○	CEILING OUTLET																							
–○	BRACKET OUTLET																							
⊕	CONVENIENCE OUTLET DUPLEX																							
⊙	FLOOR OUTLET																							
▲	SPECIAL PURPOSE OUTLET OIL BURNER ETC.																							
⊕R	RANGE OUTLET																							
⊗	VENTILATING FAN OUTLET																							
⊖WP	CONVENIENCE OUTLET WEATHERPROOF																							
–R	RADIO OUTLET																							
–○	CLOCK OUTLET																							
–○HN	ILLUMINATED HOUSE NUMBER																							
$	LIGHTING SWITCH																							
$3	THREE WAY SWITCH																							
$P	SWITCH AND PILOT																							
$WP	SWITCH WEATHERPROOF																							
♀	BELL AND TRANSFORMER																							
–/–	CIRCUIT BREAKER																							
◁	TELEPHONE OUTLET																							

RECAP OF OUTLETS

_____ Ceiling outlets ____ Bracket outlets   _____ Double wall plugs   _____ Floor outlets

_____ Switch outlets ____ 3 way switch outlets   _____ Switch and Pilots   _____ W. proof switches

_____ Clock outlets ____ Radio outlets   _____ Bell and Transformer_____ Telephone outlets

_____ Fan outlets   ____ Range outlets   _____ Yard outlets   _____ Heating outlets

The electric entrance service shall be three-wires with _____ampere capacity, installed in accordance with the National Electrical Code or the local ordinance, whichever applies. The type of switches shall be _____ .
The electrical contractor shall include items specified under "Built-Ins".

ELECTRIC FIXTURES

Electric light fixtures to the value of $_____ , including installation of same, shall be furnished by contractor. Any cost in excess of this amount shall be paid by the owner and any cost lower than this amount shall be credited owner. _____

_____

_____

FIGURE 7-5 (cont'd)

WINDOW SHADES

The amount of $_____ is allowed for window shades. Any cost in excess of this amount shall be paid by owner and any cost lower than this amount shall be credited to the owner.

CLEANING UP

The contractor *shall or shall not* remove all debris from the premises when the job is completed. The contractor *shall or shall not* clean all window glass when job is completed.

_____

_____

GARAGE

Foundation _____ Floor 1-2-4 Mix_____ Apron 1-2-4 Mix_____ Thickness _____

Sheathing _____ Wall Covering_____ Roof Shingles _____

Service Door_____ Driveway_____ Electric Wiring_____ Painting_____

Garage Door *shall or shall not* be the hinged type _____

Garage Door *shall or shall not* be the overhead type_____

Garage Door *shall or shall not* be mechanically operated _____

_____

FIREPLACES

Fireplace, if any, shall be as shown herein. Specify type of mantel on page 2 or 6.

MISCELLANEOUS

(Describe items if any, not mentioned in specifications or shown on plans.)

_____

_____

_____

_____

_____

_____

_____

_____

_____

_____

_____

_____

_____

_____

_____

FIGURE 7–5 (cont'd)
BUILDING CONTRACT

WE, THE UNDERSIGNED, have read the foregoing specifications, prepared in duplicate, and accept them as correct and hereby acknowledge receipt of one copy for each party hereto.

THIS AGREEMENT, made this _____ day of _____ , 19 ___ , by

and between _____ , hereinafter called

the Contractor, and_____ , hereinafter called the Owners, WITNESSETH:

That the Contractor and Owner for the consideration hereinafter named agree as follows:

ARTICLE I. The Contractor agrees to provide the materials as specified and to perform all the work shown on the drawing and subscribed in the specifications and to do everything required by the General Conditions of the Contract, the Specifications and the Drawings.

ARTICLE II. The Contractor agrees that the work under this contract shall be substantially

completed the_____ day of_____ .

ARTICLE III. The Owner agrees to pay the Contractor in current funds for the performance

of the contract_____ Dollars ($ _____), subject to any additions or deductions to the General Conditions of the Contract agreed upon in writing, and to make payments on account hereof upon presentation of proper lien waivers, as the

work progresses and as follows: _____

_____

_____

_____

It is agreed that the completion of the work covered in this contract is contingent upon strikes, lockouts, delay of common carriers, laws or government regulations or any other circumstances or conditions beyond the control of the contractor.

ARTICLE IV. The Contractor and the Owner agree that the General Conditions, the Specifications and the Drawings, together with this agreement form the contract, as if hereto attached.

The Contractor and Owners for themselves, their successors, executors, administrators and assigns, hereby agree to the full performance of the covenants herein contained.

IN WITNESS WHEREOF, They have executed this agreement the day and year first above written.

_____ Contractor _____
(Witness)

_____ Owner _____
(Witness)

_____

.12.

FIGURE 7-5 (cont'd)

Authority for Change in Contract

By mutual agreement between . . .

_____(Contractor)

and_____(Owner)

the following changes, alterations, additions or substitutions are to be made in the work or materials called for in the plans and specifications which are a part of the Building Contract signed by the above named parties.

on_____ 19_____

_____

_____

_____

_____

These changes will (cost or save) $_____
which amount will be added to or subtracted from the next regular payment, or if agreed upon, at the time of final payment, under the terms of the above mentioned contract.

Contractor_____

Owner_____

_____ 19_____

Notify Mortgagee of any additions to, or deductions from the contract price.

Authority for Change in Contract

By mutual agreement between . . .

_____(Contractor)

and_____(Owner)

the following changes, alterations, additions or substitutions are to be made in the work or materials called for in the plans and specifications which are a part of the Building Contract signed by the above named parties.

on_____ 19_____

_____

_____

_____

_____

These changes will (cost or save) $_____
which amount will be added to or subtracted from the next regular payment, or if agreed upon, at the time of final payment, under the terms of the above mentioned contract.

Contractor_____

Owner_____

_____ 19_____

Notify Mortgagee of any additions to, or deductions from the contract price.

HOME PLAN BOOK CO.
Larson-Reitz, Publishers
1596 Selby Ave.
St. Paul 4, Minn.
Printed in U.S.A.
All Rights Reserved

Building Laws

Building laws are designed to make a building safe and control the building material. For example, if a garage is attached to the house, the building law might say that the common wall between the house and garage must have a fire rating or fireproofing. The garage may be considered a hazardous area because of the gasoline in the automobile's tank, and some protection must be provided to save the house if there is a fire in the garage. The entire state may be under the same building laws, which means that the building laws will apply no matter the city or town in which the house is being built.

Zoning Laws

Control and use of land to avoid conjestion and to ensure safety to all people who use buildings fall under the zoning laws. Building use such as residential, commercial, manufacturing, professional, and industrial are controlled by zoning laws. If a lot has a residential zone, only a building for that purpose or use can be built on that particular land. The use of the building must conform to the zoning of the lot (Fig. 7–6).

FIGURE 7–6a   *Zoning plan.*

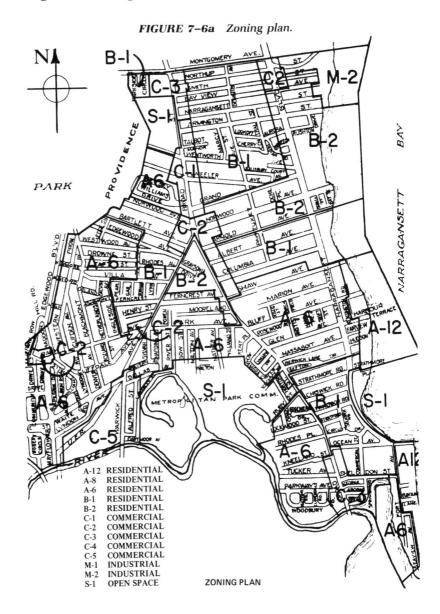

A-12	RESIDENTIAL
A-8	RESIDENTIAL
A-6	RESIDENTIAL
B-1	RESIDENTIAL
B-2	RESIDENTIAL
C-1	COMMERCIAL
C-2	COMMERCIAL
C-3	COMMERCIAL
C-4	COMMERCIAL
C-5	COMMERCIAL
M-1	INDUSTRIAL
M-2	INDUSTRIAL
S-1	OPEN SPACE

ZONING PLAN

ZONING

Districts	Intended Primarily for the Use of
Residential A-80	Single-family dwellings on lots not served by public water and of minimum areas of 80,000 square feet
Residential A-20	Single-family dwellings on lots of minimum areas of 20,000 square feet
Residential A-12	Single-family dwellings on lots of minimum areas of 12,000 square feet
Residential A-8	Single-family dwellings on lots of minimum areas of 8,000 square feet
Residential A-6	Single-family dwellings on lots of minimum areas of 6,000 square feet
Residential B-1	Single-family and two-family dwellings
Residential B-2	Single-, two- and multi-family dwellings
Commercial C-1	Office business
Commercial C-2	Neighborhood business
Commercial C-3	General business
Commercial C-4	Highway business
Commercial C-5	Heavy business, industry
Industrial M-1	Restricted industry
Industrial M-2	General industry
Open Space S-1	Uses containing high proportion of open space or natural character
Planned districts	Uses in buildings arranged in an efficient, harmonious and convenient manner on sites

FIGURE 7–6b *Zoning regulations.*

It is possible to change the zoning of a lot for a particular use by petitioning to the zoning board of review. Evidence is presented to the board as to why the zoning of a particular piece of land should be changed. The zoning board may or may not grant a change, called a *variance.* Only if the variance is granted can a particular type of building be constructed on that land.

Another area of zoning laws controls the location of a building on the property or lot. The law will state what the distance must be from the front property line to the building, and the size of the side and rear yards—in addition to a host of other laws.

Building Drawings

A set of drawings for a building is nothing more than a graphic message, like a painting or a photograph of an idea from the designer to the builder. This graphic message is communicated by way of lines and symbols, and once learned, these symbols apply to any building plans. These symbols have been adopted universally, so that no matter who designed the building, the plans will read in the same way (Fig. 7–7).

A set of building plans consists of three types of drawings. First are the basic *building plans,* a set of horizontal planes. If you imagine a building cut midpoint at window height, remove the upper portion, and look down on the remaining portion—that is a building plan. There will be one plan for each floor of the building and a plan of the lot or property as a flying bird would see it.

FIGURE 7-7 *Architectural and mechanical symbols.*

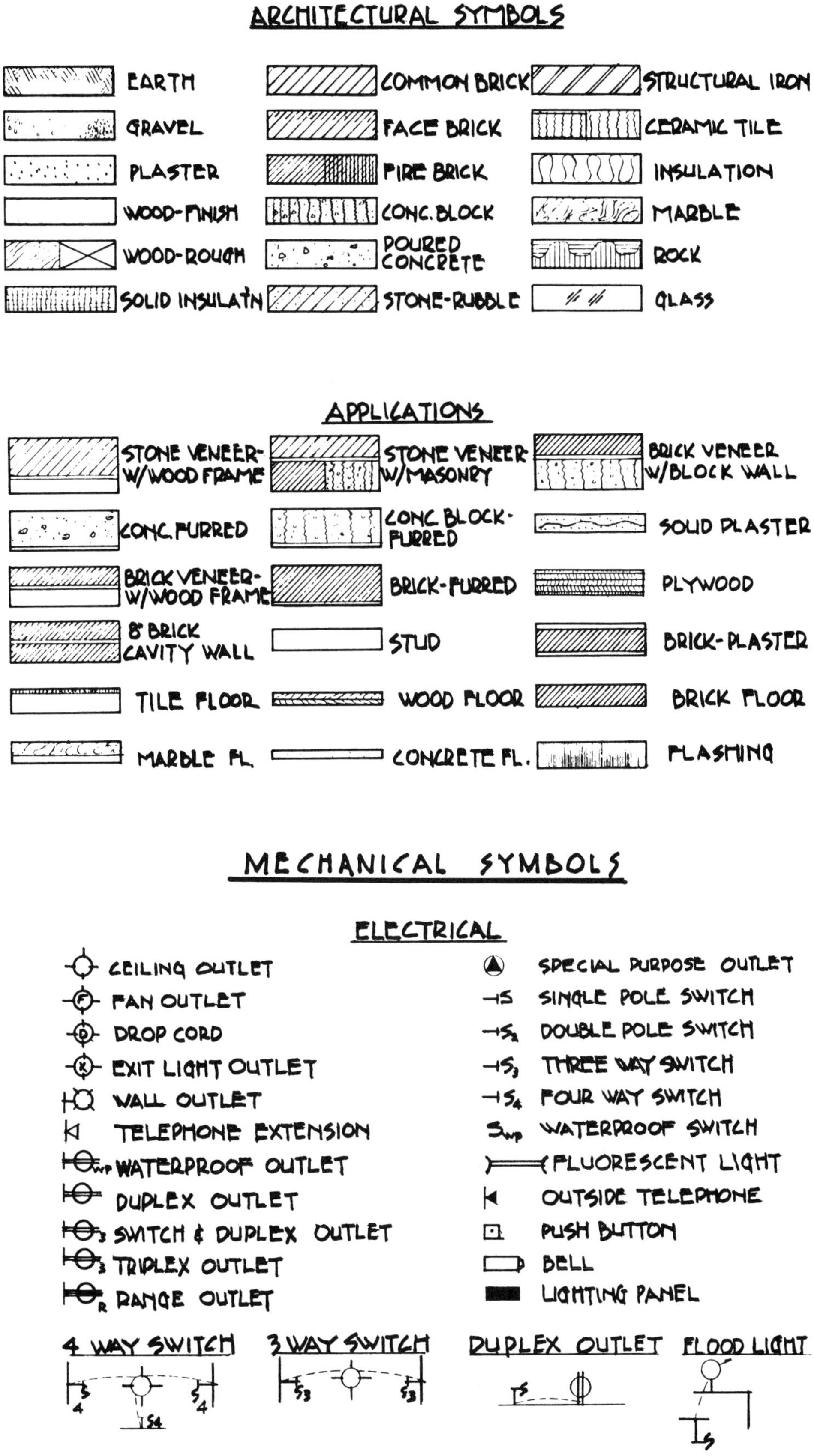

ARCHITECTURAL SYMBOLS

EARTH — COMMON BRICK — STRUCTURAL IRON
GRAVEL — FACE BRICK — CERAMIC TILE
PLASTER — FIRE BRICK — INSULATION
WOOD-FINISH — CONC. BLOCK — MARBLE
WOOD-ROUGH — POURED CONCRETE — ROCK
SOLID INSULATN — STONE-RUBBLE — GLASS

APPLICATIONS

STONE VENEER-W/WOOD FRAME — STONE VENEER W/MASONRY — BRICK VENEER W/BLOCK WALL
CONC. FURRED — CONC BLOCK-FURRED — SOLID PLASTER
BRICK VENEER-W/WOOD FRAME — BRICK-FURRED — PLYWOOD
8" BRICK CAVITY WALL — STUD — BRICK-PLASTER
TILE FLOOR — WOOD FLOOR — BRICK FLOOR
MARBLE FL. — CONCRETE FL. — FLASHING

MECHANICAL SYMBOLS

ELECTRICAL

CEILING OUTLET — SPECIAL PURPOSE OUTLET
FAN OUTLET — SINGLE POLE SWITCH
DROP CORD — DOUBLE POLE SWITCH
EXIT LIGHT OUTLET — THREE WAY SWITCH
WALL OUTLET — FOUR WAY SWITCH
TELEPHONE EXTENSION — WATERPROOF SWITCH
WATERPROOF OUTLET — FLUORESCENT LIGHT
DUPLEX OUTLET — OUTSIDE TELEPHONE
SWITCH & DUPLEX OUTLET — PUSH BUTTON
TRIPLEX OUTLET — BELL
RANGE OUTLET — LIGHTING PANEL

4 WAY SWITCH   3 WAY SWITCH   DUPLEX OUTLET   FLOOD LIGHT

HEATING

⌐ DUCT-PLAN VIEW   CONVECTOR RECESSED

⊠ RADIATOR   ─┼─ T CONNECTION

— SUPPLY LINE   ELBOW

— RETURN LINE   ● RISER

SUPPLY DUCT   ⊙ RETURN

RETURN DUCT   REGISTER

CONVECTOR PROJECTING

PLUMBING

—— COLD WATER LINE   ⓗⓦ HOT WATER TANK

---- HOT WATER LINE   ⊙ SOIL PIPE-FRAME WALL

─×─×─ GAS LINE   PIPE CHASE-BRICK WALL

─•─•─ REFRIGERATOR LINE   ▢ LAUNDRY TUB

✕ FLOOR DRAIN   ▢▢ KITCHEN SINK

CLEANOUT   ▭ BATHTUB

WATERCLOSET

FIGURE 7-7   (cont'd)

The second type of drawing is the *elevation*. This is a vertical picture of one plane only and only one side of the building is shown at a time. It may be the entire outside of one side of the building. It may also be any interior wall of any room or a part of a wall. As a wall is seen in looking at it, so it will be drawn on paper at a scale less than full size.

The third type of drawing is known as a *section* or *detail*. This is drawn in a vertical plane showing a wall completely through with all parts not visible when the wall is completed. Also, parts of a construction detail are shown to clear up any possible doubt as to how the wall is to be constructed. In other words, if a wall were cut vertically with a head-on view, it would show all the parts of the wall and how the parts are constructed and assembled together.

Scale Drawings

All building drawings are drawn to a convenient scale; otherwise, the paper would have to be as large as the building. The scale must be small enough to fit on a convenient-size sheet of paper and large enough to show details. The most popular scales are $\frac{1}{8}'' = 1'-0''$, $\frac{1}{2}'' = 1'-0''$, $\frac{1}{4}'' = 1'-0''$, $\frac{3}{8}'' = 1'-0''$, $1\frac{1}{2}'' = 1'-0''$, $3'' = 1'-0''$, and at times full size. In all cases, the scale will be noted on the drawings. If, for example, the drawing indicated $\frac{1}{2} = 1'-0''$, it means that every $\frac{1}{2}$ in. an actual measurement on the drawing is $1'-0''$ full size, so that if we measured 1 in. on the drawing, the actual full-size dimension is $2'-0''$ (Fig. 7-8).

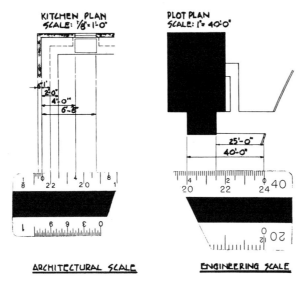

KITCHEN PLAN
SCALE: ⅛"=1'-0"

FIGURE 7-8   *Scale reading.*

Plot Plan

A complete set of drawings will consist of several sheets, usually in order of sequence of building or construction. The first sheet will be the plot plan, which will show the size of the building lot; locating the building on the lot; contour elevations (the level or terrain of the lot, including trees); locating utilities (water, sewer, gas, and electric), curb, and compass bearing or direction of north; scale of drawing; dimension of property lines, including angles; street name; and lot and plat numbers (Fig. 7–9, page 132).

   The plot plan will show garage, walks, and landscaping, if any. It is usually the first sheet in the complete set of plans, showing the ground level or contour elevations before starting construction and at the completion of construction. The ground level is important because the level of the floor of the house must be established in relation to the level of the ground. The contour elevations or ground will dictate if we need to cut or fill the ground to change the shape; it will also indicate the levels of all floors in the house. It becomes much too expensive to make changes after construction has begun. The plot plan thus should give all the information needed regarding the site or lot. Because of the amount of information and size of objects shown, this sheet may be drawn at a different scale, usually $1'' = 10'$ or $1'' = 20'$ because the entire lot, which may be 100 ft or more in any one dimension, must be shown, and all sheets within the set should be of the same size.

Foundation or Basement Plan

The next sheet will be the foundation plan or basement floor plan. If the building has a basement, this sheet will be called a basement plan. If the building does not have a basement, it will be called a foundation plan (Fig. 7–10). Here

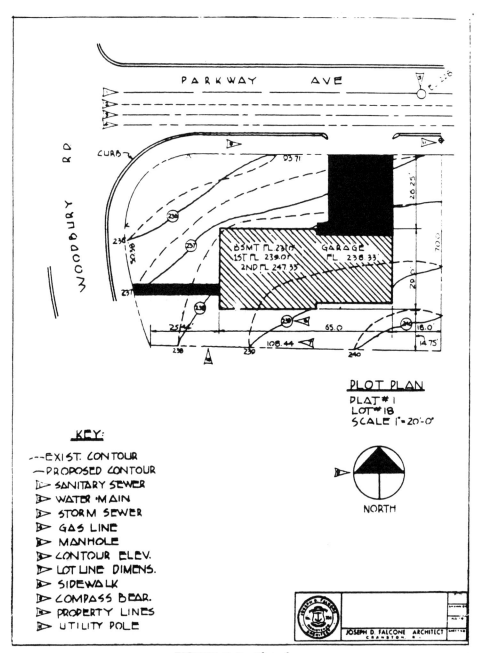

FIGURE 7–9   Plot plan.

the size of the foundation is shown with dimensions on the outer perimeter
of the walls. The plan will also show the locations of all windows in the basement; the size of the main beam that supports the floor above, which in turn
is supported by columns; and the size and spacing of the columns. The main
beam will support what are called floor joists. These will be 2 in. in width and
anywhere from 8 to 12 in. in height. They will be noted on the plans as
$2'' \times 8''$–$16''$ O.C. This means that the floor joists are 2 in. thick and 8 in. high,
spaced 16 in. on center (that is, 16 in. apart) and are placed in a vertical position with the larger dimension up. One end of each floor joist is supported by
the outer foundation wall, and the end is supported by the main beam. The
floor joists holds up the partitions above. Also shown will be stairs, chimney,
laundry sinks, and the thickness of the concrete floor and bulkhead, if any.

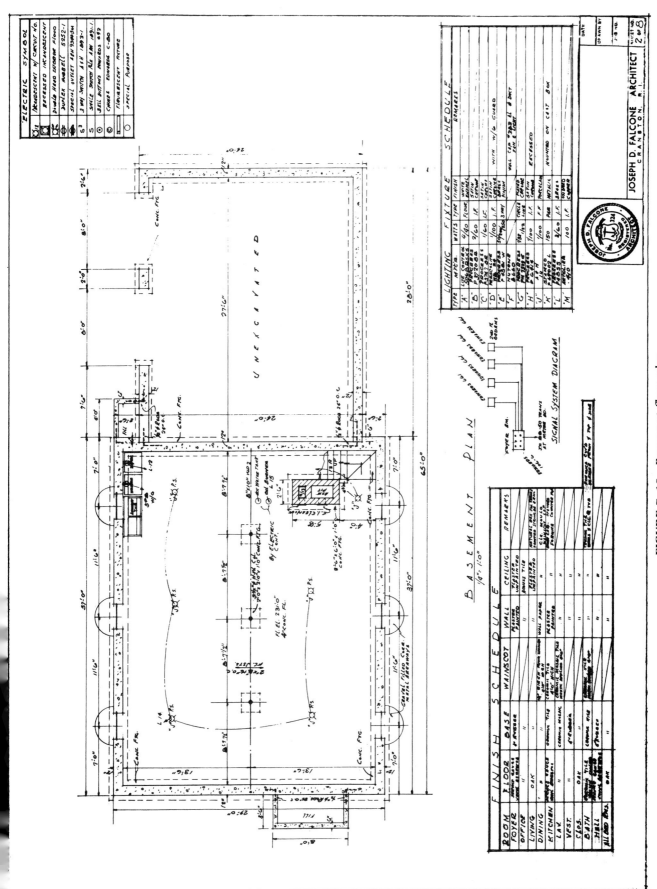

FIGURE 7-10 Basement floor plan.

This plan gives only horizontal dimensions, no vertical dimensions. If there is no basement, we simply read a foundation plan, which will show a wall and related information. This plan is usually drawn at a scale of $\frac{1}{4}'' = 1'-0''$.

First-Floor Plan

Next in line will be the first-floor plan, which is read the same way as the basement plan with the same horizontal cut through the windows (Fig. 7–11). This will show all the rooms at this level. Also shown will be the bath and all plumbing fixtures. The kitchen will show the location, shape, and size of upper and lower cabinet units, sink, refrigerator, range, dishwasher, windows, and closets. This plan will show the size of all doors, windows, fireplaces, and stairs. Dimensions locating all partitions or walls within the building will be shown. All dimensions on plans are taken from center to center of interior walls and outside to center of exterior walls. If there is a garage, it will show on this plan, including the size and location of doors and windows. Porches will also be seen on the first-floor plan, as will exterior stairs, doors, partitions, closets, bedrooms, and bath.

Electric plugs, called duplex convenience outlets, will be shown as well as electric lights, switches, and wiring. This plan also shows the first-floor ceiling or second-floor framing, indicated as $2'' \times 8''–16''$ a.c. floor joists. The closets show shelves and poles.

The example in Fig. 7–11 indicates exterior brick-finish walls for the house and garage, shown by the symbol ▨. All dimensions for doors and windows are taken to the center of the unit. A window schedule will indicate the size of the windows. The door sizes are indicated on the plan as $2'-6'' \times 6'-6''$, which means that the door will be $2'-6''$ wide and $6'-6''$ high. Also shown on Figure 6–12 is the baseboard heating, indicated as $22'-0''$ radiation, which means that the baseboard will be $22'-0''$ long.

Second-Floor Plan

The second floor will be next in sequence and is read the same as noted for the first floor. It, too, shows all the windows, stairs, doors, partitions, closets, bedrooms, and bath (Fig. 7–12). From the second-floor plan looking through the window of bedroom 3 will be shown the roof of the garage. The roof over the front door will be seen from bedroom 2.

Exterior Elevations

The elevations or vertical drawings will show a separate drawing for each of the four sides of the exterior of the house. They will be labeled East Elevation, West Elevation, and South Elevation, or Front Elevation, Rear Elevation, Left

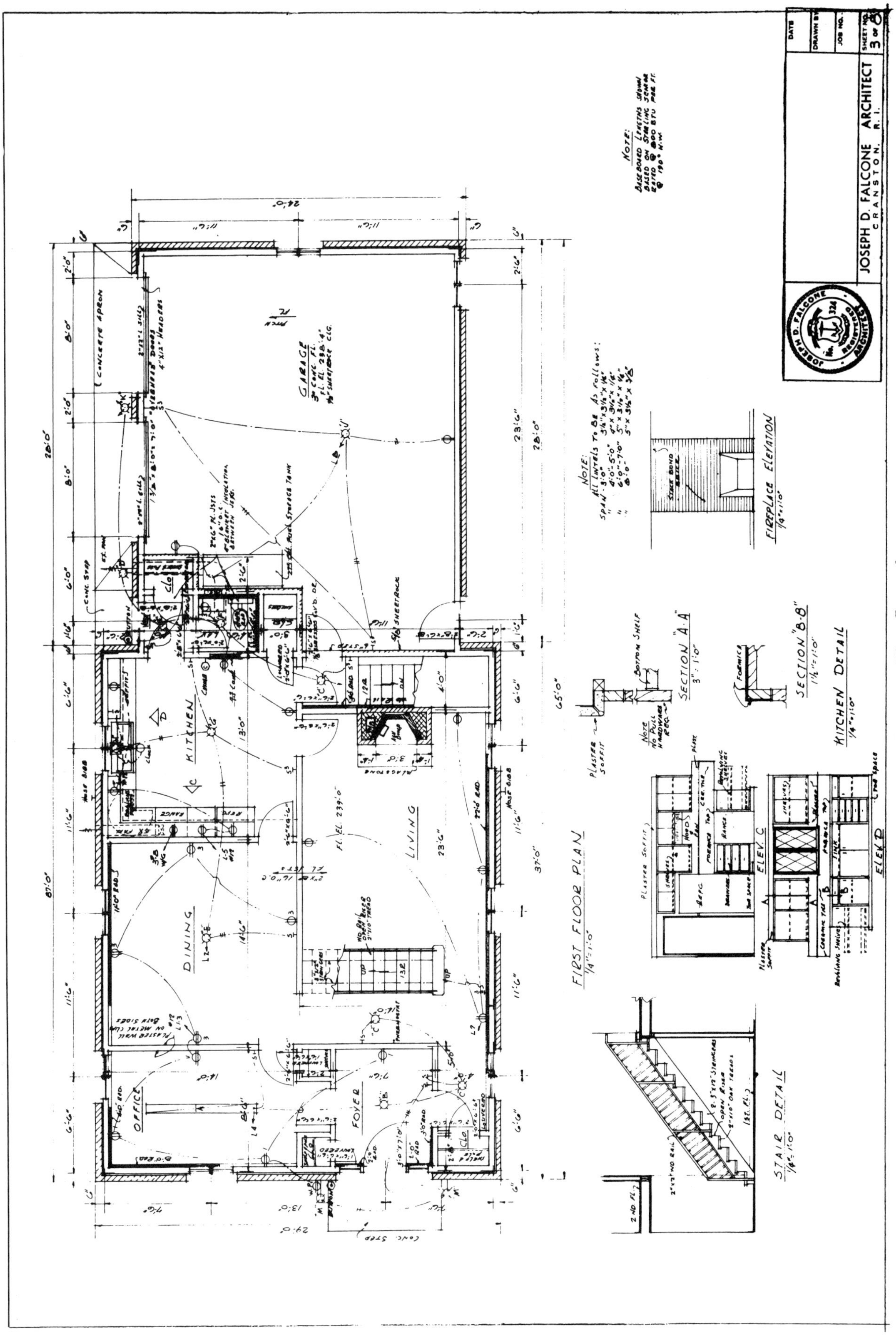

FIGURE 7-11 First-floor plan.

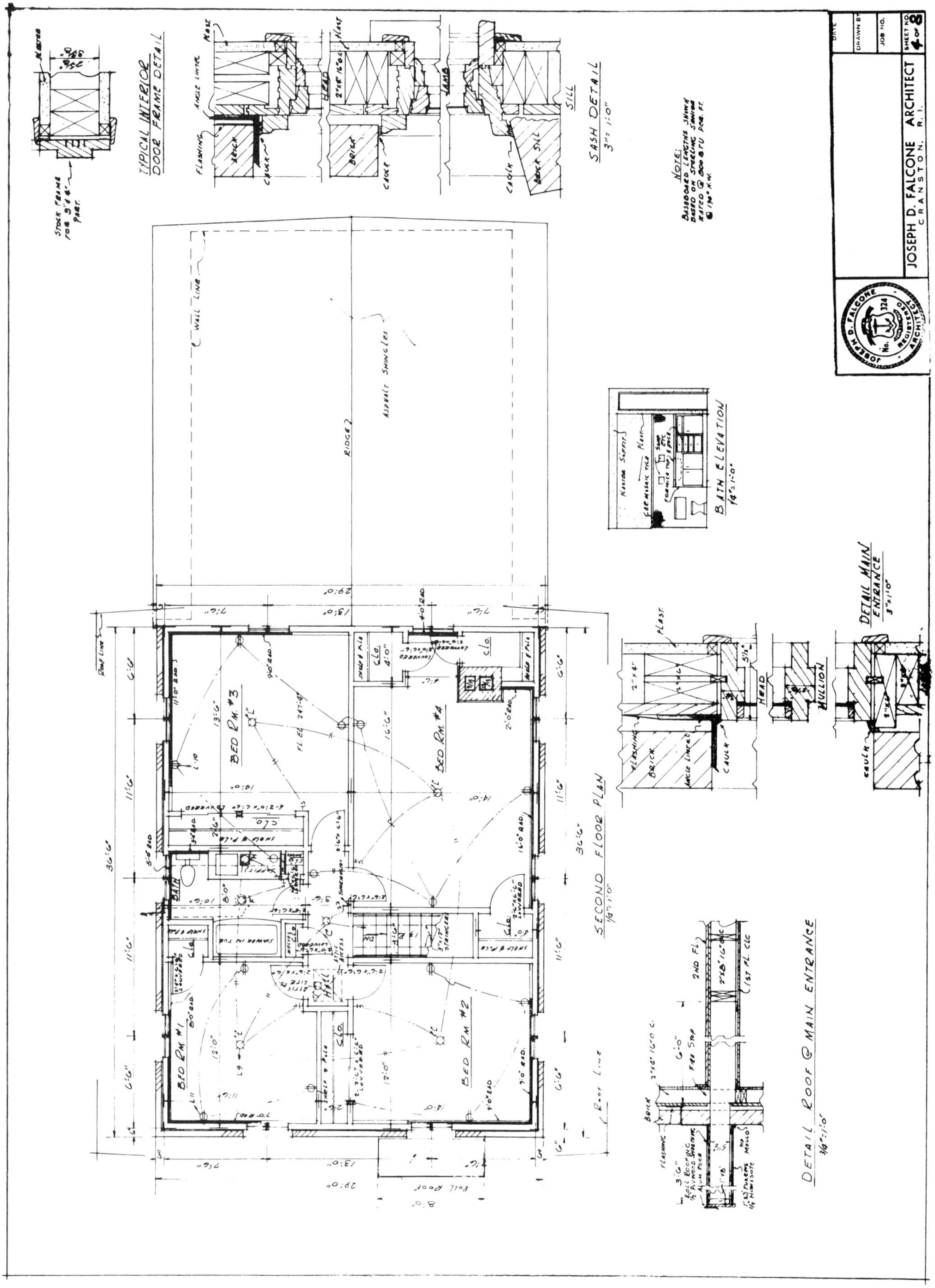

FIGURE 7-12 Second-floor plan.

Elevation, and Right Elevation, again drawn at a scale of $\frac{1}{4}'' = 1'\text{-}0''$. By examining this drawing the entire side from the basement up to and including the roof will be shown. The floor lines are shown by a dotted dashed line and labeled by the respective floor, such as Basement Floor, First Floor, or Second Floor. The type and size of windows are shown: "type" means style, such as double hung, casement, sliding or gliding, awning, or vent; and "size" means height and width. The configuration of the windows will also be shown in terms of number and size of panes of glass. The design of all exterior doors will be shown on these drawings, as will the material finish on the exterior walls, such as wood shingles, clapboards, or brick. This drawing will tell the distance from the grade or ground to the first floor and the basement. All dashed lines are objects not directly visible. For example, all information below ground, such as foundation, basement windows, floor of basement, bulkhead, and so on, will be shown dashed because direct view of these items is obstructed by the ground. The drawing will also show the design of the chimney, including type, material, and height. The ground or finish-grade elevations (that is, ground level) will also be shown. The elevations will tell the types of gutters and conductors as well as the design of the roof overhang (Figs. 7–13 to 7–15).

Sections and Details

The final drawing in the series will show how the building is put together. This drawing is called a section or detail. Picture mentally a completed house, cut the house in half completely from the roof to foundation, remove one half, look head-on at the other half, and it will show how the complete building is constructed (Fig. 7–16). This drawing will show the foundation, walls, floors, and roof. It will show what the parts of the building are and how they are assembled. The distance from floor to floor will be shown, as will the roof pitch, and the sizes of the beam, floor joists, and roof rafters will be shown. The upper part of Fig. 7–16 shows how the roof trusses are assembled. The lower part of Fig. 7–16 is a section through the garage. The left side of Fig. 7–16 is a section through the house. These building sections are drawn at a scale of $\frac{1}{4}'' = 1'\text{-}0''$. The roof truss details are drawn at a scale $1\frac{1}{2}'' = 1'\text{-}0''$. Basically that is all there is to reading a set of plans.

Copies

A set of plans is copied from the original set that the drafter has drawn on a special kind of transparent paper using a special type of pencil determined by the quality of the paper. When the drawings are completed, they are reproduced or copied somewhat like photos from a negative. The original drawings, being the "negative," are placed over a chemically treated paper and run through a machine which prints by way of a strong light penetrating all but the lines of the drawing. This light transfers the image onto the printing paper, which after leaving the printer, is run through a developing agent. The chemical coating on the paper turns white as a direct result of the exposure to

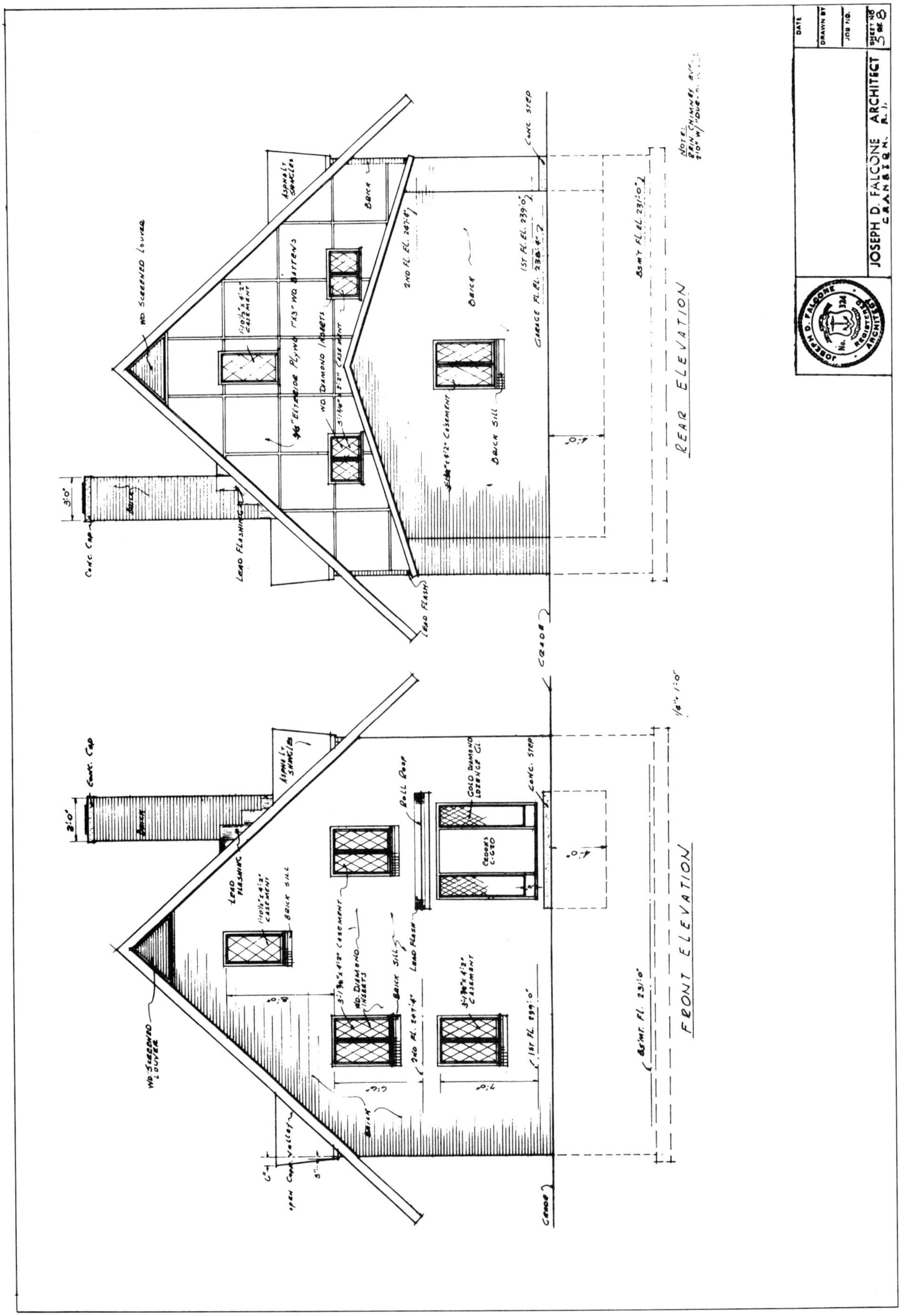

FIGURE 7-13 Front and rear elevations.

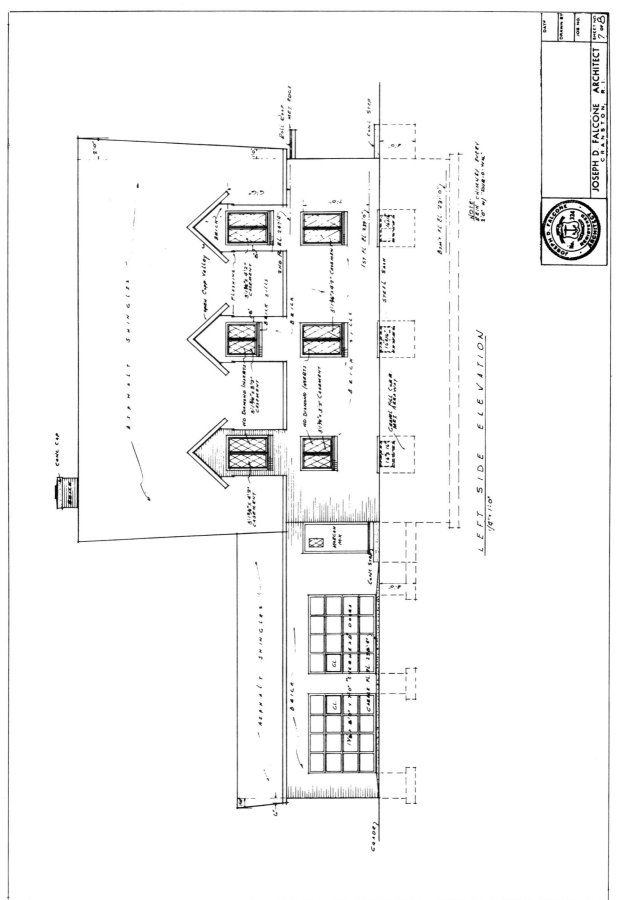

FIGURE 7–14 *Left side elevation.*

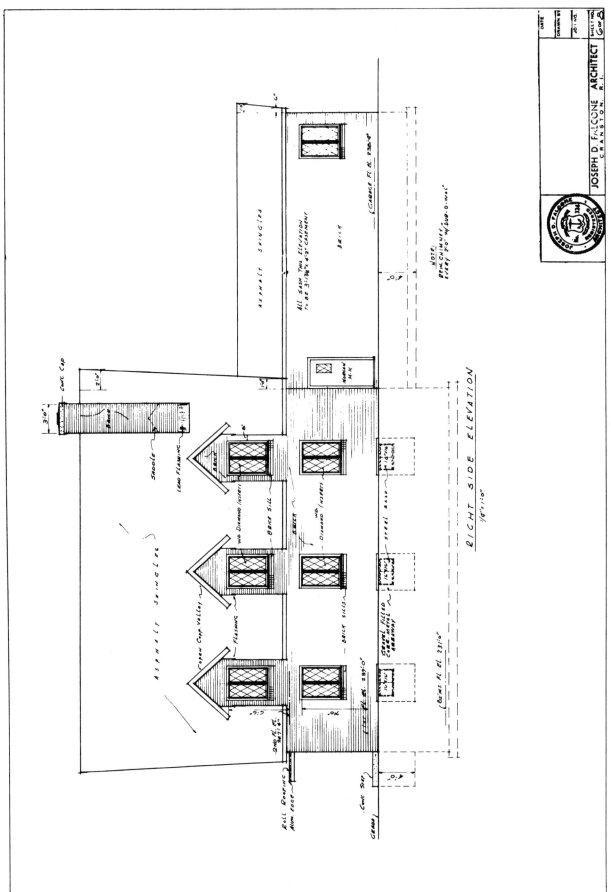

FIGURE 7-15 Right side elevation.

140

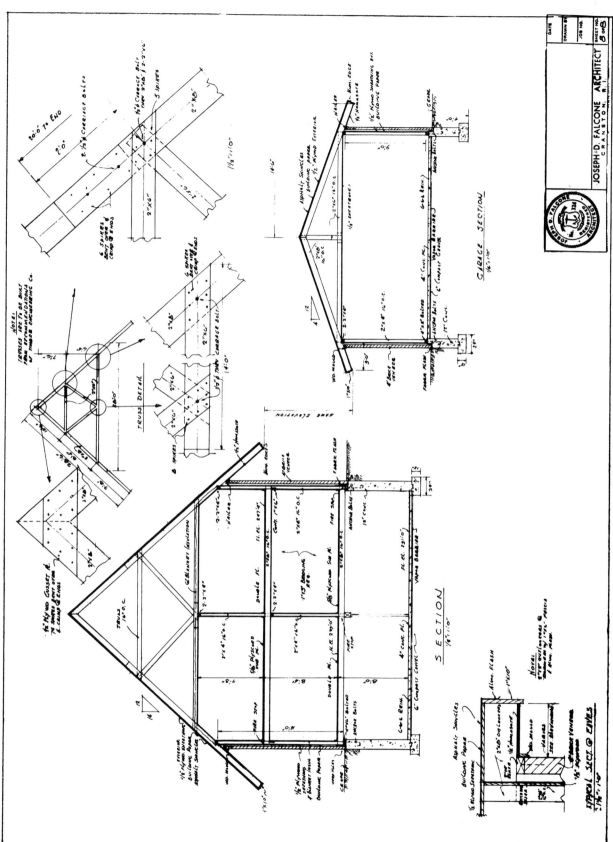

FIGURE 7-16 Sections.

141

the chemical, but the lines on the drawing are blue. Any number of copies can be made from an original set of drawings. A more popular term for the reproduction is *blueprinting*, although this term is obsolete because of the current techniques used in reproduction.

QUESTIONS

7–1. Name three types of drawings in a set of building plans.
1. _____
2. _____
3. _____

7–2. Drawing a house to scale means changing the physical dimensions of the house.
True or False

7–3. Define *plot plan*. _____
_____

7–4. Contours of land measure the size of the lot.
True or False

7–5. Define *elevation drawings*. _____
_____

7–6. Original drawings are reproduced by taking pictures with a film and camera.
True or False

7–7. Reproduction of drawings is called _____

7–8. Define the following symbols.

_____
_____

7–9. The symbol ——W—— indicates hot water pipe.
True or False

7–10. Show the symbol for a duplex outlet. _____

8

Mechanical System

Introduction

The mechanical system of a building consists of plumbing, heating, ventilation, air conditioning, and electrical. At this stage of construction, after all the interior stud partitions are in place and before finishing of walls, floors, or ceilings has been completed, all mechanical facilities, such as piping and wiring or ductwork to support the mechanical facilities, are "roughed in" in the partitions, where they will be concealed. The finish installation of the mechanical systems, such as plumbing fixtures, heating, grills, baseboard, convectors or radiators, lighting fixtures, switches, plugs, and plates are not installed until the floors, walls, and ceilings are finished. All lines must be tested for leaks or breaks before the finish is completed. Making repairs later will require that the finish be removed in order to expose the problem for correction. For economy, careful planning in arranging the plumbing fixtures must be employed. Simplification of arrangement dictates clustering of plumbing fixtures on a common wall or wet wall. Where there is more than one story, fixtures are located above each other to utilize common piping for water, waste, and vents.

Plumbing

Water Lines

The cost of installation of a public water supply is less than the cost of installation of a private water supply. In the case of a public water supply, the town or city will have a record of the water facilities, including the size of the water main, depth below the surface, and the pressure of the water. For a private home, all that is required is to run a ¾-in. or larger main from the public supply to the house deep enough to protect the pipe from the frost. This pipe is usually made of copper. The utility company will make the connection from the main street to a shutoff at the property line. Installation from that point into the house is the responsibility of the homeowner. When the line is brought into the house, the utility company will install a water meter, and from the meter, the water is distributed throughout the house. In the building of the foundation, a chase or opening is installed to receive the water pipe.

If a public water supply is not available, a private water system must be planned. In nature, water is seldom free of impurities. The pure vapor in the atmosphere may collect airborne bacteria. Percolation through the earth filters the water, causing it to lose most of the bacteria but to pick up salts or gases. Some are harmful and some are not. In some parts of the central states, methane gas is found in groundwater. Calcium and magnesium in the form of sulfates or carbonates as well as iron are common. Earth strata and minerals vary from community to community.

Water containing large amounts of calcium and magnesium salts is called hard water and sudsing from soaps is difficult. Rainwater is soft and suds easily. A glass of water that looks clear may contain millions of dangerous organisms. Contaminated water can cause typhoid fever, dysentery, diarrhea, and intestinal disorders as well as several varieties of intestinal worms. Sand, soft sandstone, or sand and gravel substrata as a rule will yield the safest water.

The most important requirement is to keep at least 100 ft away from any private sewage system and preferably to locate the well on high ground (check the local code). All well water should be analyzed for chemical content and purity. This will dictate what type of treatment to use. As a rule, this analysis will be done by local health officials. New wells must be disinfected and kept sealed. If a water softener is necessary, there are several complete packages on the market. The most satisfactory method is to pass the water through zeolite, which is a special type of sand. Another product for filtering water is charcoal. The minimum amount of water should be 50 gallons per day per person for domestic use. In addition to the well, a water pump is necessary. These fall into five categories: plunger or reciprocating type, turbine, centrifugal, rotary, and ejector (Fig. 8–1). The pump not only pushes or pulls water from the well into the house, but also provides pressure to allow the water to flow through the pipes within the house. In most cases, a storage water tank is included in the package. A tank can cause a problem with condensation (Fig. 8–2), one solution to which is to set the tank over a sand bed to collect the condensation without causing a problem. A hand pump over the well can be very convenient when electric power is lost. If a hand pump is installed, it should be the completely enclosed type.

When the source of water supply is brought into the house, a water main valve must be installed to enable shutting off the water supply within the house to make pipe repairs. From the main water line, a branch is connected to the domestic hot water tank if the water is not heated as an integral part of the hot water heating system. This tank should be large enough to hold at least a 1-hour supply of hot water at the rate of 8 gallons per hour per person. All hot water tanks should have a pressure relief valve to prevent excessive pressure due to overheated water throwing off steam inside the tank (Fig. 8–3).

Galvanized pipe is mild steel sometimes containing small quantities of copper and molybdenum to increase resistance to corrosion for longer life.

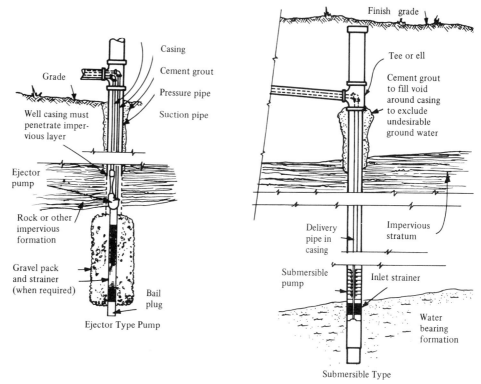

FIGURE 8–1   Water pumps (courtesy Department of Housing and Urban Development).

FIGURE 8–2   Well installation (courtesy Department of Housing and Urban Development).

SHALLOW WELL INSTALLATION

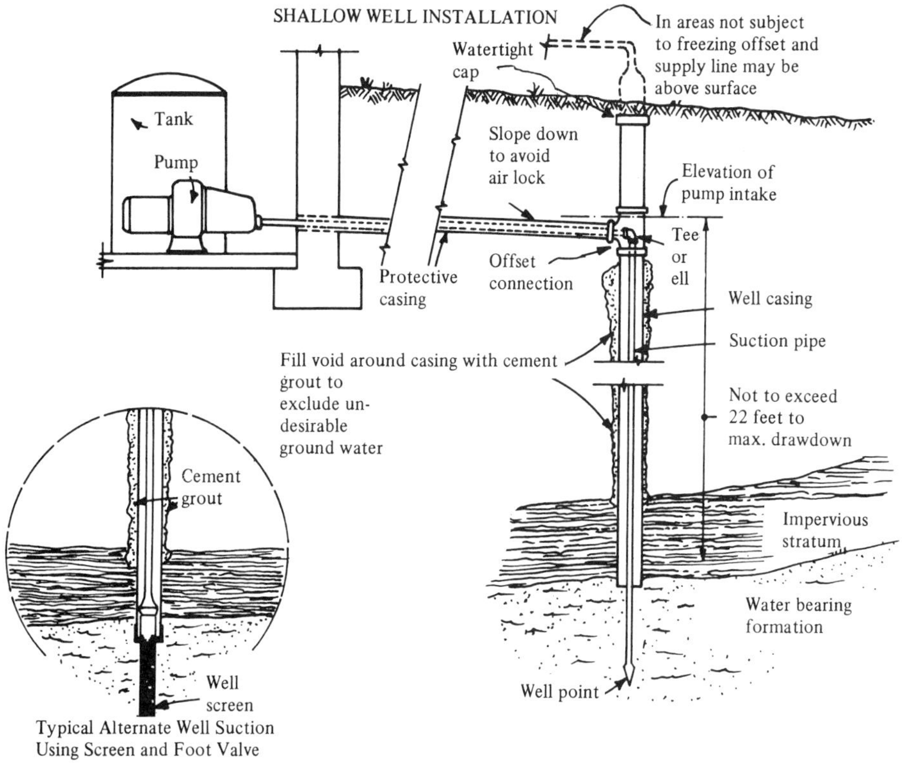

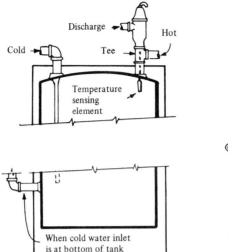
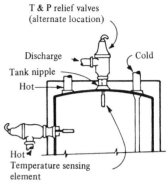

FIGURE 8-3   Domestic hot water tank (courtesy of Housing and Urban Development).

Wrought iron is made of puddled iron almost entirely free of impurities which lead to corrosion. This pipe is called "genuine wrought iron" and should be galvanized. Brass piping is available in yellow brass, containing 67% copper and 33% zinc. Copper is available in three types: K, L, and M. Type K is designed for underground service and where corrosion conditions are severe, type L is designed for general plumbing purposes, and type M is for use with soldered joints and fittings and is generally used for residential plumbing. Types K and L come in hard or soft tempers; type M is hard only and requires fittings at all turns. Soft copper comes in coils and can be shaped to turn corners but is also easily punctured and damaged.

Cold water lines will condense, causing water to drip from the surface of the pipe, which may cause damage to the ceiling. To avoid this, the pipe should be covered with insulation. Hot water pipes should also be insulated but for a different reason: to avoid rapid cooling of water, which would cause an extra energy demand.

Fittings required for piping joints include couplings for straight-line connection, elbows for 45° turns and 90° turns, and tees for branches (Fig. 8-4). Types of fittings are threaded or screwed, flanged, soldered, bronzed, welded, or compression. Screw connections are used for pipe up to 4 in. or more in diameter. Pipe size is always given in inside dimension. The thread on the outside of the pipe is called the male connection and the thread on the inside of the pipe is called the female connection. Flanged connections are fittings

FIGURE 8-4   Pipe connections.

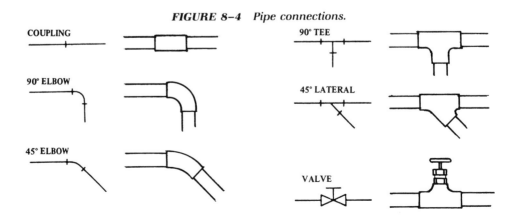

with projecting rims or flanges. They are tightened over the pipe by a screwed fitting and bolted to a gasket or seal to prevent leaks. There is also a slip flange connection type of fitting, which is a pipe with the end spread out to a larger diameter by a special tool. A nut is slipped over the pipe before enlarging the end and the mate has a flanged screwed connection joining the two together. This type of connection is usually used with copper pipe. The soldered joint consists of a fitting that is inserted over the pipe ends, joining the ends together. The connection is heated with a torch and solder is applied to the connection. The solder fills the space between the pipe and the fitting and is distributed by capillary attraction over the entire surface of the joint between the pipe and the fitting. It is impossible to solder a joint with water in the pipe; the pipe must be completely dry.

Control of water through pipes is accomplished with gate valves, check valves, and globe valves. Gate valves are used to shut off the water supply completely, globe valves are used to throttle the flow of water, and check valves are used to prevent water from flowing in the wrong direction and also when there is a possibility of water flowing in reverse because of back pressure. Other valves are cock, bibb, and faucet. Faucets are used in plumbing fixtures, such as sinks, lavatories, and tubs. Valves for connecting to garden hose are called hose bibbs or sill cock. All piping should be properly supported with pipe hangers. These are brackets attached directly to wood holding the pipe in position. Hangers should be spaced about 10'-0" apart. Copper pipe is supported with copper hangers.

To trace the route of a water supply from the street to the house, the local water utility authority, upon request, will excavate the street to open or expose the water main and install a tap or connection to the property line (Fig. 8-5). A gooseneck type of fitting is installed to allow for settlement of the pipe. Two valves, a corporation cock and a curb cock, are located on the line. The curb cock has a long stem reaching up to the level of the ground so that water can be disconnected without entering the home or without excavation. This

FIGURE 8–5 *Hot and cold water lines (from Ernest R. Weidhass,* Architectural Drafting and Design, © *1972 by Allyn and Bacon, Inc. Reprinted with permission).*

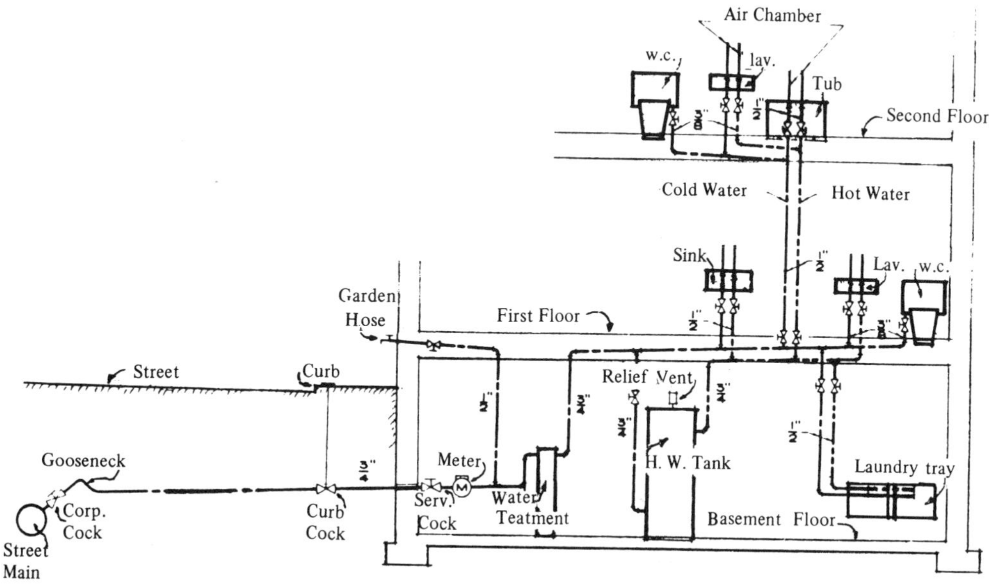

completes the work of the utility authority; from here on the owner is responsible. From the curb cock $\frac{3}{4}$-in. copper tubing is installed below the frostline in a trench to the building and, immediately inside the building, a service cock or valve is installed which is used to shut off the water throughout the entire building. Following the service valve is a water meter, which measures the amount of water consumed. Following the meter is a drain valve for removing or draining all the water in the piping within the house. If a water softener is used, hose bibbs can be connected without going through the water softener; otherwise, the water softener is connected next in line and from there to the source of the hot water supply. A $\frac{3}{4}$-in. cold water line is installed in the basement ceiling and $\frac{1}{2}$-in. lines directly to the fixtures. Manufacturers' catalogs on selection of plumbing fixtures will list the spacing and height above the floor for all water lines. Each pipe or riser is installed 2'-0" higher than the fixture, with the ends capped to provide an air chamber to reduce knocking or hammering of water lines. Valves are installed under each riser so that repairs can be made without shutting off the water for the entire house.

The hot water system has a $\frac{3}{4}$-in. pipe installed in the basement ceiling and $\frac{1}{2}$-in. lines directly to the fixtures. (Hot water tanks will collect sediment and rust the bottom. Water needs to be drained at least once a year.) The cold water enters the tank, leaving at about 130°F. There is a setting at the tank to adjust water temperature.

If water is from a private source, the corporation cock, curb cock, and water meter are not required. All else remains the same. At least 6 in. of space must be maintained between the hot and cold water piping so that the temperature in either pipe is not affected by the other. When installing the riser to the fixtures, the cold water line is always on the right side.

Waste Lines

Local codes for plumbing require a minimum distance for vents from doors or windows, minimum pipe size, and height above roof. Cleanouts are provided in waste lines to clean out the line if blockage should occur (Fig. 8–6). These are located at the foot of each rise and at the change of direction of pipe. The maximum distance between cleanouts in horizontal lines is about 50'-0". A cleanout is a threaded plug that is removable for pipe access to release any

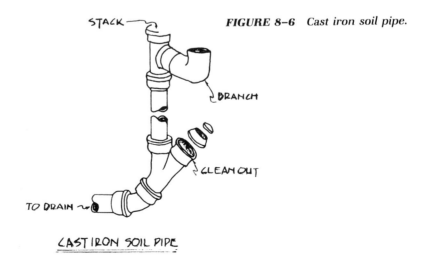

FIGURE 8–6 *Cast iron soil pipe.*

CAST IRON SOIL PIPE

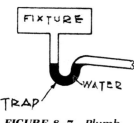

FIGURE 8-7 *Plumbing trap.*

blockage. Sewer or waste lines produce offensive and harmful gases that would permeate the entire house through the fixtures unless a trap were installed. Traps are nothing more than an offset in the waste pipe designed to retain water, which then forms a seal (Fig. 8–7). Traps must be installed under all plumbing fixtures except the water closet; water in the bowl acts as a built-in trap. Vent stacks through the roof discharge gases to the outside.

The main soil pipe in residential construction is 4-in. pipe and the branch waste and vents usually are 1½- or 2-in. pipe. To minimize friction, all waste drainage lines should be as straight and direct as possible (Fig. 8–8). Changes in direction of drains should be made with easy bends so as not to restrict flow. Standard plumbing fittings used are: T or 90° bend, Y or 45° bend, TY ⅙ bend, ⅛ bend, ¹⁄₁₆ bend, and ¼ bend. T fittings should be used for waste lines and can also be used for vent lines. Pipes of different sizes are connected by a reducer or increaser fitting.

Flashing of vent line through the roof is accomplished with a preformed sheet of copper flashing, caulked into the pipe, and turned under the roof covering. All points must be gas- and watertight. In addition to cast iron piping, vetrified clay pipe and wrought iron are used. Becoming more popular is polyvinyl chloride (PVC) with sealed slip joints of special mastic.

Pipes carrying waste are not under pressure and depend on gravity for removing waste. The minimum pitch of slope of pipe is ⅛ in. per foot to facilitate even flow. To prevent decomposition of waste in the pipe, air circulation through the waste piping must be provided. The air circulation dilutes poisonous gases, retards pipe corrosion, and maintains a balanced atmospheric pressure in the system. This is accomplished by extending air or vent stacks up through the roof.

FIGURE 8-8 *Waste lines (from Ernest R. Weidhass,* Architectural Drafting and Design, *© 1972 by Allyn and Bacon, Inc. Fig. 3 on p. 288. Reprinted with permission).*

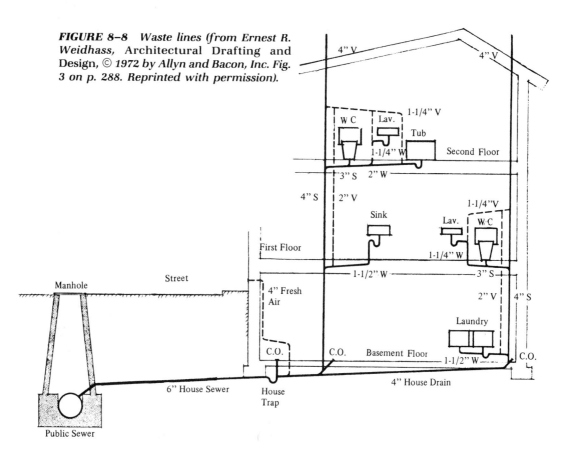

Private Disposal System

When public sewers are not available, a private system is built (Fig. 8–9). Operation of the system is simple. Waste from the house is directed to a septic tank (Fig. 8–10), which is built of concrete or fiberglass. In the tank bacteria convert waste solids to liquid. The liquid flows into a distribution system that distributes the liquid into a wide underground area. Between the sun evapo-

FIGURE 8–9   Private disposal system (courtesy Department of Housing and Urban Development).

(1) Drain tile laid with covered separated joints

(2) Pipe laid on undisturbed earth with tight joints

Absorption field trenches

Earth backfill

Gravel, crushed stone.

Gravel, crushed stone or slag filter material.

2"

16"

3'–0" max.

Provide separation from backfill by covering with straw, building paper, etc.

Detail - Absorption Trench

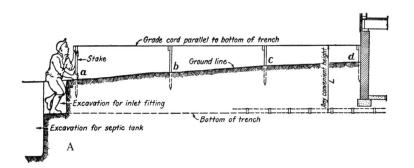

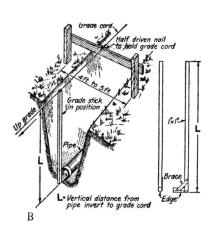

Establishing grade for sewer. A, 2- by 4-inch stakes are set each side of the trench at convenient distances a, b, c, and d. Then a board is nailed horizontally on the stakes at d, at a convenient height above the bottom of the trench, that is, the bottom of the sewer leaving the house. A board is nailed likewise to the stakes at a, the same height above the inlet to the tank that d is above the bottom of the trench. Similarly, boards are set at b and c by sighting from a to d so the tops of the intermediate boards will be in line. B, The exact grade of the sewer is obtained by measuring from the grade cord with the 1- by 1-inch stick, shown in detail. The length of the stick must equal the height of the board above sewer at d.

FIGURE 8–10 *Septic tank (courtesy Department of Housing and Urban Development).*

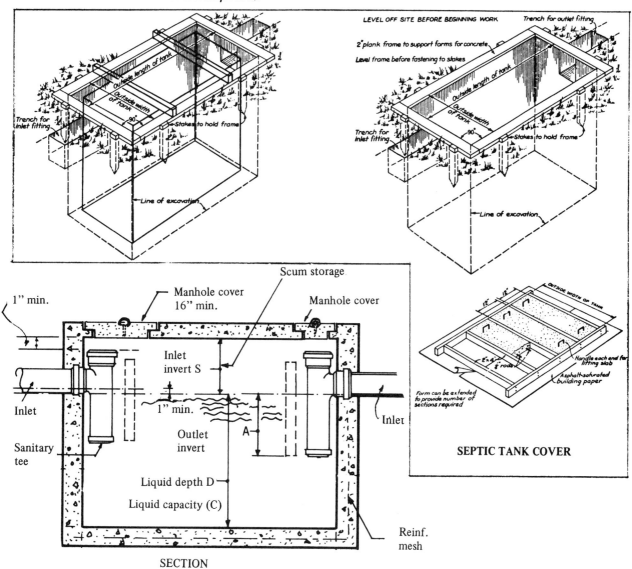

SEPTIC TANK COVER

SECTION

A - Approx. 40% of the depth D.
D - Not less than 30" depth. Greater than 6 ft. should not
    be considered in tank capacity.
S - Not less than 15% of the liquid capacity C.

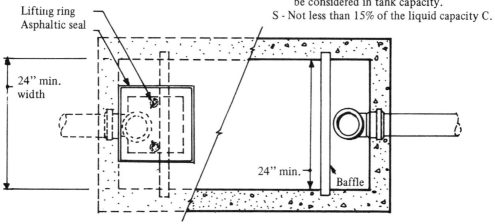

PLAN

rating the liquid and the ground absorbing the liquid, the system is very functional. The size of the system depends on local codes and the number of people it is designed to serve. It also depends on the condition of the soil, which is determined by a percolation test. The procedure is to separate the solids from the liquids by sedimentation. The natural disintegration of sewage is divided into two stages: putrefaction and oxidation. The first stage will produce ammonia, carbon dioxide gas, and hydrogen sulfide, which causes dark discolorations. As the process continues, methane gas is produced and the solids change to humus and decompose no more. A lack of oxygen causes a slow but continuous decay by means of anaerobic bacteria. The ammonia is oxidized to nitrates and the sulfur compounds to sulfate (plant food). The process then consists of moving the solids to a receptacle (septic tank), where they putrefy, and then leading the liquid into the soil or drain field, where it oxidizes without odor or danger to health. Later, bacteria act to break down the solids, resulting in sludge which needs to be removed from the tank about every three years.

The tile lines in the distribution system are placed on a gravel and crushed stone bed and are about $\frac{1}{4}$ in. apart with open joints. These are placed about 16 in. below the surface of the ground and are sloped about $\frac{1}{2}$ in. per foot. The length and size of tile are determined by local code based on the number of occupants and the absorption rate of the soil. Usually, from 100 to 300 ft of tile is required for the average residence.

Detergents will interfere with the bacterial action in the septic tanks. Waste from washing machines should empty into a separate drainage system. Watertight or sealed wells should be at least 100 ft away from sewage drainage systems. No structure of any type or a driveway is allowed over a disposal system. Avoid swampy land, muck soil, flowerbeds, vegetable gardens, roadways, or pavements in locating disposal systems. Porous soil, in a location where the disposal field will not be disturbed, yet may be easily inspected, is most suitable. The system should run in as straight a line as possible in the same direction as the sewer pipe leaving the house. The exception to this is on slopes, where it is necessary to run the disposal field across the slope to slow the flow and allow absorption. While laying out the system, it is wise to plan for later extension of the disposal field. The depth of tank depends on the inlet grade level from the house. The grade should be 1 in. for every 4 ft of pitch. The minimum-size tank for any house should be 500 gallons. The larger the tank, the more efficient it is. A tank 50% larger than minimum will double the time between cleanouts. The depth should be at least 5'-0", regardless of other dimensions. If garbage disposal is used, the tank should be 5% larger than minimum.

Gas Piping

Since gas is highly dangerous, all joints must be leakproof. Gas is supplied by the public utility company or stored in tanks on the site. The utility is responsible for piping to the building, including the gas meter. From that point it becomes the responsibility of the owner to run gas piping to the appliance or fixture. If gas is supplied at high pressure, a pressure-regulating valve is furnished and installed by the utility company. A shutoff valve is placed on the main line to shut off the entire system, in addition to each fixture having a valve.

Gas piping should be of best quality standard black wrought iron, or steel pipe. The fittings should be of galvanized, malleable iron with cocks and valves of brass. A certain amount of moisture is contained in gas and all pipes should be straight without sags and pitched back so that condensation will flow back into the service pipe, or the piping should be dropped. Gas piping should not be bent; changes in direction are made with screw couplings, and changes in pipe size with reducing fittings. Connections at fixtures should be made with flexible pipe to allow for positioning the fixture or appliance.

Heating Piping

Heat is transferred from warm to cold surfaces by three methods: radiation, convection, or conduction. Radiation heat flows through space to a cooler surface in the same way that light travels. The air is not warm, but the cooler object it strikes becomes warm. An open fire in a fireplace is an example of radiation. Convection heat is caused by a warm surface heating the air around it. The warm air rises and cooler air takes its place, causing a convection of current. Hot air registers are an example of convection heat. Conduction heat moves through a solid material. Frying eggs in a pan is an example of conduction heat.

Air heat requires a series of metal ducts to distribute the heat throughout the house (Fig. 8–11). If air conditioning is planned, air heat would be the most economical choice of heat because the same metal ducts are used for heating and cooling. If any other type of heating system is used with air conditioning, a separate ducting system will need to be installed in addition to the heating system.

The fuel needed for any heating system is oil, wood, gas, electricity, coal, or sun. Insulation plays a very important part in heating and cooling. Heat is measured in Btu (British thermal units); 1 Btu is the amount of heat required to raise the temperature of 1 pound of water 1 degree Fahrenheit. Basically, the purpose is to design a heating system to supply the heat lost in a given space and to maintain the required temperature within that space. Heat flows from a high temperature to a low temperature. Warm objects lose heat to cold objects. In the case of a heated house, the warmed air inside is attracted to the cold air outside, and that loss must be replaced by the heating system. The outside wall of the house serves as a barrier between the warm and the cold, and heat loss or retention depends on the construction of the external walls.

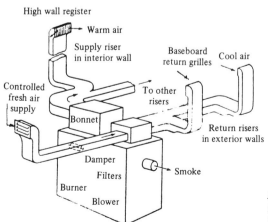

FIGURE 8–11 Heating ducts (courtesy Department of Housing and Urban Development).

There is no heat loss between adjacent walls if each room is heated to the same temperature. Wall effectiveness is the ability of a certain building material to resist the flow of heat. All building materials have a heat loss factor. Lower heat loss numbers indicate good insulation. The heat loss factors are known as heat transmission coefficients, K factors, or U factors. Heat transmission coefficients vary from 0.07 for well-insulated walls to 1.13 for glass and doors. Degree temperature is the difference between the inside room temperature and the coldest temperature likely to occur in a given locality expressed in Fahrenheit degrees. It is common practice to use 70°F for inside design temperature. The outside temperature is not the coldest ever recorded—that would be uneconomical. Heating units such as furnaces or boilers are rated in Btu capacity, and the results of the heat loss formula will determine the number of Btu or size of heating unit. Another factor to be considered in designing a system is infiltration, which is the amount of heat loss through doors, windows, cracks, and fireplaces.

Humidity control is a contributing factor toward comfort and health in a properly designed heating system. Humidity is the amount of moisture in the air related to the temperature level. The air will hold more water when the temperature is high. A comfortable level is about 50% when the temperature is about 72°F. During the winter months, the moisture content indoors is low. If there is no moisture in the air, throats and skin will be irritated, and furniture can crack and separate at the joints. Even a higher-temperature setting of the thermostat will not provide comfort when the relative humidity is low. In the summer, too much moisture is a problem. Wood will expand, drawers and doors will not operate properly, and water is likely to condense. This condition will cause severe damage to woodwork. Humidity is also added to house through bathing, showers, and cooking. If too much humidity is present, a dehumidifier will remove water from the air. Warm air heating systems have a built-in controlled humidifier.

Air, unless replaced through circulation, will become stale, stagnant, and unhealthy. Provision should be made to provide fresh circulated air throughout the house. Air contains dust and foreign particles and therefore should be filtered. Warm air heating systems have a built-in filtering system. Other systems can have electronic air cleaning grids which will remove 95% of the foreign matter from the air.

Thermostats control the temperature of all types of heating systems, and heating systems can be split to provide many separate thermostats controlling certain parts of the house. Thermostats should be located on an inside wall free from cold, drafts, or heat from lamps.

Electricity

In planning an electrical system, safety must be of prime concern. Electricity passes through wires, creating heat. If undersized wires are used, not only is the system inefficient but the electricity passing through the wire will overload the service, resulting in a breakdown and melting of the protective coating or insulation covering the wires, and creating a hazard and possible fire. Minimum requirements are given in local codes and the National Electrical Code® .

Electrical Terminology

Ampere   Unit of current to measure the amount of electricity passing through wire.

Circuit   Two or more wires from a source of electrical supply to one or more outlets and return.

Circuit breaker   A switch that stops or shuts off the flow of electricity at the source of supply.

Conductor   Wire that carries electricity.

Fuse   A safety device at the electrical supply source that melts, cutting off the flow of electricity.

Ground   A connection between electricity and earth, minimizing the danger of electric shock and damage from electrical storm, such as lightning.

Horsepower   A unit for measuring work, such as that done by electric motors (1 hp = 745 watts)

Kilowatt   1000 watts.

Kilowatt hour   1000 watts per hour (utilities charge by the kilowatthour).

Outlet   Electric plug, switch, or light.

Receptacle   Electric plug.

Service entrance   Electric wires from outside (utility company) the building to a distribution or electric panel.

Service panel   Steel box containing fuses or circuit breakers from which the main electric service distributes electricity throughout a building.

Short circuit   An incorrect wire connection.

Volt   Measure or push of electric current.

Watt   Measure of electric power used by an appliance.

The heart of an electrical system is the distribution panel, which is made of metal and attached to the wall or built in, containing a number of fuses or circuit breakers (Fig. 8–12). All electricity must be grounded by running a wire from the panel to a water pipe or ground terminal. At the point on the house where the wires are attached is an electric meter. From the meter, the wires are attached to the panel inside the house. The wires can be copper or aluminum, overhead or underground. The minimum service required should be 100 amperes.

Wires are furnished to the home by the local electric company. These wires supply 240 and 120 volts, single phase, 60 cycles of alternating current and should be at least 10′-0″ above the ground at the point of house attachment. The size of the distribution panel is determined by the total electrical load in the house plus an allowance for future loads. From the electrical distribution box, branch circuits are extended to various parts of the house through either a circuit breaker or a fuse-type panel (Fig. 8–13). Branch circuits carry different electrical loads, depending on the work that it is required to do, ranging from 15 to 50 amperes. The wires used from the distribution panel to the branch circuits are sized according to the service performed. A single cable consists of two or three insulated wires all wrapped into one. These wires have numbers stamped on the wrapping indicating the number of wires in the cable and the diameter of the wire. For example, 12/2 indicates two wires of No. 12

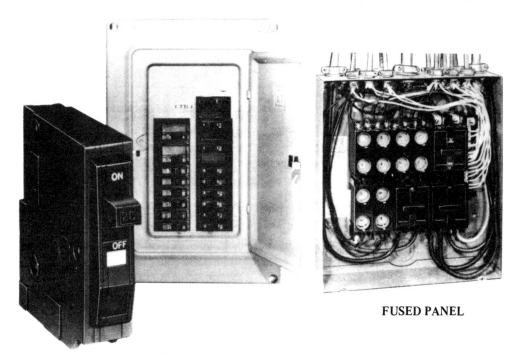

CIRCUIT BREAKER PANEL

FUSED PANEL

FIGURE 8–12   *Electric panels.*

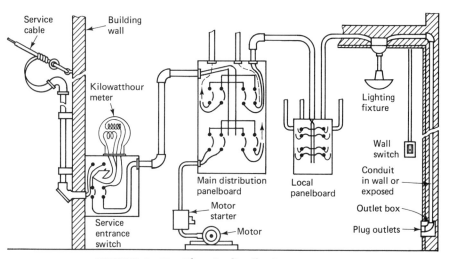

FIGURE 8–13   *Electric distribution system.*

gauge. The larger the wire, the smaller the number. The minimum-size wire for residential work is No. 14 gauge. Two types of wire covering are available: non-metallic sheath cable (Romax), which is a flexible cable covering of plastic or fabric, and metal armored cable (BX), which is a steel spiral covering not recommended in damp places (Fig. 8–14).

All outlets, such as lights, switches, and plugs, must be installed in an electrical box. There are three types of electrical boxes: square, hexagon, and outlet (Fig. 8–15). The outlet box is used for switches and plugs, which are attached directly to the wall studs flush with the finish wall material. The hexagon box is generally used for hanging electrical lighting fixtures, which are attached directly to the studs or ceiling joists, protruding from the joist or

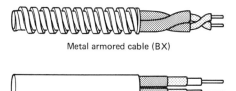

Metal armored cable (BX)

Non-metallic sheath cable (ROMAX)

Electric wires

FIGURE 8-14   Electric wire.

FIGURE 8-15   Junction boxes.

stud the thickness of the finish. The square box and the hexagon box are used to splice wires together. Under no circumstances should electrical wire be spliced with tape and left exposed. They must be placed in a square or hexagonal junction box. The two wires to be spliced are held together with a wire nut which locks and twists the two wires together. All wiring is brought into any of these boxes and the switches, plugs, or lighting fixtures are connected at or to the box. Plastic boxes are also available.

Low-Voltage System

Another type of electrical system for residential use is called a low-voltage system. This is a 24-volt system controlling switches through a relay. Bell wire can be used for low-voltage wiring and there is no danger of electrical shock. All outlets can be controlled from a central station. Lights can be controlled from one or more stations.

Ventilation

Crawl Spaces

All crawl spaces under houses without basements and other unexcavated spaces under porches, breezeways, and patios or other appendages should be ventilated by openings in the foundation walls. Such spaces should be provided with access panels so that they may be inspected easily. The vent openings should have a net area not less than 2 square feet for each 100 linear feet of exterior wall, plus ⅓ square foot for each 100 square feet of crawl space. Open-

ings should be arranged to provide cross ventilation and covered with corrosion-resistant wire mesh, not less than ¼ in. or more than ½ in. in any
dimension. Unventilated, inaccessible spaces should not be permitted (Fig.
8–16). When soil in crawl spaces is noticeably damp, it should be covered with
a layer of impervious material, such as 15-lb asphalt-saturated felt or poly-
ethelene. The ground surface should be leveled and the cover material turned
at walls and piers and lapped at least 2 in., but need not be sealed.

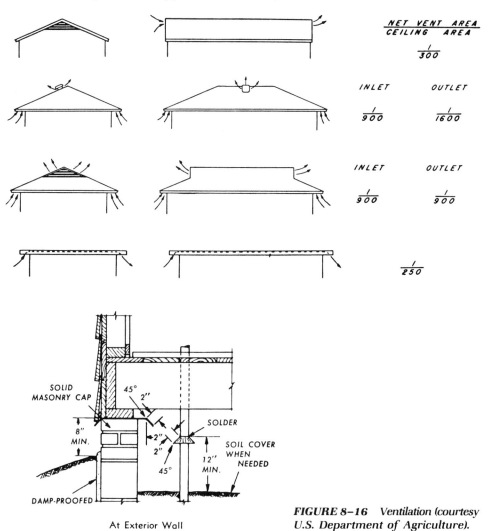

FIGURE 8–16   Ventilation (courtesy
U.S. Department of Agriculture).

Attic Spaces

To eliminate the problem of moisture condensation on roof framing in cold
weather and to permit the escape of heat in hot weather, ventilation of all
spaces is required. For gable roofs, screened louvers generally are provided,
and the net area of the opening should be about 1/300 of the area of the ceiling
below. When a ¾-in. slot is provided beneath the eaves, the ventilating area
may be reduced to 1/900. For hip roofs, it is customary to provide a ¾-in. slot
beneath the eaves and a sheet metal ventilator near the ridge, in which case
the net area of the inlet should be 1/900, and that of the outlet 1/1600 of the
area of the ceiling below. For flat roofs, blocking and bridging should be ar-

ranged to prevent interference with movement of air. Such roofs may be ventilated along overhanging eaves on the basis of net area of opening equal to
1/250 of the area of the ceiling below.

In cold climates when winter temperature customarily falls below 0 °F,
walls of all insulated dwellings should have a vapor barrier applied to the
warm side of the walls. Where a water-resistant building paper is used between sheathing and siding, or where a water-resistant material is incorporated into the sheathing, it should be a "breathing-type" material, except in
climates where winter temperatures commonly fall below − 20 °F.

Vapor barriers should be installed carefully to provide a complete envelope, preventing moisture vapor produced inside the structure from entering
enclosed spaces where condensation might occur. The principle of vapor protection is to make the warm side of the wall as vapor-tight as possible and the
cold side permeable enough to permit the passage of moisture vapor to the
outside, yet provide sufficient resistance to cold air infiltration and penetration of wind-driven rain.

Solar Energy

Solar heat is not new; it was the first kind of heat experienced by humans.
Solar heating will generally provide most heat in the spring and fall, when
the heating load is light and the sun is brightest. Conventional heating systems, which are designed to heat a house to 70 °F when the outside temperature is 0 °F, work at only about one-third capacity during the 10-month heating
season (in some parts of the country). A solar system designed with a smaller
capacity than that of a conventional system will take the heating load for a
large percentage of the heating time. The number of Btu of heat falling per
hour from the sun on 1 square foot of surface is called *insolation.*

Heat generated from the sun, measured in Btu per hour, is partially lost
through the atmosphere. A portion is scattered by contact with air, smoke,
moisture, and dust, and absorbed by water vapor, carbon dioxide, and ozone.
The remainder of energy striking the earth is called direct solar radiation.
When this radiation strikes a surface, part of it is absorbed and part is transmitted through the material or surface. This surface will also radiate heat to
the atmosphere. The energy used for heating comes from the sun, but only
40% of it is efficient; 60% is lost as described.

The sun is the most practical energy source. It is constant, nonpolluting,
and there is no cost. Its life span is infinite and in every 24 hours the amount
of energy reaching the earth from the sun is 5000 times more than the sum of
all energy sources on earth. Solar energy, which is sometimes intermittent,
reaches us in two forms: direct and diffused. Direct radiation casts a shadow
from the sun; diffused radiation is dispersed or reflected and does not cast a
shadow. The average intensity of solar energy will deliver about 100 to 200
Btu for every square feet of ground. An entire nation's energy needs could be
filled by the sun.

Solar energy could reduce air pollution by 385,000 tons of solid waste per
week or 20,000,000 tons annually. The simplest form of solar heating, called
direct or passive, converts sunlight into thermal energy within the space to be
heated. The technique is to install large south-facing windows that trap direct
solar radiation during the winter daylight hours and store it in the walls, giv-

ing it back into the room when the sun sets. The other form of solar heating is the indirect system, converting sunlight into thermal energy outside the building. This system requires a means of collecting and storing the heat until ready for distribution. The heart of the indirect system consists of solar collection panels, which gather solar radiation and intensify it to heat water or air which is piped to a conventional system.

There are two types of collectors in an indirect system: concentration and flat plate (Fig. 8–17). The concentration collector consists of a highly reflective curved surface which focuses sunlight on to a radiation-absorbing area. The collectors can reach temperatures of 250 °F. They are dish-shaped with a tracking system following the sun's rays. Flat-plate collectors are more popular because they absorb, diffuse, and direct sunlight. In simple terms, these collectors are large flat trays or panels of water or air covered with glass or plastic to create a concentration of heat, which in turn heats the water or air. The surfaces of these panels are coated with an absorbent material to soak up the rays of the sun. The panels are about $4'-0'' \times 8'-0''$ and are mounted on a roof or on the ground tilted to capture the most direct radiation. The back side of the panels is insulated. The heated water is carried through the collectors into a storage tank large enough to hold 2 day's supply of heat. The heat is transferred to the room by convection, circulating the heated water in the storage tank through the conventional heating system of baseboard, convectors or radiators, or water coils in a warm air ducting system.

Heat from the air system is stored in large bins of stone. Domestic hot water is preheated by cold water passing through the storage tank and heating

FIGURE 8–17 (courtesy Daystar Corporation).

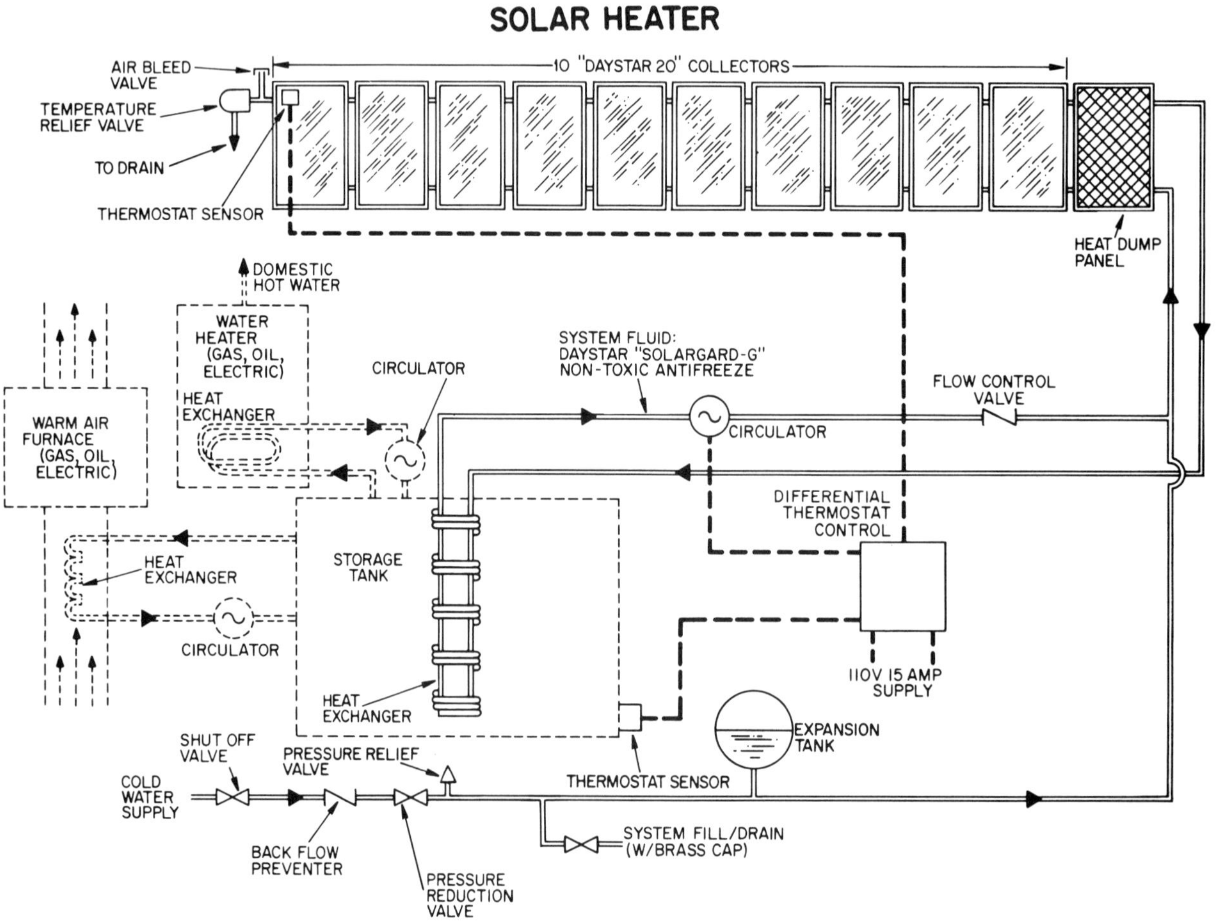

SOLAR HEATER

it up to 145 °F. In addition to domestic hot water, the system is capable of heating water in swimming pools and whirlpools. Solar energy can also be used to cool a building. Cooling is designed to drive an absorptive chiller by hot water.

Air Conditioning

The process of air conditioning is simply a matter of drawing heat from the air and replacing it with cooler air. Human comfort is a matter of temperature and humidity—the two are inseparable (Fig. 8–18). If the air is dry (low humidity), perspiration easily evaporates and cools the skin. Therefore, dehumidification is necessary for comfort in air conditioning. This is what the air-conditioning machinery does. A summer temperature of 75 °F at a relative humidity of 60% is comfortable. Indoor temperatures in the summer should not be more than 15 °F below the outdoor temperature to avoid an unpleasant chill upon entering the building or the feeling of intense heat when leaving the building.

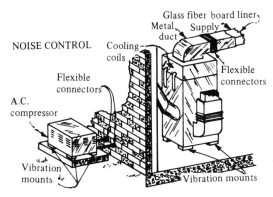

FIGURE 8–18 *Central air conditioner (courtesy Department of Housing and Urban Development).*

Ventilation, humidity, and temperature are all important to human comfort. For satisfactory results, air should move about 25 ft per minute. Air conditioners are continually changing the air by introducing fresh air from outdoors and exhausting stale air containing carbon dioxide, reduced oxygen, and unpleasant odors. This stale air is not recirculated in the house but is discharged directly to the outside. A complete air change every 15 minutes is desirable. In most cases, infiltration in homes provides a satisfactory amount of fresh air to make the change. The air needs to be filtered to remove impurities; the dry type of filter is the most common.

Warm air heating is most adaptable for central air conditioning using the same ducts for heating and cooling, and the same filter and blower (Fig. 8–19). Supply ducts must be insulated with air conditioning because of condensation forming on the surface of the metal and the loss of cooled air. If a separate air-conditioning system is installed, that is, not part of the heating system, all the equipment that is part of a warm air heating system will need to be installed in addition to other equipment. A hot water or steam system can also be employed as air conditioning by circulating chilled water through the piping system with a water chiller. In this case, blowers are installed on the convectors to circulate the warm air over the chilled air coils.

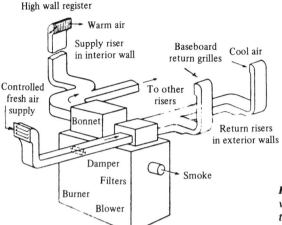

High wall register

Warm air

Supply riser
in interior wall

Baseboard
return grilles

Cool air

Controlled
fresh air
supply

To other
risers

Bonnet

Return risers
in exterior walls

Damper

Filters

Smoke

Burner

Blower

FIGURE 8-19 Duct system for warm-air heating and cooling (courtesy Department of Housing and Urban Development).

As winter heat is lost through a building, so summer heat enters by transmission through floors, walls, glass, and ceiling in addition to cracks around doors and windows. Latent heat must also be considered. This is heat within the house generated by cooking, which generates about 1200 Btu per hour, and people, who produce about 300 Btu per hour. Motors from refrigerators, dishwashers, and similar equipment also generate heat. Lights contribute about 3.5 Btu per hour for each watt of electricity.

Cooling units are rated by tons of refrigeration. A ton is equivalent to 12,000 Btu per hour. One horsepower of electricity is required for each ton of air conditioning. The mechanical makeup of an air-conditioning system is composed of the evaporator, which absorbs heat and vaporizes the refrigerant. This unit must be placed in the house and if part of the warm air heating system, is contained in the plenum directly connected to the furnace. The other unit, a condenser, gives off heat and must be placed outdoors. It may be installed inside but must be on an outside wall discharging the heat outdoors. A dual unit combines heating and cooling and a single unit, cooling only.

Heating

Warm Air Heat

Air is heated in a furnace and forced to all parts of the house through ducts, called supply ducts, by a fan or blower (Fig. 8-20). Air is returned through the return ducts back to the furnace, where it is filtered, humidified, and reheated and the process is repeated. This heated air provides a quick source of heat. There are three types of warm air heating units: the standard up-flow furnace, designed for basement installation with ducts overhead; the counterflow furnace, designed for basementless or main-floor installation, with ducts below the floor, such as in crawl spaces; and the horizontal furnace, which can be suspended in a crawl space or attic. The metal ducts are designed to fit between the joists and studs. There should be a supply and a return duct in all rooms except the kitchen and bath. These rooms need only a supply, to prevent odors from being pulled through the rest of the house. The main and largest duct is called a trunkline, and smaller ducts are branched off from the trunk

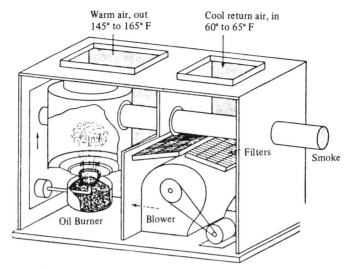

Warm air, out
145° to 165° F

Cool return air, in
60° to 65° F

Filters

Smoke

Oil Burner

Blower

FIGURE 8–20 *Mechanical warm-air heating furnace (courtesy Department of Housing and Urban Development).*

to various rooms in the house (Fig. 8–21). The farther from the furnace, the smaller the duct size, because the amount of air it is required to move is less. Ducts can be rectangular or round. The ends of ducts terminate in the room in either a grille or a register. The registers are adjustable to control the flow of heat in balancing the system. Sometimes baseboard registers are used to distribute the heat over a wider area. Warm air heating (not in conjunction with air conditioning) requires that the registers be located close to the floor (Fig. 8–22). If the system is designed for air conditioning as well as heating, the supply registers are close to the floor and the return registers are close to the ceiling. The theory is that hot air rises and is drawn into the return register for conditioning and recycling.

Where warm air supply outlets are installed low on exterior walls, room air temperatures are largely unaffected by location of the return air intakes. However, returns placed above the occupied space, either high in the inside wall or in the ceiling, are preferred because air motion (drafts) in the occupied zone is then less noticeable. For year-round air conditioning, high returns also reduce stratification of cool air by drawing off the warm air.

Underfloor plenum systems are similar to perimeter duct systems with respect to arrangement and location of heating unit and floor supply registers; however, with the omission of the connecting ductwork, the entire crawl space is maintained at furnace air temperatures (Fig. 8–23). Thus duct costs are reduced somewhat and the entire floor is kept warm, but heat loss by transmission and leakage is increased substantially and musty odors may develop unless the crawl space is moisture proofed.

Perimeter system ducts are usually embedded in concrete. By being embedded, heat is transmitted from the ducts directly to the concrete, thereby warming the cold concrete floor slab. The ducts may also be installed in a crawl space or in a basement, thereby warming the space under the floor, for greater comfort.

Perimeter systems should not be installed in slabs-on-ground located in swales or flat, low-lying areas where there is a possibility of (1) flooding, (2) high groundwater after rains, (3) subsurface springs, or excessive moisture in the ground (poor drainage) (Fig. 8–24). Drain tiles installed outside the house at the footings will help to alleviate some of these moisture problems provided that there is a good outfall or a reliable automatic sump pump system.

FIGURE 8–21 *Air heating ducts (courtesy Department of Housing and Urban Development).*

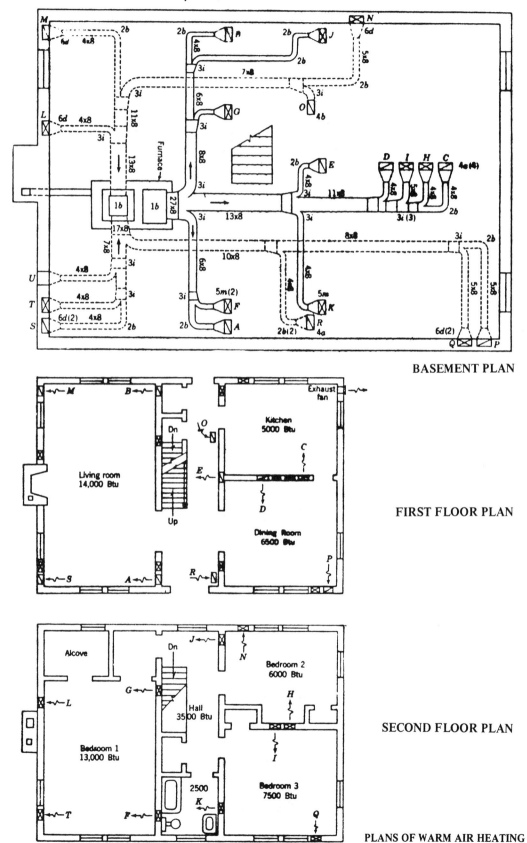

BASEMENT PLAN

FIRST FLOOR PLAN

SECOND FLOOR PLAN

PLANS OF WARM AIR HEATING

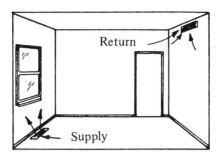

FIGURE 8–22 *Air supply and return location (courtesy Department of Housing and Urban Development).*

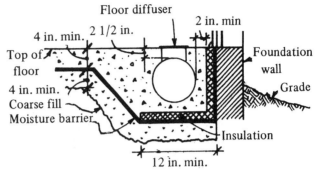

FIGURE 8–23 *Underfloor warm-air heating (courtesy Department of Housing and Urban Development).*

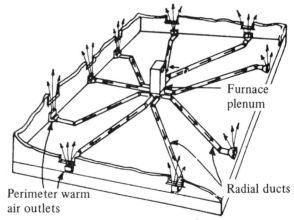

FIGURE 8–24 *Air heating perimeter system (courtesy Department of Housing and Urban Development).*

Hydronic—Hot Water

A hot water, or hydronic, heating system consists of a boiler to heat water to 200 to 215 °F, then to pump it into pipes carrying the hot water to the radiators, baseboards, or convectors (Fig. 8–25). In a one-pipe system, the cooled water is returned to the boiler for reheating. (Fig. 8–26). A two-pipe system of hot water heat is more expensive but more efficient (Fig. 8–27). The principle is the same as the one-pipe system except that the cooled water is returned to the boiler through the independent piping system. The boiler is equipped with

FIGURE 8–25   Hot-water heat controls (courtesy Department of Housing and Urban Development).

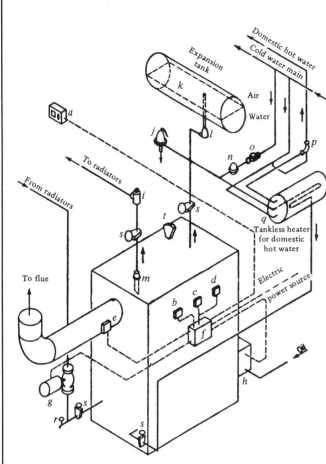

the boiler water is hot enough (above 160 ° F).

(h) Oil Burner. Reheat may be needed for a number of reasons. From lack of use the boiler water may have cooled below 160° F. The water may have been cooled in making domestic hot water. Finally, when circulation starts, cold radiator water is returned to the boiler and needs to be heated.

(i) Flow-Control Valve   The precise temperature control possible in forced circulation systems is assured by the flow-control valve, which closes when the pump stops, thus preventing gravity circulation which would result in a further rise in room temperature. In principle it is a check valve.

(j) Pressure-Relief Valve   When the pressure in the system exceeds 30 lb. per sq. in., the spring-loaded valve opens, bleeding water out of the pipes and relieving the pressure which might otherwise cause breakage. It should be placed where its discharge will do no damage. With proper system design and adjustment it should not operate except in an emergency.

(k) Expansion Tank. This is sometimes known as a compression tank in closed systems. A cushion of air remains in the top of the tank to adjust for the varying volume of water in the system as the temperature changes.

(l) and (m) Tank and Boiler Air-Control Fittings   Much of the air in the system is eliminated at once by these fittings, which lead the air to the expansion tank. Air accumulating in the boiler cannot leave through the dip tube (m) but finds its way to (l), where it is led to the top of the expansion tank.

(n) Pressure-Reducing Valve   This is the automatic fill valve. It opens when the pressure in the system drops below 12 lb. per sq. in. and closes with a check action against higher pressures. It keeps the system full.

(o) Check Valve. In an emergency where pressure-relief valve (j) did not open and the pressure-reducing valve failed in its checking action, the check valve (o) prevents the boiler from putting the house cold water system under pressure that would be dangerous.

(p) Tempering Valve   This mixing valve operates automatically by a mechanical thermostat to add cold water in sufficient quantities to deliver the domestic hot water at exactly the required temperature.

(q) Tankless Heater. This generates domestic hot water for use in the various plumbing fixtures.

(r) Drain. At this or other low points means of draining the system must be provided.

(s) Gate Valve. The location of gate valves is determined by the need for shutting off sections of the system for repair or servicing without draining the entire water content. Their selection in preference to globe valves is due to the smaller resistance they offer to the passage of water.

(t) Temperature and Pressure Gauge. The operating pressure of the system may be observed as a check on the operation and setting of the pressure-relief valve and on the cushioning effect of the compression tank. Observation of the boiler temperature is a check on the operation of the aquastat which sets this temperature.

CONTROLS – HOT WATER HEATING

(a) House Thermostat. When the room air temperature falls below the setting of the thermostat, the house thermostat turns on the pump and oil burner simultaneously. When satisfied it turns them both off.

(b) Low-Limit Control. This control turns on the oil burner when the boiler water falls below a chosen temperature (about 160° F).

(c) High-Limit Control. "Runaway" performance is prevented by this device, which turns off the oil burner when the boiler water starts to exceed a chosen high temperature (often about 200° F).

(d) Reverse-Acting Control. To prevent the circulation of cold water in the radiators, this control stops the circulating pump when the water falls below 160° F until the burner has had time to raise the temperature again to the desired degree.

(e) Stack-Temperature Control. After the burner starts, the stack-temperature control waits for the resulting rise in the stack temperature. If it does not come in a short time, it turns off the burner which has failed to ignite. This is a safety control.

(f) Junction Box and Relays. This central control station transmits the impulses of the controls previously described.

(g) Circulating Pump   This electrically driven centrifugal pump turns on whenever heat is called for and

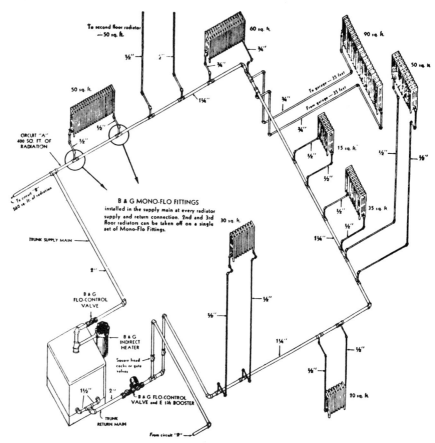

FIGURE 8-26 *One-pipe hot-water heating system (courtesy Department of Housing and Urban Development).*

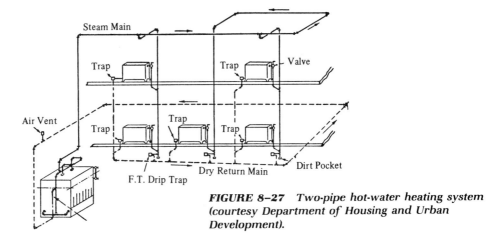

FIGURE 8-27 *Two-pipe hot-water heating system (courtesy Department of Housing and Urban Development).*

an expansion tank to compensate for variations of water volume at different temperatures and to relieve air pockets. In addition, each system offers an uninterrupted supply of domestic hot water as a part of the heating system. The piping may be wrought iron, black steel, or copper.

A third system of hot water heat, called series loop (Fig. 8-28), consists of a single continuous baseboard radiator around the entire exterior wall of the house. Pipes drop under the floor at doors and rise again. There is no individual control with this type of heat. Either the entire house is heated or none of it.

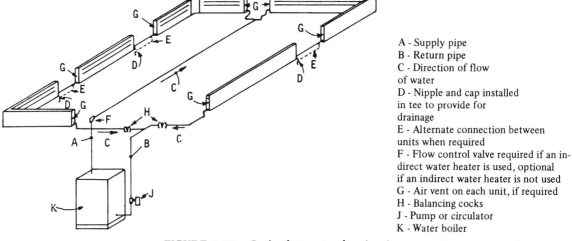

A - Supply pipe
B - Return pipe
C - Direction of flow
of water
D - Nipple and cap installed
in tee to provide for
drainage
E - Alternate connection between
units when required
F - Flow control valve required if an in-
direct water heater is used, optional
if an indirect water heater is not used
G - Air vent on each unit, if required
H - Balancing cocks
J - Pump or circulator
K - Water boiler

*FIGURE 8–28 Series hot-water heating (courtesy Department of
Housing and Urban Development).*

In a series-loop forced hot water system, the water flows through each
consecutive heating element and individual units cannot be valved. To control
heat output, each unit should be equipped with a manually adjustable air
damper, and each circuit must be equipped with an adjusting cock.

In all types of hot water heat, radiators have a large exposed surface to
allow the heat to radiate to the room. If convectors are used, they draw in cool
air from the bottom, warm the air by contact with the surface of the hot convector, and force it out into the room again. Convectors can be wall recessed to
increase floor space. Baseboard units may be radiant or convector type. Any
system of hot water heating is slow in heating the elements, but they cool off
more slowly when the heat is turned down or off. Where radiator, convector,
or baseboard enclosures are installed in an outside wall, insulation must be
provided to reduce excessive heat losses (Fig. 8–29).

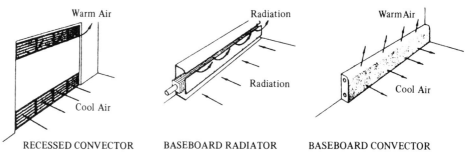

RECESSED CONVECTOR   BASEBOARD RADIATOR   BASEBOARD CONVECTOR

*FIGURE 8–29 Types of heating delivery (courtesy Department of
Housing and Urban Development).*

Radiant Heat

Radiant heat can also be called hydronic. It is similar to hot water heat, but
instead of radiators, a serpentine endless line or coil of tubing is concealed in
the floor or ceiling (Fig. 8–30). Radiant heat does not depend on air movement:
it passes directly to the object or person, making it one of the most comfortable

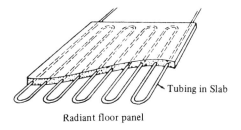

Radiant floor panel

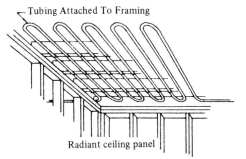

Radiant ceiling panel

FIGURE 8–30 Radiant heat (courtesy Department of Housing and Urban Development).

types of heating systems. Should a leak develop in the lines, it means tearing down the floor or ceiling to make repairs; for that reason the system must be thoroughly tested before any surface is finished. In effect, a radiant heating system acts as one large radiator.

Hot water is circulated through the pipes embedded in the floor or ceiling as in a hot water heating system. This system is primarily but not necessarily used in a house without a basement and is completely concealed. Electricity may also be employed in a radiant heating system. Preassembled heating panels are designed to be installed in the ceiling under the finish. This type of heating is like a giant toaster in the ceiling.

Heat Pump

A dual system of heating and cooling is produced by a heat pump. Basically, it is a refrigeration unit which pumps natural heat or water to be heated from the outside air. Heat pumps work on the principle that outside air contains heat, which is pumped into the house by electricity to heat it and in summer, is pumped out to cool it. A heat pump may not be practical for cold climates because when the outside temperature drops below 30 °F, the efficiency of the system drops. This necessitates a supplementary heating system. The system is more efficient for cooling than for heating. A heat pump employs a water-to-water and air-to-air heat exchanger system. If a water system is used, an economical source of uniform temperature must be available for the heat exchanger. Heated water is distributed through a conventional hot water piping system. In the air-to-air system, air is distributed similar to a warm air heating system, utilizing metal ducts.

The heat pump is a packaged unit which can be located outdoors or may have two cabinets, one inside and one outside, called a remote unit. The operation of the heat pump draws outside air or water into the unit, the refrigerant in the evaporator absorbs the heat, and a compressor pumps the refrigerant to a high temperature and pressure. A condensor gives off the heat to the outside air, creating a heating cycle.

Comparison of Heating Systems

TYPE OF HEATING SYSTEM	ADVANTAGES	DISADVANTAGES
Warm air	Quick heat	Ducts takes up basement headroom
	No radiators or convectors to take up floor space	Ducts convey dust and sound
	Air conditioning and humidification possible	Flue action increases fire danger
		Separate hot water heater required
Hot water	Cannot freeze	
	Low installation cost	
	Low-temperature heat possible for mild weather	
		Retains heat during periods when no longer required
		Slow to heat up
		Radiators require two lines
		Must be drained to avoid freezing when not in use
Radiant	No visible heating device	
		Slow response to heatneeds
		Air conditioning must be separate unit
	Good temperature distribution	Repair costly
Steam (one pipe)	Radiators require only one line	Large pipes required
		Sloping pipes take up basement headroom
		Inefficient time and pressure required to vent air from radiators
		Water hammer
Electric		Operation cost high in many locations
	Low installation cost	
		Heavy insulation required
	Individual room control	
	Clean, silent operation	
Solar		
	Low operation cost	Supplemental heating system necessary

Electric Heat

The least expensive heating system to install is electric heat. It requires no space for boilers or furnaces, nor is a chimney necessary. It has individual room control, is clean, but may not be the least expensive to operate. Proper insulation is the key to an efficient electric heating system. Basically there are three types of electric heat. The first is electric resistance cable, consisting of covered wire cables heated by electricity and concealed in the floor or ceiling. The wires are made in the exact length that will provide the necessary wattage. The finish ceiling or floor conceals this system. The second system consists of electric panels, prefabricated finished ceiling panels that cover the entire ceiling. They can be painted, plastered, or papered. In the third type, baseboard, convector heaters consisting of heating elements are enclosed in a metal baseboard. The top and bottom are slotted to allow air to circulate. The value of electricity converted to heat loss is that 1 watt of electricity equals 3.41 Btu.

QUESTIONS

8-1. Name three methods of transferring heat.

1. _____
2. _____
3. _____

8-2. Two types of heat are wet heat and dry heat.
True or False

8-3. Warm air is attracted to cold air.
True or False

8-4. Infiltration is which of the following?
(a) Filtering heat
(b) Introducing outside air
(c) Maintaining a constant temperature
(d) None of the above

8-5. Name two types of hot water heat.

1. _____
2. _____

8-6. Radiant heat is the least comfortable type of heat.
True or False

8-7. Warm air heat is delivered by which of the following?
(a) Wires
(b) Pipes
(c) Ducts
(d) All of the above

8-8. Solar heat has a limited fuel supply.
True or False

8-9. Electric heat is the least expensive to install.
True or False

8–10. Name three types of fuel used for heat.

1. _____
2. _____
3. _____

8–11. Moisture is contained in gas piping.
True or False

8–12. Hot water heating systems can also be used for air conditioning.
True or False

8–13. What is an evaporator? _____
_____

8–14. A heat pump can be used for heating and cooling.
True or False

8–15. What is the difference between solar heat and hot water heat? _____
_____

8–16. Water can be hard or soft.
True or False

8–17. Name the types of piping material used for water installation. _____
_____

8–18. What is a cleanout? _____

8–19. Define *percolation test.* _____
_____

8–20. Define the following terms.
(a) Watt _____
(b) Volt _____
(c) Ampere _____
(d) Kilowatt _____

9

Construction Details

Introduction

Most homes built in North America are of wood frame construction, principally because frame construction costs less than other types of construction. Wood is more versatile to shape and form than are most other building materials. A well-built wood frame house is one of the most lasting types of construction.

When trees are felled in the forest and delivered to a lumber mill, the logs are cut to a full dimension, such as 2 in. $\times$ 4 in. This green lumber is put into a kiln or oven for drying, called *seasoning*. During the drying process, the lumber shrinks through moisture evaporation and a 2 in. $\times$ 4 in. board becomes a $1\frac{5}{8}$ in. $\times$ $3\frac{5}{8}$ in. board. Lumber lengths are sized in 2-ft intervals. This is true of all seasoned lumber, framing and finish, except plywood and composition panels. A 1-in.-thick by 12-in.-wide board is $\frac{3}{4}$ in. thick and $11\frac{1}{2}$ in. wide. The length is not affected. A 12 to 20% moisture content in lumber is allowed for framing lumber and 3 to 8% for interior finish lumber. The drying-out process or seasoning causes the walls of fiber cells to shrink. There is constant movement in wood, which varies with the seasons.

In the winter months the heat within a house causes the wood to shrink because moisture is absorbed by the heat. The summer months has a reverse effect on wood, causing it to absorb moisture, with a consequent swelling effect. The movement between the two can be as much as $\frac{1}{4}$ in.

Decay in wood is caused by fungi which penetrate the wood, feeding the cells and breaking down the wood. Four requirements are necessary for fungi growth: air, moisture, food, and favorable temperatures. Remove any of these and fungi cannot exist; thus the wood will be preserved for long periods of time. Preservation can be accomplished in several ways. One is to impregnate the wood with poison, including such commercial preservatives as coal tar or zinc chloride. Painting wood is another way of preserving it.

Besides decay, there are other defects in wood which affect the acceptability from a standpoint of strength, durability, and appearance. These are known as shakes, checks, knots, wane, and pitch pockets. All these defects are graded by the National Lumber Manufacturers Association, together with the U.S. Department of Agriculture, into various grades meeting specific requirements regarding strength. This is important because all wood is not of the same strength but varies according to species. This grading, called *stress grading,* indicates the amount of load the wood will support. For this reason a specific species of wood or woods is desirable for framing. Grading also separates wood into yard lumber, which is a general purpose or utility grade; structural lumber, used primarily for load bearing; and factory or shop lumber, used for finish work and millwork such as doors, windows, and moldings. Lumber is sold by the board foot. To compute board feet, divide the sectional area in inches by 12 and multiply by the length in feet. For example, a 2 × 4 that is 8′-0″ long is figured as follows: $\dfrac{2 \times 4 \times 8}{12} = 5\frac{1}{3}$ board feet

Terminology

Before any construction work is begun, it is important to know the terms and phrases used in communication. This terminology has become universal and is used throughout the building trades. Some of the terms have a history which makes them easier to understand. The term "wood framing" comes to us from the New England colonists, as do "collar beam," "sole plate," and "ridge board." The Greeks gave us "freeze," "plinth," and "details." Some terms are named after their shape, such as "box sill," a sill shaped like a box. Other terms come from use or position in a building, such as "footing," "foundation," and "baseboard."

Following is a list of common terms used in construction:

Airway A space between roof insulation and roof boards for the movement of air.

Alligatoring A coarse checking pattern characterized by slipping a new paint coating over the old coating to the extent that the old coating can be seen through the fissures.

Anchor bolts Bolts to secure a wooden sill plate to a concrete or masonry floor or wall.

Apron The flat member of the inside trim of a window placed against the wall immediately beneath the stool.

Areaway An open subsurface space adjacent to a building used to admit light or air or as a means of access to a basement.

Asphalt Most native asphalt is a resudue from evaporated petroleum. It is insoluble in water but soluble in gasoline and melts when heated. Used widely in buildings for waterproofing roof coverings of many types, exterior wall coverings, flooring tile, and the like.

Astragal A molding, attached to one of a pair of swinging doors, against which the other door strikes.

Attic ventilators In houses, screened openings provided to ventilate an attic space. They are located in the soffit areas as inlet ventilators and in the gable end or along the ridge as outlet ventilators. They can also consist of power-driven fans used as an exhaust system *See also* Louver.

Backband   A simple molding sometimes used around the outer edge of a plain rectangular casing as a decorative feature.

Backfill   The replacement of excavated earth into a trench around and against a basement foundation.

Balusters   Usually, small vertical members in a railing used between a top rail and the stair treads or a bottom rail.

Balustrade   A railing made of balusters, top rail, and sometimes bottom rail, used on the edge of stairs, balconies, and porches.

Barge board   A decorative board covering the projecting rafter (fly rafter) of the gable end. At the cornice, this member is a facia board.

Base (baseboard)   A board placed against the wall around a room next to the floor to provide a proper finish between the floor and the wall.

Base molding   Molding used to trim the upper edge of interior baseboard.

Base shoe   Molding used next to the floor on interior baseboard.

Batten   Narrow strips of wood used to cover joints or as decorative vertical members over plywood or wide boards.

Batter board   One of a pair of horizontal boards nailed to posts set at the corners of an excavation, used to indicate the desired level; also as a fastening for stretched strings to indicate the outlines of foundation walls.

Bay window   Any window space projecting outward from the walls of a building, either square or polygonal in plan.

Beam   A structural member transversely supporting a load.

Bearing partition   A partition that supports any vertical load in addition to its own weight.

Bearing wall   A wall that supports any vertical load in addition to its own weight.

Bed molding   Molding used in an angle, as between the overhanging cornice, or eaves, of a building and the sidewalls.

Blind-nailing   Nailing such that the nailheads are not visible on the face of the work—usually at the tongue of matched boards.

Blind stop   Rectangular molding, usually ¾ by 1⅜ in. or more in width, used in the assembly of a window frame. Serves as a stop for storm and screen or combination windows and to resist air infiltration.

Blue stain   A bluish or grayish discoloration of sapwood caused by the growth of certain moldlike fungi on the surface and in the interior of a piece, made possible by the same conditions that favor the growth of other fungi.

Bodied linseed oil   Linseed oil that has been thickened in viscosity by suitable processing with heat or chemicals. Bodied oils are obtainable in a great range in viscosity, from a little greater than that of raw oil to just short of a jellied condition.

Boiled linseed oil   Linseed oil in which enough lead, manganese, or cobalt salts have been incorporated to make the oil harden more rapidly when spread in thin coatings.

Bolster   A short horizontal timber or steel beam on top of a column to support and decrease the span of beams or girders.

Boston ridge A method of applying asphalt or wood shingles at the ridge or at the hips of a roof as a finish.

Brace An inclined piece of framing lumber applied to wall or floor to stiffen the structure. Often used on walls as temporary bracing until framing has been completed.

Brick veneer A facing of brick laid against and fastened to sheathing of a frame wall or tile wall construction.

Bridging Small wood or metal members that are inserted in a diagonal position between the floor joists at midspan to act as both tension and compression members for the purpose of bracing the joists and spreading the action of loads.

Buck Often used in reference to rough frame opening members; door bucks used in reference to metal door frame.

Built-up roof A roofing composed of three to five layers of asphalt felt laminated with coal tar, pitch, or asphalt. The top is finished with crushed slag or gravel. Generally used on flat or low-pitched roofs.

Butt joint The junction where the ends of two timbers or other members meet in a square-cut joint.

Cant strip A triangular piece of lumber used at the junction of a flat deck and a wall to prevent cracking of the roofing that is applied over it.

Cap The upper member of a column, pilaster, door cornice, molding, and the like.

Casement frames and sash Frames of wood or metal enclosing part or all of the sash, which may be opened by means of hinges affixed to the vertical edges.

Casting Molding of various widths and thicknesses used to trim door and window openings at the jambs.

Cement, Keene's A white finish plaster that produces an extremely durable wall. Because of its density, it excels for use in bathrooms and kitchens and is also used extensively for the finish coat in auditoriums, public buildings, and other places where walls may be subjected to unusually hard wear or abuse.

Checking Fissures that appear with age in many exterior paint coatings, at first superficial, but which in time may penetrate entirely through the coating.

Checkrails Meeting rails sufficiently thicker than a window to fill the opening between the top and bottom sash made by the parting stop in the frame of double-hung windows. They are usually beveled.

Collar beam Nominal 1- or 2-in.-thick members connecting opposite roof rafters. They serve to stiffen the roof structure.

Column In architecture: A perpendicular supporting member, circular or rectangular in section, usually consisting of a base, shaft, and capital.

Combination doors or windows Combination doors or windows used over regular openings. They provide winter insulation and summer protection and often have self-storing or removable glass and screen inserts. This eliminates the need for handling a different unit each season.

Concrete plain Concrete either without reinforcement, or reinforced only for shrinkage or temperature changes.

Condensation In a building: Beads or drops of water (frequently, frost in extremely cold weather) that accumulate on the inside of the exterior covering of a building when warm, moisture-laden air from the interior reaches a point where the temperature no longer permits the air to sustain the moisture it holds.

Conduit, electrical   A pipe, usually metal, in which wire is installed.

Construction, drywall   A type of construction in which the interior wall finish is applied in a dry condition, generally in the form of sheet material as contrasted to plaster.

Construction, frame   A type of construction in which the structural parts are wood or depend on a wood frame for support.

Coped joint   *See* Scribing.

Corbel   To build out one or more courses of brick or stone from the face of a wall.

Corner bead   A strip of formed sheet metal, sometimes combined with a strip of metal lath, placed on corners before plastering to reinforce them. Also, a strip of wood finish three-quarters-round or angular placed over a plastered corner for protection.

Corner braces   Diagonal braces at the corners of frame structure to stiffen and strengthen the wall.

Cornerite   Metal-mesh lath cut into strips and bent to a right angle. Used in interior corners of walls and ceilings on lath to prevent cracks in plastering.

Cornice   Overhang of a pitched roof at the eave line, usually consisting of a facia board, a soffit for a closed cornice, and appropriate moldings.

Cornice return   That portion of the cornice that returns on the gable end of a house.

Counterflashing   A flashing usually used on chimneys at the roofline to cover shingle flashing and to prevent moisture entry.

Cove molding   A molding with a concave face used as trim or to finish interior corners.

Crawl space   A shallow space below the living quarters of a basementless house, normally by the foundation wall.

Cricket   A small drainage-diverting roof structure of single or double slope placed at the junction of larger surfaces that meet at an angle, such as above chimney.

Cross-bridging   Diagonal bracing between adjacent floor joists, placed near the center of the joist span.

Crown molding   A molding used on cornice or wherever an interior angle is to be covered.

Cut-in brace   Nominal 2-in.-thick members, usually 2 × 4's, cut in between each stud diagonally.

Dado   A rectangular groove across the width of a board or plank. In interior decoration, a special type of wall treatment.

Decay   Disintegration of wood or other substance through the action of fungi.

Deck paint   An enamel with a high degree of resistance to mechanical wear, designed for use on such surfaces as porch floors.

Density   The mass of substance in a unit volume.

Dewpoint   Temperature at which a vapor begins to deposit as a liquid. Applies especially to water in the atmosphere.

Dimension   *See* Lumber dimension.

Direct nailing To nail perpendicular to the initial surface or to the junction of the pieces joined. Also termed "face nailing."

Doorjamb, interior The surrounding case into which and out of which a door closes and opens. It consists of two upright pieces, called side jambs, and a horizontal head jamb.

Dormer An opening in a sloping roof, the framing of which projects out to form a vertical wall suitable for windows or other openings.

Downspout A pipe, usually of metal, for carrying rainwater from roof gutters.

Dressed and matched (tongue and groove) Boards or planks machined in such a manner that there is a groove on one edge and a corresponding tongue on the other.

Drier paint Usually, oil-soluble soaps of such metals as lead, manganese, or cobalt, which, in small proportions, hasten the oxidation and hardening (drying) of the drying oils in paints.

Drip A member of a cornice or other horizontal exterior finish course that has a projection beyond the other parts for throwing off water. A groove in the underside of a sill or drip cap to cause water to drop off on the outer edge instead of drawing back and running down the face of the building.

Drip cap A molding placed on the exterior top side of a door or window frame to cause water to drip beyond the outside of the frame.

Drywall Interior covering material, such as gypsum board, which is applied in large sheets or panels.

Ducts In a house, usually round or rectangular metal pipes for distributing warm air from the heating plant to rooms, or air from a conditioning device or as cold air returns. Ducts are also made of asbestos and composition materials.

Eaves The margin or lower part of a roof projecting over the wall.

Expansion joint A bituminous fiber strip used to separate blocks or units of concrete to prevent cracking due to expansion as a result of temperature changes. Also used on concrete slabs.

Facia (fascia) A flat board, band, or face, used sometimes by itself but usually in combination with moldings, often located at the outer face of the cornice.

Filler (wood) A heavily pigmented preparation used for filling and leveling off the pores in open-pored woods.

Fire resistive In the absence of a specific ruling by the authority having jurisdiction, applies to materials for construction not combustile in the temperatures of ordinary fires and that will withstand such fires without serious impairment of their usefulness for at least 1 hour.

Fire-retardant chemical A chemical or preparation of chemicals used to reduce flammability or to retard spread of flame.

Firestop A solid, tight closure of a concealed space, placed to prevent the spread of fire and smoke through such a space.

Fishplate A wood or plywood piece used to fasten the ends of two members together with nails or bolts at a butt joint. Sometimes used at the junction of opposite rafters near the ridge line.

Flagstone (flagging or flags) Flat stones, from 1 to 4 in. thick, used for rustic walks, steps, and floors.

Flashing Sheet metal or other material used in roof and wall construction to protect a building from water seepage.

Flat paint An interior paint that contains a high proportion of pigment and dries to a flat or lusterless finish.

Flue The space or passage in a chimney through which smoke, gas, or fumes ascend. Each passage is called a flue, which together with any others and the surrounding masonry make up the chimney.

Flue lining Fire clay or terra-cotta pipe, round or square, usually made in all ordinary flue sizes and in 2-ft lengths, used for the inner lining of chimneys with the brick or masonry work around the outside. Flue lining in chimneys runs from about a foot below the flue connection to the top of the chimney.

Fly rafters End rafters of the gable overhang, supported by roof sheathing and lookouts.

Footing A masonry section, usually concrete, in a rectangular form wider than the bottom of the foundation wall or pier that it supports.

Foundation The supporting portion of a structure below the first-floor construction, or below grade, including the footings.

Framing, balloon A system of framing a building in which all vertical structure elements of the bearing walls and partitions consist of single pieces extending from the top of the foundation sill plate to the room plate and to which all floor joists are fastened.

Framing, platform A system of framing a building in which floor joists of each story rest on the top plates of the story below or on the foundation sill for the first story, and the bearing walls and partitions rest on the subfloor of each story.

Frieze In house construction, a horizontal member connecting the top of the siding with the soffit of the cornice.

Frostline The depth of frost penetration in soil. This depth varies in different parts of the country. Footings should be placed below this depth to prevent movement.

Fungi, wood Microscopic plants that live in damp wood and cause mold, stain, and decay.

Fungicide A chemical that is poisonous to fungi.

Furring Strips of wood or metal applied to a wall or other surface to even it and normally to serve as a fastening base for finish material.

Gable In house construction, the portion of the roof above the eave line of a double-sloped roof.

Gable end An end wall having the shape of an "A."

Girder A large or principal beam of wood or steel used to support concentrated loads at isolated points along its length.

Gloss (paint or enamel) A paint or enamel that contains a relatively low portion of pigment and dries to a sheen or luster.

Gloss enamel A finishing material made of varnish and sufficient pigments to provide opacity and color but little or no pigment of low opacity. Such an enamel forms a hard coating with maximum smoothness of surface and a high degree of gloss.

Grain The direction size, arrangement, appearance, or quality of the fibers in wood.

Grain, edge (vertical) Edge-grain lumber has been sawed parallel to the pitch of the log and approximately at right angles to the growth rings; that is, the rings form an angle of 45° or more with the surface of the piece.

Grain, flat Flat-grain lumber has been sawed parallel to the pitch of the log and approximately tangent to the growth rings; that is, the rings form an angle of less than 45° with the surface of the piece.

Grain, quartersawn Another term for "edge grain."

Grounds Guides used around openings and at the floor line to end plaster. They can consist of narrow strips of wood or wide subjambs at interior doorways. They provide a level plaster line for installation of casing and other trim.

Grout Mortar made of such consistency (by adding water) that it will just flow into the joints and cavities of the masonry work and fill them solid.

Gusset A flat wood, plywood, or similar type of member used to provide a connection at the intersection of wood members. Most commonly used at joints of wood trusses. They are fastened by nails, screws, bolts, or adhesives.

Gutter (eave trough) A shallow channel or conduit of metal or wood set below and along the eaves of a house to catch and carry off rainwater from the roof.

Gypsum plaster Gypsum formulated to be used with the addition of sand and water for base-coat plaster.

Header (1) A beam placed perpendicular to joists and to which joists are nailed in framing for chimney, stairway, or other opening; (2) a wood lintel.

Hearth The inner or outer floor of a fireplace, usually made of brick, tile, or stone.

Heartwood The wood extending from the pith to the sapwood, the cells of which no longer participate in the life processes of the tree.

Hip The external angle formed by the meeting of two sloping sides of a roof.

Hip roof A roof that rises by inclined planes from all four sides of a building.

Humidifier A device designed to increase the humidity within a room or a house by means of the discharge of water vapor. They may consist of individual room-sized units or larger units attached to the heating plant to condition an entire house.

I-beam A steel beam with a cross section resembling the letter "I" It is used for long spans as basement beams or over wide wall openings, such as a double garage door, when wall and roof loads are imposed on the opening.

INR (Impact Noise Rating) A single-figure rating that provides an estimate of the impact sound-insulating performance of a floor–ceiling assembly.

Insulation, thermal Any material high in resistance to heat transmission that when placed in the walls, ceiling, or floors of a structure will reduce the rate of heat flow.

Insulation board, rigid A structural building board made of coarse wood or cane fiber in $\frac{1}{2}$- and $\frac{25}{32}$-in. thicknesses. It can be obtained in various-sized sheets, in various densities, and with several treatments.

Interior finish Material used to cover the interior framed areas, or materials of walls and ceilings.

Jack rafter   A rafter that spans the distance from the wallplate to a hip, or from a valley to a ridge.

Jamb   The side and head lining of a doorway, window, or other opening.

Joint   The space between the adjacent surfaces of two members or components joined and held together by nails, glue, cement, mortar, or other means.

Joint cement   A powder that is usually mixed with water and used for joint treatment in a gypsum-wallboard finish. Often called Spackle.

Joist   One of a series of parallel beams, usually 2 in. in thickness, used to support floor and ceiling loads, and supported in turn by larger beams, girders, or bearing walls.

Kiln-dried lumber   Lumber that has been kiln dried often to a moisture content of 6 to 12%.

Knot   In lumber, the portion of a branch or limb of a tree that appears on the edge or face of the piece.

Landing   A platform between flights of stairs or at the termination of a flight of stairs.

Lath   A building material of wood, metal, gypsum, or insulating board that is fastened to the frame of a building to act as a plaster base.

Lattice   A framework of crossed wood or metal strips.

Leader   *See* Downspout.

Ledger strip   A strip of lumber nailed along the bottom of the side of a girder on which joists rest.

Let-in brace   Nominal 1-in.-thick boards applied diagonally into notched studs.

Light   Space in a window sash for a single pane of glass. Also, a pane of glass.

Lintel   A horizontal structural member that supports the load over an opening such as a door or window.

Lookout   A short wood bracket or cantilever to support an overhang portion of a roof or the like, usually concealed from view.

Louver   An opening with a series of horizontal slats arranged to permit ventilation but to exclude rain, sunlight, or vision.

Lumber   Lumber is the product of the sawmill and planning mill not further manufactured other than by sawing, resawing, and passing lengthwise through a standard planing machine, crosscutting to length and matching.

Lumber, boards   Yard lumber less than 2 in. thick and 2 more inches wide.

Lumber dimension   Yard lumber from 2 in. to, but not including, 5 in. thick and 2 or more inches wide. Includes joists, rafters, studs, plank, and small timbers.

Lumber, dressed size   The dimension of lumber after shrinking from green dimension and after machining to size or pattern.

Lumber, matched   Lumber that is dressed and shaped on one edge in a grooved pattern and on the other in a tongued pattern.

Lumber, shiplap   Lumber that is edge dressed to make a close rabbeted or lapped joint.

Lumber, timbers   Yard lumber 5 or more inches in least dimension. Includes beams, stringers, posts, caps, sills, girders, and purlins.

Lumber, yard   Lumber of those grades, sizes, and patterns which are generally intended for ordinary construction, such as framework.

Mantel   The shelf above a fireplace. Also used in referring to the decorative trim around a fireplace opening.

Masonry   Stone, brick, concrete, hollow-tile, concrete-block, gypsum-block, or similar building units or materials or a combination of the same, bonded together with mortar.

Mastic   A pasty material used as a cement (as for setting tile) or a protective coating (as for thermal insulation or waterproofing).

Metal lath   Sheets of metal that are slit and drawn out to form openings. Used as a plaster base for walls and ceilings and as reinforcing over other forms of plaster base.

Millwork   Generally all building materials made of finished wood and manufactured in millwork plants and planing mills are included inder the term "millwork." It includes such items as inside and outside doors, window and doorframes, blinds, porchwork, mantels, panelwork, stairways, moldings, and interior trim.

Miter joint   The joint of two pieces at an angle that bisects the joining angle.

Moisture content of wood   Weight of the water contained in the wood.

Molding   A wood strip having a curved or projecting surface used for decorative purposes.

Mortise   A slot cut into a board, plank, or timber, usually edgewise, to receive the tenon of another board, to form a joint.

Mullion   A vertical bar or divider in the frame between windows, doors, or other openings.

Muntin   A small member that divides the glass or openings of sash or doors.

Natural finish   A transparent finish that does not seriously alter the original color or grain of the natural wood. Natural finishes are usually provided by sealers, oils, varnishes, water-repellent preservatives, and other similar materials.

Newel   A post to which the end of a stair railing or balustrade is fastened. Also, any post to which a railing or balustrade is fastened.

Nonbearing wall   A wall supporting no load other than its own weight.

Nosing   The projecting edge of a molding or drip. Usually applied to the projecting molding on the edge of a stair tread.

Notch   A crosswise rabbet at the end of a board.

O.C. (on center)   The measurement of spacing for studs, rafters, joists, and the like in a building from the center of one member to the center of the next.

O.G. (ogee)   A molding with a profile in the form of a letter S; having the outline of a reversed curve.

Outrigger   An extension of a rafter beyond the wall line. Usually, a smaller member nailed to a larger rafter to form a cornice or roof overhang.

Paint   A combination of pigments with suitable thinners or oils to provide decorative and protective coatings.

Panel   A thin flat piece of wood, plywood, or similar material, framed by stiles and rails as in a door or fitted into grooves of thicker material with molded edges.

Paper, building   A general term for papers, felts, and similar sheet materials used in buildings.

Paper sheathing   A building material, generally paper or felt, used in wall and roof construction as a protection against the passage of air and moisture.

Parting stop or strip   A small wood piece used in the side and head jambs of double-hung windows to separate upper and lower sash.

Partition   A wall that subdivides spaces of a building.

Penny   As applied to nails, the term serves as a measure of nail length and is abbreviated by the letter d.

Perm   A measure of water vapor movement through a material.

Pier   A column of masonry, usually rectangular in horizontal cross section, used to support other structural members.

Pigment   A powdered solid in suitable degree of subdivision for use in paint or enamel.

Pitch   The incline slope of a roof or the ratio of the total rise to the total width of a house; for example, an 8-ft rise and 24-ft width is a one-third pitch roof. Roof slope is expressed in inches or rise per foot of run.

Pitch pocket   An opening extending parallel to the annual rings of growth, which usually contains, or has contained, either solid or liquid pitch.

Pith   The small, soft core at the original center of a tree around which wood formation takes place.

Plaster grounds   Strips of wood used as guides or strike-off edges around window and door openings and at the base of walls.

Plate   Sill plate: a horizontal member anchored to a wall. Sole plate: bottom horizontal member of a frame wall. Top plate: horizontal member of a frame wall supporting ceiling joists, rafters, or other members.

Plough   To cut a lengthwise groove in a board or plank.

Plumb   Exactly perpendicular; vertical.

Ply   A term to denote the number of thicknesses or layers of roofing felt, veneer in plywood, or layers in built-up materials.

Plywood   A piece of wood made of three or more layers of veneer joined with glue, and usually laid with the grain of adjoining plies at right angles. Almost always, an odd number of plies are used.

Pores   Wood cells of comparatively large diameter that have open ends and are set one above the other to form continues tubes. The openings of the vessels on the surface of a piece of wood are referred to as pores.

Preservative   Any substance that for a reasonable length of time will prevent the action of wood-destroying fungi, borers of various kinds, and similar destructive agents when the wood has been properly coated or impregnated with it.

Primer   The first coat of paint in a paint job that consists of two or more coats; also the paint used for such a first coat.

Putty   A type of cement usually made of whiting and boiled linseed oil, beaten or kneaded to the consistency of dough, and used in sealing glass in sash, filling small holes and crevices in wood, and for similar purposes.

Quarter round   A small molding that has the cross section of a quarter circle.

Rabbet   A rectangular longitudinal groove cut in the corner edge of a board or plank.

Radiant heating   A method of heating, usually consisting of a forced hot water system with pipes placed in the floor, wall, or ceiling; or with electrically heated panels.

Rafter   One of a series of structural members of a roof designed to support roof loads. The rafters of a flat roof are sometimes called roof joists.

Rafter, hip   A rafter that forms the intersection of an external roof angle.

Rafter, valley   A rafter that forms the intersection of an internal roof angle.

Rail   Cross members of panel doors or of a sash. Also the upper and lower members, as a balustrade or staircase extending from one vertical support, such as a post, to another.

Rake   Trim members that run parallel to the roof slop and form the finish between the wall and a gable roof extension.

Raw linseed oil   The crude product processed from flaxseed and usually without much subsequent treatment.

Reflective insulation   Sheet material with one or both surfaces of comparatively low heat loss, such as aluminum foil. When used in building construction the surfaces face air spaces, reducing the radiation across the air space.

Reinforcing   Steel rods or metal fabric placed in concrete slabs, beams, or columns to increase their strength.

Relative humidity   The amount of water vapor in the atmosphere, expressed as a percentage of maximum quantity that could be present at a given temperature.

Resorcinol glue   A glue that is high in both wet and dry strength and resistant to high temperatures. It is used for gluing lumber or assembly joints that must withstand severe service conditions.

Ribbon (girt)   Normally, a 1 × 4 inch board let into the studs horizontally to support ceiling or second-floor joists.

Ridge   The horizontal line at the junction of the top edges of two sloping roof surfaces.

Ridge board   The board placed on edge at the ridge of the roof into which the upper ends of the rafters are fastened.

Rise   In stairs, the vertical height of a step or flight of stairs.

Riser   Each of the vertical boards closing the spaces between the treads of stairways.

Roll roofing   Roofing material, composed of the fiber and saturated with asphalt.

Roof sheathing   The boards or sheet material fastened to the roof rafters on which roof covering is laid.

Rubber-emulsion paint   Paint, the vehicle of which consists of rubber or synthetic rubber dispersed in fine droplets in water.

Run   In stairs, the net width of a step or the horizontal distance covered by a flight of stairs.

Saddle   Two sloping surfaces meeting in a horizontal ridge, used between the back side of chimney, or other vertical surface, and a sloping roof.

Sand float finish   Lime mixed with sand, resulting in a textured finish.

Sapwood The outer zone of wood, next to the bark. In the living tree it contains some living cells (the heartwood contains none), as well as dead and dying cells. In most species, it is lighter in color than the heartwood. In all species, it is lacking in decay resistance.

Sash A single light frame containing one or more lights of glass.

Sash balance A device, usually operated by a spring or tension designed to counterbalance double-hung sash.

Saturated felt Felt impregnated with tar or asphalt.

Scratch coat The first coat of plaster, which is scratched to form a bond for the second coat.

Screed A small strip of wood, usually the thickness of the plaster coat, used as a guide for plastering.

Scribing Fitting woodwork to an irregular surface. In moldings, cutting the end of one piece to fit the molded face of the other.

Sealer A finishing material, either clear or pigmented, that is usually applied directly over uncoated wood.

Seasoning Removing moisture from green wood.

Semigloss (paint or enamel) A paint or enamel made with a slight insufficiency of nonvolatile vehicle so that the coating, when dry, has some luster but is not very glossy.

Shake A thick, handsplit shingle; usually edge-grained.

Sheathing The structural covering, usually wood boards or plywood, used over studs or rafters of a structure.

Sheathing paper *See* Paper, sheathing.

Sheet metal work All components of a house employing sheet metal, such as flashing, gutters, and downspouts.

Shellac A transparent coating made by dissolving lac, a resinous secretion of the lac bug (a scale insect that thrives in tropical countries, especially India), in alcohol.

Shingles Roof covering of asphalt, asbestos, wood, tile, slate, or other material cut to stock lengths, widths, and thicknesses.

Shingles, siding Various kinds of shingles, such as wood shingles or shakes and nonwood shingles, that are used over sheathing for exterior sidewall covering.

Shiplap *See* Lumber, shiplap.

Shutter Usually lightweight louvered or flush wood or nonwood frames in the form of doors located at each side of a window. Some are made to close over the window for protection; others are fastened to the wall as a decorative device.

Siding The finish covering of the outside wall of a frame building.

Siding, bevel (lap siding) Wedge-shaped boards used as horizontal siding in a lapped pattern.

Sill The lowest member of the frame of a structure, resting on the foundation and supporting the floor joists or the uprights of the wall. The member forming the lower side of an opening, such as a door or window sill.

Sleeper Usually, a wood member embedded in concrete, as in a floor, that serves to support and to fasten other flooring.

Soffit Usually, the underside of an overhanging cornice.

Soil cover (ground cover) A light covering of plastic film, roll roofing, or similar material used over the soil in crawl spaces of buildings to minimize moisture permeation of the area.

Soil stack A general term for the vertical main of a system of soil, waste, or vent piping.

Sole (sole plate) *See* Plate.

Solid bridging A solid member placed between adjacent floor joists near the center of the span.

Span The distance between structural support, such as walls, columns, piers, beams, girders, and trusses.

Splash block A small masonry block laid with the top close to the ground surface to receive roof drainage from downspouts and to carry it away from the building.

Square A unit of measure—100 square feet—usually applied to roofing material and sidewall coverings.

Stain, shingle A form of oil paint, very thin in consistency, intended for coloring wood with rough surfaces, such as shingles.

Stair carriage Supporting member for stair treads. Usually a 2-in. plank notched to receive the treads; sometimes called "rough horse."

Stair landings *See* Landing.

Stair rise *See* Rise.

STC (Sound Transmission Class) A measure of sound stopping of ordinary noise.

Stile An upright framing member in a panel door.

Stool A flat molding fitted over the window sill between jambs and contacting the bottom rail of the lower sash.

Storm sash (storm window) An extra window usually placed on the outside of an existing one as additional protection against cold weather.

Story That part of a building between any floor and the floor or roof next above.

String, stringer A timber or other support for cross members in floors or ceilings. In stairs, the support on which the stair treads rest.

Strip flooring Wood flooring consisting of narrow, matched strips.

Stucco Most commonly refers to an outside plaster made with portland cement as its base.

Stud One of a series of slender wood or metal vertical structural members placed as supporting elements in walls and partitions.

Subfloor Boards or plywood laid on joists over which a finish floor is to be laid.

Suspended ceiling A ceiling system supported by hanging it from the overhead structural framing.

Tail beam A relatively short beam or joist supported in a wall on one end and by a header at the other.

Termites Insects that superficially resemble ants in size, general appearance, and habit of living colonies.

Termite shield A shield, usually of noncorrodible metal, placed in or on a foundation wall or other mass of masonry or around pipes to prevent passage of termites.

Terneplate   Sheet iron or sheet coated with an alloy of lead and tin.

Threshold   A strip of wood or metal with beveled edges used over the finish floor and the sill of exterior doors.

Toenailing   To drive a nail at a slant with the initial surface to permit it to penetrate into a second member.

Tongue and groove   *See* Dressed and matched.

Tread   The horizontal board in a stairway on which the foot is placed.

Trim   The finish materials in a building, such as moldings, applied around openings.

Trimmer   A beam or joist to which a header is nailed in framing for a chimney, stairway, or other opening.

Truss   A frame or jointed structure designed to act as a beam of long span.

Turpentine   A volatile oil used as a thinner in paints and as a solvent in varnishes.

Undercoat   A coating applied prior to the finishing or top coats of a paint job. It may be the first of two or the second of three coats. In some usage it may be synonymous with priming coat.

Underlayment   A material placed under finish coverings, such as flooring, or shingles, to provide a smooth, even surface for applying the finish.

Valley   The internal angle formed by the junction of two sloping sides of a roof.

Vapor barrier   Material used to retard the movement of water vapor into walls and prevent condensation in them.

Varnish   A thickened preparation of drying oil or drying oil and resin suitable for spreading on surfaces to form continuous, transparent coatings or for mixing with pigments to make enamels.

Vehicle   The liquid portion of a finishing material; it consists of the binder (nonvolatile) and volatile thinners.

Veneer   Thin sheets of wood made by rotary cutting or slicing of a log.

Vent   A pipe or duct that allows flow of air as an inlet or outlet.

Vermiculite   A mineral closely related to mica, with the faculty of expanding on heating to form lightweight material with insulation quality.

Volatile thinner   A liquid that evaporates readily and is used to thin or reduce the consistency of finishes without altering the relative volumes of pigments and nonvolatile vehicles.

Wane   Bark, or lack of wood from any cause, on edge or corner of a piece of wood.

Water-repellent preservative   A liquid designed to penetrate wood and impart repellency and a moderate preservative protection.

Weatherstrip   Narrow or jamb-width sections of thin metal or other material to prevent infiltration of air and moisture around windows and doors.

Wood rays   Strips of cells extending radially within a tree and varying in height from a few cells in some species to 4 in. or more in oak.

Staking Out

Locating the house on the lot following dimensions on the plot plan is called staking out. This can be accomplished with the use of a measuring tape, level, and transit. The lot line location and dimension must be plotted on the ground from the building location dimensions. Each corner of the house must be located on the lot by dimensions found on the plot plan by driving a piece of 2 × 4 cut to a point on one end and driven into the ground. This must be done very carefully because from this point on, the entire house is based on these dimensions. A nail is driven into the top of the stake at the *exact* dimension of the house (Fig. 9–1).

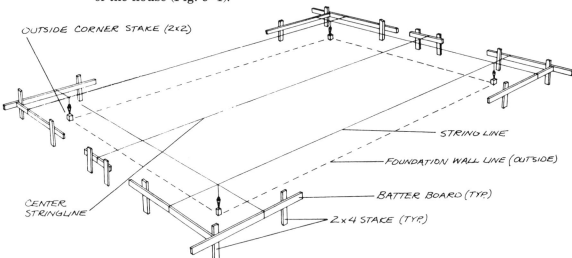

FIGURE 9–1 *Staking out a building (courtesy U.S. Department of Agriculture).*

Batter Boards

The wood stakes indicating the exact corners of the building are temporary, used only for reference, and will be removed after the installation of the batter boards. The points on these wooden stakes will be transferred to the batter boards, which are used to retain these points during excavation and construction. They will not interfere with construction and they should not be disturbed. The batter boards are installed about 4'-0" outside the perimeter of the house. Installation of batter boards consists of driving 2 × 4's about 3'-0" long with a pointed end into the ground; three are required for each corner. These should be placed about 6'-0" to 8'-0" on each side of the corner stake, forming a right angle. A 1 × 6 is nailed to the stake in a level horizontal plane at the same level. Transfer the nail point on the corner stake to the batter board by using a strong string, line, or cord stretched across the batter boards at opposite ends of the building, located directly over the nail on the corner stake. A plumb bob is used to transfer this point. The batter boards will remain in position until the foundation is completed. Once these lines are strung, they will be the exact dimensions of the outside foundation line of the house (Fig. 9–2).

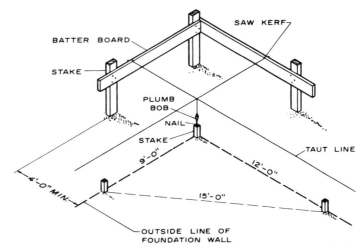

FIGURE 9-2 *Batter boards (courtesy U.S. Department of Agriculture).*

In the case of an addition, project or extend the sides of the house and square the length using batter boards on two sides only. Heights are already established by transferring the top of the existing foundation to the batter boards of the new addition.

Excavation

The strung building lines are removed during excavation to allow ample space for operating excavating equipment. The topsoil is removed first and stockpiled on-site away from the building location, to be used later for finish grading. The finish-grade elevation and existing grade elevation are established from the plot plan, and the plot plan tells the basement floor elevation or level. How deep to excavate below, the existing grade or ground is determined from this information (Fig. 9–3). Referring to the plot plan, the existing grade at the location of the house is about elevation 241. This is shown by the dashed line. The basement floor elevation is 231.0, which indicates an excavation of 10 '-0 " below the existing grade plus 1 '-0 " for the footing, for a total depth of

FIGURE 9-3 *Excavation (courtesy U.S. Department of Agriculture).*

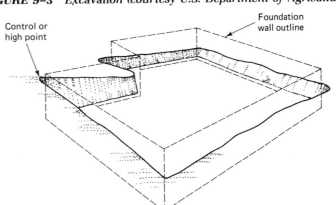

11′-0″ below the ground. The garage, which has no basement, is unexcavated; the only excavation required is a trench for the foundation of the garage, which must be below the prevailing frostline to prevent upheaval when the ground freezes. Excavation should extend about 2 ft beyond the outside foundation walls. No foundation should be set on filled land without proper compacting. The bottom of the foundation is extended down to the original undisturbed or virgin earth.

Foundation and Footings

Laying out a foundation is the critical beginning in house construction. It is a simple but extremely important process and requires careful work. The foundation must be square and level. The house location on the lot must comply with local regulations. If properly lines are in question at all, verify the location of lot-line corners by city, county, or private surveyor. Once property lines are established, it is equally vital that city, county, or state requirements be followed on location of the house with respect to the property lines. Most regulations require that a house be set back from the street property line a specified distance (often 25 to 30 ft) and that the sides of the house be set back from the adjoining property lines (often 5 to 10 ft). Carelessness in establishing property lines and allowable house location could result in extending a garage or future addition over a neighbor's property line, or in an infringement of local building-code regulations. Set the house location, based on required setbacks and other factors, such as the natural drainage pattern of the lot; then level or at least rough-clear the site.

During foundation excavation, the corner stakes and temporary leveling stakes will be removed. This stresses the importance of the leveled batter boards and string line, because corners and foundation levelness must be located using the string line.

Poured concrete footings are most commonly used for house foundations. Footings, properly sized and constructed, prevent settling or cracking of building walls. Footings must be completely level and must extend below the frostline. These requirements dictate the depth at which footings are placed.

A row of post footings will be located along the centerline of the house. These support posts and girders, which, in turn, support the floor joists (Fig. 9–4). Posts and girders are the basic structural members that support the floor

FIGURE 9–4   *Post footings (courtesy U.S. Department of Agriculture).*

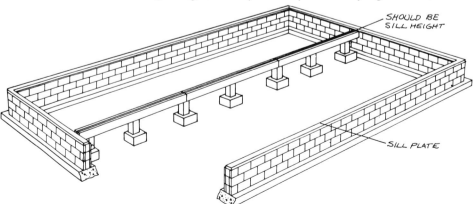

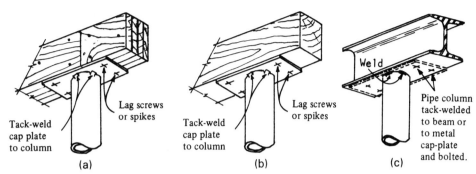

FIGURE 9–5 *Types of beams: (a) built-up beam; (b) solid beam; (c) steel beam (courtesy U.S. Department of Agriculture).*

joists along the centerline of the house. Wood posts are fastened to the girder, which rests on them.

The girders used to support floor joists are generally built up of two or more pieces of 2-in.-thick dimension lumber, solid timber, or steel beams (Fig. 9–5). House plans will specify post spacing, girder span lengths, and lumber grades.

Although the wood frame type of house is noted for its strength and resilience, adequate and properly installed footings are still as essential as they are for other types of construction. Footings should extend far enough below exterior grade to be free of frost action during winter months. Where roots of trees were removed during excavation, soil should be well compacted before footings are poured. Where poor soil conditions exist, satisfactory foundations may be provided by use of treated timber piles capped with wood or concrete sills.

Although the size of the footing will depend on the local building code, it is good practice, generally, to make the depth of the footing equal to the thickness of the foundation wall it supports. The projection of the footing should be equal to one half the thickness of the foundation wall. Usually, footings are of plain concrete. Sometimes it is necessary to use reinforced concrete where unequal soil conditions cannot be avoided, in which case engineering analysis of the footings is required.

The foundation wall may be of poured concrete or of masonry units (Fig. 9–6). Where masonry units are used, a $\frac{1}{2}$-in. coat of portland cement mortar should be applied to the exterior of the wall and then covered with two coats of asphalt. Drain tiles should also be installed around the exterior of footings and connected to a positive outfall. These measures will assure a dry basement (Fig. 9–7).

FIGURE 9–6 *Foundation footings (courtesy U.S. Department of Agriculture).*

FIGURE 9–7 *Masonry foundation scaler (courtesy U.S. Department of Agriculture).*

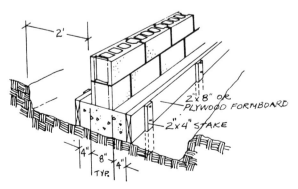

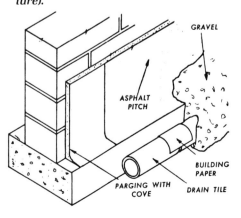

Where basements are not provided, foundations may consist of free-standing piers, piers with curtain walls between them, or piers supporting grade beams. In any of these methods, the piers and their footings must be of sufficient size to carry the weight of the house and its contents. Spacing of the piers will depend on the arrangement of the floor framing and location of load-bearing walls and partitions. A distance on the order of 8 to 12 ft is the usual practice.

Wood sills, which rest on concrete or masonry exterior walls, should be placed at least 6 in. above the exposed earth on the exterior of the building. An approved durable or treated wood should be used for this purpose (Fig. 9–8). Wood beams or girders, framing into masonry walls, should have $\frac{1}{2}$ in. of air space at the top, end, and sides, unless approved durable or treated wood is used for this purpose (Fig. 9–9).

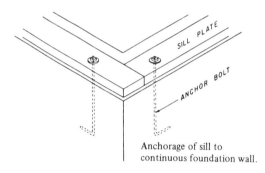

Anchorage of sill to continuous foundation wall.

FIGURE 9–8 Foundation sill (courtesy U.S. Department of Agriculture).

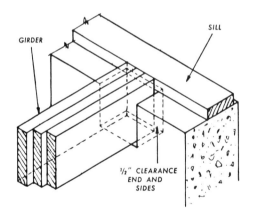

FIGURE 9–9 Wood girder (courtesy U.S. Department of Agriculture).

The crawl space under houses without basements should be ventilated by openings in the foundation walls. Such openings should have a net area of not less than 2 square feet for each 100 linear feet of exterior wall, plus $\frac{1}{3}$ square foot for each 100 square feet of crawl space. Openings should be arranged to provide cross-ventilation and should be covered with corrosion-resistant wire mesh not less than $\frac{1}{4}$ in. nor more than $\frac{1}{2}$ in. in any dimension (Fig. 9–10).

Spread Footings

There are three types of foundations: full basement, crawl space, and slab-on-grade (Fig. 9–11). They all require a spread footing. The purpose of a spread footing is to support the load in the same way that snowshoes support a person walking on snow. Wood forms must be constructed for a poured concrete spread

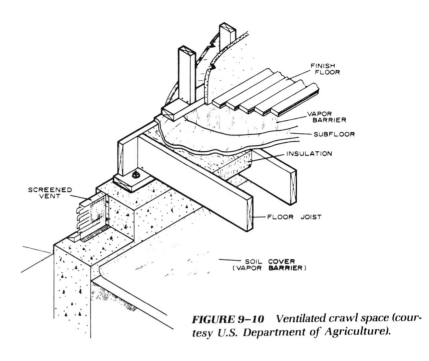

FINISH
FLOOR

VAPOR
BARRIER

SUBFLOOR

INSULATION

SCREENED
VENT

FLOOR JOIST

SOIL COVER
(VAPOR BARRIER)

FIGURE 9–10   *Ventilated crawl space (courtesy U.S. Department of Agriculture).*

FIGURE 9–11   *(a) Crawl space; (b) slab on grade [(a) and (b) courtesy U.S. Department of Agriculture].*

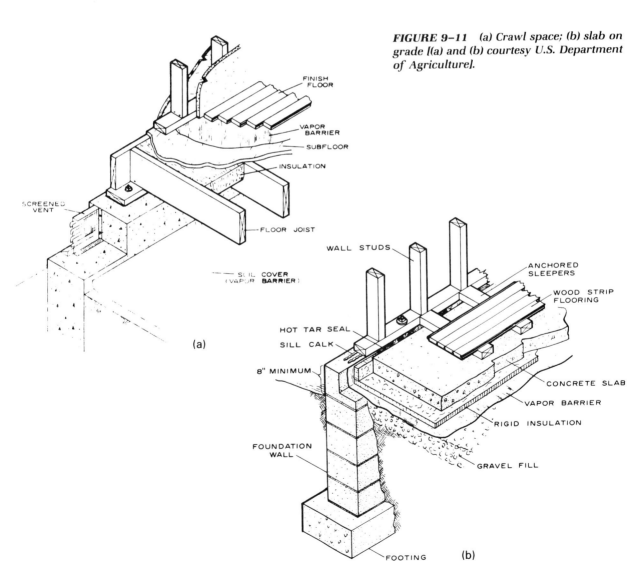

FINISH
FLOOR

VAPOR
BARRIER

SUBFLOOR

INSULATION

SCREENED
VENT

FLOOR JOIST

SOIL COVER
(VAPOR BARRIER)

(a)

WALL STUDS

ANCHORED
SLEEPERS

WOOD STRIP
FLOORING

HOT TAR SEAL

SILL CALK

8" MINIMUM

CONCRETE SLAB

VAPOR BARRIER

RIGID INSULATION

GRAVEL FILL

FOUNDATION
WALL

FOOTING

(b)

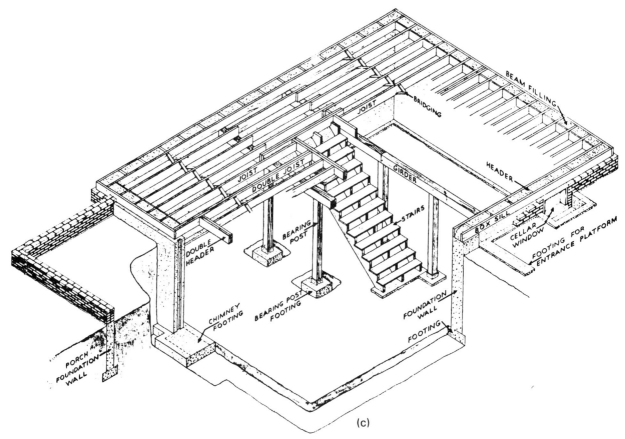

FIGURE 9-11c   Full basement (courtesy U.S. Department of Agriculture).

footing of dimensions shown in the plans (Fig. 9–12). These dimensions are for the average allowable soil-bearing capacities. The total weight of the building is being supported by the ground. It must be clearly understood that soil will support anywhere from ½ ton to 80 tons per square foot, depending on the type of soil, from sand to clay or ledge.

The soil must be firm and level when constructing the wood forms for the spread footing. The foundation must be tied to the footing to avoid sliding or slipping. This is accomplished by a key formed into the footing from a 2 × 4 with both edges beveled to facilitate removal from the form after the concrete

FIGURE 9–12   Spread footing form.

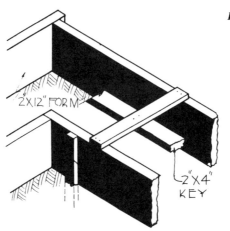

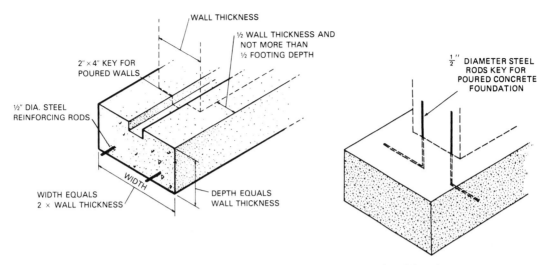

FIGURE 9–13 (a) Reinforced footing; (b) steel rod key (courtesy U.S. Department of Agriculture).

has hardened. This key is continuous, as is the spread footing around the entire perimeter of the building. Another method is to place ½-in.-diameter L-shaped steel rods into the wet concrete footing (Fig. 9–13). Stepped footings are often required on lots that are sloped. Do not exceed 2′0″ on the vertical dimensions between steps (Fig. 9–14). If concrete blocks are used for foundation, the vertical height should equal an even number of blocks in height. Usually, blocks are 8 in. high. The bottom of the footing should always be level along the horizontal, never inclined. If the foundation, or part of it, is bearing on ledge, no footing is necessary.

During construction, the weight on the footing increases, causing soil compression. This compression creates a slight movement called *settlement* of the structure. Whenever there are two or more different subsoils under various parts of the house, a variation in settlement will result in unequal movement. The round steel reinforcing rods in the footing will help to prevent this situation.

FIGURE 9–14 Stepped footing (courtesy U.S. Department of Agriculture).

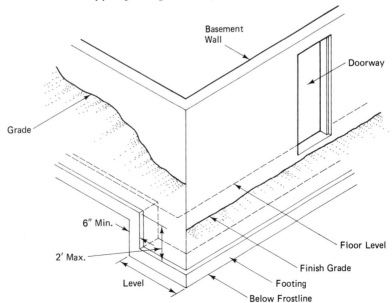

Foundations

The purpose of the foundation is to support the load of the house above and to transmit this load onto the concrete spread footing. Foundations are usually of poured concrete or concrete block 8 to 12 in. thick. (Check the local building code.) Poured concrete is recommended because the solid mass reduces the problem of water leaks or termites.

A concrete block foundation requires a $\frac{1}{2}$-in. coat of cement plaster on the outside surface of the wall. This is called parging (Fig. 9–15). The top layer of block must be filled solid with concrete at the core of the block to seal the wall against the passage of water. If the height of the block foundation wall is 10 times the thickness of the wall or larger, round steel reinforcing rods are required to strengthen the block walls. In poured concrete walls, rods may not be necessary. The majority of concrete block walls are built of 8-in.-high, 16-in.-long, and 8-in.-wide units. The actual thickness is $7\frac{5}{8}$ in. high, $15\frac{5}{8}$ in. long, and $7\frac{5}{8}$ in. wide.

For the sake of economy and good construction, care and careful planning should be excercised to avoid cutting concrete block. Wall lengths and heights should be in multiples of 8 in. to afford an even number of blocks. At beam-bearing locations, fill the core of the block solid with concrete. The mortar joints are the weakest part of the wall and should be laid in a full bed of mortar made up of portland cement mix. Corners should have intersecting block walls bonded by interlocking or lapping of alternate courses. The core should be filled with insulation to reduce heat loss. This should be a granule-type insulation that can be poured from the package into the block core. In areas subjected

FIGURE 9–15   *Wall parging (courtesy U.S. Department of Agriculture).*

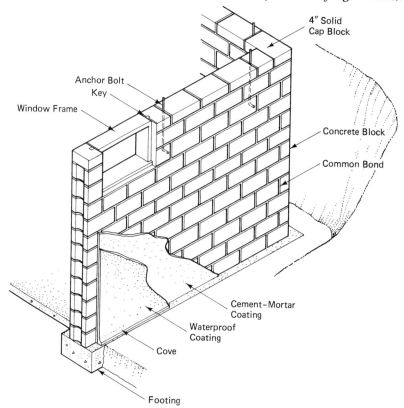

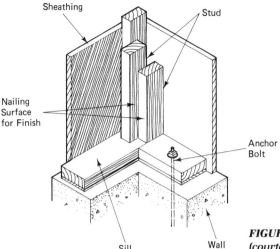

FIGURE 9–16 *Foundation anchor bolt (courtesy U.S. Department of Agriculture).*

to earthquakes, block walls should not be used for foundations unless they are reinforced with steel rods placed vertically in the block. Horizontal reinforcing should also be used in the joints or mortar beds.

Anchor bolts must be set in the top of the foundation to secure the framework to the foundation (Fig. 9–16). The anchor bolts are about 18 in. long and ½ in. in diameter, threaded on one end with a washer and nut and hooked or bent on the other end. The hooked end is inserted into the foundation with the threaded end on top. In the case of a poured concrete foundation, the anchor bolts are placed into position while the concrete is still wet, with the bolt about 4 or 5 in. above the top of wall, set 3 in. back from the outside surface of the wall, placed about 4′-0″ apart around the entire perimeter of the foundation. If the bolts are used with concrete block foundations, the hooked ends are inserted either between joints of the block or in the core before filling them with concrete. The hooked end should be locked between joints (Fig. 9–15).

In the case of a poured concrete foundation, the basement windows are installed in the forms at locations shown on plans and the concrete is poured around them. Basement windows are installed with the block walls. In either case, the tops of the windows should be in line with the top of the foundation. Window sizes should be decided before foundation work is begun, and in the case of a block wall, the sizes should be in modules with block courses without having to cut the block to fit.

Bulkheads

Outside entrances from the basement are accomplished by the use of bulkheads. These units can be purchased in a package made of steel or can be built entirely of concrete walls and stairs with metal or wood doors. The size of these units must be established before any foundation work is started because openings must be left in the foundation to receive these units. The number of stairs required in a bulkhead is determined by the vertical distance between the finished basement floor and finish grade. Allow about 6 or 8 in. above the grade for the first step to prevent water from running into the basement. If built of concrete, 8-in.- thick walls can be used reinforced with ½-in. steel rods. If built of concrete block, 8-in.-thick block can be used. The width of the stair treads should be about 10-in. wide and the risers should be no more than 8 in. high.

Waterproofing

All foundations, whether concrete or block, basement, crawl space, or slab-on-ground, should receive one or two coats of asphalt, pitch, or any preparation manufactured for this purpose applied on the outside surface of the foundation, from the footings up to within a couple of inches below the finish grade. In the case of a concrete block foundation, this is applied over the parging. This application will prevent moisture penetration through the wall. It can be applied by brush or spray.

Drain Tile

Provisions must be made to prevent water from finding its way into the basement, crawl space, or slab-on-grade. This is accomplished with the installation of a 4-in. drain line or pipe, sometimes called a French drain. The pipe is laid around the perimeter of the foundation beginning at a high point just above the top of the spread footing, pitching down a minimum of $\frac{1}{16}$ in. per foot to a runoff, catch basin, dry well, or sewer (Fig. 9–17). This pipe is laid in a 2'-0" bed of crushed stone using perforated pipe with the perforations on the bottom, or clay pipe with about $\frac{1}{4}$-in. open joints covering only the top half of the joint with asphalt paper to prevent clogging the pipe. The asphalt paper can be tied around the pipe with wire. This pipe will direct any water underground into the pipe and away from the building instead of through the wall and into the building.

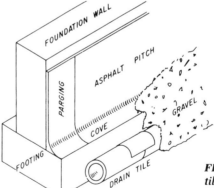

FIGURE 9–17 Foundation drain tile (courtesy U.S. Department of Agriculture).

If there is leakage, a sump pump is used to discharge the water through a window outdoors. The pump is operated electricity and is controlled by an automatic float triggered by the height of water in the pit.

Foundation Sill

The first and the most important piece of wood to be used on a home is the foundation sill, because the entire house—floors, walls, ceilings, and roof—are related directly to the foundation sill. The sill is also the closest piece of wood to the ground, which makes it more vulnerable to termite and insect attack.

Floor Framing

Floor framing consists of sills, girders, joists, and subflooring, with all members tied together in such a way as to support the loads expected on the floor and to give lateral support to the exterior walls.

Usually, beams and girders consist of solid timbers or built-up members in which nominal 2-in. pieces are nailed together with the wide faces vertical. Such pieces should be fastened together by two rows of 20d nails—one row near the top and the other near the bottom edge. Nails in each row are spaced about 32 in. apart, with end joints occurring over supports. Glued-laminated members are also frequently used. Beams and girders that are not continuous should be tied together across supports, such as columns or piers. A bearing of 4 in. on supports is recommended.

Bearing for joists should not be less than 1½ in. on wood or metal, and 3 in. on masonry. Joists should be placed so that the top edge provides an even plane for installation of the subfloor and finished floor.

Proper arrangement of headers, trimmers, and tail joists accomplishes framing of openings. Trimmers and headers should be doubled when the span of the header exceeds 4 ft. Headers, more than 6 ft long, should be supported at the ends by joist hangers or framing anchors, unless they are supported on a partition, beam, or wall. Tail joists, over 12 ft long, should be supported on framing anchors (Fig. 9–18.).

FIGURE 9–18   *Stairway framing.*

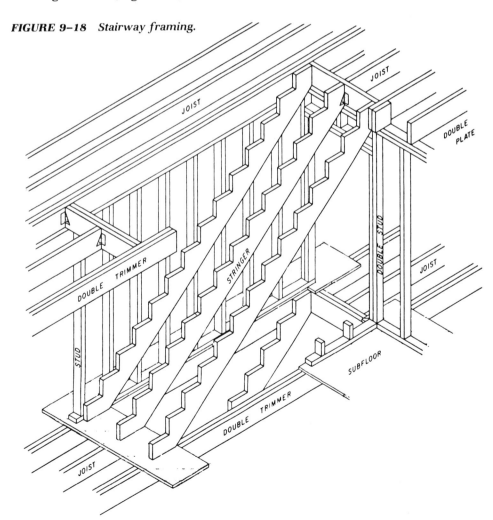

Notches for piping in the top or bottom of joists should not exceed one-sixth the depth of the joists and should not be located in the middle third of the span. Holes bored in joists for piping or electric cables should not be closer than 2 in. to the top or bottom of the joist, and the diameter of the hole should not exceed one-third the depth of the joist. Where joists are notched on the ends, the notch should not exceed one-fourth the joist depth.

Bearing partitions are usually placed directly over the girders or walls that support the floor framing (Fig. 9–19). They may be offset from such supports if the floor framing is strong enough to carry the added load. In general, bearing partitions running at right angles to joists should not be offset from main girders or walls more than the depth of the joist, unless the joists are designed to carry the extra load. When nonbearing partitions run parallel to joists, the joists should be doubled under the partitions (Fig. 9–20).

Floor joists sometimes project beyond first-story walls. When the overhanging wall is at right angles to the joists, the joists may be cantilevered over the supporting wall for the required distance (Fig. 9–21, page 202).

Where the overhanging wall is parallel to the supporting joists, a double joist may be used to support lookout joists extending over the wall line below. The double joists should be located a distance of twice the overhang back from the lower wall. Lookout joists may be framed into the double joists by means of a ledger strip, at the upper edge, or by framing anchors.

Bridging

Before the installation of the first of two layers of flooring called subflooring, cross bridging is used to stiffen the floor and spread the load over a broader area of floor. Cross bridging is done with 1 × 3 wood called furring. The ends are cut at an angle to fit snugly against the joist and are nailed with two 6d nails top and bottom, halfway between the beam and the outside wall for the entire length of the bay. Cross or diagonal bridging can be accomplished with metal as well as wood especially designed for that purpose. Another method of bridging, called solid bridging, is done with blocks of wood the same depth of the joists. Any of the described bridging is acceptable but must be nailed in place before the subflooring is installed (Fig. 9–22, page 202).

Exterior Wall Framing

Exterior wall framing should be strong and stiff enough to support the vertical loads from floors and roof. Walls should resist the lateral loads resulting from winds and, in some areas, from earthquakes. Top plates should be doubled and overlapped at the wall and bearing partition intersection. This ties the building together into a strong unit (Fig. 9–23).

Studs in gable ends should rest on wall plates with tops notched to fit the end rafter to which they are nailed (Fig. 9–24). Exterior walls should be braced by suitable sheathing. Additional strength and stiffness may be provided by 1 × 4 members let into the outside face of the studs at an angle of 45° and nailed to top and bottom plates and studs (Fig. 9–25). Sheathing should be nailed to sills, headers, studs, plates or continuous headers, and to gable end rafters.

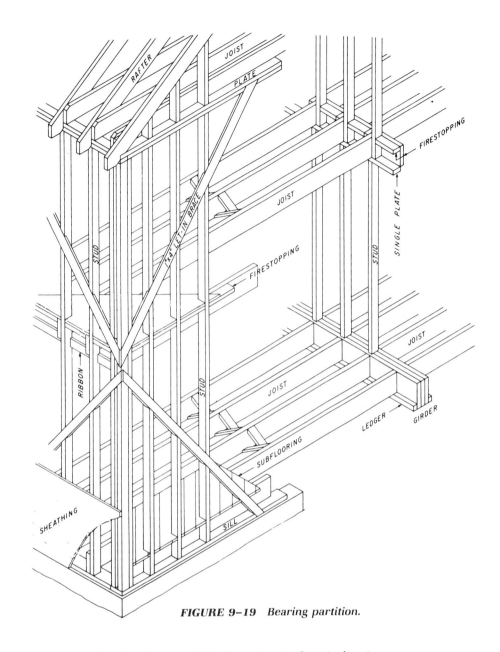

FIGURE 9-19 *Bearing partition.*

FIGURE 9-20 *Floor framing (courtesy U.S. Department of Agriculture).*

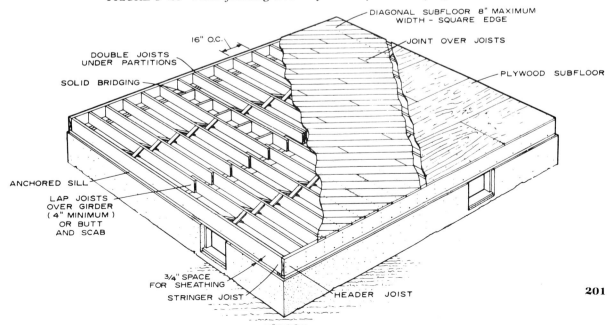

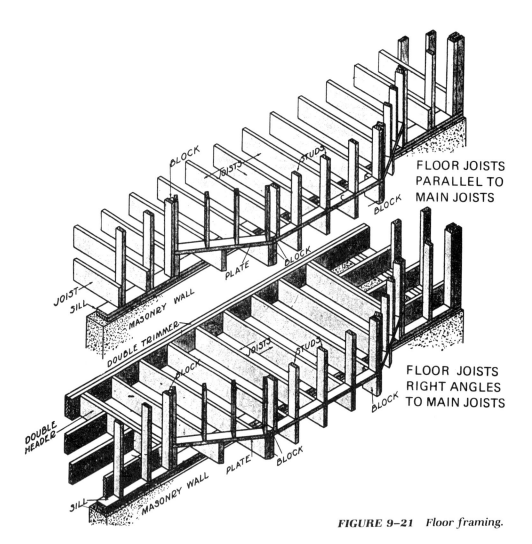

FLOOR JOISTS PARALLEL TO MAIN JOISTS

FLOOR JOISTS RIGHT ANGLES TO MAIN JOISTS

FIGURE 9–21 Floor framing.

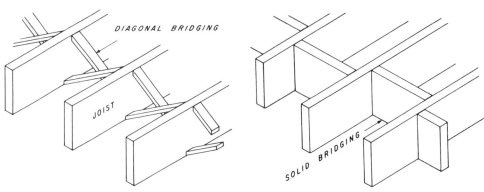

FIGURE 9–22 Bridging of floor joists: (left) diagonal bridging; (right) solid bridging.

FIGURE 9–23 Double plate.

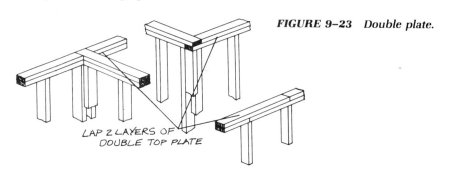

LAP 2 LAYERS OF DOUBLE TOP PLATE

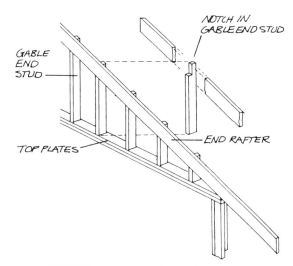

FIGURE 9–24 Notched gable studs.

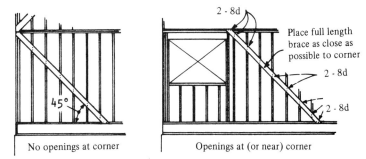

FIGURE 9–25 Corner bracing.

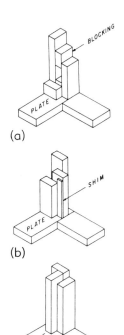

FIGURE 9–26 Corner studs.

Studs in exterior walls are placed with the wide faces perpendicular to the wall. Studs should be at least nominal 2 × 4's for one- and two-story buildings. An arrangement of multiple studs is used at the corners to provide for ready attachment of exterior and interior surface materials (Fig. 9–26).

Where doors or windows occur, provision must be made to carry the vertical load across the opening. A header of adequate size is needed. Ends of the header may be supported on studs (Fig. 9–27).

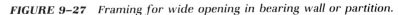

FIGURE 9–27 Framing for wide opening in bearing wall or partition.

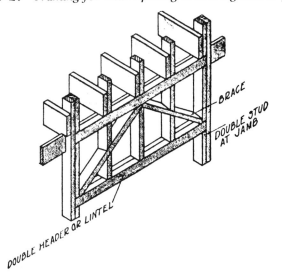

Sheathing

Weathertight walls are provided by sheathing covered on the outside with as-phalt-saturated felt weighing not less than 15 lb per 100 square feet, or with other impregnated paper having equivalent water-repellent properties. Sheathing paper must not be of a type that would act as a vapor barrier. Start-ing at the bottom of the wall, the felt should be lapped 4 in. at horizontal joints and 6 in. at vertical joints. Strips of sheathing paper about 6 in. wide are installed behind all exterior trim and around all openings.

Firestopping

All concealed spaces in wood framing are firestopped with blocking, accurately fitted to fill the opening and arranged to prevent drafts from one space to an-other (Fig. 9–28). Stud spaces should be firestopped at each floor level and at

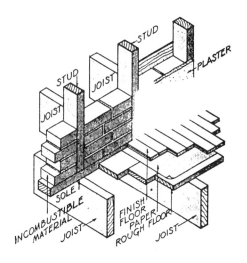

FIGURE 9–28 *Fire stops.*

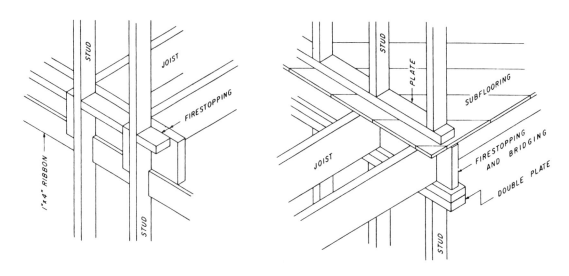

the top-story ceiling level with nominal 2-in. blocking. In many instances, sills and plates will serve this purpose, but where they are not present, additional blocking is necessary.

Stud spaces should be firestopped as required for exterior walls. Concealed spaces should be firestopped for the full depth of the joists, at the ends and over the supports, with nominal 2-in. blocking. In many cases, solid bridging will serve as firestopping. Furred spaces on masonry walls should be firestopped at each floor level and at the top ceiling level by wood blocking of sufficient thickness to fill the space, or by noncombustible material accurately fitted to the space. Spaces between wood framing, at floors and ceilings, and fireplace and chimney masonry, should be filled with noncombustible material.

Interior Partition Framing

There are two types of interior partitions: bearing partitions, which support floors, ceilings, or roofs, and nonbearing partitions, which carry only the weight of the materials in the partition. Studs should be at least nominal 2 × 4's, set with the wide dimension perpendicular to the partitions and capped with two pieces of nominal 2-in. lumber or by continuous headers which are lapped or tied into exterior walls at points of intersections. Studs supporting floors should be spaced 16 in. on center; those that support ceilings and roofs may be spaced 24 in. Where openings occur, loads should be carried across the openings by headers similar to those recommended for exterior walls.

Nonbearing Partitions

Curtain walls or room dividers are partitions not required to support anything except themselves. These are called nonbearing partitions and are built of 2 × 3 studs spaced 16 in. apart. Where these partitions run parallel to the floor joists, the joists are doubled to support the additional load of the partition (Fig. 9–29). If they are perpendicular to the floor joists, no additional support is necessary because the load is distributed over many joists.

FIGURE 9–29   Double joists.

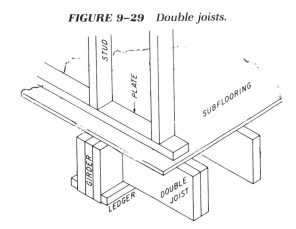

Framing Around Chimneys and Fireplaces

Wood framing should be separated from fireplace and chimney masonry, and all wood trim should have proper clearance for fireplace openings. All headers, beams, joists, and studs should be kept at least 2 in. from the outside face of chimney or fireplace masonry (Fig. 9–30). All wood mantles and similar trim should be kept at least 6 in. from the fireplace opening. Parts of the mantle which project more than 1½ in. from the face of the fireplace should have additional clearance equal to the projection.

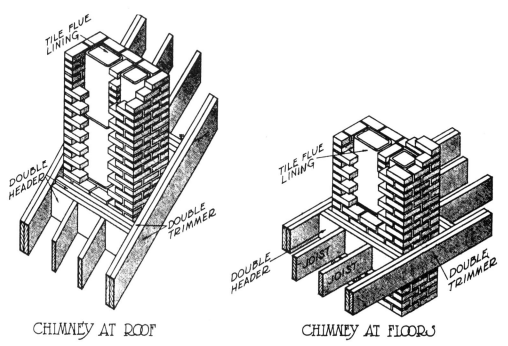

CHIMNEY AT ROOF   CHIMNEY AT FLOORS

FIGURE 9–30 *Chimney clearance.*

Termites and Carpenter Ants

The home of the termite is in the ground. The termite is attracted by wood and works its way inside, often leaving no visual sign of its presence. The first indication may be noticed too late to make it worthwhile to correct the damage. These unwanted pests can be found even in the cleanest of homes because they can be brought in with fruits, vegetables, and clothing or sometimes even by domestic pets. When they are not able to find enough food (wood) in or on the ground, they will emerge from the soil and attack the wood in buildings, taking care to avoid contact with outside air or light. They will gain entrance through any part of the wood structure in contact with the ground through openings in the foundation, around pipes and conduits or through cracks in the foundation. If none of these are available, they will construct tubes made from mud to reach the wood of the building. They work quickly and quietly, devouring and destroying all wood in their path from the inside of the wood, working their way outside. They will hollow out a board, leaving nothing but the paint. Detection is difficult. They are careful not to eat through the outside surface of the wood, even going so far as to block up any surface hole accidentally broken through. Egg laying of termites increases rapidly; two or three years after the colony is established, a colony can consist of several thousands of termites. The worker termite will leave the colony seeking wood because the principal food of termites is cellulose, the main ingredient of wood. Good construction details generally eliminate damage to wood structures. However, when such details are ignored, decay or termite damage may occur unless naturally durable heartwood or preservatively treated wood is used.

The subterranean termite is an insect that attacks in colonies and derives its nourishment from cellulosic materials such as wood, fabrics, papers, and fiberboard. To obtain nourishment the termite may attack wood structures above the ground by means of shelter tubes attached to foundation walls, piers, and other members in contact with the ground. However, only under conditions that permit the insect to establish and maintain contact with soil moisture is a colony able to penetrate and consume wood in service. This requirement indicates that a barrier separating wood from earth, supplemented by inspection, is a practical and effective method of preventing damage by termites.

Protection of wood structures to provide maximum service life involves three methods of control which can be handled by proper design and construction. One or more of the following methods may be employed: control moisture content of wood, provide effective termite barriers, and use naturally durable or treated wood.

Wood construction maintained at a moisture content of 20% or less will not decay. Optimum conditions for decay occur when moisture content is above 25%. It should be stressed that when wood is protected from water or from vapor condensation, and exposed to normal atmospheric conditions such as exist inside buildings and outdoors, its moisture content control by means of accepted design and construction details is a simple and practical method of providing protection against decay.

Although control of moisture contributes to the prevention of subterranean termite attack, the primary control method requires the use of effective barriers supplemented by periodic inspection. Termite barriers are provided by the use of accepted construction practices which drive termites into the open, where the shelter tubes can be detected by inspection. Wood structures that are provided with a recognized barrier supplemented by periodic inspection can be permanently insured against subterranean termite attack.

Protection against termites is accomplished by a barrier of toxicant sprayed beneath and around the house, which make it impossible for the termites to cross or pass. Termites above the chemical barrier will die for lack of moisture and those below it will die from lack of food. If any damage has affected the structural portion of the house, it should be replaced. This spraying should be done once a year for lasting protection.

To guard against termites, a metal shield of not less than 26 gauge of nonrusting metal such as galvanized sheet metal, copper, or aluminum should be placed between the top of the foundation and the bottom of the sill. The metal should be no less than 8 in. wide, extending out beyond the outside foundation about 1 in. with a 60° bend (Fig. 9–31).

A few simple precautions will help keep a home safe. Keep a clean yard, especially around the house. Remove all scrap lumber in contact with the ground. Have tree stumps removed as soon as possible. Do not use waste lumber or wood of any kind for fill. No portion of the wood should be in contact

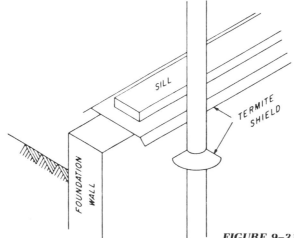

FIGURE 9–31 Termite shields on exterior wall.

with the ground. Wood posts should be sealed with preservative and bent or damaged termite shields should be repaired. Seal all foundation cracks immediately—termites will pass through a crack $\frac{1}{64}$ in. wide. A chemical spray on the exterior of the foundation of the ground will discourage termites. At least once a year have a trained termite expert inspect the house.

Carpenter ants crawl about houses and yards. They can get into food and will excavate galleries for their colony in wood. They can damage or weaken buildings, trees, poles, and posts. In the crawling stage these insects are large, black, and wingless, measuring about $\frac{1}{4}$ to $\frac{3}{8}$ in. long indoors or outdoors. They may wander anywhere, but sometimes seem to follow a specific trail marked by visible narrow path clean of any vegetation. In the winged stage a sudden flight of numerous large, black ants with darker wing veins and brownish bodies may be seen. The wings extend beyond the end of the body about half the body length. Sometimes a pile of sawdust or an accumulation of course fibrous "sawdust" will be found near a colony in a building, hollow tree, or pole. The ants carry the sawdust out in building their nests and neatly dispose of it. They do not eat wood but will damage the wood in nest building. If infested, the damaged wood will have interconnecting, irregular chambers and tunnels with clean smooth inner walls. The colonies may not be seen because the entrance may be hidden, but they can be found in any part of the house. They sometimes nest in hollow porch columns, walls, and so on. Outdoors they live in trees that are partly hollow or decaying, also in stumps, logs, poles, and posts. Termites are sometimes confused with carpenter ants. No sawdust is produced with termites because they eat the wood; ants eat foodstuffs and other insects.

The ants mate during a brief flight after leaving the parent colony. The male soon dies and the female breaks off her wings, digs a small chamber in suitable wood, seals herself in, lays her eggs, and raises her family of workers. The colony may eventually contain several queens and thousands of workers. After two or three years the colony will produce large, winged males and females who will leave the colony and start the cycle over again. Flights are common in spring and early summer.

Roof and Ceiling Framing

Roof construction should be strong to withstand anticipated snow and wind loads. Members should be securely fastened to each other to provide continuity across the building and should be anchored to exterior walls (Fig. 9–32). Fram-

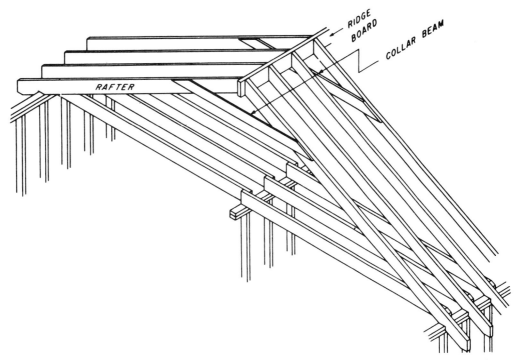

FIGURE 9–32   *Roof framing with ceiling joints parallel to rafters.*

ing will provide maximum allowable spans for ceiling joists and rafters. Ridge members may be of 1- or 2-in. lumber, but 2 in. deeper than the rafter to permit full contact with the beveled end of the rafter. Where rafters abut the ridge, they should be placed directly opposite each other and nailed to the ridge member. Rafters should be notched to fit the exterior wall plate and toenailed or secured to it by special fastenings.

Ceiling joists should be nailed to exterior walls and to the ends of rafters. Where joining over interior partitions, they should be nailed to plates and to each other. Where ceiling joists are at right angles to rafters, short joists are nailed to ends of the rafters and to the top plate, and fastened to the ceiling joists by means of metal straps or framing anchors. For this condition, subflooring is necessary to provide a tie across the building (Fig. 9–33, page 210).

The valley rafter at the intersection of two roof areas should be doubled in thickness and 2 in. deeper than the common rafter, to permit full bearing for the beveled end (Fig. 9–34, page 210). Where ridges are at different elevations, care should be taken to provide vertical support for the interior end of the lower ridge board.

Hip rafters may be of the same thickness as common rafters, but should be 2 in. deeper to permit full contact with that of the jack rafter (Fig. 9–35, page 211).

Collar beams of 1×6 in. boards should be installed in the upper third of the attic space to every third pair of rafters on pitched roofs, to hold the ridge framing together during high winds (Fig. 9–32).

Roof framing for pitched roofs may be fabricated as light trusses and installed as complete units. Framing of this type is designed according to accepted engineering practice. The various members of the truss are joined together by fasteners such as nails, nails and glue, bolts, connectors, or other framing devices (Fig. 9–36, page 211).

The use of trussed rafters eliminates the need for interior bearing partitions and usually results in more rapid installation of roof and ceiling framing.

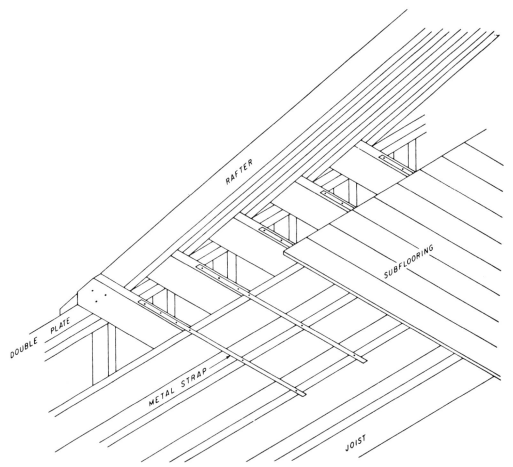

FIGURE 9–33 *Roof framing with ceiling joints at right angles to rafters.*

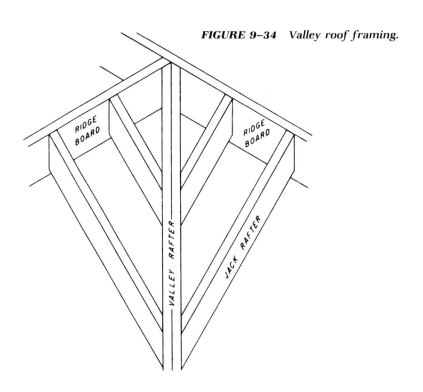

FIGURE 9–34 *Valley roof framing.*

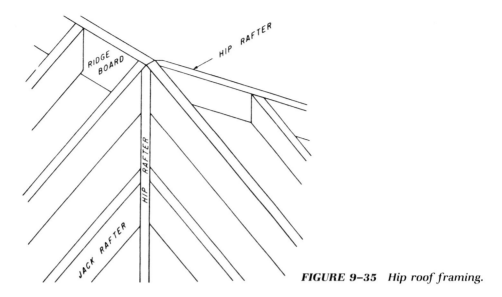

FIGURE 9-35 *Hip roof framing.*

FIGURE 9-36 *Roof truss.*

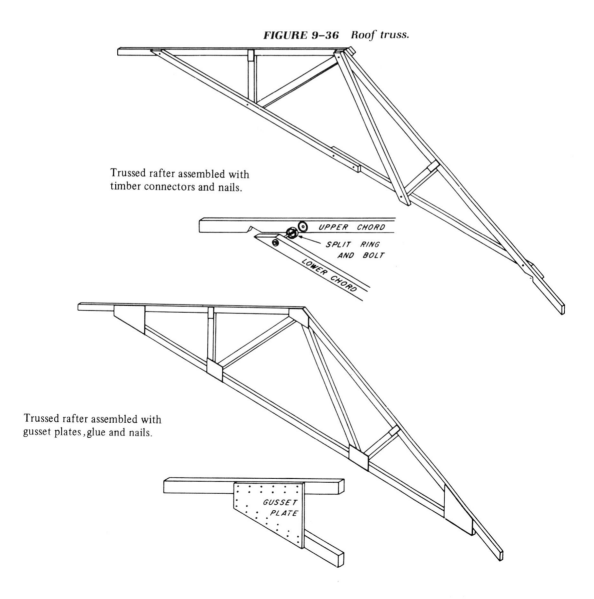

Trussed rafter assembled with timber connectors and nails.

Trussed rafter assembled with gusset plates, glue and nails.

Spacing of trussed rafters is usually 16 to 24 in., depending on the type of roof sheathing and ceiling covering used.

Where trussed rafters are used, gable ends usually are framed in the conventional manner using a common rafter to which gable end studs are nailed. Overhangs at eaves may be provided by extending the upper chords of the trusses the required distance beyond the wall or by nailing the overhang framing to the upper chords of the trusses.

Where hip and valley construction occurs, modified trussed rafters or conventional framing are used to meet this condition. In buildings with flat roofs the rafters or roof joists usually serve as ceiling joists for the space below (Fig. 9–37).

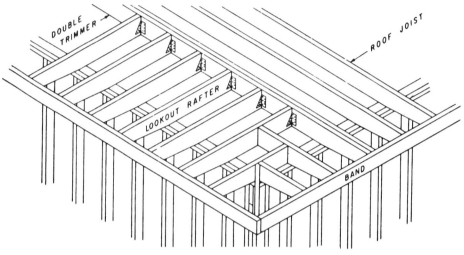

FIGURE 9–37   Cantileaver roof framing.

Design of Roofs (Fig. 9–38).

We should begin with some terms and definitions.

Gable roof   The most popular style; easy to ventilate.

Hip roof   Slightly more difficult to build because all sides are pitched.

Flat roof   The most economical and easiest to construct. A dead-level roof is not recommended. So-called "flat" roofs are pitched just enough to shed the water, about ⅛ to ¼ in. pitch per foot.

Shed roof   Similar to a flat roof, with a more pronounced pitch.

Mansard roof   Of French design; gaining in popularity but more difficult to construct.

Gambrel roof   Provides additional space on upper-level floors.

Butterfly roof   Provides more light and ventilation but may cause drainage problems.

A frame roof   Provides the dual function of walls and roof; adds more cubic footage, thus more area to heat.

The members used in roof construction, called roof rafters, are spaced 16 in. apart. In preparing or cutting the roof rafters to fit, we are concerned with

ROOF DESIGNS

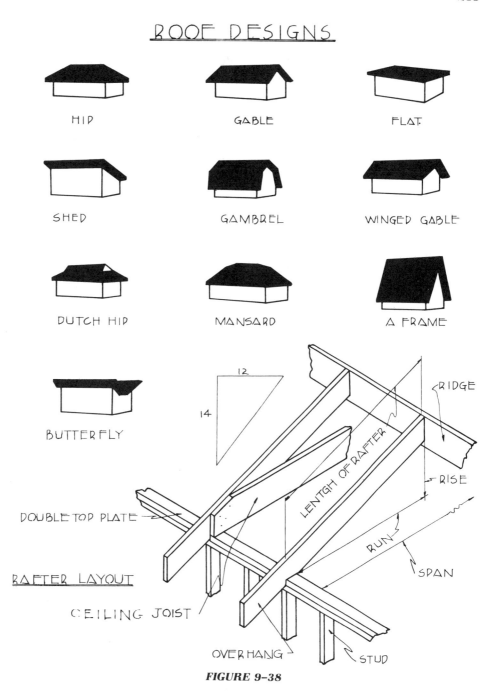

HIP   GABLE   FLAT

SHED   GAMBREL   WINGED GABLE

DUTCH HIP   MANSARD   A FRAME

BUTTERFLY

RAFTER LAYOUT

FIGURE 9-38

ridge cut or plumb cut, which is the high or center portion of the roof, and the heel or seat cut, which is at the wall line resting on the double plate. The tail cut is the overhang of the roof. The precise layout of these cuts is determined by the slope or pitch of the roof and the width or span of the building.

The rise is the vertical distance from the top of the double wall plate to the top of the roof. The span is half the span or the horizontal distance from the outside wall to the center of the roof. The span is the horizontal distance from the outside wall to the opposite outside wall. The slope or pitch of roof is indicated as

which indicates that for every 12 in. of horizontal dimension, the rise is 4 in.

Where the rafters come together at the plumb cut is called the ridge (top of roof). A ridge board is installed for the entire length of the roof between the plumb cuts. The ridge board is 2 in. wider than the roof rafters. If, for example, the roof rafters are 2 × 6's, the ridge board will be a 2 × 8.

The entire roof assembly must be braced and stiffened by installing collar beams of 1 × 6's at every other rafter. These collar beams are parallel with the ceiling joists attached halfway up the run of the roof rafter nailed to two rafters, one on each side of the roof, tying them together.

Dormers

A structure projecting above the roof slope with a vertical wall is a dormer. Its chief purpose is to allow light and ventilation, more space, and to enhance the aesthetics of the roof. The design of the roof of a dormer can be shed roof, gable roof, or hip roof and is constructed much like the main roof. The wall ends of the dormer are resting on the main roof rafters, which are doubled at that point (Fig. 9–39).

FIGURE 9–39a *Shed dormer.*

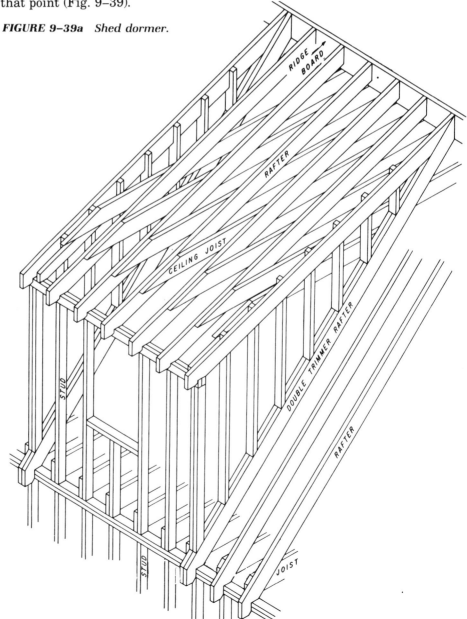

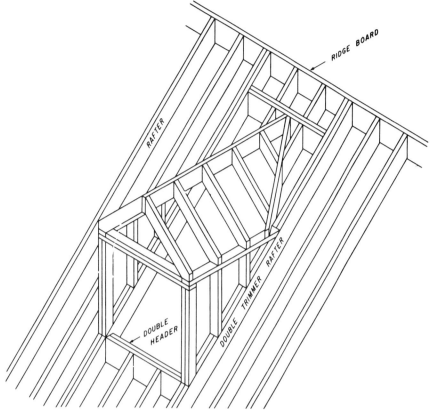

FIGURE 9–39b   *Gable dormer.*

Plank-and-Beam Framing

The plank-and-beam method of framing floors and roofs has been used in heavy timber buildings for many years. The adaptation of this system to residential construction has raised many technical questions from designers and builders concerning details of application, advantages and limitations, construction details, and structural requirements for the plank-and-beam method of framing.

Whereas conventional framing utilizes joists, rafters, and studs spaced 12 to 24 in. on center, the plank-and-beam method requires fewer and larger pieces spaced farther apart (Fig. 9–40). In plank-and-beam framing, plank subfloors or roofs, usually of 2-in. nominal thickness, are supported on beams spaced up to 8 ft apart (Fig. 9–41). The ends of the beams are supported on posts or piers. Wall spaces between posts are provided with supplementary framing to the extent required for attachment of exterior and interior finish. This supplementary framing and its covering also serve to provide lateral bracing for the building.

The most successful plank-and-beam houses are those which are designed from the beginning for this method of framing. Such a procedure permits the correlation of the structural framework with the exterior dimensions of the house, the location of doors and windows, and the location of interior parti-

FIGURE 9–40a *Plank-and-beam framing compared with conventional framing.*

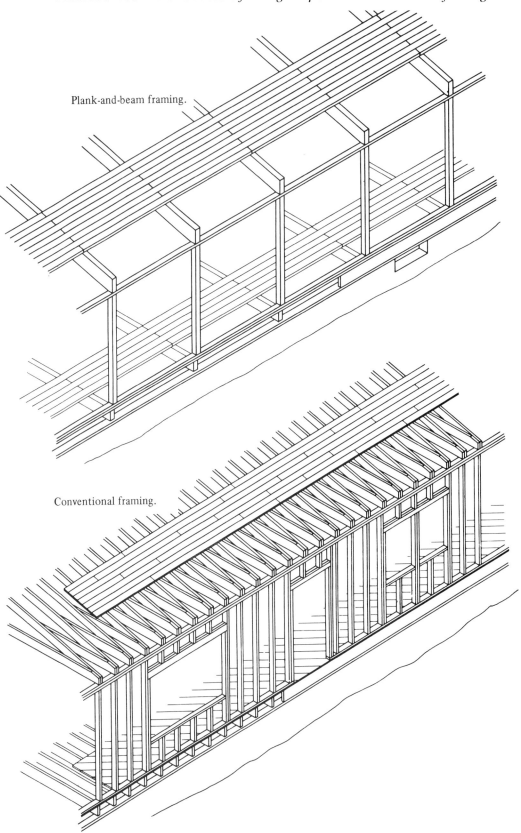

Plank-and-beam framing.

Conventional framing.

FIGURE 9–40b *Plank-and-beam framing combined with conventional framing in two-story house.*

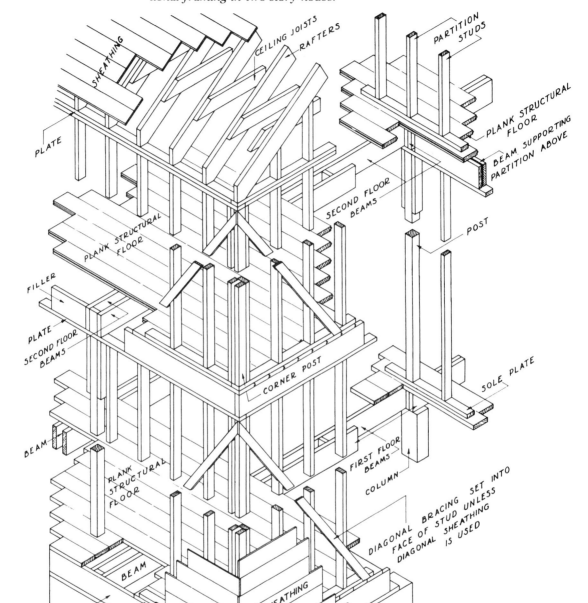

FIGURE 9–41 *Plank-and-beam, one story.*

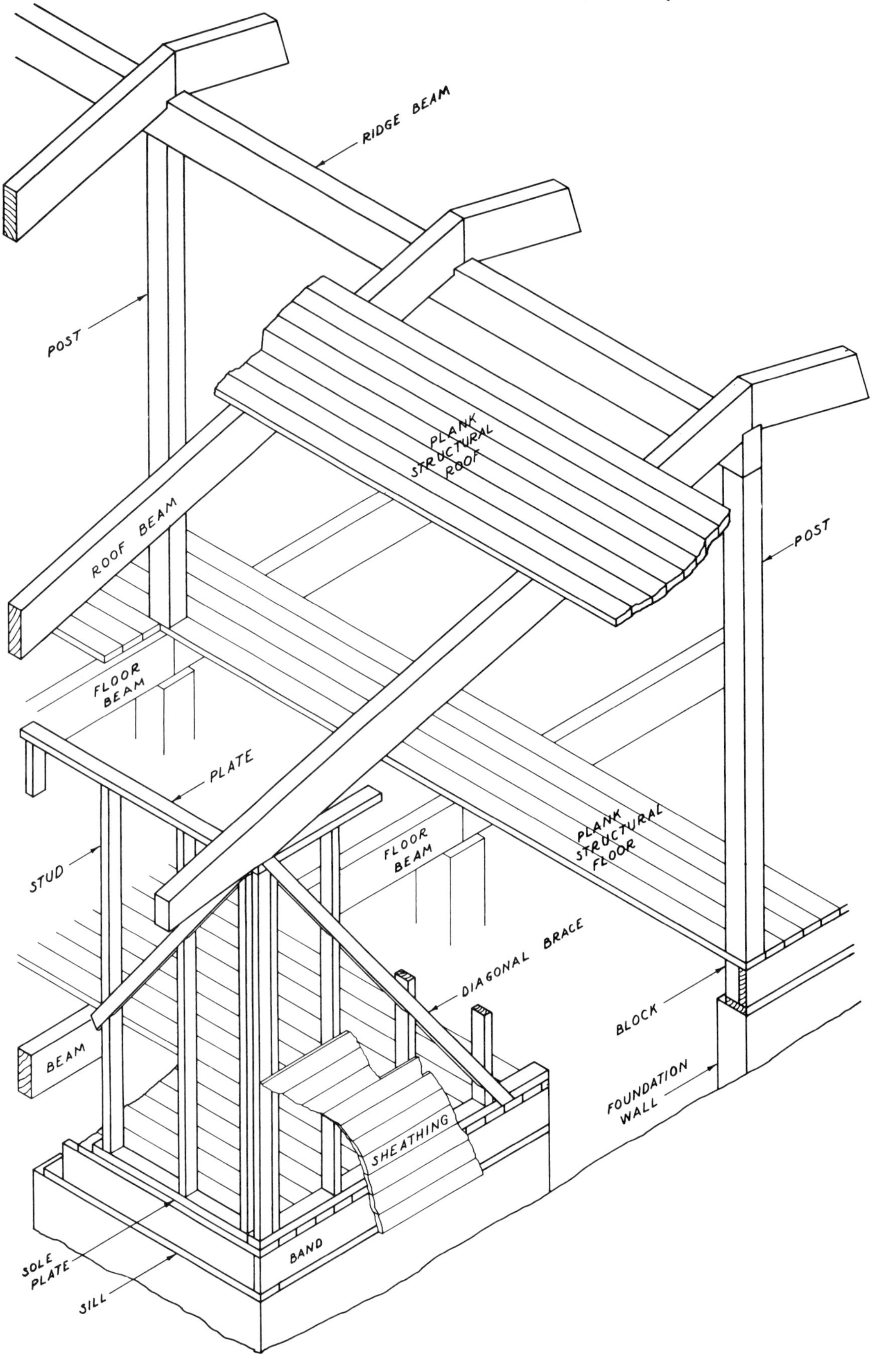

tions. Proper study of these features in the early stages will contribute much to simplified framing.

The most efficient use of 2-in. plank occurs when it is continuous over more than one span (Fig. 9–42). Where standard lengths of lumber are used, such as 12, 14, or 16 ft, beam spacings of 6, 7, or 8 ft are indicated, and this has bearing on the overall dimensions of the house. Where end joints in the plank are allowed to occur between supports, random-length planks may be used and the beam spacing adjusted to fit the dimensions of the house.

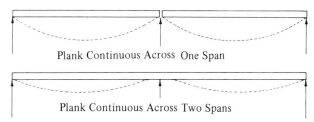

Plank Continuous Across One Span

Plank Continuous Across Two Spans

FIGURE 9–42   *Wood plank span.*

Windows and doors should be located between posts in exterior walls to eliminate the need for headers over the openings. The wide spacing between posts permits ample opportunity for large glass areas. However, a sufficient amount of solid wall should be present to provide adequate lateral bracing.

A combination of conventional framing with plank-and-beam framing is sometimes used. Where the two adjoin each other side by side, no particular problems are encountered. Where a plank-and-beam floor or roof is supported on a stud wall, a post should be placed under the end of the beam to carry the concentrated load. Where conventional roof framing is used with plank-and-beam construction, a header should be installed to carry the load from the rafters to the posts.

There are many advantages to be gained through the use of the plank-and-beam system of framing. Perhaps the most outstanding is the distinctive architectural effect provided by the exposed plank-and-beam ceiling. In many houses the roof plank serves as the ceiling, thereby providing added height to living areas with no increase in cost. Where planks are selected for appearance, no further ceiling treatment is needed except the application of a stain, sealer, or paint, and this results in quite a saving in cost (Fig. 9–43).

Well-planned plank-and-beam framing permits substantial savings in labor. The pieces are larger and there are fewer of them than in conventional framing. Cross-bridging of joists is eliminated entirely. Larger and fewer nails are required. All of this adds up to labor saving at the job site.

In plank-and-beam framing, the ceiling height is measured to the underside of the plank, whereas in conventional construction, it is measured to the underside of the joists. The difference between the thickness of the plank and the depth of the joists results in a reduction in the volume of the building. It also reduces the height of the exterior walls.

There are limitations on the use of the plank-and-beam system, but they are readily resolved through careful study in the planning stage. When this is done, the parts of the house fit together very quickly and easily. The plank floors are designed for moderate uniform loads and are not intended to carry heavy concentrated loads. Where such loads occur as those for bearing partitions, bathtubs, and refrigerators, additional framing is needed beneath the planks to transmit the loads to the beams (Fig. 9–44).

In moderate climates, the insulation provided by the nominal 2-in. plank is usually adequate. In colder climates, additional insulation is often desired

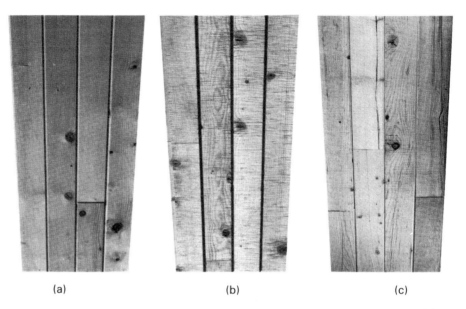

(a)   (b)   (c)

FIGURE 9–43   *Wood plank grades: (a) premium; (b) architectural; (c) California rustic.*

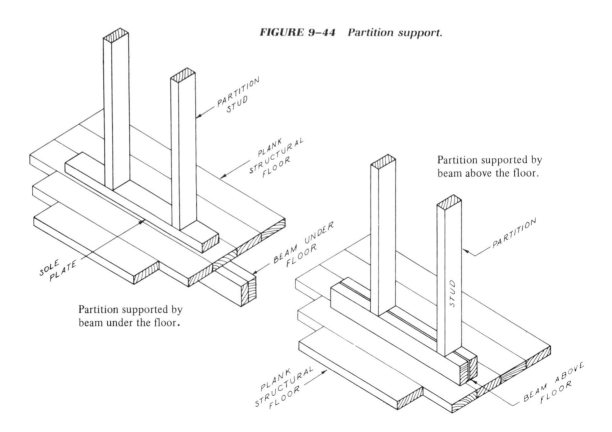

FIGURE 9–44   *Partition support.*

Partition supported by beam above the floor.

Partition supported by beam under the floor.

and this may be installed in the amount needed to meet local conditions. Insulation may be applied to the underside of the planks, in which case its appearance is a factor. The insulation may also be installed on top of the planks, where it should be in rigid form. This type is usually laid in mastic and limited to a roof slope of 3-in-12 (3/12) or lower. A vapor barrier between the wood plank and the insulation is recommended.

Location of the electrical distribution system may present a problem because of the lack of concealed spaces in the ceiling. However, the main supporting beams may be made of several pieces of 2-in. lumber and separated by short blocking, which provides a space to accommodate electrical cable and pipes for other uses (Fig. 9–45). Solid beams may be routed along their top surfaces for this purpose. Concealed spaces in the supplementary wall framing provide ample space for wall outlets and electrical cable.

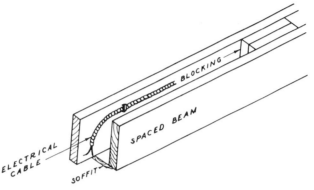

FIGURE 9–45   False beam.

The plank-and-beam system is essentially a skeleton framework. Planks are designed to support a moderate load, uniformly distributed. This is carried to the beams, which in turn transmit their loads to posts which are supported on the foundation.

Foundations for plank-and-beam framing may be continuous walls or piers, supported on adequate footings. With posts spaced up to 8 ft apart in exterior walls, this system is well adapted to pier foundations for houses without basements.

Posts should be of adequate size to carry the load and large enough to provide full bearing for the ends of beams. In general, posts should be at least nominal 4 × 4's. Where the ends of beams abut over a post, a dimension of 6 in. parallel to the beams is recommended for the post. The posts may be solid or made up of several pieces of 2-in. lumber well spiked together.

Beams may be solid or glued laminated pieces, or may be built up of several thinner pieces securely nailed to each other or to spacer blocks between them. When built-up beams are used, a cover plate attached to the underside provides the appearance of a solid piece. Fastening of beams to posts is accomplished by framing anchors or angle clips.

Since the 2-in. plank floor or roof frequently serves as the finish ceiling for the room below, appearance as well as structural requirements of the plank should be considered. For the purpose of distributing load, tongue-and-groove or grooved-for-spline lumber is recommended (Fig. 9–46). To provide a pleasing appearance, a reasonably good grade of lumber should be selected and it should be sufficiently seasoned to meet the requirements of service conditions so as to avoid large cracks at the joints.

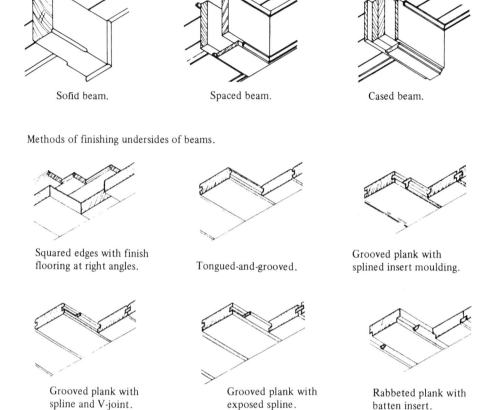

Solid beam.   Spaced beam.   Cased beam.

Methods of finishing undersides of beams.

Squared edges with finish   Tongued-and-grooved.   Grooved plank with
flooring at right angles.   splined insert moulding.

Grooved plank with   Grooved plank with   Rabbeted plank with
spline and V-joint.   exposed spline.   batten insert.

FIGURE 9–46   Joint treatment.

In laying the plank, greater advantage can be taken of the strength and stiffness of the material by making the planks continuous over more than one span. For example, using the same span and uniform load in each case, a plank that is continuous over two spans is nearly two and one-half times as stiff as a plank that extends over a single span.

The finish floor should be laid at right angles to the plank subfloor, using the same procedure as that followed in conventional construction. Where the underside of plank is to serve as a ceiling, care is needed to make sure that flooring nails do not penetrate through the plank.

Partitions in the plank-and-beam system usually will be nonbearing. Where bearing partitions occur, they should be placed over beams and the beams enlarged to carry the added load. If this is not possible, supplementary beams must be placed in the floor framing arrangement. Nonbearing partitions, which are parallel to the planks, should have support to carry this load to the beams. This may be accomplished by using two pieces of 2 × 4's set on edge as the sole plate. Where openings occur in the partition, the two pieces may be placed under the plank floor and supported on the beams by framing anchors. Where the nonbearing partition is at right angles to the planks, no supplementary framing is needed since the partition load will be distributed across a number of planks. As in conventional framing, lateral bracing is required in the exterior walls to provide resistance against wind forces. In plank-and-beam framing, this is accomplished by installing solid panels at appropriate intervals wherein the supplementary wall framing and the posts are all tied together by diagonal bracing or suitable sheathing.

Wall and Roof Sheathing

When the walls and roof framing are completed, sheathing must be applied over the wall studs and roof rafters (Fig. 9–47). The sheathing provides rigidity to the frame and provides a surface for applying the finish roof and walls. Material used for sheathing is 4 × 8 plywood or composition board (check local codes for minimum thickness). The joints are located over the center of the stud or rafter, and sheathing is fitted carefully at valleys, hips, and ridges are nailed securely. Common boards may be nailed diagonally for extra strength, but there is also greater waste because of angle cutting.

If plywood sheathing is used, it must be nailed with the face grain perpendicular to the studs or rafters, with end joints directly over the center of a stud or rafter, again breaking up the joints. Sheathing should be applied to the walls before the roof is installed to reinforce the frame of the building.

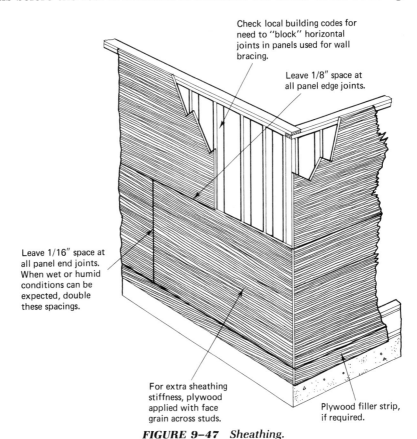

FIGURE 9–47   Sheathing.

Roof Construction

Covering Materials

Materials for covering roofs are classified by weight per 100 square feet, called a square (100 square feet = 1 square). For example, a 30-lb roofing paper or felt weights 30 lb per 100 square feet. Roof construction and finish consists of a number of operations which must be followed in proper sequence. Materials used for roofing include built-up roofing, asphalt shingles, wood shingles, mineral fiber shingles, slate shingles, tile, roll roofing, galvanized metal, aluminum, terne, and copper. The selection of roofing material is influenced by initial cost, maintenance, durability, aesthetics, and roof pitch or slope. Local building codes may prohibit certain materials because of fire hazard or wind resistance. Moisture control is an important consideration in avoiding roof failures. Sometimes moisture vapor from the lower floors, rising to the attic, will be chilled below its dew point and will condense on the underside of the roof deck or sheathing, causing the sheathing to warp and buckle. Louvered openings constructed under the eaves in the gables will prevent this problem (Fig. 9–48).

One of several materials used in roofing is tar, which is a familiar word but has different meanings for different people. To many, tar is a black adhesive liquid or plastic substance. However, it is much more than that. Tar is a hydrocarbon and an organic compound obtained from coal. The coal is heated to a very high temperature, which cracks the molecules into gas. This gas is further distilled, refined, and separated into products known as creosote, used for chemical oils used in manufacturing drugs, dyes, paints, varnishes, cosmet-

FIGURE 9–48 *Attic and roof ventilation.*

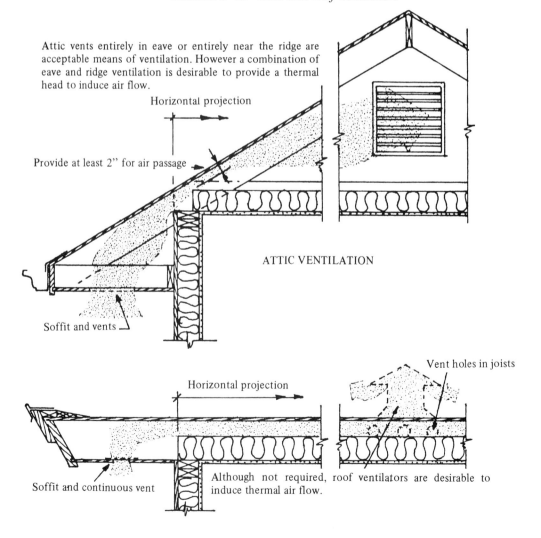

ics, plastics and synthetic rubber, and pitches used for roofing materials and waterproofing compounds. Coal tar roofing pitch has superb water- and corrosive-resistance qualities as well as being an excellent adhesion for fusing roofing felts. All roofing material must be stored in a dry place prior to application and off the ground, preferably on a platform covered with waterproof coverings. Store rolls of felt and paper on end to avoid deforming or damaging.

Built-up Roofing.   Also called tar and gravel roofing, this type is used on a flat roof or a pitch not to exceed 3/12 (Fig. 9–49).

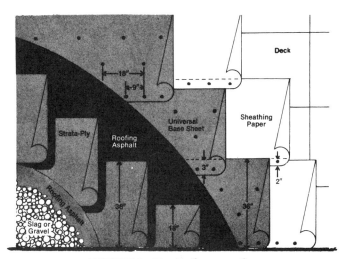

FIGURE 9–49   Built-up roof.

Roll Roofing.   This type of roofing consists of felt or paper saturated with asphalt surfaced with mineral granules. The rolls are available 36 in. wide weighing from 15 to 120 lb a square. This style of roof can be used with any roof pitch, including flat roofs (Fig. 9–50). Reroofing over an existing roof is not recommended. Better results will be obtained by removing the old roof and constructing a new one. The heavier the paper, the longer the service of the roof. A common weight for this type roofing is 90-lb mineral surfaced.

Asphalt Shingles.   This type of roofing consists of saturated felt coated with multicolored granules manufactured into strips of different shape and size (Fig. 9–51). The most popular is the square butt shingle 12 in. wide and 36 in. long with slotted butts to simulate individual shingles. The portion of shingles exposed is termed "to the weather" and the average exposure is about 5 in. There are many qualities of asphalt shingles, determined by weight, from 180 to 380 lb per square. Needless to say, the heavier the shingles, the longer the life or service. An average weight is 235 lb per square. When using asphalt shingles, the roof pitch or slope must be 4 in. or greater.

Some shingles are self-sealing by means of several spots of asphalt above the tabs. This will allow the shingles to fuse to each other. Nails used on asphalt shingles are $1\frac{1}{4}$-in. galvanized roofing nails. The succeeding courses will cover the nails of each course. Three tab shingles require four nails per strip. It is not necessary to remove old asphalt shingles for reroofing except for more than one course. Apply new roofing over the old, using longer nails. The average life of an asphalt shingle roof is 20 to 25 years.

FIGURE 9–50 Rool roofing (courtesy Asphalt Roofing Manufacturers Association).

PRODUCT	Approximate Shipping Weight		Squares Per Package	Length	Width	Selvage	Exposure
	Per Roll	Per Square					
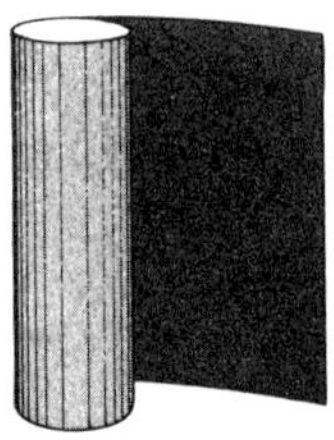 Mineral surface roll	75# to 90#	75# to 90#	1	36' to 38'	36"	2" to 4"	32" to 34"
 Mineral surface roll (double coverage)	55# to 70#	110# to 140#	½	36'	36"	19"	17"
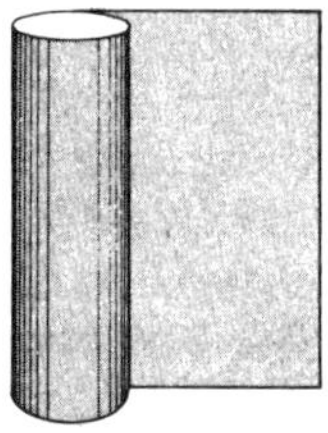 Smooth surface roll	50# to 86#	40# to 65#	1 to 2	36' to 72'	36"	2"	34"
 Saturated felt (non-perforated)	45# to 60#	11# to 30#	2 to 4	72' to 144'	36"	2" to 19"	17" to 34"

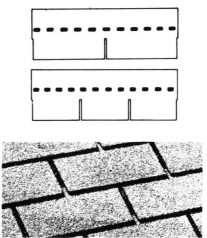

FIGURE 9–51   *Asphalt shingles.*

Wood Shingles.   This type of roofing may not be acceptable in certain areas because they may be a fire hazard. Some wood shingles are treated to meet fire safety requirements. There are two types of wood shingles, machine sawed and handsplit, both made from western red cedar, redwood, and cyprus, all highly decay-resistant woods. Machine-sawed shingles are 16, 18, and 24 in. long in random widths, tapered with $\frac{1}{2}$- to $\frac{3}{4}$-in.-thick butts. They are graded No. 1, 2, or 3 according to knots and defects (Fig. 9–52, page 228). Handsplit shingles, sometimes called shakes, vary in thickness with butts ranging from $\frac{5}{8}$″ to $1\frac{1}{4}$ in. thick with lengths of 24, 32, and 36 in. with random widths (Fig. 9–53, page 229).

The minimum roof pitch is 3/12 and the exposure of wood shingles depends on the roof pitch or slope, varying from 3 to 7 in. exposure. Wood shingles are normally applied in straight single courses but may vary to achieve special effects for thatch, serrated, weave, and ocean.

Handsplit Shakes with Roof Sheathing.   Red cedar handsplit shakes may be applied over open or solid sheathing. When spaced sheathing is used, 1 × 4's (or wider) are spaced on centers equal to the weather exposure at which the shakes are to be laid, but never more than 10 in. In areas where wind-driven snow conditions prevail, a solid roof deck is recommended.

Proper weather exposure is important. As a general rule, a $7\frac{1}{2}$-in. exposure is recommended for 18-in. shakes and a 10-in. exposure for 24-in. shakes. Valley and flashing metals that have proved reliable in a particular region should be used. It is important that valley metals be used whose longevity will match that for which cedar is renowned. Metal valley sheets should be center-crimped, of 20-in. minimum width, and for longer life should be underlaid with a strip of 30-lb roofing felt applied over the sheathing with a good grade of metal paint. Either field-applied or preformed factory-made hip and ridge units may be used. Weather exposures should be the same as for roof shakes (Fig. 9–54, page 230).

Slate Shingles.   This type of roofing material is a natural quarried rock product split into thin sheets used for roof covering. The marked cleavage of the slate rock lends itself to a natural, irregular, and pleasing roof surface with natural color variations from blacks and grays, blues and greens, and browns and reds. A slate roof will usually outlast the life of the building (Fig. 9–55, page 231). They require a larger or stronger roof framing system because of the weight of the shingles, and the roof pitch should be no less than 6 in.

FIGURE 9–52 Wood shingles (courtesy Red Cedar Shingle & Handsplit Shake Bureau).

● Valleys should extend far enough under the shingles to insure complete drainage, with water-stop as shown if necessary.

● How the recommended modified "Boston" hip is made.

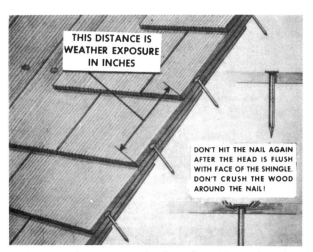

● Proper weather exposure and nailing will provide a 3-ply roof.

● Drip from gables and the formation of icicles can be prevented by this simple expedient.

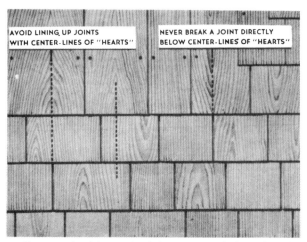

● Flat-grain shingles in Red Label and No. 3 Black Label grades should be properly applied as shown above.

● In over-roofing, new flashings should be placed around chimneys without removing the old.

RTIGRADE RED CEDAR SHINGLES

GRADE	Length	Thickness (at Butt)	No. of Courses Per Bundle	Bdls/Cartons Per Square		Description
o. 1 BLUE LABEL	16" (Fivex) 18" (Perfections) 24" (Royals)	.40" .45" .50"	20/20 18/18 13/14	4 bdls. 4 bdls. 4 bdls.		The premium grade of shingles for roofs and sidewalls. These top-grade shingles are 100% heartwood ... 100% clear and 100% edge-grain.
o. 2 RED LABEL	16" (Fivex) 18" (Perfections) 24" (Royals)	.40" .45" .50"	20/20 18/18 13/14	4 bdls. 4 bdls. 4 bdls.		A proper grade for some applications. Not less than 10" clear on 16" shingles, 11" clear on 18" shingles and 16" clear on 24" shingles. Flat grain and limited sapwood are permitted in this grade.
o. 3 BLACK LABEL	16" (Fivex) 18" (Perfections) 24" (Royals)	.40" .45" .50"	20/20 18/18 13/14	4 bdls. 4 bdls. 4 bdls.		A utility grade for economy applications and secondary buildings. Not less than 6" clear on 16" and 18" shingles, 10" clear on 24" shingles.
o. 4 UNDER-COURSING	16" (Fivex) 18" (Perfections)	.40" .45"	14/14 or 20/20 14/14 or 18/18	2 bdls. 2 bdls. 2 bdls. 2 bdls.		A utility grade for undercoursing on double-coursed sidewall applications or for interior accent walls.
o. 1 or o. 2 REBUTTED-REJOINTED	16" (Fivex) 18" (Perfections) 24" (Royals)	.40" .45" .50"	33/33 28/28 13/14	1 carton 1 carton 4 bdls.		Same specifications as above for No. 1 and No. 2 grades but machine trimmed for exactly parallel edges with butts sawn at precise right angles. For sidewall application where tightly fitting joints are desired. Also available with smooth sanded face.

PITCH	Maximum exposure recommended for roofs:								
	NO. 1 BLUE LABEL			NO. 2 RED LABEL			NO. 3 BLACK LABEL		
	16"	18"	24"	16"	18"	24"	16"	18"	24"
IN 12 TO 4 IN 12	3¾"	4¼"	5¾"	3½"	4"	5½"	3"	3½"	5"
IN 12 AND STEEPER	5"	5½"	7½"	4"	4½"	6½"	3½"	4"	5½"

LENGTH AND THICKNESS	Approximate coverage of one square (4 bundles) of shingles based on following weather exposures																										
	3½"	4"	4½"	5"	5½"	6"	6½"	7"	7½"	8"	8½"	9"	9½"	10"	10½"	11"	11½"	12"	12½"	13"	13½"	14"	14½"	15"	15½"	16"
" x 5/2"	70	80	90	100*	110	120	130	140	150‡	160	170	180	190	200	210	220	230	240†	....	....	....	....	....	....	....	....
" x 5/2¼"	....	72½	81½	90½	100*	109	118	127	136	145½	154½	163½	172½	181½	191	200	209	218	227	236	245½	254½	....	....	....	....
" x 4/2"	....	....	....	....	80	86½	93	100*	106½	113	120	126½	133	140	146½	153	160	166½	173	180	186½	193	200	206½	213†	

ES: *Maximum exposure recommended for roofs.   ‡Maximum exposure recommended for single-coursing No. 1 grades on sidewalls. Reduce exposure for No. 2 grades.
     †Maximum exposure recommended for double-coursing No. 1 grades on sidewalls.

RTI-SPLIT RED CEDAR HANDSPLIT SHAKES

GRADE	Length and Thickness	18" Pack**		Description
		# Courses Per Bdl.	# Bdls. Per Sq.	
o. 1 HANDSPLIT & RESAWN	15" Starter-Finish 18" x ½" Mediums 18" x ¾" Heavies 24" x ⅜" 24" x ½" Mediums 24" x ¾" Heavies	9/9 9/9 9/9 9/9 9/9 9/9	5 5 5 5 5 5	 These shakes have split faces and sawn backs. Cedar logs are first cut into desired lengths. Blanks or boards of proper thickness are split and then run diagonally through a bandsaw to produce two tapered shakes from each blank.
o. 1 TAPERSPLIT	24" x ½"	9/9	5	 Produced largely by hand, using a sharp-bladed steel froe and a wooden mallet. The natural shingle-like taper is achieved by reversing the block, end-for-end, with each split.
o. 1 STRAIGHT-SPLIT	18" x ⅜" True-Edge* 18" x ⅜" 24" x ⅜"	**20" Pack** 14 Straight 19 Straight 16 Straight	4 5 5	Produced in the same manner as tapersplit shakes except that by splitting from the same end of the block, the shakes acquire the same thickness throughout.

E: * Exclusively sidewall product, with parallel edges.
   ** Pack used for majority of shakes.

SHAKE TYPE, LENGTH AND THICKNESS	Approximate coverage (in sq. ft.) of one square, when shakes are applied with ½" spacing, at following weather exposures, in inches (h):						
	5½"	7½"	8½"	10"	11½"	16"	
3" x ½" Handsplit-and-Resawn Mediums (a)	55(b)	75(c)	85(d)	100	....	....	
3" x ¾" Handsplit-and-Resawn Heavies (a)	55(b)	75(c)	85(d)	100	....	....	
4" x ⅜" Handsplit	....	75(e)	85	100(f)	115(d)	....	
4" x ½" Handsplit-and-Resawn Mediums	....	75(b)	85	100(c)	115(d)	....	
4" x ¾" Handsplit-and-Resawn Heavies	....	75(b)	85	100(c)	115(d)	....	
4" x ½" Tapersplit	....	75(b)	85	100(c)	115(d)	....	
3" x ⅜" True-Edge Straight-Split	....	....	....	....	....	112(g)	
3" x ⅜" Straight-Split	65(b)	90(c)	100(d)	....	....	....	
4" x ⅜" Straight-Split	....	75(b)	85	100(c)	115(d)	....	
5" Starter-Finish Course	Use supplementary with shakes applied not over 10" weather exposure.						

(a) 5 bundles will cover 100 sq. ft. roof area when used as starter-finish course at 10" weather exposure; 6 bundles will cover 100 sq. ft. wall area at 8½" exposure; 7 bundles will cover 100 sq. ft. roof area at 7½" weather exposure; see footnote (h).

(b) Maximum recommended weather exposure for 3-ply roof construction.

(c) Maximum recommended weather exposure for 2-ply roof construction.

(d) Maximum recommended weather exposure for single-coursed wall construction.

(e) Maximum recommended weather exposure for application on roof pitches between 4-in-12 and 8-in-12.

(f) Maximum recommended weather exposure for application on roof pitches of 8-in-12 and steeper.

(g) Maximum recommended weather exposure for double-coursed wall construction.

(h) All coverage based on ½" spacing between shakes.

Roofs

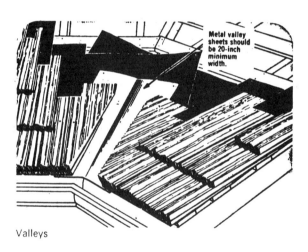

Valleys

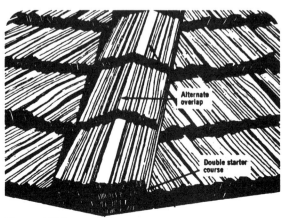

Hips and Ridges

FIGURE 9-54 Wood shake roofing (courtesy Red Cedar Shingle & Handsplit Shake Bureau).

FIGURE 9–55 Slate shingles (courtesy Hilltop Slate Inc.).

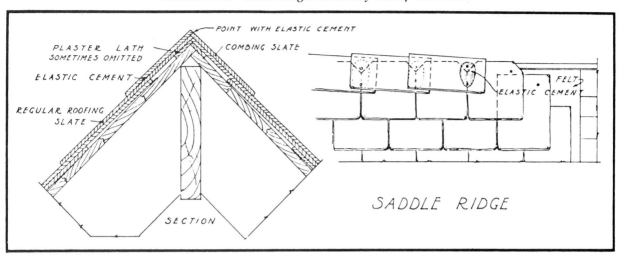

LAYING SLATE

Smooth and Rough Slates

LOCATION OF NAIL HOLES

SLATE ROOFING

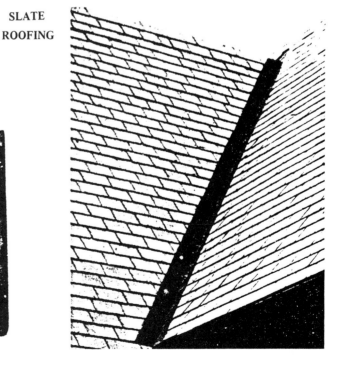

OPEN VALLEY

Tile Roofing. This roofing style has a Mediterranean–Spanish motif. There are two general categories of clay roofing tile: flat and roll type. The flat type varies from simple pieces to pieces with interlocking sections. Roll type is formed in many shapes, from semicircular to pan shape. All are preholed for nailing (Fig. 9–56).

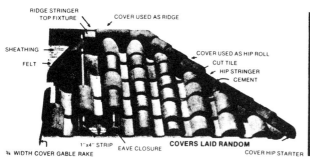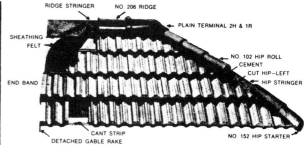

FIGURE 9–56   *Tile roofing (courtesy Ludowici-Celadon).*

Metal Roofing. For this type of roofing there is a wide choice of material, including copper, aluminum, galvanized iron, and terne. Of the metals used for roofing, copper is perhaps the most expensive and most lasting, requiring little maintenance (Fig. 9–57). It will weather to a greenish color called a patina. There are three types of joints for copper roofing: batten, flat, and standing. Batten seams are formed by nailing 2 × 2 wood strip in the direction of the slope or pitch, about 24 in. apart. Metal lengths are placed between the battens and bent up along the edge of the wooden batten to form a pan down

FIGURE 9–57   *Metal roofing.*

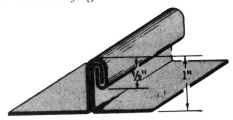

STANDING SEAM
Standing seams are used to join long dimensions of sheet lead in the direction of roof slope. Sheets should be not more than 16 square feet in area and are usually 3 lb. (3/64 inch thick) in weight.

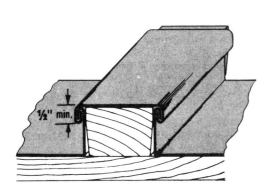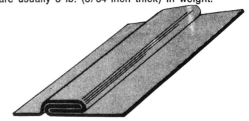

BATTEN SEAM
Batten seams are generally used for large sloping areas and are applicable to the same type of roofing applications as standing seams. They may be used alone or combined with standing seams to create patterns for architectural effect.

FLAT SEAM
Flat seams are usually auxiliary seams used in conjunction with either standing or batten seams. Their function is to close the cross seams at right angles to the roof slope. They should always be formed in the direction of flow.

STRUCTURAL DETAILS

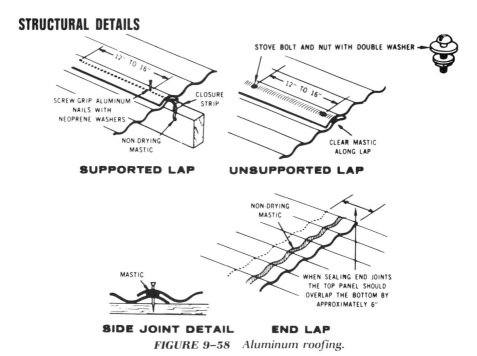

FIGURE 9-58   Aluminum roofing.

the slope of the roof. Cleats of the same metal are nailed to the edge of the batten and formed into a lock joint. The flat joints are soldered. A standing seam is formed by turning up one edge $1\frac{1}{2}$ in. and the adjoining edge $1\frac{1}{4}$ in. The two are bent and locked together without solder, held to the roof by cleats as in the method described above. Flat seams are simply soldered at adjoining pieces.

Aluminum: Aluminum roofing is generally made up of corrugated or fluted panels. Aluminum is not recommended in areas of saltwater spray. Aluminum should not come in direct contact with other metals because of a chemical action taking place which will break down the metal (Fig. 9-58). Both surfaces of unlike metals are coated with heavy asphalt paint or mastic.

Galvanized Metal: Sheets of 26 or 28 gauge metal should be coated with zinc of no less than 2 oz per square foot. End laps should be no less than 8 in. Lead-headed nails or galvanized nails with lead washers should be used. Galvanized metal roofing has a limited life span with an economical cost factor.

Terne Metal: Terne is copper-bearing sheet steel. The sheets are dip coated in a mixture of 80% lead and 20% tin. Grades are expressed in terms of weight of coating, the best being 40 lb. A wide variety of widths is available in 50-ft rolls. For best results, a terne metal roof must be painted with an iron oxide linseed oil–based primer as a base coat over which any good-quality exterior paint may be applied.

Flashing

Any object projecting through the roof, such as a chimney, piping, or skylight must be sealed against leakage with material called flashing. This is accomplished with lead, aluminum, copper, or fabric-reinforced paper or felt. Flashing is also used to join roofs to walls and valleys (Fig. 9-59).

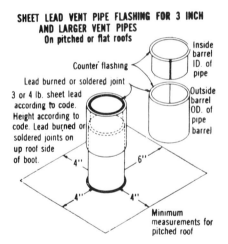

SHEET LEAD VENT PIPE FLASHING FOR 3 INCH AND LARGER VENT PIPES
On pitched or flat roofs

Counter flashing

Lead burned or soldered joint

3 or 4 lb. sheet lead according to code. Height according to code. Lead burned or soldered joints on up roof side of boot.

Inside barrel ID. of pipe

Outside barrel OD. of pipe barrel

4"   6"

4"   4"

Minimum measurements for pitched roof

FIGURE 9–59   Flashing.

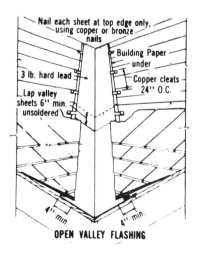

Nail each sheet at top edge only, using copper or bronze nails

Building Paper under

3 lb. hard lead

Copper cleats 24" O.C.

Lap valley sheets 6" min. unsoldered

4" min.   4" min.

OPEN VALLEY FLASHING

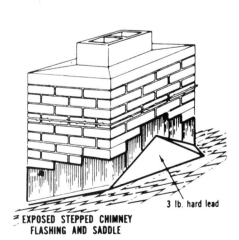

3 lb. hard lead

EXPOSED STEPPED CHIMNEY FLASHING AND SADDLE

FIGURE 9–59 (cont'd)

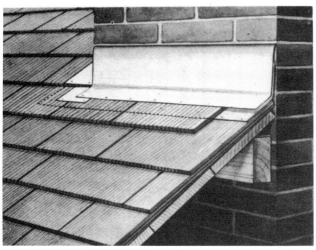

● Flashings at chimneys must be carefully placed to prevent leakage.

● Flashings and counter flashings are required against brick walls, but for wood walls, flashings in shingle lengths are completely satisfactory.

3 nails →

2 sheet metal screws with neoprene washers in slotted holes

4" lap

RAKE LAP

Metal cap flashing

Roofing cemented to wall

8 holes in cover plates punched for nailing

8"

COVER PLATE

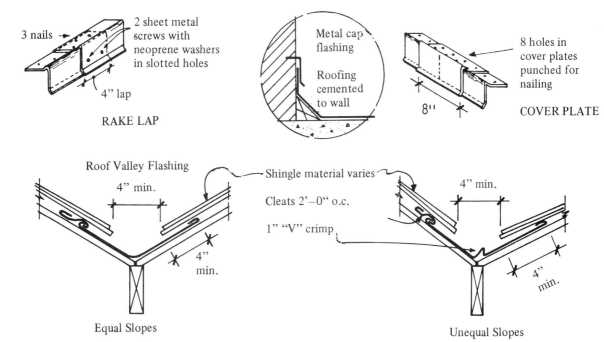

Roof Valley Flashing

4" min.

4" min.

Shingle material varies

Cleats 2'–0" o.c.

1" "V" crimp

4" min.

4" min.

Equal Slopes

Unequal Slopes

OPEN VALLEY FLASHING

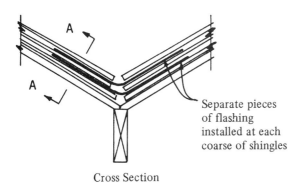

A

A

Separate pieces of flashing installed at each coarse of shingles

Cross Section

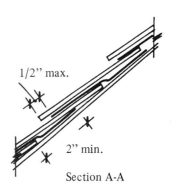

1/2" max.

2" min.

Section A-A

FIGURE 9-60 Cornice details.

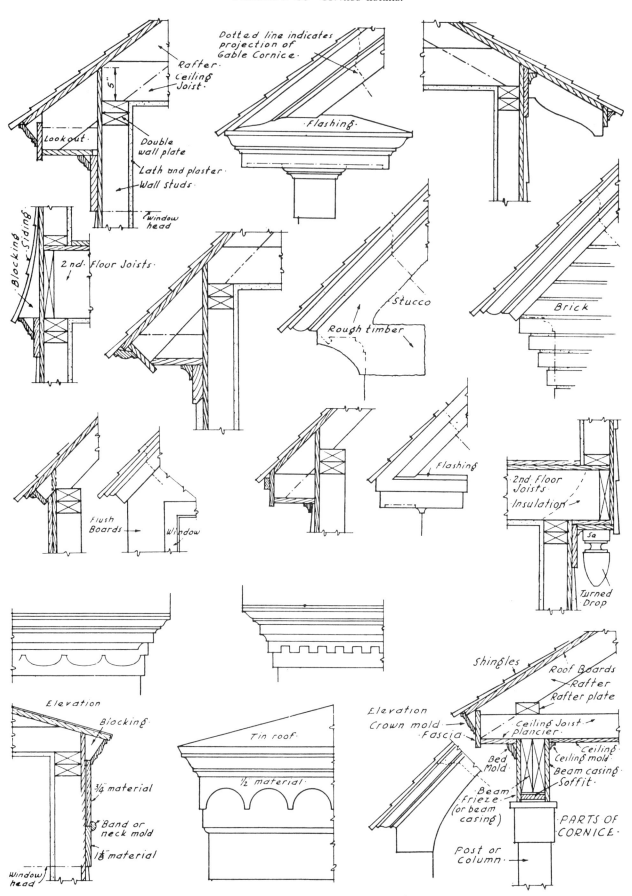

236

Cornices

The finish at the edge of the roof overhang is called a cornice or eave. The purpose is to close the intersection of walls and roof and to carry away from the building water which flows from the roof, preventing it from entering the building. The character of the building is strongly expressed in the design of the cornice, which may take a great variety of designs (Fig. 9–60). The projection of the roof may be wide or narrow, exposed or concealed, reflect a classic or a modern design, and may include gutters and/or conductors or not. The construction at the ends or gables of the roof is relatively simple because no water is carried off the roof at that point. The roof sheathing is extended just enough to allow moldings to be placed under the roof sheathing and rested against the gable. This molding is called a frieze and crown molding. The roof overhang is quite a different matter and a little more involved, because in addition to several moldings, a gutter (if used) must be installed. The gutter can be wood, aluminum, copper, or galvanized metal, hanging or built-in. The purpose of the gutter is to carry the water away from the building with conductors or downspouts (Fig. 9–61).

FIGURE 9–61 *Cornice and gutter construction.*

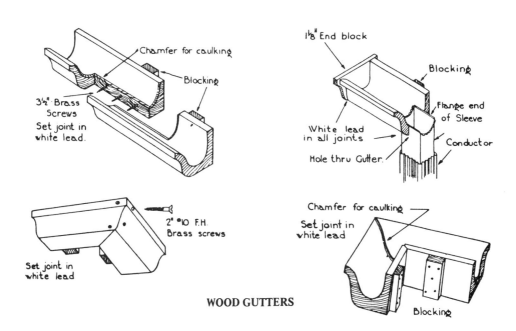

CORNICE CONSTRUCTION DETAIL

WOOD GUTTERS

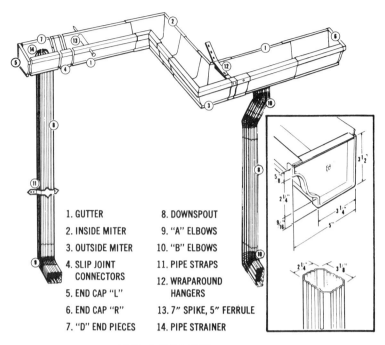

1. GUTTER   8. DOWNSPOUT
2. INSIDE MITER   9. "A" ELBOWS
3. OUTSIDE MITER   10. "B" ELBOWS
4. SLIP JOINT   11. PIPE STRAPS
   CONNECTORS   12. WRAPAROUND
5. END CAP "L"   HANGERS
6. END CAP "R"   13. 7" SPIKE, 5" FERRULE
7. "D" END PIECES   14. PIPE STRAINER

METAL GUTTERS
FIGURE 9–61   (cont'd)

There are so many ways of constructing a cornice that only a general description can be given in naming the parts. Gutter sizes are 6 by 4 in. and conductor sizes are 3 by 2 in. All gutters must pitch ever so slightly toward the conductors to allow water to run off. Gutters can be a troublespot, especially in colder climates. Ice buildup in gutters can cause a backup, and if the ice forces itself under the shingles, there may be a leak in the walls. The freezing and thawing action causes the water to be forced under the roof because the normal flow of water through the conductors via the gutters is blocked with ice. Hanging the gutters free of the building will help with this problem, and a better way is not to install any gutters. No harm will come from allowing the water to fall from the roof onto the ground; at worse, the ground may erode a bit. This can be resolved by placing a row of brick, crushed stone, or landscaping at that point on the ground, and with the proper grade pitch away from the building, the water will flow away.

Exterior Finishes

Stucco

Many stucco surfaces fail because of faulty application. Stucco is a plaster product with cement added used on the exterior surface of buildings, and comes in a great variety of colors and textures. Properly installed, it requires little or no maintenance. Any movement in the wall upon which stucco is applied will cause cracking. The secret of success is to minimize movement in the walls (Fig. 9–62). The furring strips act as a separator between the wall and the stucco and reduce wall movement.

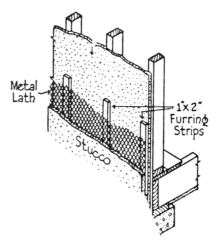

FIGURE 9–62 Stucco.

Stucco should not be applied when the temperature is 32 ° F or colder. It is a three-coat application, consisting of a scratch coat, which is the first coat; a brown coat, which is the second coat; and the finish or third coat. The finish coat is what produces the desired texture by smoothing or floating the surface with a wooden or metal trowel. Mixtures of sand or crushed stone may be thrown against the surface of the finish coat before it hardens to produce a sand or pebble finish.

A rustproof metal bead is applied at the bottom of the stucco wall to act as a stop and metal beads are also used on the exterior corners to protect the corners from breaking. These beads are installed with galvanized wire, wired to the metal lath before the first coat is applied. All metal or nails used for stucco should be rustproof. The bottom of stucco should extend $\frac{1}{2}$ in. below the top of the foundation.

Wood Shingles and Shakes

A continuous 1 × 3 wood furring strip is nailed along the entire perimeter of the walls over the paper with the bottom of the furring strip even with the bottom of the foundation wood sill. This strip is used as a starting course for the shingles to allow the first course to slope. The first course of wood shingles should be doubled. All courses should line with the top of all door frames and window frames and with the bottom of all windows. If there is a slight difference in the courses' dimensions, it will not be noticeable. The exposure may vary from 5 to 6 in.

There are several ways of treating corners. Interior corners can be resolved by nailing a $1\frac{1}{8} \times 1\frac{1}{8}$ in. finish wood strip in the corner and butting the shingles to it, or by alternating the shingle courses to avoid a straight-line joint. A third method is to use rustproof preformed metal corner pieces. Exterior corners can be treated by metal pieces, alternating the joints or by a 1 × 4 corner board (Fig. 9–63, page 240).

Red cedar shingles, grooved sidewall shakes, and handsplit shakes are well equipped by nature to endure without a protective finish or stain. In this state, the wood will eventually weather to a silver or dark gray. The speed of change and final shade depend mainly on atmosphere and climate conditions. Bleaching agents may be applied, in which case the wood will turn an antique silver gray. So-called natural finishes, which are lightly pigmented and maintain the original appearance of the wood, are available commercially. Stains,

FIGURE 9–63   *Wood siding.*

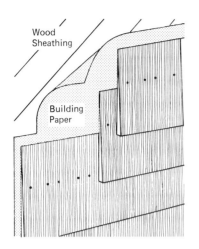

Wood Sheathing

Building Paper

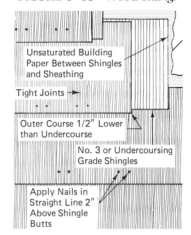

Unsaturated Building Paper Between Shingles and Sheathing

Tight Joints

Outer Course 1/2" Lower than Undercourse

No. 3 or Undercoursing Grade Shingles

Apply Nails in Straight Line 2" Above Shingle Butts

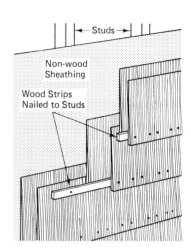

Studs

Non-wood Sheathing

Wood Strips Nailed to Studs

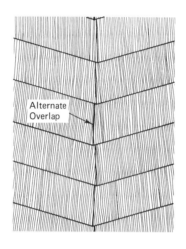

Alternate Overlap

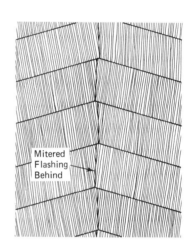

Mitered Flashing Behind

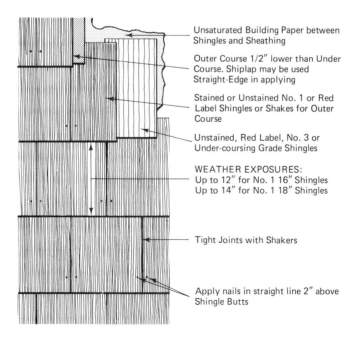

Unsaturated Building Paper between Shingles and Sheathing

Outer Course 1/2" lower than Under Course. Shiplap may be used Straight-Edge in applying

Stained or Unstained No. 1 or Red Label Shingles or Shakes for Outer Course

Unstained, Red Label, No. 3 or Under-coursing Grade Shingles

WEATHER EXPOSURES:
Up to 12" for No. 1 16" Shingles
Up to 14" for No. 1 18" Shingles

Tight Joints with Shakers

Apply nails in straight line 2" above Shingle Butts

whether heavy or semitransparent, are readily "absorbed" by cedar, and paints are most suitable, too.

As with shingle sidewalls, the double-course application requires an extra undercourse at the foundation line. Grooved sidewall shakes are also available in 4- and 8-ft-wide panels, for even faster application. Grooved sidewall shakes are marketed in a wide variety of factory-applied colors, ranging from delicate pastels to dark browns and greens. They are also available prime-coated for finish treatment after they are applied.

Since grooved-sidewall shakes are basically a rebutted-rejointed shingle with a machine-grooved surface, many of the requirements for shingle-sidewall application apply. But grooved-sidewall shakes are always applied double-coursed. This procedure yields a deep shadow line nearly 1 in. at the butt and greater coverage at lower cost, since extended weather exposures are possible over the undercourse of low-grade shingles. As with shingle sidewalls, the double-course application requires an extra undercourse at the foundation line. For even faster application, grooved-sidewall shakes are also available in 4- and 8-ft-wide panels.

Rebutted and rejoined shingles are shingles whose edges have been machine trimmed so as to be exactly parallel, with butts retrimmed at precisely right angles. They are used on sidewalls with tight-fitting joints to give a strong horizontal line. Available with the natural "sawed" face or with one face sanded smooth, they may be applied single or double coursed. Rebutted-rejointed shingles weather beautifully in the natural state. But they are often stained or painted, with excellent results.

Brick and Stone Veneer

The foundation and foundation wood sill construction will change slightly if masonry veneer is planned. In this case the foundation wood sill is flush with the inside foundation wall and a 6-in. shelf is constructed on the outside of the foundation wall to support the veneer. The level of the shelf should be about 6 in. below the finish grade. The face of the veneer is in line with the outside foundation. Conventional brick is $2\frac{1}{2}$ in. high, 4 in. deep, and 8 in. long. The 4-in. dimension rests on the shelf. Brick is made of a natural clay product of the dimensions indicated above. This mold is baked in an oven or kiln. The moisture evaporates, shrinking the brick to about $2\frac{1}{4}$ in. high, $3\frac{5}{8}$ in. deep, and $7\frac{5}{8}$ in. long (Fig. 9–64, page 242).

The veneer can be carried to any height on the wall or walls. If carried only partway up, the top of the veneer must be capped to look finished. This is accomplished by turning the brick on end or by using some form of flat stone as a cap (Fig. 9–65, page 242). The brick is $3\frac{5}{8}$ in. deep and the shelf is 6 in. deep, which leaves a cavity of $2\frac{3}{8}$ in. behind the brick wall or between the back of the brick and the wall sheathing. This cavity or void is important and must be left as is. It is designed to prevent water from penetrating the wall. Moisture and water will penetrate the veneer and fall behind the veneer into the cavity and be carried away through holes in the joints of the brick near the bottom called weep holes. The weep holes are installed in the brick courses at or near the bottom (one row only). This area is also flashed to prevent the water from entering below the brick coursing.

Brick or stone used in this fashion will not support itself laterally without falling over and therefore must be supported by the stud wall. It also serves

Frame Wall with Masonry Veneer Base

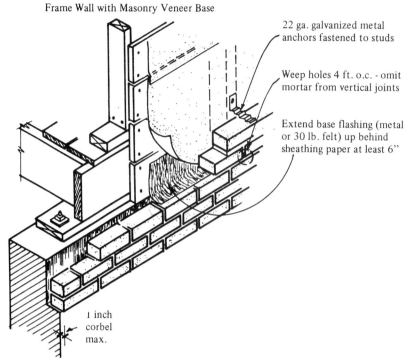

22 ga. galvanized metal anchors fastened to studs

Weep holes 4 ft. o.c. - omit mortar from vertical joints

Extend base flashing (metal or 30 lb. felt) up behind sheathing paper at least 6''

1 inch corbel max.

FIGURE 9–64 *Brick veneer.*

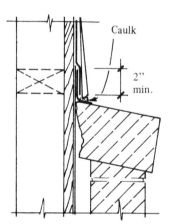

Caulk

2'' min.

FIGURE 9–65 *Brick veneer sill.*

no structural function but acts only as a curtain wall or veneer. If the veneer were to be removed, the building will remain standing. The veneer must be tied to the stud walls or wood frame with galvanized metal ties. These ties are nailed to the stud wall and bent at a mortar joint and embedded into the mortar, locking the veneer to the stud wall. Ties are installed every third course in height spaced about 16 in. apart. A wood molding is applied at the doors and windows to seal the space between the brick and the doors and windows. Later, this irregular brick line is sealed with caulking compound. Veneer coursing should be planned to line with the tops of all openings. The brick height should not be cut to fit. The window and door sills can be of brick laid on edge with a slope similar to the cap mentioned earlier. The angle of the slope will allow the sill top to line with a course. If brick is continued above the top openings, a steel angle or lintel is used to support the brick. Usually, a $5 \times 3\frac{1}{2} \times \frac{5}{16}$ in. angle (for normal spans), bearing at least 4 in. on both sides

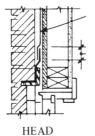

Lap sheathing paper over flashing as shown. Where sheathing paper is not required, extend flashing up behind sheathing.

Turn up flashing 2" minimum.

Extend metal flashing sufficiently at jambs to prevent penetration of water at these points.

HEAD

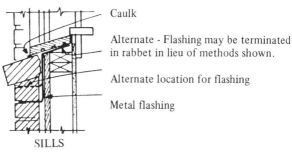

Caulk

Alternate - Flashing may be terminated in rabbet in lieu of methods shown.

Alternate location for flashing

Metal flashing

SILLS

FIGURE 9–66   Brick veneer flashing.

of opening is used to support the brick, such as over doors, windows, or any other type of opening. Flashing is installed between the back of the brick and the angle to seal the void, preventing water from entering or leaking through to the inside. Flashing is also required at the sill between the underside of the wood window sill and the joint between the last course and the masonry sill (Fig. 9–66).

Brick is available in many colors, textures, and patterns and are sold in lots of 1000. Sometimes the symbol "M" is used to represent 1000. Brick takes on a natural clay color, but sometimes earth colors are added to the mix to form a blend of colors. Two types of brick are used in construction. The first and most expensive, face brick, used for a finish. The second type, common brick, is less expensive and is used only as a filler or backup; it is not visible when the wall is completed. Common brick is sometimes molded from concrete. For veneer purposes, a hard-burned moisture-resistant brick should be used.

Patterns of brick coursing include common bond, English bond, Flemish bond, and stack bond (Fig. 9–67, page 244). A stretcher course is brick laid with the 8-in. surface exposed, in a header course the 2-in. surface is exposed, and a soldier course is brick on end with the 8-in. surface in a vertical position. Common bond consists of five stretcher courses and one header course, with the pattern repeated over and over. English Bond is one header course and one stretched course. Flemish bond coursing is alternating headers and stretchers in the same row. Stack bond is simply lining up all joints, vertically and horizontally.

Often, white stains appear on the surface of a brick wall. These stains, caused by the water dissolving in sodium lime and magnesium (the mortar), are called efflorescence. They can be removed easily by washing with diluted muriatic acid using a special brush.

Sandstone and limestone are commonly used for stone veneer. Ready-mix mortars are available in which enough water is simply added to make the mix a working consistency, or mortar is mixed by using one part portland cement, three parts sand, and 15% by volume hydrated lime. The installation of brick

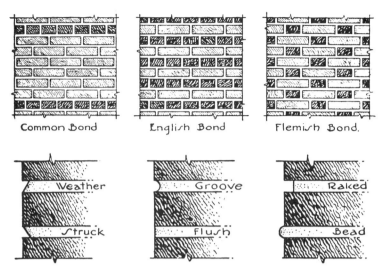

FIGURE 9–67 *Brick coursing.*

is similar to that of block. Existing homes without shelved foundations can be veneered by installing a continuous $4 \times 6 \times \frac{3}{8}$ in. galvanized angle lagged to the foundation just a few courses below the finish grade level. Lag bolts should be galvanized and installed about $4'-0''$ apart.

Horizontal Siding

Several exterior wall surface products are termed horizontal siding. They include clapboards, bevel siding, novelty siding, and lap siding (Fig. 9–68). Redwood, western cedar, and cypress require no finish and can be allowed to be exposed and natural. Any other wood species require paint or stain. Bevel siding or clapboards are used widely in present-day residential construction. Units are cut to varying widths ranging from 4 to 12 in. and a butt thickness of $\frac{1}{2}$ to $\frac{3}{4}$ in. with lapping courses of from 1 to 2 in. The wider the siding, the more exposure of the courses there will be. All nails are exposed with this type of siding and should be rustproof; if not, rust will bleed to the surface and stain the finish. Lap siding is similar to beveled siding without the bevel; novelty siding is a tongue-and-groove siding sometimes used without sheathing (nailing directly to studs) mostly for vacation homes or garages and offers an economical way to cover exterior walls.

FIGURE 9–68 *Wood siding.*

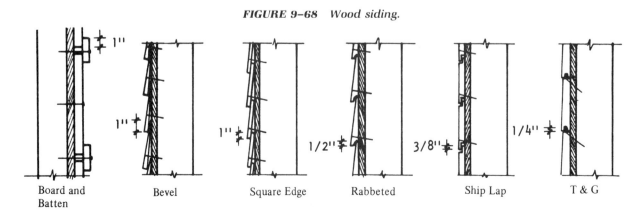

Vertical Siding and Plywood

V joint, tongue and groove, battens, and lap joint are some of the designs available for vertical siding. The siding may be plain or rough sawed, of matched or patterned boards, square edge or plywood, or of notched or solid boards (Fig. 9–69). Plywood should be sealed at all edges before installation and solid boards should not be more than 8 in. wide nailed with two 8d nails about 4′–0″ apart. As with other siding, all should extend about ½ in. below the top of the foundation with the starter panel and sheathing covered with paper. Battens are narrow pieces of wood covering the vertical joints of siding, either plywood or wide square-edge boards. Battens are nailed to only one side of the siding to allow for movement during expansion and construction.

FIGURE 9–69   *Exterior wood siding.*

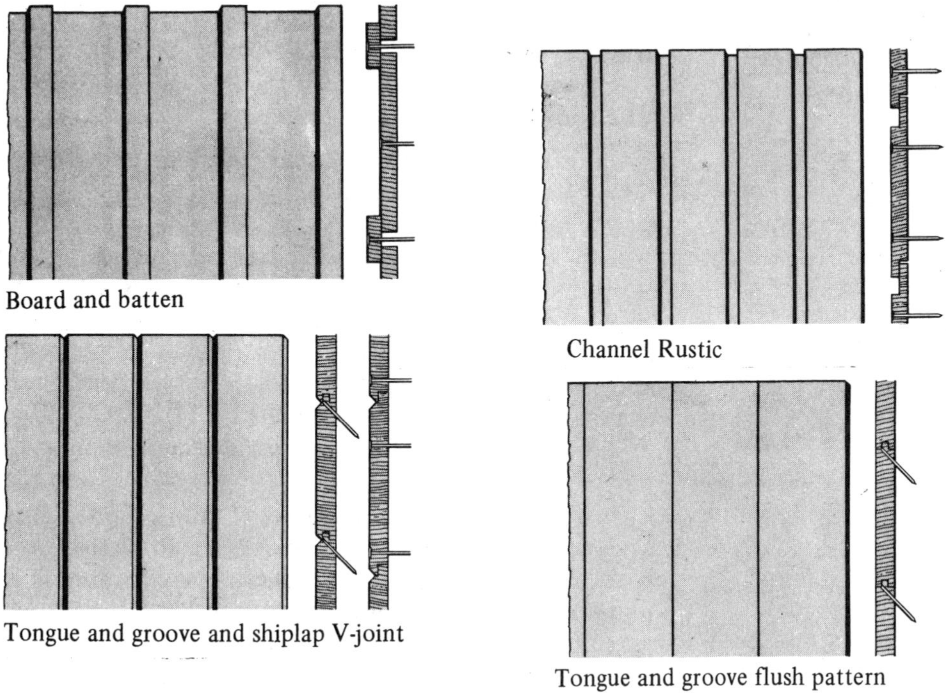

Board and batten

Channel Rustic

Tongue and groove and shiplap V-joint

Tongue and groove flush pattern

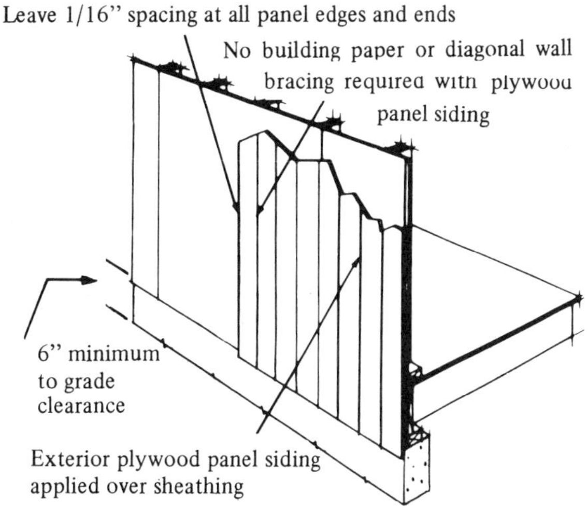

Leave 1/16" spacing at all panel edges and ends

No building paper or diagonal wall bracing required with plywood panel siding

6" minimum to grade clearance

Exterior plywood panel siding applied over sheathing

Composition Siding

Panels vary from $\frac{3}{8}$ to $\frac{5}{8}$ in. thick, up to 4′–0″ wide, and 9′–0″ long, made in various patterns such as reverse board, battens, V groove, lap, flat, horizontal, or vertical. They are available in unpainted, primed, or factory finished.

Re-Siding

Practically any of the siding described can be used for remodeling or re-siding over old siding without removing the old siding. The wood trim may have to be modified or built out to accommodate the added wall thickness, and additional moldings may have to be used around doors and windows.

Aluminum and Vinyl Siding

For alterations of homes without insulation in the walls, aluminum or vinyl siding offers the best opportunity (Fig. 9–70). There is no need to remove old siding. Some aluminum or vinyl siding has a factory-applied insulation sandwiched between the panels. These units are manufactured in double courses of panels in clapboard design in lengths up to 12′–6″. Panels are also available for vertical installation. Either way, there is a wide selection of color and texture, all of which are blind nailed. Special shapes are available for trim work, and this material can be cut easily with a hacksaw or sheet metal shears. Courses are 4 or 8 in. wide in the horizontal direction and about 12 in. wide in the vertical. Special aluminum fasteners must be used with $1\frac{1}{2}$-in. rustproof nails.

One of the disadvantages of aluminum siding is that it dents and scratches easily and cannot be repaired successfully without replacing the panel. Putting a ladder against aluminum siding is difficult without denting and any object thrown against the siding can cause damage.

Vinyl siding is a PVC (polyvinyl chloride) product installed in much the same manner as aluminum siding, with all the same accessories, patterns, textures, and sizes as aluminum. Like aluminum, these panels require no painting or maintenance. Vinyl will not scratch but ultraviolet rays (sunshine) may discolor the finish.

Acoustical Treatment

Acoustical treatment in residential construction is designed primarily for comfort. To be effective, the comfort takes into account hearing and sound. The three subjective points of sound are degree of loudness, pitch of sound, and quality of sound. Loudness is a measure of sound energy per second. Pitch measures the frequency of sound or tone and tells if it is a high sound or low sound. All of this is measured in decibels, or rate of sound, and once we know how many of the noises we want to shut out, we can design accordingly by

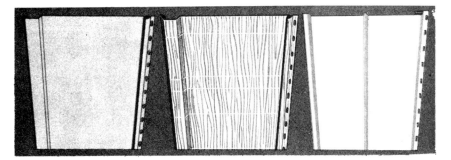

12-INCH VERTICAL   **V-GROOVE**

Inside Corner Post

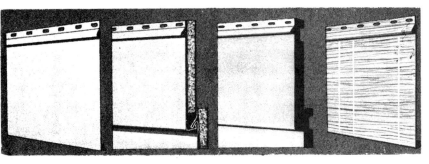

8-INCH HORIZONTAL

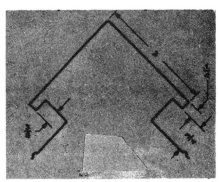

Outsidé Corner Post

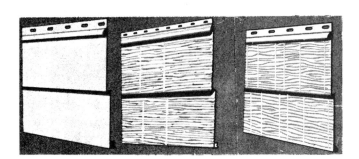

DOUBLE 4-INCH HORIZONTAL

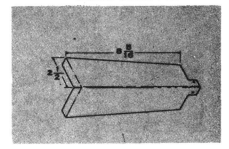

Outside Corner Cap

FIGURE 9–70   Vinyl and aluminum siding.

selecting building material that has been tested for sound absorption. Unwanted noise is unpleasant, reduces efficiency, and can cause fatigue. The types of residential noises that can be annoying come from conversation, television, record/tape players, radios, typewriters, musical instruments, vacuum cleaners, dish and clothes washers, washing machines, poorly designed plumbing, heating, ventilation, and air-conditioning systems, power tools, and kitchen appliances. When sound is generated within a room, sound waves strike the walls, floors, and ceilings, causing these surfaces to vibrate like a diaphragm or drum, reproducing these sounds on the opposite side of the room, reflected back into the room. The remainder of the sound is absorbed by the surfaces. As sound moves through a surface or barrier, its intensity is reduced by an action called Sound Transmission Loss (STL). The transmission loss of a surface depends on the material, design, and quality of construction. Another system used for rating sound is the Sound Transmission Class (STC). The higher the number rating, the better the sound barrier.

Walls

One of the most effective sound barrier partitions is a double partition with insulation between the studs (Fig. 9–71). The purpose is to separate the finish on both sides of the wall to prevent sound from transmitting through the partition and into the room. Each wall finish has its own row of studs. A second method, not as effective, is called the spring clip method. Metal spring clips are nailed to a single stud wall on both sides of the studs. Gypsum wallboard is clipped or attached to the spring clips, separating the finish wall surface from the studs.

Care must be taken if doors are installed in the partition because the wall treatment is no better than the door treatment for soundproofing. Double rabbetted door frames are used with two solid-core doors in the frame, one at each side of the wall. Both doors should be weatherstripped to prevent sound from leaking through. Windows also need to be soundproofed with double glazing and a neoprene strip to hold both panes of glass in place.

FIGURE 9–71   *Acoustical treatment at walls.*

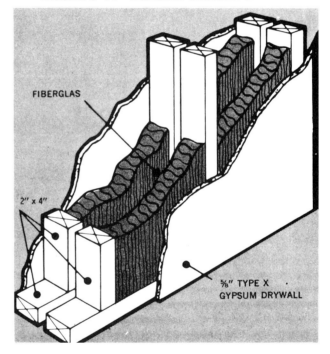

SPRING CLIP   **RESILIENT METAL CLIP**

Floors and Ceilings

Wall treatment is not enough. Floors and ceilings must also be treated because sound will telegraph through these surfaces as well. In new construction, the wall should be separated from the floor and ceiling by installing a neoprene gasket between the shoe and the subfloor and the same gasket between the ceiling and the plate (Fig. 9–72). The partition is literally floating free of the floor and ceiling. Suspended acoustical ceilings, carpeted floor, upholstered furniture, heavy drapes, and soft wall finishes such as cork, carpet, acoustical wall panels, drapes, perforated or porous fiberboard, and acoustical plaster will help to absorb sound.

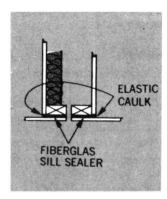

FIGURE 9–72 Acoustical treatment at floors.

An existing room can be soundproofed by floating another floor over the existing floor, separating the two with a fiberglass wood blanket. The walls can be soundproofed by building a separate second wall as explained above.

Insulation

There is no secret to saving energy, but there are limits as to how much energy can be saved in a home, because energy is required for comfort in heating, cooling, and lighting. Our purpose is to conserve and not use more than is required to meet these needs. The types of energy used in heating and cooling are gas (natural or artificial), oil, and electricity. Solar energy must have a supplementary backup system and is not yet designed as a main source of energy.

The amount of heat that is lost through various factors within a house is calculated and the conclusion is a rated heating unit in number of Btu. This heat loss is determined by area of building; area of glass; area of exterior walls; type of building material used in construction of the walls, floor, and ceiling; and heat loss through cracks, known as infiltration. The smaller the Btu capacity, the smaller the unit and consequently the less energy required. The idea is to heat the building to a desired temperature and to sustain or maintain that temperature with a minimum of heat loss. There are several ways to reduce this heat loss.

Warm air is attracted to cold air, so that when a door is opened, cold air does not come in, warm air goes out. Our purpose is to reduce, as much as possible, this heat loss by making a building as tight as practical by the use of insulation, weatherstripping, storm windows and doors, and so on, to hold in as much heat as we can.

Reduce the ratio of exterior wall surface to floor area by carefully dimensioning the overall size of the house attached. Garages and carports will reduce heat loss. Reducing the ceiling height from 8′–0″ to 7′–6″ will save about 400 Btu. The following suggestions are based on an average-sized house with about 1200 square feet of floor space. As near a square as possible in house shape can save as much as 600 Btu. Another 1000 Btu can be gained by avoiding H-, L-, and T-shaped houses. Reducing the window area to about 10% of the floor area can save about 3000 Btu. Installing double glazing or storm sash will save another 6000 Btu. Raising the sill height of the windows will not only provide for better natural light but helps keep the house cooler in the summer because of the roof overhang. The quality of windows affects the heat loss. A poorly fitted window with no weatherstripping can cause as much as five times the infiltration of that of an average better-fitted window. In terms of heat loss, this can be as much as 25,000 Btu. Storm sash alone will save about 3500 Btu.

Saving energy for air conditioning must also be considered, and the use of storm sash or double glazing is necessary to keep heat out, thereby reducing the load on the air-conditioning equipment. A 30-ft roof overhang is an important part of energy conservation, in that it will reduce heat in the summer and help reduce heat loss in the winter by as much as 1200 Btu. The average house has two exterior doors, and if storm doors are installed, as much as another 600 Btu can be saved; further, if these doors have interlocking weatherstripping, an additional 1400 Btu is gained.

In cold climates, attaching the garage or carport on the northerly exposure, and in hot climates on the easterly exposure, will help conserve energy. Trees help by providing shade in the summer and act as a buffer in winter. Air-conditioning compressors should be located in the shade to help increase compressor efficiency. In a ventilated crawl space, install operating vents that can be closed in winter. A vapor barrier and perimeter insulation under a concrete floor slab in basementless houses will reduce energy costs. Uninsulated heating ducts in nonlivable areas such as a crawl space will help keep the area warm in that heat loss through the ducts will warm the floor above; however, if the ducts are insulated, that heat loss could be avoided. In a full-basement house with an average of 2′–0″ of basement wall exposure above ground, heat loss through a 12-in.-thick foundation wall would be about 10,000 Btu. By installing 1½-in. insulation on the interior of the exterior walls, approximately 1300 Btu can be saved.

Insulation is rated by thermal factor or R value, which is the resistance of the material to heat flowing through the insulation. The higher the R value, the greater the insulating value. There are many types, forms, and thicknesses of insulation. Insulation is light in weight because the principal ingredient is air. The air is trapped by hundreds of tiny cells. The material forming the cells may be mineral, glass, fibers, vegetable, wood, cotton, corn or sugarcane stalks, animal hair, or a variety of chemicals or foams. There are many different types of insulation: rigid, blanket or batt, loose (or fill), reflective, and foam (Fig. 9–73).

Rigid. This is board-type insulation measuring generally 24 in. by 88 in. and in thicknesses of ½ in. up to 3½ in. It is made of various mineral, wood, and vegetable products and glass. It is used principally over foundations, under

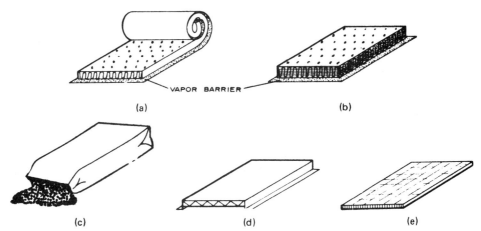

FIGURE 9–73 *Types of insulation: (a) blanket; (b) batt; (c) fill; (d) reflective (one type); (e) rigid (courtesy U.S. Department of Agriculture).*

FIGURE 9–74 *Rigid insulation (courtesy Pittsburgh Corning Corporation).*

concrete floors on grade, and on flat roofs. It is also formed to fit the core of masonry units, such as concrete block (Fig. 9–74).

Blanket or Batt.   This insulation can be in the shape of a batt or blanket. Batt insulation is 15 in. and 23 in. wide and 2 and 4 ft long in thicknesses from 2 to 12 in. Blanket or batt insulation is manufactured of loosely felted mats of vegetable or mineral fibers. Blanket insulation can be faced with a variety of covers, including a vapor barrier, or it can be unfaced (Fig. 9–75).

Loose (or Fill).   This type is made from various materials in bulk form, is free flowing, and is either blown or poured in place between the studs, rafters,

Rips or tears in vapor barriers should be patched after installation. Always install vapor barriers toward the warm-in-winter side of the construction.

Stuff pink insulation in small spaces between studs and in small cracks around doors and window framing to help eliminate heat leaks.

Exterior Walls

In room additions, insulate exterior walls with faced insulation stapled in place with vapor barrier facing on warm-in-winter side. Or, unfaced insulation can be used with a separate vapor barrier of either polyethylene or foil-backed gypsum board.

Basement Walls

Insulate basement walls by installing framework of studs or furring strips against masonry walls. Nail bottom plate directly to floor and top plate to joists above. Install pink insulation between studs or furring strips.

Walls Between Heated and Unheated Areas

Insulate walls between heated and unheated areas by placing pink insulation between studs with vapor barrier facing warm-in-winter side. Staple facing at top and hold in place with bowed wire, chicken wire, criss-crossed wires or other methods.

Unfloored Attics

Lay pink Fiberglas insulation between the joists of your attic. If there is no insulation now, use faced insulation with the vapor barrier facing down. If you're adding more insulation, use unfaced Fiberglas insulation. Be sure your insulation covers the top plate but doesn't block any air vents at the eaves.

Unfinished Ceilings

Install faced Fiberglas insulation between joists of an unfinished ceiling by stapling flanges to inside of joists. Unfaced insulation is simply pushed into place and a separate vapor barrier of either polyethylene film or foil-backed gypsum board installed.

Floors

Install pink Fiberglas insulation with the vapor barrier facing upward toward the heated area. Use bowed wire, chicken wire, criss-crossed wire, or other methods to hold the insulation in place.

Small details that make a big difference

The more complete and uniform you make the insulation barrier around your home, the greater the savings and comfort. The precautions shown will pay big dividends.

Insulation installed behind pipes and electrical outlets can help eliminate frozen pipes and drafts around outlets.

FIGURE 9–75   Blanket insulation (courtesy Pittsburgh Corning Corporation).

or joists. This type of insulation is best used in homes being altered or remodeled, where the framework is not exposed. It is manufactured from glass, rock wool, wood fibers, bark, cork, vermiculite, perlite, gypsum, and sawdust. Holes need to be made in the exterior wall to blow the insulation in place; the holes are later patched. The blown-in procedure will fill the spaces between the studs, rafters, or joists. This type of insulation can also be poured in the core of concrete block. There is no built-in vapor barrier with loose insulation. A separate barrier must be installed.

Reflective. This is usually a single-sheet type of insulation using mostly aluminum foil. It acts as a vapor barrier as well and is designed to reflect the heat inside the building. Frequently, this single sheet of reflective insulation is part of another type of insulation, such as a batt or blanket. It is also attached to wallboard, gypsum lath, and other types as rigid insulation. In summer, the reflective insulation will reflect the heat from the sun back outside the wall, making the building cooler inside. In winter the reflective insulation will reflect the heat from the house back into the house, helping to keep the house warm. To be effective, this type of insulation must have at least a $\frac{3}{4}$-in. air space around it. If it is in contact with any other building material, it will not be reflective.

Foam. Most commonly a urea-formaldehyde resin, this insulation is pumped into walls between studs of new and existing buildings. Foam is also manufactured as rigid-board insulation. Like the loose or poured-in type, foam is best used on houses that are being altered or remodeled, where the framework is not exposed. Holes are made in the wall and the foam insulation is pumped into the space between the studs in liquid form, which solidifies in about 10 hours. It cures in about 30 days. The holes in the exterior walls are later patched.

Condensation

One of the biggest headaches a homeowner can face is the problem of condensation. The headache can be cured, usually easily and cheaply, by means of vapor barriers and ventilation. But very few people understand the mechanics of vapor barriers, ventilation, and condensation.

Paint failure on exterior walls is very often caused by water vapor from inside the home. As excess water builds up indoors during the cold season, it migrates outward and condenses on the cold house siding. It soaks the wood, stains the siding, and causes peeling paint. Or the vapor may try to push right on out through the paint, causing blisters.

Excess water vapor migrates to an unheated attic in the winter. There it condenses and forms ice. Over the winter months, the ice builds up. When warm weather comes, the ice melts. It drips down to the ceiling below and causes damage. Water vapor condenses in a cold wall cavity and soaks the insulation. This makes the insulation less effective. Heating costs rise. Water vapor migrates outward and condenses on the cold inner face of a brick veneer wall. It then soaks through the bricks, leaching out salts in the bricks and depositing a white powdery stain called efflorescence on the outer face of the wall. All these problems and others, including rot and decay, can be eliminated with a proper vapor barrier, and in some cases, minimal ventilation. Ideally, both barrier and ventilation would have been built into the house during construction.

A vapor barrier is anything that restricts the passage of water vapor. It may be a plastic film, aluminum foil fastened to insulation batts, special types of paper, even certain kinds of paint. The primary location for a vapor barrier is between any heated area and the cold area next to it. The important thing to remember is that the barrier always goes on the warm side of that floor, ceiling, or wall, because that stops the migration of the vapor before it can reach a cold surface, where it will condense and cause damage.

Windows and Energy Saving

New generations of glass and recent advances in frame design and construction are only some of the factors that have helped bring windows to the point where many wooden and aluminum models now on the market have U values in a high range. Windows perform six energy functions: solar heating, daylighting, shading, insulation, air tightness, and ventilation.

Glass

There are three basic varieties of glass:

1. Plain, clear glass is the least energy efficient type.
2. Glass that absorbs heat, absorbs the sun's rays, and reradiates the energy, chiefly to the outside.
3. Reflective, or high-performance glass, controls the amount of light and heat that passes through it from as low as 8% to nearly any degree of solar radiation desired. This type can be tinted silver, gold, gray, blue, or bronze on the outside without coloring the light that passes through it to the interior. The color offers obvious design uses in addition to their primary energy control role.

Multiple glazing improves the efficiency of all three types of glass, since it is essentially a means of providing insulation. Glass is a good conductor of heat, and multiple glazing provides insulating air space to reduce heat losses. The greatest reduction in U values with the most efficiency takes place when the space between the glass panels is between $\frac{3}{16}$ and $\frac{5}{8}$ of an inch in width. Triple glazing is more effective then double glazing with the same overall width. Triple glazing with two $\frac{1}{4}$-in. air spaces has a U value of 0.47 compared to 0.58 for double glazing with a single $\frac{1}{2}$-in. air space. Even greater efficiency is possible: an uncoated triple-glazed window with two $\frac{1}{2}$-in. air spaces has a U value of 0.36.

Ceiling and Wall Treatment

Ceilings

One of the least expensive ways of finishing a ceiling is with acoustical tile. There are basically three construction methods in doing this: cement to a solid sound surface; apply to 1×3 wood furring strips spaced 12 in. apart; and use suspended or lay-in panels called tees with a metal suspension system. The selection of texture, color, and tile size is varied: 12×12 in., 12×24 in., and 24×48 in. in thickness of $\frac{1}{2}$ and $\frac{5}{8}$ in. made of mineral fiber, asbestos, or fiberglass (Fig. 9–76).

FIGURE 9–76   *Acoustical tile ceiling: (a) cemented; (b) wood furring; (c) suspended.*

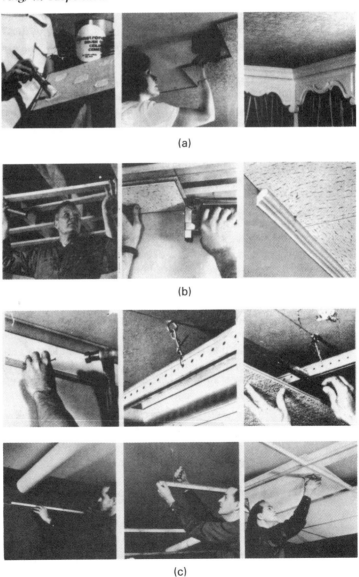

(a)

(b)

(c)

Exposed Wood Plank

Unlike most conventional ceilings in wood frame construction, in plank and beam construction the plank or wooden ceiling is a structural part of the framing system in conjunction with the structural wooden beams, all of which are exposed for a finished ceiling. With this type of system, no further finish is required on the wood (Fig. 9–43).

Prefinished Plywood

One of the richest-looking and most attractive interior wall finishes is prefinished plywood. The sizes of plywood panels are $\frac{3}{16}$ and $\frac{1}{4}$ in. thick in a width of 4'-0" with lengths of 7'-0" and 8'-0". One of the advantages of prefinished plywood is the ease of maintenance; all that is required is an application of paste wax about every six months. The material is available in nutmeg, oak, birch, elm, pecan, pine, cherry, hickory, cedar, cypress, cottonwood, teak, rosewood, butternut, redwood, chestnut, mahogany, and other woods and in random width, grooved, V grooved, channel grooved, random scoring, and pegged. Finishes range from antique to shadows, plank, tonings, and embossed.

The way a log is cut determines the finish surface of the panel; plain sliced will give a subdued grain appearance, whereas rotary cut will accentuate the grain with a finger-grain appearance. In alteration work, if the existing wall is sound and secure, the panels can be applied directly to the wall surface. This material can be applied either by nailing or with ready-to-use adhesive.

Composition Paneling

These panels are made by several manufacturers and can be had in simulated wood grain finish, stone, brick and several designs of deeply dimensional textures. All panels are mirror images with no variation in grain or color. These panels are for interior use only and the application is similar to that of plywood.

Hardwood is a man-made wood product, also known as pressed wood or board, composition board, fiber board, flakeboard, and other descriptive or brandname products. Basically, this material is made from wood residue—fiber, chips, flakes, particles, and shavings—to produce a usable by-product from materials wasted or leftover in processing or manufacturing lumber and plywood. Hardboard is a smooth panel with knots or grain, yet is made almost entirely of natural wood cellulose for strength. The fibers are rearranged to provide special properties of hardness and density. Hardboard will not crack or splinter, check craze, or flake and is impact resistant. The panels are available in sizes up to 4'-0" wide and 8'-0" long, in thicknesses from $\frac{1}{8}$ to $\frac{1}{4}$ in., surfaced smooth on one or both sides.

Wood Fiber Substrate

Processed wood fiber (particleboard, hardboard) wall panels are available with grain-printed vinyl or paper overlays, or printed face surface. These prefinished panels are rigid, appealing, and economical. Thicknesses range from $\frac{1}{8}$ to $\frac{1}{4}$ in.

Groove Treatment

Most vertical wall panelings are "random-grooved," with grooves falling on 16 in. centers so that nailing over studs will be consistent.

Other groove treatments included uniform spacing (4, 8, 16 in.) and cross-scored grooves randomly spaced to give a "plank effect." Grooves are generally striped darker than the panel surface.

Grooves are cut or embossed into the panel in V grooves or channel grooves. Less expensive panels sometimes have a groove just "striped" on the surface (Fig. 9–77).

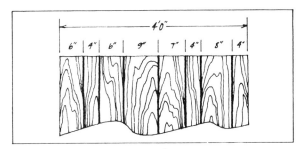

FIGURE 9–77   Prefinished plywood grooves.

Hardboard paneling

Panels of ⅛-in. thick hardboard are designed to perform well when applied to flat interior surfaces above grade. They should not be used below grade, especially over masonry walls.

To prevent warping, ⅛-in. hardboard panels must be solidly supported (backed) by plywood, drywall (plasterboard), or sound, dry plaster construction. Fastening direct to studs or over furring strips is not recommended.

Fiberglass Paneling

Fiberlass panels 4′-0″ × 8′-0″ simulate brick, stone, and wood. The panels are fingered for joining, pretrimmed, and precut ready for installation with no cutting or sawing except closing. The seams or joints on the mortar line are filled with a special compound to match the panels. The panels are applied with a special adhesive backing pressed into place and nailed at the mortar joints about 12 in. apart along every other joint line.

Laminated Plastic

Laminated plastic in many colors and patterns is available from several companies. It consists of several layers of kraft paper impregnated with resins fused together in a press at a pressure of more than 1000 lb per inch and a temperature of 250 °F. Patterns are printed and protected by a plastic coating. This product is manufactured in four different types: type I for counters and tables, type II for tabletops and sink tops, type III for furniture and walls, and type IV for paneling and doors. Sheet sizes are $4'$-$0'' \times 8'$-$0''$ and larger and care must be used in handling because they break very easily. Laminated plastic must be applied to a solid backing preferably plywood, with a special adhesive brushed on the back side of the panel. It is ideally suited for kitchen countertops and walls. Metal moldings are used for interior and exterior corners.

Factory Vinyl-Surfaced Plasterboard

Another wall covering is plasterboard with vinyl surfacing preapplied at the factory in a thickness of $\frac{1}{2}$ in. thick and $8'$-$0''$, $9'$-$0''$, and $10'$-$0''$ lengths. Woodgrain patterns come in both square edges and beveled edges. There are two basic methods of applying this material over a solid backing: nailing and adhesive. Nailing, with color-coded nailheads to match the fabric, is done along the entire perimeter of the panel with nails positioned about 12 in. apart. Adhesive is applied with a caulking gun similar to that for plywood panels, including nailing at the top and bottom of the panel. The adhesive is special, as recommended by the manufacturer. The colors and patterns are as varied as for sheet-rolled vinyl, the only difference being that they are factory applied to a plasterboard backing. Trim accessories are matching color metal molding used at exterior corners and trimming around doors and windows, and around top and bottom moldings.

Vinyl Wallcovering and Paper

Vinyl is a chemical product made into a wall covering in designs ranging from plain to prints and embossings. In texture it varies from relatively smooth to deep three-dimensional effects. There are three qualities of vinyl wall covering: type I, light duty, weighing a minimum of 7oz per square yard, for use in areas exposed to normal ordinary wear; type II, medium duty, with a minimum weight of 13 oz per square yard, used for walls with better wearing quality with deeper and more attractive embossing; and type III, heavy duty, with a minimum weight of 22 oz per square yard, used for walls with heavy traffic, such as lobbies and corridors in public buildings. Vinyl wallcovering generally comes in rolls of 54 in. widthin.

Vinyl wall covering must be applied on a smooth-surfaced wall such as plaster or drywall in sound condition. Masonry block or concrete walls can be used if filled with plaster or cement rubbed smooth. If applying on a painted surface, all loose paint and scale must be removed. If application is over a new plaster or drywall surface, a coat of sizing will be necessary to fill the pores of the wall, affording the paste greater holding power.

Architectural Paneling

Genuine solid wood veneer cut paper thin in widths up to 24 in. and lengths up to $22'$-$0''$ is available in a wide variety of wood species. This product is a wall covering applied similar to vinyl wall covering. The wood finish is raw and requires finishing after installation by sanding slightly.

Interior Planking

Solid wood ½ and ¾ in. thick, 4 to 12 in. wide in random widths, V groove, square edge, channel rustic, spaced boards, and finger joined, to be applied vertically or horizontally, is available in prefinished or unfinished redwood, walnut, oak, ash, cypress, butternut, cottonwood, pecan, cherry, and pine. It may be applied directly over studs for new work and over existing wall surfaces in remodeling work with no preparation of existing wall. All planking is tongue and grooved.

Ceramic Tile

A clay product in thicknesses of ¼, ⁵⁄₁₆, ½, and ⁷⁄₁₆ in., ceramic tile has a variety of finishes, including glazed, unglazed, slip-proof, and matte. Ceramic tile has only a light coating finish, whereas ceramic mosaic tile has the finish through the total thickness of the tile. Tile is made with a fine-grained body impervious to water, stain, dent, and frost. Mosiacs, which have tile sizes of 1×1 in., 2×1 in., and 2×2 in., are mounted on a prespaced backing sheet of 12×12 in., ready for application. Ceramic tiles are larger and depending on the size, may or may not be mounted on a backing sheet. Tile must be handled carefully, as they break or chip easily. Colors and patterns are available in a very wide range in both types, including murals. A solid backing surface is necessary for the application of ceramic tile. A ready-to-use adhesive is applied to the surface with a notched trowel. Apply one sheet at a time or one tile at a time, taking care to space the units properly for uniformity.

Drywall

Plaster sandwiched between two layers of heavy paper, also known as plasterboard, sheetrock, or gypsum board, is a construction technique known as drywall. The panels are available in thicknesses of ¼, ⅜, ½, and ⅝ in. and 4′-0″ in width. Lengths are 8′-0″, 10′-0″, 12′-0″, and 14′-0″. Drywall walls and ceilings have a number of advantages:

1. Excellent sound isolation can be obtained by separate framing of the two sides of the wall, fastening the wallboard over a sound control material, such as another wallboard, and including sound-absorbing materials in the wall cavity.
2. Drywall makes strong high-quality walls and ceilings with good dimensional stability. The surfaces may be easily decorated and refinished during their long life.
3. Drywall products are readily available and relatively easy to apply. They are the least expensive wall surfacing materials available that offer a structurally sound, fire-resistant interior finish.

Paint and Stain

Before any painting or staining is done, the surface must be sanded to remove dirt and scratches, and if the surface is damaged or dented, a wood filler must be used to make repairs. Stains highlight the variations in wood grain and color; therefore, the surface must be clean, dry, and smooth, and free of all fingerprints, smudges, and pencil marks. Open-grained woods, such as mahogany, oak, and walnut, must be filled with a paste filler and allowed to dry overnight. Close-grained woods, such as birch, maple, and pine, require no filler. Stain must be stirred thoroughly before use.

Painting will require one coat of primer (for new work) and two coats of finish material. On old work, the finish should be sanded to allow the paint to adhere to the surface. Latex or water-based paint is not recommended over an oil-based paint.

The proper brush and application is essential to a good-quality paint job. As a rule, 1 gallon of paint will cover between 400 and 500 square feet of surface. A pure bristle brush should be used for oil-based paint, a nylon brush for latex paint, and a polyester brush for general purposes. The proper brush size is important to a good finish. Latex paints can be cleaned from brushes with ammoniated water, oil-based paint requires paint thinner or turpentine for cleaning. When not in use, brushes should be stored with the handle down.

Defective paint surfaces have many causes. Peeling and blistering are caused by a loss of adhesion brought about by moisture getting behind a film of paint and pushing out, trying to escape. Protected areas pose more of a problem than open areas because the water is slow to dry and the likelihood of damage is increased. Wood and wood composition materials are constantly moving, expanding, and contracting, and this constant movement breaks the film and adhesion of paint, causing an opening for water to penetrate and lock in behind the paint, resulting in peeling and blistering. If the trapped water freezes, it will result in further damage.

Anything that affects the relationship of paint film to the surface it touches will affect adhesion and cause peeling, including air borne dust, dirt, or chemicals not visible to the naked eye. The previous coat of paint has chemical by-products which can cause breakdown of the new coat, especially with latex paints. The contact surface of a coat of paint is important, which is why it is diffucult to obtain a good coat of paint on a smooth hard surface.

Floor Treatment

Wood Parquet and Block Flooring

Parquet and block flooring is hardwood, factory finished, applied over concrete or wood with ready-to-use mastic. It offers a wide variety of species and patterns to choose from with ease of maintenance. The units or panels are completely unitized for fast, simple installation. The wood species available include white oak, red oak, pecan, black walnut, hard maple, cherry, cedar, teak, and a variety of other woods (Fig. 9–78).

FIGURE 9–78 *Parquet wood floor.*

PRODUCT DESCRIPTION AND PATTERN	PANEL SIZE	GRADE	SPECIES
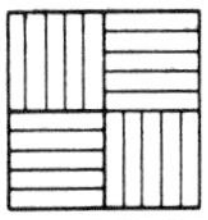 STANDARD Pattern Unfinished—Paper-Faced	5/16" x 19" x 19" 16 equal alternating squares 5/16" x 12" x 12" 4 equal alternating squares	Premium Select Rustic	Cherry—Maple Red Oak—White Oak—Cedar—Pecan—Walnut Rhodesian Teak Angelique (Guiana Teak) Panga-Panga
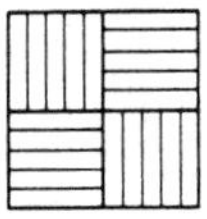 STANDARD Pattern Unfinished—WebBack or Mesh-Back	5/16" x 19" x 19" 16 equal alternating squares 5/16" x 11" x 11" 4 equal alternating squares	Premium Select Rustic Select & Better (Par & Better) Rustic	Red Oak—White Oak Pecan Red and White Oak
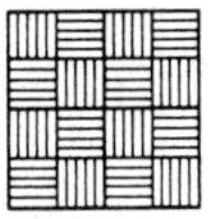 STANDARD Pattern Unfinished—WebBack (For Industrial Use)	5/16" x 19" x 19" 16 equal alternating squares 9/16" x 19" x 19" 16 equal alternating squares	Select & Better (Par & Better) Select Rustic & Better Rustic	Maple—Red Oak White Oak Pecan
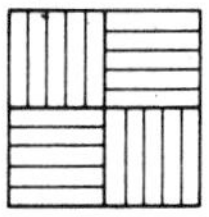 STANDARD Pattern Unfinished WebBack (For Industrial Use)	11/16" x 11" x 11" 4 equal alternating squares ¾" x 12-11/16" x 12-11/16" 4 equal alternating squares	Select & Better (Par & Better) Industrial & Better (Rustic & Better)	Red Oak—Maple
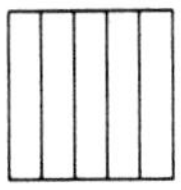 STANDARD Pattern Factory-Finished (Available in various colors)	5/16" x 6⅜" x 6⅜" 5/16" x 6½" x 6½" individual unit	Choice Natural & Better Natural Cabin	Oak—Walnut Pecan—Maple
 STANDARD Pattern Factory-Finished Foam-Back Tile	5/16" x 6½" x 6½" individual units . . . ⅛" foam, 2 lb. density	Natural & Better Natural Cabin	Oak—Pecan Maple
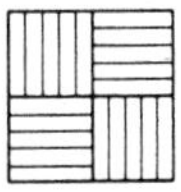 ANTIQUE TEXTURED (Factory-finished and Unfinished)—Kerfsawn Various colors available	5/16" x 6⅜" x 6⅜" individual squares 5/16" x 6½" x 6½" individual squares 5/16" x 11" x 11" 4 equal alternating squares	Select Natural & Better Select & Better (Par & Better)	Red Oak & White Oak Red Oak & White Oak
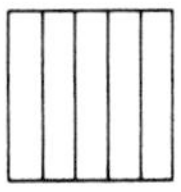 ANTIQUE TEXTURED (Factory-finished and Unfinished)—Wire brushed Various colors available	5/16" x 6⅜" x 6⅜" 5/16" x 6½" x 6½" individual squares	Natural & Better	Oak
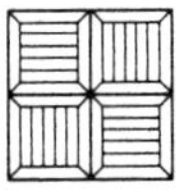 MONTICELLO Pattern Unfinished—Paper-Faced	5/16" x 13¼" x 13¼" 4 equal alternating squares	Select & Better (Par & Better)	Angelique (Guiana Teak) Red Oak—White Oak Panga-Panga—Black Walnut
 HADDON HALL Pattern Unfinished—Paper-Faced	5/16" x 13¼" x 13¼" 4 equal squares	Select & Better (Par & Better)	Angelique (Guiana Teak) Red Oak—White Oak Panga-Panga—Black Walnut
 HERRINGBONE Pattern Unfinished—Paper-Faced	5/16" x 14⅛" x 18⅛" (Approximate overall) 2 - "V" shape courses wide and 11 slats long	Select & Better (Par & Better)	Angelique (Guiana Teak) Red Oak—White Oak Panga-Panga—Black Walnut
 SAXONY Pattern Unfinished—Paper-Faced	5/16" x 19" x 19" 4 equal squares on diagonal and 8 equal half squares	Select & Better (Par & Better)	Angelique (Guiana Teak) Red Oak—White Oak Panga-Panga—Black Walnut
 CANTERBURY Pattern Unfinished—Paper-Faced	5/16" x 13¼" x 13¼" 4 equal alternating squares with diagonal center slats	Select & Better (Par & Better)	Angelique (Guiana Teak) Red Oak—White Oak Panga-Panga—Black Walnut
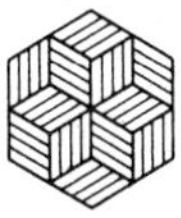 RHOMBS Pattern Unfinished—Paper-Faced	Hexagonal Shape 5/16" x 15⅛" x 15⅛" 12 equal Rhomboids	Select & Better (Par & Better)	Red Oak & White Oak
 BASKET WEAVE Pattern Unfinished—Paper-Faced	5/16" x 15-1/5" x 19" 4 runs of 3 slats and 5 slats alternating	Select & Better (Par & Better)	Angelique (Guiana Teak) Red Oak—White Oak Panga-Panga—Black Walnut
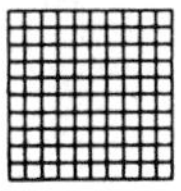 ITALIAN & DOMINO Pattern Unfinished—Paper-Faced	5/16" x 19" x 19" 400 equal size pieces butt-jointed	Premium Par & Select	Black Walnut Angelique (Guiana Teak) Maple—Red Oak White Oak

Plank and Strip Flooring

Plank and strip must be laid one piece at a time. The sizes vary from 2 to 8 in. wide, $\frac{3}{8}$ and $\frac{3}{4}$ in. thick, and 1'-0" to 5'-0" long: blind nailed, keyed, pegged, or screwed, prefinished or unfinished with beveled edges, in oak, maple, beech, birch, pecan, teak, walnut, and other exotic woods. This flooring can be applied over wood or concrete.

Pegged flooring is predrilled with countersunk holes on the top surface of the floor. The flooring is then screwed through the top predrilled holes into the subfloor and the holes are plugged with prefitted wood plugs.

Resilient Flooring

Resilient flooring includes sheet vinyl, vinyl asbestos, linoleum, and vinyl composition. Sheet vinyls are among the most popular flooring materials. The vinyl content allows them to be very colorful and adds to their ability to resist wear, grease and alkalis, and stains and scratches, and allows for easy cleaning. The design is on the surface only. Rolls come in 6'-0" and 12'-0" widths and thicknesses of 0.160, 0.090, 0.080, 0.070, 0.075, 0.065 in. The material can be used below or above ground.

Carpet

Carpet is made by inserting face yarn or tufts through premanufactured backing by use of needles. Yarns are held in place by coating the back with latex and a secondary backing is applied to add body and stability. A variety of textures is possible.

A woven carpet will be one of three styles: velvet, Axminster, or Wilton. The face and back are formed by the interweaving of warp and weft yarns. The warp yarns run lengthwise and usually consist of chain, stuffer, and pile yarns. The weft yarns are "shot" run across the width. The weft yarns bind in the pile and weave in the stuffer and chain yarns, which form the carpet back.

Velvet is the simplest of all carpet weaves. Pile is formed as the loom loops warp yarns over wires inserted across the loom. Pile height is determined by the height of the wire inserted. Velvets are traditionally known for smooth-cut pile plush or loop pile textures, but can also create high–low loop or cut–uncut textures. Usually carpet is solid, moresque, or striped in color.

Tile

The heading "tile" includes ceramic mosaic tile, slate, bluestone, flagstone, quarry tile, and terrazzo. Terrazzo is a concrete mix with marble chips mixed in. After setting, the entire floor is ground with a grinding machine for a smooth, even, colorful finish. Quarry tile is installed the same as ceramic tile. Slate, bluestone, and flagstone must be prefitted before installation over a concrete base.

QUESTIONS

9–1. Define *bridging.* _____

_____

9–2. Batter boards are used to mix the lumber in framing.
True or False

9–3. Name three types of foundations.
1. _____
2. _____
3. _____

9–4. Floor joists are used to:
(a) Support finish flooring
(b) Support finish under the floor
(c) Floor framing

9–5. Exterior walls are built only of wood.
True or False

9–6. Carpenter ants do which of the following?
(a) Eat wood
(b) Tunnel in wood
(c) Rot wood

9–7. The design of a roof framing system has no part in the selection of roof covering.
True or False

9–8. Define *plank-and-beam framing.* _____

_____

9–9. Name three types of roof covering material.
1. _____
2. _____
3. _____

9–10. Define *cornice.* _____

_____

9–11. Veneer is a solid mass of finish.
True or False

9–12. Define *composition siding.* _____

_____

9–13. Name three types of insulation.
1. _____
2. _____
3. _____

9–14. Name five types of interior finish material.
1. _____
2. _____
3. _____
4. _____
5. _____

9–15. Name three types of interior floor finish.
1. _____
2. _____
3. _____

10

Nonresidential Building

Introduction

There are differences in the design of commercial and residential buildings. Some small commercial buildings use the same type of wood framing as that used for residential buildings. Most commercial buildings, however, are constructed of concrete, light steel framing, masonry, curtain walls (which are not supporting), and many types of roofing other than that used on residential construction, such as tar and gravel (sometimes called built-up roofing), single-ply roofing, metal roofing, and other roofing materials.

More professionals are involved in commercial buildings: architects, civil engineers, surveyors, structural engineers, electrical engineers, mechanical engineers, estimators, and project or construction managers. In addition, more drawings are required in commercial design, including drawings designed by the civil, structural, electrical, and mechanical engineers, all members of the team working with the architect. A great deal of research and many meetings with the owners are necessary in the preliminary design stage. Each building use requires a great deal of study by the architect to make certain that the needs of the owner are met. A step-by-step construction sequence will be presented, based on the design of a retail commercial building, to illustrate the entire range of activities.

Building Preliminaries

The owner purchased land and decided to build a retail minimall. An architect was selected, an agreement was reached between the owner and the architect, and a contract was signed.

264

Before any design is begun, the architect must study the building and zoning codes. A construction budget is established by the owner and the building study is then ready to be started. Next, preliminary drawings, consisting of simple plans and elevations, are completed. Changes are then made based on the owner's requirements, and the studies are approved. Work is now ready to begin based on the contract and final drawings.

Foundation (Fig. 10-1)

Examination of the foundation plans shows a semicircular building. This may prove to be a little expensive to build because of its shape, but careful examination shows that the foundation has been designed on tangents to a circle, making a series of straight lines. The tangents have dimensions of 18'-0", 17'-0", and 8'-0". The angle at the 44'-0" dimension at the end of the building is parallel with the rear property lot line. This can be seen by examining the plot plan. The angles at the corners of the building are shown and must add up to 360°. In the building's midcenter is a projection designed to break up the wide expanse of the building front line. The foundation consists of 12-in.-thick concrete walls supported by 12×24 in. continuous concrete footing, shown by dashed lines under the foundation. Before designing the foundation, soil tests were run on the building site, which determined the size of the footing and foundation. The overall building size is 117'-6" on the rear side, 175'-0" on the front side, 40'-0" on one end, and 44'-0" on the other end. Since there is no basement, the note "Unexcavated" means "Do not remove the earth from inside the building." The radius of 116'-0" is given to help the contractor establish the tangents to the circle. The foundation plan is drawn to a scale of $\frac{1}{8}$" = 1'-0".

The front projection dimensions of 37'-0" and 68'-0" are given to help confirm the building's shape and dimensions. The building size was determined on the basis of budget and number of parking spaces, which is dictated by the building laws, and the maximum lot coverage, which is also mandated by law.

Floor Plan (Fig. 10-1)

If the foundation plan and floor plan are placed one over the other, the dimension and shape of the building will be seen to be the same. There are 10 retail units in the building, all of which are of equal width except for the last unit on the right, which is a little wider. The building laws require that two doors be present for each retail unit. This is indicated by a front door, no. 1, and a rear door, no. 2. The law also requires that the door swing out, in the direction of travel, to facilitate leaving the building in the event of an emergency. To the left or right of each front door is glass, which takes up most of the front wall of each unit. The small room labeled "T" in the rear of each unit is a toilet. The building laws in some states require that toilets be designed to accommodate physically handicapped people. There must be room enough to turn wheelchairs around in the toilet room.

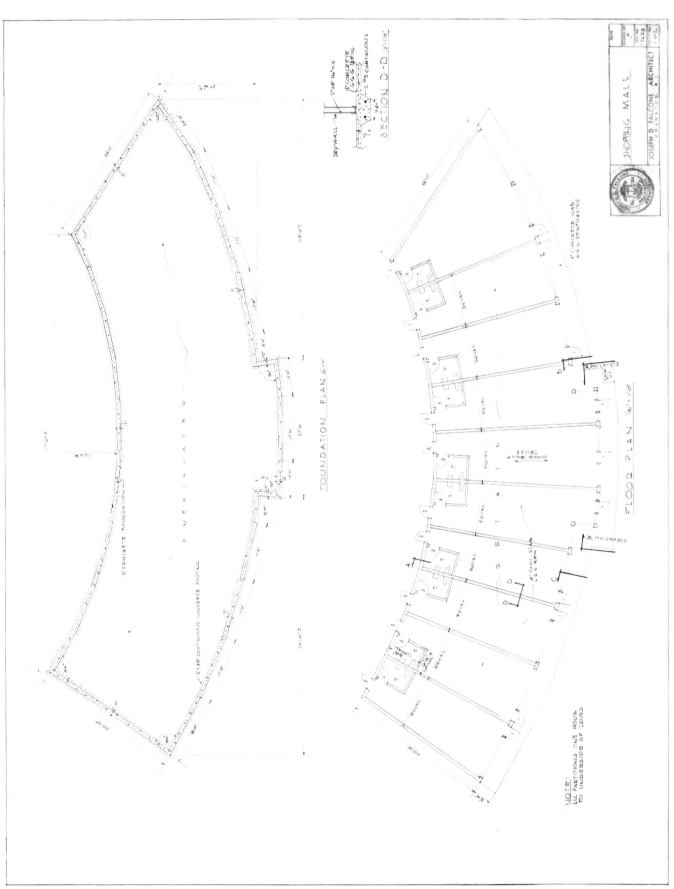

FIGURE 10-1

266

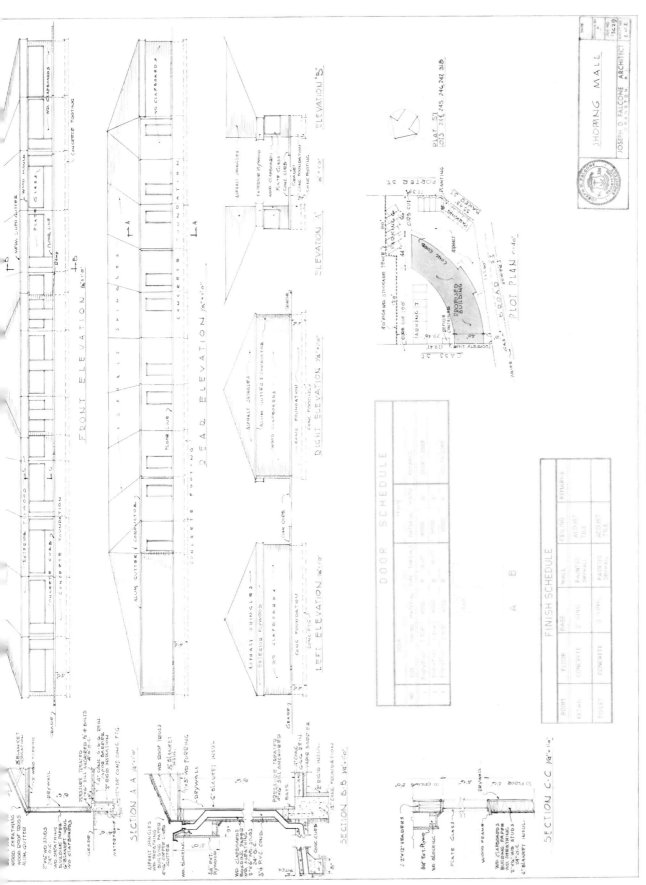

FIGURE 10-2

267

In front of the building is a continuous concrete curb 5′-0″ wide, level with the floor of the retail units and one step above the ground. Also note the ramp up for physically handicapped people and for easy access to the building. The lower left side of the plan has a note which reads: "All partitions one hour." The law in most states requires that each unit have a fire protection wall from the floor to the ceiling. The "one hour" means that the construction of this wall is such that a fire could burn for 1 hour before it would penetrate the wall.

Since there is no basement in this building, the floor is 4-in.-thick concrete placed on the ground over a vapor barrier to prevent the ground moisture from penetrating the concrete floor into the building. The floor has steel embedded into the concrete, a checkerboard-shaped wire termed 6-6-6, which means a wire grid 6 in. apart in both directions and No. 6 gauge wire in thickness.

Because of the added weight of the interior walls resting on the concrete floor, the concrete floor at those points must be increased in thickness to prevent the concrete floor from cracking. Section D-D shows the floor thickness of these points. In addition to the installation of 6-6-6 wire reinforcing, there are two $\frac{5}{8}$-in.-diameter steel rods placed into the concrete to keep it from cracking. The interior walls are built of 2 × 4 studs, wood or metal, placed 16 in. apart with $\frac{5}{8}$-in. drywall on both sides. The roof and ceiling is built as one unit in the shape of a truss supported by the exterior walls. It was the owner's decision not to have any interior columns in the building, allowing a tenant to lease more than one unit simply by removing the dividing partition.

Elevations (Fig. 10-2)

All exterior walls of the building must be drawn. These are labeled Front Elevation, Rear Elevation, Left Elevation, Right Elevation, Elevation A, and Elevation B.

Front Elevation

The front elevation is drawn at $\frac{1}{8}″ = 1′-0″$ and shows the entire front of the building. The grade is the ground and all information below the ground is shown by a dashed line which includes the 12-in.-thick foundation wall, and the parallel dashed lines under the foundation wall represent the spread footing, which is 12 in. deep and 2 ft wide. The distance from the ground to the bottom of the spread footing is 4′-0″. Above the ground and at ground level is a 6-in.-high concrete curb continuous along the entire front of the building.

The vertical lines between the doors are the tangents to the circular building. These vertical lines start on top of the curb and end at the ridge of the roof. Each unit has a glass front and door. The glass front is labeled PL glass, which means plate glass of $\frac{1}{4}$ in. thick. The distance from the floor to the bottom of the glass and the top of the glass is shown on section C-C.

The front of the building is covered with wood clapboards and the roof is covered with asphalt shingles. The floor line is also indicated to get a proper perspective on the different heights of the building. The wide space above the doors and windows is called the fascia and in this case is used for signs. No chimney is shown at roof level; this means that the building is heated by electricity.

Rear Elevation

The rear elevation is the opposite side of the front elevation, which is also drawn at $\frac{1}{8}'' = 1'\text{-}0''$. The same foundation and footings are shown. Each door leads to a unit which is the rear door used for delivery and workers. The walls are covered with wood clapboards as in the front and the roof is covered with asphalt shingles, as in the front.

Careful examination of all sides will show that gutters and conductors are installed only at the rear of the building. These are of aluminum. At the extreme right of the rear elevation, the fascia is different from the rear fascia but the same as that at the front of the building. This is really the end of the building; we are seeing it at an angle because of the shape. The vertical lines separating the door are tangents to the circle, much as in the front elevation.

Left Elevation

The left elevation is the side seen standing from the front of the building, the left side. It is also drawn at $\frac{1}{8}'' = 1'\text{-}0''$ scale. The fascia shown at the front elevation is continued on this side because it is visible from the street. Like the other two sides, the foundation is shown below the ground with dotted lines and each part is labeled. The concrete curb is visible one step above the ground on the right side of this elevation.

Right Elevation

The right elevation is not visible from the street, and since it faces the rear of the property, the roof overhang is similar to that in the rear of the building. As in the left elevation, the foundation, footing, and curb are also shown.

Elevations A and B

It is seen by examining the floor plan that the center of the building on the front side has a projection beyond the main building line which measures $37'\text{-}0''$ long by $7'\text{-}0''$ wide. The front of the projection is shown on the front elevation, but the $7'\text{-}0''$ sides must also be shown. This is what is drawn at elevation A and elevation B. Elevation A shows the left side of the projection and elevation B shows the right side of the projection. The gable roof frames into the main roof, which is covered with asphalt shingles. Like other elevations, the foundation is shown $4'\text{-}0''$ below the grade or ground and the same concrete curb is shown on these elevations. The plate glass, shown as PL, is the same as that shown on the floor plan. This completes all elevations. It is now clear what the contractor is to provide to complete the exterior of the building.

Sections (Fig. 10-2)

Floor plans and elevations do not provide enough information for a builder to complete a project. More data are required, including sections. As many sections will be drawn as are necessary to communicate to the builder the idea of the building. This commercial building requires three different sections: A-A, B-B, and C-C. These are wall sections showing the composition or material used in completing various walls of the building. The location of the section is indicated on the plan and the elevations.

Section A-A

Section A-A shows the composition of the rear wall of the building drawn at a scale of $\frac{1}{4}'' = 1'-0''$. $4'-0''$ below the grade is the bottom of the continuous 12×24 in. concrete footing to help spread the building load over a wider surface of the ground. On top of the spread footing is a 12-in.-thick concrete foundation wall up to a height of 6 in. above the floor. The shelf on the inside of the foundation wall is at floor height. Inside the foundation wall is a 2-in. rigid insulation to reduce the heat loss. The floor of the building is a 4-in.-thick concrete floor reinforced with 6-6-6 wire mesh. Under the concrete floor and on top of the ground is a vapor barrier of plastic or polyethylene to prevent ground moisture from entering the building through the concrete floor. In addition, over the vapor barrier and under the concrete floor is 2-in. rigid insulation 2 ft wide along the entire foundation perimeter. The purpose of this insulation is to prevent heat loss from the building.

Before the concrete foundation hardens, $\frac{1}{2}$-in.-diameter anchor bolts $18''$ long $4'-0''$ apart are placed into the wet, soft concrete to anchor the foundation wood sill to the foundation top, which will be installed later. The outside of the foundation wall is covered with a waterproof coating to prevent groundwater from entering through the foundation wall. This completes the foundation.

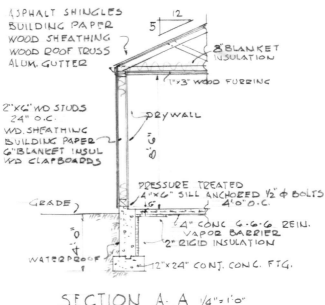

SECTION A-A ¼"=1'0"

The exterior wall framing is supported by the concrete foundation, beginning with a pressure-treated 4 × 6 in. wood sill with holes drilled to mate with the location of the anchor bolts. This is called the foundation sill. The step back in the concrete foundation top is as wide as the 4 × 6 in. sill, which is 6 in. The 2 × 6 in. exterior wall studs are nailed to the top of the foundation sill spaced 24 in. apart. The length of the studs determines the ceiling height inside the building.

Nailed on the inside of the exterior walls is ½-in. drywall which can be plastered, painted, or papered. The exterior stud walls are covered with wood sheathing, which in most cases is ⅝-in. plywood. Over the plywood is building paper and the finish exterior wall is covered with wood clapboards. Later, 6-in. blanket insulation is installed between the studs. That completes the outside wall assembly except for painting or staining the clapboards. Sitting on top of the double wall plate are wood trusses supported by the exterior walls. These trusses, which are prebuilt, make up the roof and the ceiling and are spaced 16 in. apart. The roof pitch is indicated as 12/5, and the wood sheathing, which is ½-in. plywood, is nailed to the top of the trusses. The application that completes the roof is the installation of asphalt shingles over the roof sheathing or building paper. Like the walls, the ceiling is insulated with 8-in. insulation. This type of roof framing permits freedom from partitions or walls inside the building, giving tenants the option of space without interior walls. The interior walls carry no loads; they only divide the space. These walls, built of 2 × 4 studs placed 16 in. apart, are covered with fire-rated drywall or gypsum board designed to give 1 hour of protection in the event of fire. This is a requirement in most local building codes. Under the roof truss at the ceiling level are nailed wood 1 × 3's spaced 16 in. apart, called *furring*. Drywall is used on the ceiling, secured to the furring.

To complete the outside, all that remains to be done is to install the aluminum gutters and downspouts. The location of the downspouts is shown on the rear elevation. The water draining from the roof falls into the gutter, down the downspouts, and onto the ground.

Section B-B

Section B-B shows a built-in gutter with an internal (between the studs) downspout of 3-in.-diameter PVC turning under the concrete curb and leading onto the ground. The 2'-0"-wide fascia, spaced for signs, projects 9 in. out from the exterior building line. The front wall remaining is of the same construction as the rear wall, except for the concrete curb, which is 4 in. thick reinforced with 6-6-6 steel wire and is the same length as the building. It projects 5'-0" out from the front building wall. Section B-B is cut through the solid front wall, where there is no glass or door.

Section C-C

The only difference between section B-B and section C-C is the location of the front wall where the section is cut. Section C-C is cut through the glass line and shows the height of glass above the floor as 2'-6" and a glass height of 4'-6". The detail shows how the glass is secured to the wall by a wood frame.

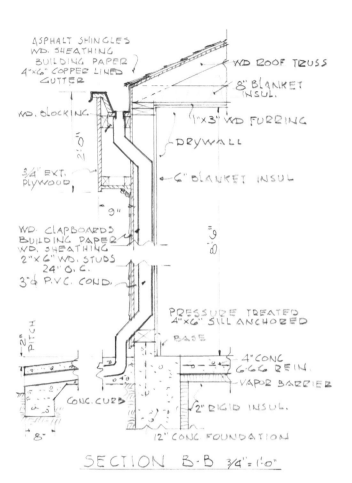

ASPHALT SHINGLES
WD. SHEATHING
BUILDING PAPER
4"x6" COPPER LINED GUTTER

WD ROOF TRUSS

8" BLANKET INSUL.

WD. BLOCKING

1"x3" WD FURRING

DRYWALL

2'-0"

3/4" EXT. PLYWOOD

6" BLANKET INSUL

9"

WD. CLAPBOARDS
BUILDING PAPER
WD. SHEATHING
2"x6" WD. STUDS 24" O.C.
3"∅ P.V.C. COND.

8'-9"

PRESSURE TREATED
4"x6" SILL ANCHORED
BASE

2" PITCH

4" CONC
6-6-6 REIN.

VAPOR BARRIER

2" RIGID INSUL.

CONC. CURB

8"

12" CONC FOUNDATION

SECTION B·B 3/4"=1'·0"

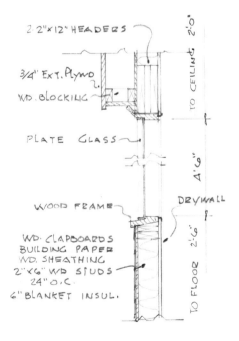

2·2"x12" HEADERS

2'-0"

TO CEILING

3/4" EXT. PLYWD
WD. BLOCKING

PLATE GLASS

9'-4"

DRYWALL

WOOD FRAME

WD. CLAPBOARDS
BUILDING PAPER
WD. SHEATHING
2"x6" WD STUDS 24" O.C.
6" BLANKET INSUL.

2'-6"

TO FLOOR

SECTION C·C 3/4"=1'·0"

Schedules (Fig. 10-2)

The plans are not complete without door and finish schedules. Each door has a number shown on the floor plan. The doors are listed in a door schedule by door number. The size thickness, and material of each door are listed.

Many door designs are available. The designs chosen for this project are found listed under "type" as A or B. Elevations for types A and B are given in the door schedule.

The type of threshold must be included in a door schedule. If there is no threshold, the space is left blank. Details of the door frame must also be included in the schedule. The material of the frame and the width of the frame are indicated. The remarks column will include information on door closers and door quality.

The finish schedule lists the finish on the floor, base, wall, and ceiling of each room.

Plot Plan (Fig. 10-2)

The building plans are useless unless the contractor knows exactly where the building is to be built. This is what the plot plan discloses. It is drawn at a scale of $1'' = 40'$, which is much smaller than all the other scales used in the plans.

The lot and plot numbers are given together with the street names. Here the property borders on four streets: Cass, Broad, Baker, and Porter. The compass bearing shows the direction of north, and the dimensions of all property lines are indicated.

The building dimensions and location on the property must be given. All parking spaces are shown on the plan, along with the asphalt paving. A refuse container for tenants' waste is shown on Cass Street. Curb cuts are shown on Broad and Porter Streets. There is evergreen planting on Baker Street, and the rear of the property has a $4'$-$0''$-high stockade fence.

QUESTIONS

10-1. In designing a building, what are some of the first steps an architect must take?

1. _____
2. _____
3. _____
4. _____

10-2. Continuous concrete footings help a building to:
   (a) Become stable
   (b) Prevent foundation settlement
   (c) Support the weight of the building
   (d) All of the above
   (e) None of the above

10–3. All exterior doors for public buildings must swing in.
True or False

10–4. Why are toilet facilities for physically handicapped persons different from other toilet facilities? _____

_____

10–5. What is a fire wall? _____

_____

10–6. To prevent concrete from cracking, which of the following precautions must be used?
(a) Reinforce the concrete
(b) Compact the earth
(c) Use a stronger concrete mix
(d) Use a thicker concrete floor

10–7. What is the purpose of drawing sections of a building? _____

_____

10–8. What is the purpose of a vapor barrier? _____

_____

10–9. Anchor bolts hold a building to the ground.
True or False

10–10. Define *door and finish schedule.* _____

10–11. What information does a plot plan give? _____

11

Specifications

Introduction

It is impossible to draft all the information necessary to construct a building on a set of plans. Additional information is necessary to communicate properly with the builder. This additional information comprises what are called specifications. Specifications are exactly what they sound like: every part of a building must be delineated specifically. Specifications control the quality of a building by telling the contractor what type of building material is to be used. Specifications can be in the form of notes on the drawings or they can be $8\frac{1}{2} \times 11$ in. printed sheets which accompany the plans.

The specifications are legal documents that become part of the plans. A plan may show a brick wall—which alone is not enough information. It must be supplemented by the specifications, which will specify the size, color, and texture of brick. A wooden stud wall in a plan is not enough—the specifications will describe the species and quality of the studs. Every product of the building material must be specified, including quality, model number, and several companies that manufacture the product. Once the quality of the product has been established, the contractor has a choice of several companies from whom the product can be purchased.

Format

A professional organization called the Construction Specification Institute has as its purpose the establishment of uniformity in the writing of specifications. Work to be performed on a building is divided into categories. The system was devised to meet a consistent arrangement familiar to architects and the building trades.

The system has 16 categories or divisions. These are, in turn, broken down into sections, each of which has a number. The main divisions are as follows:

0. Bidding and Contract Requirements (Fig. 11–1)
1. General Requirements
2. Site Work
3. Concrete (Fig. 11–2)
4. Masonry
5. Metals
6. Wood and Plastics
7. Thermal and Moisture Protection
8. Doors and Windows
9. Finishes
10. Specialties
11. Equipment
12. Furnishings
13. Special Construction
14. Conveying Systems
15. Mechanical
16. Electrical

Under the main division, Building and Contract Requirements, is included nontechnical information or information that relates to contractural agreements rather than building material quality. These are agreements that include the architect, owner, and builder and are to be considered as contracts for other than material quality. The information contained in the specifications should agree with the information contained on the drawings. If a contradiction or discrepancy is found, the specifications usually prevail. The material contained in the specifications comes from the manufacturer of the building material or product selected.

FIGURE 11–1

*General Conditions of the Contract for Construction
(courtesy The American Institute of Architects),
pages 277 to 300.*

FIGURE 11–2

*Specifications: Concrete, Forms, and Reinforcment,
pages 301 to 304.*

FIGURE 11–1

T H E A M E R I C A N I N S T I T U T E O F A R C H I T E C T S

AIA Document A201

General Conditions of the Contract for Construction

THIS DOCUMENT HAS IMPORTANT LEGAL CONSEQUENCES; CONSULTATION WITH AN ATTORNEY IS ENCOURAGED WITH RESPECT TO ITS MODIFICATION

1987 EDITION
TABLE OF ARTICLES

This document has been approved and endorsed by the Associated General Contractors of America.

FIGURE 11–1   *(cont'd)*

INDEX

FIGURE 11–1 *(cont'd)*

FIGURE 11–1   (cont'd)

FIGURE 11-1 (cont'd)

FIGURE 11–1 (cont'd)

GENERAL CONDITIONS OF THE CONTRACT FOR CONSTRUCTION

ARTICLE 1
GENERAL PROVISIONS

1.1 BASIC DEFINITIONS

1.1.1 THE CONTRACT DOCUMENTS

The Contract Documents consist of the Agreement between Owner and Contractor (hereinafter the Agreement), Conditions of the Contract (General, Supplementary and other Conditions), Drawings, Specifications, addenda issued prior to execution of the Contract, other documents listed in the Agreement and Modifications issued after execution of the Contract. A Modification is (1) a written amendment to the Contract signed by both parties, (2) a Change Order, (3) a Construction Change Directive or (4) a written order for a minor change in the Work issued by the Architect. Unless specifically enumerated in the Agreement, the Contract Documents do not include other documents such as bidding requirements (advertisement or invitation to bid, Instructions to Bidders, sample forms, the Contractor's bid or portions of addenda relating to bidding requirements).

1.1.2 THE CONTRACT

The Contract Documents form the Contract for Construction. The Contract represents the entire and integrated agreement between the parties hereto and supersedes prior negotiations, representations or agreements, either written or oral. The Contract may be amended or modified only by a Modification. The Contract Documents shall not be construed to create a contractual relationship of any kind (1) between the Architect and Contractor, (2) between the Owner and a Subcontractor or Sub-subcontractor or (3) between any persons or entities other than the Owner and Contractor. The Architect shall, however, be entitled to performance and enforcement of obligations under the Contract intended to facilitate performance of the Architect's duties.

1.1.3 THE WORK

The term "Work" means the construction and services required by the Contract Documents, whether completed or partially completed, and includes all other labor, materials, equipment and services provided or to be provided by the Contractor to fulfill the Contractor's obligations. The Work may constitute the whole or a part of the Project.

1.1.4 THE PROJECT

The Project is the total construction of which the Work performed under the Contract Documents may be the whole or a part and which may include construction by the Owner or by separate contractors.

1.1.5 THE DRAWINGS

The Drawings are the graphic and pictorial portions of the Contract Documents, wherever located and whenever issued, showing the design, location and dimensions of the Work, generally including plans, elevations, sections, details, schedules and diagrams.

1.1.6 THE SPECIFICATIONS

The Specifications are that portion of the Contract Documents consisting of the written requirements for materials, equip-

ment, construction systems, standards and workmanship for the Work, and performance of related services.

1.1.7 THE PROJECT MANUAL

The Project Manual is the volume usually assembled for the Work which may include the bidding requirements, sample forms, Conditions of the Contract and Specifications.

1.2 EXECUTION, CORRELATION AND INTENT

1.2.1 The Contract Documents shall be signed by the Owner and Contractor as provided in the Agreement. If either the Owner or Contractor or both do not sign all the Contract Documents, the Architect shall identify such unsigned Documents upon request.

1.2.2 Execution of the Contract by the Contractor is a representation that the Contractor has visited the site, become familiar with local conditions under which the Work is to be performed and correlated personal observations with requirements of the Contract Documents.

1.2.3 The intent of the Contract Documents is to include all items necessary for the proper execution and completion of the Work by the Contractor. The Contract Documents are complementary, and what is required by one shall be as binding as if required by all; performance by the Contractor shall be required only to the extent consistent with the Contract Documents and reasonably inferable from them as being necessary to produce the intended results.

1.2.4 Organization of the Specifications into divisions, sections and articles, and arrangement of Drawings shall not control the Contractor in dividing the Work among Subcontractors or in establishing the extent of Work to be performed by any trade.

1.2.5 Unless otherwise stated in the Contract Documents, words which have well-known technical or construction industry meanings are used in the Contract Documents in accordance with such recognized meanings.

1.3 OWNERSHIP AND USE OF ARCHITECT'S DRAWINGS, SPECIFICATIONS AND OTHER DOCUMENTS

1.3.1 The Drawings, Specifications and other documents prepared by the Architect are instruments of the Architect's service through which the Work to be executed by the Contractor is described. The Contractor may retain one contract record set. Neither the Contractor nor any Subcontractor, Sub-subcontractor or material or equipment supplier shall own or claim a copyright in the Drawings, Specifications and other documents prepared by the Architect, and unless otherwise indicated the Architect shall be deemed the author of them and will retain all common law, statutory and other reserved rights, in addition to the copyright. All copies of them, except the Contractor's record set, shall be returned or suitably accounted for to the Architect, on request, upon completion of the Work. The Drawings, Specifications and other documents prepared by the Architect, and copies thereof furnished to the Contractor, are for use solely with respect to this Project. They are not to be used by the Contractor or any Subcontractor, Sub-subcontractor or material or equipment supplier on other projects or for additions to this Project outside the scope of the

FIGURE 11–1 (cont'd)

Work without the specific written consent of the Owner and Architect. The Contractor, Subcontractors, Sub-subcontractors and material or equipment suppliers are granted a limited license to use and reproduce applicable portions of the Drawings, Specifications and other documents prepared by the Architect appropriate to and for use in the execution of their Work under the Contract Documents. All copies made under this license shall bear the statutory copyright notice, if any, shown on the Drawings, Specifications and other documents prepared by the Architect. Submittal or distribution to meet official regulatory requirements or for other purposes in connection with this Project is not to be construed as publication in derogation of the Architect's copyright or other reserved rights.

1.4 CAPITALIZATION

1.4.1 Terms capitalized in these General Conditions include those which are (1) specifically defined, (2) the titles of numbered articles and identified references to Paragraphs, Subparagraphs and Clauses in the document or (3) the titles of other documents published by the American Institute of Architects.

1.5 INTERPRETATION

1.5.1 In the interest of brevity the Contract Documents frequently omit modifying words such as "all" and "any" and articles such as "the" and "an," but the fact that a modifier or an article is absent from one statement and appears in another is not intended to affect the interpretation of either statement.

ARTICLE 2

OWNER

2.1 DEFINITION

2.1.1 The Owner is the person or entity identified as such in the Agreement and is referred to throughout the Contract Documents as if singular in number. The term "Owner" means the Owner or the Owner's authorized representative.

2.1.2 The Owner upon reasonable written request shall furnish to the Contractor in writing information which is necessary and relevant for the Contractor to evaluate, give notice of or enforce mechanic's lien rights. Such information shall include a correct statement of the record legal title to the property on which the Project is located, usually referred to as the site, and the Owner's interest therein at the time of execution of the Agreement and, within five days after any change, information of such change in title, recorded or unrecorded.

2.2 INFORMATION AND SERVICES REQUIRED OF THE OWNER

2.2.1 The Owner shall, at the request of the Contractor, prior to execution of the Agreement and promptly from time to time thereafter, furnish to the Contractor reasonable evidence that financial arrangements have been made to fulfill the Owner's obligations under the Contract. *[Note: Unless such reasonable evidence were furnished on request prior to the execution of the Agreement, the prospective contractor would not be required to execute the Agreement or to commence the Work.]*

2.2.2 The Owner shall furnish surveys describing physical characteristics, legal limitations and utility locations for the site of the Project, and a legal description of the site.

2.2.3 Except for permits and fees which are the responsibility of the Contractor under the Contract Documents, the Owner shall secure and pay for necessary approvals, easements, assess-ments and charges required for construction, use or occupancy of permanent structures or for permanent changes in existing facilities.

2.2.4 Information or services under the Owner's control shall be furnished by the Owner with reasonable promptness to avoid delay in orderly progress of the Work.

2.2.5 Unless otherwise provided in the Contract Documents, the Contractor will be furnished, free of charge, such copies of Drawings and Project Manuals as are reasonably necessary for execution of the Work.

2.2.6 The foregoing are in addition to other duties and responsibilities of the Owner enumerated herein and especially those in respect to Article 6 (Construction by Owner or by Separate Contractors), Article 9 (Payments and Completion) and Article 11 (Insurance and Bonds).

2.3 OWNER'S RIGHT TO STOP THE WORK

2.3.1 If the Contractor fails to correct Work which is not in accordance with the requirements of the Contract Documents as required by Paragraph 12.2 or persistently fails to carry out Work in accordance with the Contract Documents, the Owner, by written order signed personally or by an agent specifically so empowered by the Owner in writing, may order the Contractor to stop the Work, or any portion thereof, until the cause for such order has been eliminated; however, the right of the Owner to stop the Work shall not give rise to a duty on the part of the Owner to exercise this right for the benefit of the Contractor or any other person or entity, except to the extent required by Subparagraph 6.1.3.

2.4 OWNER'S RIGHT TO CARRY OUT THE WORK

2.4.1 If the Contractor defaults or neglects to carry out the Work in accordance with the Contract Documents and fails within a seven-day period after receipt of written notice from the Owner to commence and continue correction of such default or neglect with diligence and promptness, the Owner may after such seven-day period give the Contractor a second written notice to correct such deficiencies within a second seven-day period. If the Contractor within such second seven-day period after receipt of such second notice fails to commence and continue to correct any deficiencies, the Owner may, without prejudice to other remedies the Owner may have, correct such deficiencies. In such case an appropriate Change Order shall be issued deducting from payments then or thereafter due the Contractor the cost of correcting such deficiencies, including compensation for the Architect's additional services and expenses made necessary by such default, neglect or failure. Such action by the Owner and amounts charged to the Contractor are both subject to prior approval of the Architect. If payments then or thereafter due the Contractor are not sufficient to cover such amounts, the Contractor shall pay the difference to the Owner.

ARTICLE 3

CONTRACTOR

3.1 DEFINITION

3.1.1 The Contractor is the person or entity identified as such in the Agreement and is referred to throughout the Contract Documents as if singular in number. The term "Contractor" means the Contractor or the Contractor's authorized representative.

FIGURE 11–1 (cont'd)

3.2 REVIEW OF CONTRACT DOCUMENTS AND FIELD CONDITIONS BY CONTRACTOR

3.2.1 The Contractor shall carefully study and compare the Contract Documents with each other and with information furnished by the Owner pursuant to Subparagraph 2.2.2 and shall at once report to the Architect errors, inconsistencies or omissions discovered. The Contractor shall not be liable to the Owner or Architect for damage resulting from errors, inconsistencies or omissions in the Contract Documents unless the Contractor recognized such error, inconsistency or omission and knowingly failed to report it to the Architect. If the Contractor performs any construction activity knowing it involves a recognized error, inconsistency or omission in the Contract Documents without such notice to the Architect, the Contractor shall assume appropriate responsibility for such performance and shall bear an appropriate amount of the attributable costs for correction.

3.2.2 The Contractor shall take field measurements and verify field conditions and shall carefully compare such field measurements and conditions and other information known to the Contractor with the Contract Documents before commencing activities. Errors, inconsistencies or omissions discovered shall be reported to the Architect at once.

3.2.3 The Contractor shall perform the Work in accordance with the Contract Documents and submittals approved pursuant to Paragraph 3.12.

3.3 SUPERVISION AND CONSTRUCTION PROCEDURES

3.3.1 The Contractor shall supervise and direct the Work, using the Contractor's best skill and attention. The Contractor shall be solely responsible for and have control over construction means, methods, techniques, sequences and procedures and for coordinating all portions of the Work under the Contract, unless Contract Documents give other specific instructions concerning these matters.

3.3.2 The Contractor shall be responsible to the Owner for acts and omissions of the Contractor's employees, Subcontractors and their agents and employees, and other persons performing portions of the Work under a contract with the Contractor.

3.3.3 The Contractor shall not be relieved of obligations to perform the Work in accordance with the Contract Documents either by activities or duties of the Architect in the Architect's administration of the Contract, or by tests, inspections or approvals required or performed by persons other than the Contractor.

3.3.4 The Contractor shall be responsible for inspection of portions of Work already performed under this Contract to determine that such portions are in proper condition to receive subsequent Work.

3.4 LABOR AND MATERIALS

3.4.1 Unless otherwise provided in the Contract Documents, the Contractor shall provide and pay for labor, materials, equipment, tools, construction equipment and machinery, water, heat, utilities, transportation, and other facilities and services necessary for proper execution and completion of the Work, whether temporary or permanent and whether or not incorporated or to be incorporated in the Work.

3.4.2 The Contractor shall enforce strict discipline and good order among the Contractor's employees and other persons carrying out the Contract. The Contractor shall not permit employment of unfit persons or persons not skilled in tasks assigned to them.

3.5 WARRANTY

3.5.1 The Contractor warrants to the Owner and Architect that materials and equipment furnished under the Contract will be of good quality and new unless otherwise required or permitted by the Contract Documents, that the Work will be free from defects not inherent in the quality required or permitted, and that the Work will conform with the requirements of the Contract Documents. Work not conforming to these requirements, including substitutions not properly approved and authorized, may be considered defective. The Contractor's warranty excludes remedy for damage or defect caused by abuse, modifications not executed by the Contractor, improper or insufficient maintenance, improper operation, or normal wear and tear under normal usage. If required by the Architect, the Contractor shall furnish satisfactory evidence as to the kind and quality of materials and equipment.

3.6 TAXES

3.6.1 The Contractor shall pay sales, consumer, use and similar taxes for the Work or portions thereof provided by the Contractor which are legally enacted when bids are received or negotiations concluded, whether or not yet effective or merely scheduled to go into effect.

3.7 PERMITS, FEES AND NOTICES

3.7.1 Unless otherwise provided in the Contract Documents, the Contractor shall secure and pay for the building permit and other permits and governmental fees, licenses and inspections necessary for proper execution and completion of the Work which are customarily secured after execution of the Contract and which are legally required when bids are received or negotiations concluded.

3.7.2 The Contractor shall comply with and give notices required by laws, ordinances, rules, regulations and lawful orders of public authorities bearing on performance of the Work.

3.7.3 It is not the Contractor's responsibility to ascertain that the Contract Documents are in accordance with applicable laws, statutes, ordinances, building codes, and rules and regulations. However, if the Contractor observes that portions of the Contract Documents are at variance therewith, the Contractor shall promptly notify the Architect and Owner in writing, and necessary changes shall be accomplished by appropriate Modification.

3.7.4 If the Contractor performs Work knowing it to be contrary to laws, statutes, ordinances, building codes, and rules and regulations without such notice to the Architect and Owner, the Contractor shall assume full responsibility for such Work and shall bear the attributable costs.

3.8 ALLOWANCES

3.8.1 The Contractor shall include in the Contract Sum all allowances stated in the Contract Documents. Items covered by allowances shall be supplied for such amounts and by such persons or entities as the Owner may direct, but the Contractor shall not be required to employ persons or entities against which the Contractor makes reasonable objection.

3.8.2 Unless otherwise provided in the Contract Documents:

.1 materials and equipment under an allowance shall be selected promptly by the Owner to avoid delay in the Work;

.2 allowances shall cover the cost to the Contractor of materials and equipment delivered at the site and all required taxes, less applicable trade discounts;

AIA DOCUMENT A201 • GENERAL CONDITIONS OF THE CONTRACT FOR CONSTRUCTION • FOURTEENTH EDITION
AIA® • ©1987 THE AMERICAN INSTITUTE OF ARCHITECTS, 1735 NEW YORK AVENUE, N.W., WASHINGTON, D.C. 20006

FIGURE 11–1 (cont'd)

.3 Contractor's costs for unloading and handling at the site, labor, installation costs, overhead, profit and other expenses contemplated for stated allowance amounts shall be included in the Contract Sum and not in the allowances;

.4 whenever costs are more than or less than allowances, the Contract Sum shall be adjusted accordingly by Change Order. The amount of the Change Order shall reflect (1) the difference between actual costs and the allowances under Clause 3.8.2.2 and (2) changes in Contractor's costs under Clause 3.8.2.3.

3.9 SUPERINTENDENT

3.9.1 The Contractor shall employ a competent superintendent and necessary assistants who shall be in attendance at the Project site during performance of the Work. The superintendent shall represent the Contractor, and communications given to the superintendent shall be as binding as if given to the Contractor. Important communications shall be confirmed in writing. Other communications shall be similarly confirmed on written request in each case.

3.10 CONTRACTOR'S CONSTRUCTION SCHEDULES

3.10.1 The Contractor, promptly after being awarded the Contract, shall prepare and submit for the Owner's and Architect's information a Contractor's construction schedule for the Work. The schedule shall not exceed time limits current under the Contract Documents, shall be revised at appropriate intervals as required by the conditions of the Work and Project, shall be related to the entire Project to the extent required by the Contract Documents, and shall provide for expeditious and practicable execution of the Work.

3.10.2 The Contractor shall prepare and keep current, for the Architect's approval, a schedule of submittals which is coordinated with the Contractor's construction schedule and allows the Architect reasonable time to review submittals.

3.10.3 The Contractor shall conform to the most recent schedules.

3.11 DOCUMENTS AND SAMPLES AT THE SITE

3.11.1 The Contractor shall maintain at the site for the Owner one record copy of the Drawings, Specifications, addenda, Change Orders and other Modifications, in good order and marked currently to record changes and selections made during construction, and in addition approved Shop Drawings, Product Data, Samples and similar required submittals. These shall be available to the Architect and shall be delivered to the Architect for submittal to the Owner upon completion of the Work.

3.12 SHOP DRAWINGS, PRODUCT DATA AND SAMPLES

3.12.1 Shop Drawings are drawings, diagrams, schedules and other data specially prepared for the Work by the Contractor or a Subcontractor, Sub-subcontractor, manufacturer, supplier or distributor to illustrate some portion of the Work.

3.12.2 Product Data are illustrations, standard schedules, performance charts, instructions, brochures, diagrams and other information furnished by the Contractor to illustrate materials or equipment for some portion of the Work.

3.12.3 Samples are physical examples which illustrate materials, equipment or workmanship and establish standards by which the Work will be judged.

3.12.4 Shop Drawings, Product Data, Samples and similar submittals are not Contract Documents. The purpose of their submittal is to demonstrate for those portions of the Work for

which submittals are required the way the Contractor proposes to conform to the information given and the design concept expressed in the Contract Documents. Review by the Architect is subject to the limitations of Subparagraph 4.2.7.

3.12.5 The Contractor shall review, approve and submit to the Architect Shop Drawings, Product Data, Samples and similar submittals required by the Contract Documents with reasonable promptness and in such sequence as to cause no delay in the Work or in the activities of the Owner or of separate contractors. Submittals made by the Contractor which are not required by the Contract Documents may be returned without action.

3.12.6 The Contractor shall perform no portion of the Work requiring submittal and review of Shop Drawings, Product Data, Samples or similar submittals until the respective submittal has been approved by the Architect. Such Work shall be in accordance with approved submittals.

3.12.7 By approving and submitting Shop Drawings, Product Data, Samples and similar submittals, the Contractor represents that the Contractor has determined and verified materials, field measurements and field construction criteria related thereto, or will do so, and has checked and coordinated the information contained within such submittals with the requirements of the Work and of the Contract Documents.

3.12.8 The Contractor shall not be relieved of responsibility for deviations from requirements of the Contract Documents by the Architect's approval of Shop Drawings, Product Data, Samples or similar submittals unless the Contractor has specifically informed the Architect in writing of such deviation at the time of submittal and the Architect has given written approval to the specific deviation. The Contractor shall not be relieved of responsibility for errors or omissions in Shop Drawings, Product Data, Samples or similar submittals by the Architect's approval thereof.

3.12.9 The Contractor shall direct specific attention, in writing or on resubmitted Shop Drawings, Product Data, Samples or similar submittals, to revisions other than those requested by the Architect on previous submittals.

3.12.10 Informational submittals upon which the Architect is not expected to take responsive action may be so identified in the Contract Documents.

3.12.11 When professional certification of performance criteria of materials, systems or equipment is required by the Contract Documents, the Architect shall be entitled to rely upon the accuracy and completeness of such calculations and certifications.

3.13 USE OF SITE

3.13.1 The Contractor shall confine operations at the site to areas permitted by law, ordinances, permits and the Contract Documents and shall not unreasonably encumber the site with materials or equipment.

3.14 CUTTING AND PATCHING

3.14.1 The Contractor shall be responsible for cutting, fitting or patching required to complete the Work or to make its parts fit together properly.

3.14.2 The Contractor shall not damage or endanger a portion of the Work or fully or partially completed construction of the Owner or separate contractors by cutting, patching or otherwise altering such construction, or by excavation. The Contractor shall not cut or otherwise alter such construction by the

FIGURE 11–1 (cont'd)

Owner or a separate contractor except with written consent of the Owner and of such separate contractor; such consent shall not be unreasonably withheld. The Contractor shall not unreasonably withhold from the Owner or a separate contractor the Contractor's consent to cutting or otherwise altering the Work.

3.15 CLEANING UP

3.15.1 The Contractor shall keep the premises and surrounding area free from accumulation of waste materials or rubbish caused by operations under the Contract. At completion of the Work the Contractor shall remove from and about the Project waste materials, rubbish, the Contractor's tools, construction equipment, machinery and surplus materials.

3.15.2 If the Contractor fails to clean up as provided in the Contract Documents, the Owner may do so and the cost thereof shall be charged to the Contractor.

3.16 ACCESS TO WORK

3.16.1 The Contractor shall provide the Owner and Architect access to the Work in preparation and progress wherever located.

3.17 ROYALTIES AND PATENTS

3.17.1 The Contractor shall pay all royalties and license fees. The Contractor shall defend suits or claims for infringement of patent rights and shall hold the Owner and Architect harmless from loss on account thereof, but shall not be responsible for such defense or loss when a particular design, process or product of a particular manufacturer or manufacturers is required by the Contract Documents. However, if the Contractor has reason to believe that the required design, process or product is an infringement of a patent, the Contractor shall be responsible for such loss unless such information is promptly furnished to the Architect.

3.18 INDEMNIFICATION

3.18.1 To the fullest extent permitted by law, the Contractor shall indemnify and hold harmless the Owner, Architect, Architect's consultants, and agents and employees of any of them from and against claims, damages, losses and expenses, including but not limited to attorneys' fees, arising out of or resulting from performance of the Work, provided that such claim, damage, loss or expense is attributable to bodily injury, sickness, disease or death, or to injury to or destruction of tangible property (other than the Work itself) including loss of use resulting therefrom, but only to the extent caused in whole or in part by negligent acts or omissions of the Contractor, a Subcontractor, anyone directly or indirectly employed by them or anyone for whose acts they may be liable, regardless of whether or not such claim, damage, loss or expense is caused in part by a party indemnified hereunder. Such obligation shall not be construed to negate, abridge, or reduce other rights or obligations of indemnity which would otherwise exist as to a party or person described in this Paragraph 3.18.

3.18.2 In claims against any person or entity indemnified under this Paragraph 3.18 by an employee of the Contractor, a Subcontractor, anyone directly or indirectly employed by them or anyone for whose acts they may be liable, the indemnification obligation under this Paragraph 3.18 shall not be limited by a limitation on amount or type of damages, compensation or benefits payable by or for the Contractor or a Subcontractor under workers' or workmen's compensation acts, disability benefit acts or other employee benefit acts.

3.18.3 The obligations of the Contractor under this Paragraph 3.18 shall not extend to the liability of the Architect, the Archi-

tect's consultants, and agents and employees of any of them arising out of (1) the preparation or approval of maps, drawings, opinions, reports, surveys, Change Orders, designs or specifications, or (2) the giving of or the failure to give directions or instructions by the Architect, the Architect's consultants, and agents and employees of any of them provided such giving or failure to give is the primary cause of the injury or damage.

ARTICLE 4

ADMINISTRATION OF THE CONTRACT

4.1 ARCHITECT

4.1.1 The Architect is the person lawfully licensed to practice architecture or an entity lawfully practicing architecture identified as such in the Agreement and is referred to throughout the Contract Documents as if singular in number. The term "Architect" means the Architect or the Architect's authorized representative.

4.1.2 Duties, responsibilities and limitations of authority of the Architect as set forth in the Contract Documents shall not be restricted, modified or extended without written consent of the Owner, Contractor and Architect. Consent shall not be unreasonably withheld.

4.1.3 In case of termination of employment of the Architect, the Owner shall appoint an architect against whom the Contractor makes no reasonable objection and whose status under the Contract Documents shall be that of the former architect.

4.1.4 Disputes arising under Subparagraphs 4.1.2 and 4.1.3 shall be subject to arbitration.

4.2 ARCHITECT'S ADMINISTRATION OF THE CONTRACT

4.2.1 The Architect will provide administration of the Contract as described in the Contract Documents, and will be the Owner's representative (1) during construction, (2) until final payment is due and (3) with the Owner's concurrence, from time to time during the correction period described in Paragraph 12.2. The Architect will advise and consult with the Owner. The Architect will have authority to act on behalf of the Owner only to the extent provided in the Contract Documents, unless otherwise modified by written instrument in accordance with other provisions of the Contract.

4.2.2 The Architect will visit the site at intervals appropriate to the stage of construction to become generally familiar with the progress and quality of the completed Work and to determine in general if the Work is being performed in a manner indicating that the Work, when completed, will be in accordance with the Contract Documents. However, the Architect will not be required to make exhaustive or continuous on-site inspections to check quality or quantity of the Work. On the basis of on-site observations as an architect, the Architect will keep the Owner informed of progress of the Work, and will endeavor to guard the Owner against defects and deficiencies in the Work.

4.2.3 The Architect will not have control over or charge of and will not be responsible for construction means, methods, techniques, sequences or procedures, or for safety precautions and programs in connection with the Work, since these are solely the Contractor's responsibility as provided in Paragraph 3.3. The Architect will not be responsible for the Contractor's failure to carry out the Work in accordance with the Contract Documents. The Architect will not have control over or charge of and will not be responsible for acts or omissions of the Con-

FIGURE 11–1 (cont'd)

tractor, Subcontractors, or their agents or employees, or of any other persons performing portions of the Work.

4.2.4 Communications Facilitating Contract Administration. Except as otherwise provided in the Contract Documents or when direct communications have been specially authorized, the Owner and Contractor shall endeavor to communicate through the Architect. Communications by and with the Architect's consultants shall be through the Architect. Communications by and with Subcontractors and material suppliers shall be through the Contractor. Communications by and with separate contractors shall be through the Owner.

4.2.5 Based on the Architect's observations and evaluations of the Contractor's Applications for Payment, the Architect will review and certify the amounts due the Contractor and will issue Certificates for Payment in such amounts.

4.2.6 The Architect will have authority to reject Work which does not conform to the Contract Documents. Whenever the Architect considers it necessary or advisable for implementation of the intent of the Contract Documents, the Architect will have authority to require additional inspection or testing of the Work in accordance with Subparagraphs 13.5.2 and 13.5.3, whether or not such Work is fabricated, installed or completed. However, neither this authority of the Architect nor a decision made in good faith either to exercise or not to exercise such authority shall give rise to a duty or responsibility of the Architect to the Contractor, Subcontractors, material and equipment suppliers, their agents or employees, or other persons performing portions of the Work.

4.2.7 The Architect will review and approve or take other appropriate action upon the Contractor's submittals such as Shop Drawings, Product Data and Samples, but only for the limited purpose of checking for conformance with information given and the design concept expressed in the Contract Documents. The Architect's action will be taken with such reasonable promptness as to cause no delay in the Work or in the activities of the Owner, Contractor or separate contractors, while allowing sufficient time in the Architect's professional judgment to permit adequate review. Review of such submittals is not conducted for the purpose of determining the accuracy and completeness of other details such as dimensions and quantities, or for substantiating instructions for installation or performance of equipment or systems, all of which remain the responsibility of the Contractor as required by the Contract Documents. The Architect's review of the Contractor's submittals shall not relieve the Contractor of the obligations under Paragraphs 3.3, 3.5 and 3.12. The Architect's review shall not constitute approval of safety precautions or, unless otherwise specifically stated by the Architect, of any construction means, methods, techniques, sequences or procedures. The Architect's approval of a specific item shall not indicate approval of an assembly of which the item is a component.

4.2.8 The Architect will prepare Change Orders and Construction Change Directives, and may authorize minor changes in the Work as provided in Paragraph 7.4.

4.2.9 The Architect will conduct inspections to determine the date or dates of Substantial Completion and the date of final completion, will receive and forward to the Owner for the Owner's review and records written warranties and related documents required by the Contract and assembled by the Contractor, and will issue a final Certificate for Payment upon compliance with the requirements of the Contract Documents.

4.2.10 If the Owner and Architect agree, the Architect will provide one or more project representatives to assist in carrying out the Architect's responsibilities at the site. The duties, responsibilities and limitations of authority of such project representatives shall be as set forth in an exhibit to be incorporated in the Contract Documents.

4.2.11 The Architect will interpret and decide matters concerning performance under and requirements of the Contract Documents on written request of either the Owner or Contractor. The Architect's response to such requests will be made with reasonable promptness and within any time limits agreed upon. If no agreement is made concerning the time within which interpretations required of the Architect shall be furnished in compliance with this Paragraph 4.2, then delay shall not be recognized on account of failure by the Architect to furnish such interpretations until 15 days after written request is made for them.

4.2.12 Interpretations and decisions of the Architect will be consistent with the intent of and reasonably inferable from the Contract Documents and will be in writing or in the form of drawings. When making such interpretations and decisions, the Architect will endeavor to secure faithful performance by both Owner and Contractor, will not show partiality to either and will not be liable for results of interpretations or decisions so rendered in good faith.

4.2.13 The Architect's decisions on matters relating to aesthetic effect will be final if consistent with the intent expressed in the Contract Documents.

4.3   CLAIMS AND DISPUTES

4.3.1 Definition. A Claim is a demand or assertion by one of the parties seeking, as a matter of right, adjustment or interpretation of Contract terms, payment of money, extension of time or other relief with respect to the terms of the Contract. The term "Claim" also includes other disputes and matters in question between the Owner and Contractor arising out of or relating to the Contract. Claims must be made by written notice. The responsibility to substantiate Claims shall rest with the party making the Claim.

4.3.2 Decision of Architect. Claims, including those alleging an error or omission by the Architect, shall be referred initially to the Architect for action as provided in Paragraph 4.4. A decision by the Architect, as provided in Subparagraph 4.4.4, shall be required as a condition precedent to arbitration or litigation of a Claim between the Contractor and Owner as to all such matters arising prior to the date final payment is due, regardless of (1) whether such matters relate to execution and progress of the Work or (2) the extent to which the Work has been completed. The decision by the Architect in response to a Claim shall not be a condition precedent to arbitration or litigation in the event (1) the position of Architect is vacant, (2) the Architect has not received evidence or has failed to render a decision within agreed time limits, (3) the Architect has failed to take action required under Subparagraph 4.4.4 within 30 days after the Claim is made, (4) 45 days have passed after the Claim has been referred to the Architect or (5) the Claim relates to a mechanic's lien.

4.3.3 Time Limits on Claims. Claims by either party must be made within 21 days after occurrence of the event giving rise to such Claim or within 21 days after the claimant first recognizes the condition giving rise to the Claim, whichever is later. Claims must be made by written notice. An additional Claim made after the initial Claim has been implemented by Change Order will not be considered unless submitted in a timely manner.

FIGURE 11–1   *(cont'd)*

4.3.4 Continuing Contract Performance. Pending final resolution of a Claim including arbitration, unless otherwise agreed in writing the Contractor shall proceed diligently with performance of the Contract and the Owner shall continue to make payments in accordance with the Contract Documents.

4.3.5 Waiver of Claims: Final Payment. The making of final payment shall constitute a waiver of Claims by the Owner except those arising from:

> **.1** liens, Claims, security interests or encumbrances arising out of the Contract and unsettled;
>
> **.2** failure of the Work to comply with the requirements of the Contract Documents; or
>
> **.3** terms of special warranties required by the Contract Documents.

4.3.6 Claims for Concealed or Unknown Conditions. If conditions are encountered at the site which are (1) subsurface or otherwise concealed physical conditions which differ materially from those indicated in the Contract Documents or (2) unknown physical conditions of an unusual nature, which differ materially from those ordinarily found to exist and generally recognized as inherent in construction activities of the character provided for in the Contract Documents, then notice by the observing party shall be given to the other party promptly before conditions are disturbed and in no event later than 21 days after first observance of the conditions. The Architect will promptly investigate such conditions and, if they differ materially and cause an increase or decrease in the Contractor's cost of, or time required for, performance of any part of the Work, will recommend an equitable adjustment in the Contract Sum or Contract Time, or both. If the Architect determines that the conditions at the site are not materially different from those indicated in the Contract Documents and that no change in the terms of the Contract is justified, the Architect shall so notify the Owner and Contractor in writing, stating the reasons. Claims by either party in opposition to such determination must be made within 21 days after the Architect has given notice of the decision. If the Owner and Contractor cannot agree on an adjustment in the Contract Sum or Contract Time, the adjustment shall be referred to the Architect for initial determination, subject to further proceedings pursuant to Paragraph 4.4.

4.3.7 Claims for Additional Cost. If the Contractor wishes to make Claim for an increase in the Contract Sum, written notice as provided herein shall be given before proceeding to execute the Work. Prior notice is not required for Claims relating to an emergency endangering life or property arising under Paragraph 10.3. If the Contractor believes additional cost is involved for reasons including but not limited to (1) a written interpretation from the Architect, (2) an order by the Owner to stop the Work where the Contractor was not at fault, (3) a written order for a minor change in the Work issued by the Architect, (4) failure of payment by the Owner, (5) termination of the Contract by the Owner, (6) Owner's suspension or (7) other reasonable grounds, Claim shall be filed in accordance with the procedure established herein.

4.3.8   Claims for Additional Time

4.3.8.1 If the Contractor wishes to make Claim for an increase in the Contract Time, written notice as provided herein shall be given. The Contractor's Claim shall include an estimate of cost and of probable effect of delay on progress of the Work. In the case of a continuing delay only one Claim is necessary.

4.3.8.2 If adverse weather conditions are the basis for a Claim for additional time, such Claim shall be documented by data substantiating that weather conditions were abnormal for the period of time and could not have been reasonably anticipated, and that weather conditions had an adverse effect on the scheduled construction.

4.3.9 Injury or Damage to Person or Property. If either party to the Contract suffers injury or damage to person or property because of an act or omission of the other party, of any of the other party's employees or agents, or of others for whose acts such party is legally liable, written notice of such injury or damage, whether or not insured, shall be given to the other party within a reasonable time not exceeding 21 days after first observance. The notice shall provide sufficient detail to enable the other party to investigate the matter. If a Claim for additional cost or time related to this Claim is to be asserted, it shall be filed as provided in Subparagraphs 4.3.7 or 4.3.8.

4.4   RESOLUTION OF CLAIMS AND DISPUTES

4.4.1 The Architect will review Claims and take one or more of the following preliminary actions within ten days of receipt of a Claim: (1) request additional supporting data from the claimant, (2) submit a schedule to the parties indicating when the Architect expects to take action, (3) reject the Claim in whole or in part, stating reasons for rejection, (4) recommend approval of the Claim by the other party or (5) suggest a compromise. The Architect may also, but is not obligated to, notify the surety, if any, of the nature and amount of the Claim.

4.4.2 If a Claim has been resolved, the Architect will prepare or obtain appropriate documentation.

4.4.3 If a Claim has not been resolved, the party making the Claim shall, within ten days after the Architect's preliminary response, take one or more of the following actions: (1) submit additional supporting data requested by the Architect, (2) modify the initial Claim or (3) notify the Architect that the initial Claim stands.

4.4.4 If a Claim has not been resolved after consideration of the foregoing and of further evidence presented by the parties or requested by the Architect, the Architect will notify the parties in writing that the Architect's decision will be made within seven days, which decision shall be final and binding on the parties but subject to arbitration. Upon expiration of such time period, the Architect will render to the parties the Architect's written decision relative to the Claim, including any change in the Contract Sum or Contract Time or both. If there is a surety and there appears to be a possibility of a Contractor's default, the Architect may, but is not obligated to, notify the surety and request the surety's assistance in resolving the controversy.

4.5   ARBITRATION

4.5.1 Controversies and Claims Subject to Arbitration. Any controversy or Claim arising out of or related to the Contract, or the breach thereof, shall be settled by arbitration in accordance with the Construction Industry Arbitration Rules of the American Arbitration Association, and judgment upon the award rendered by the arbitrator or arbitrators may be entered in any court having jurisdiction thereof, except controversies or Claims relating to aesthetic effect and except those waived as provided for in Subparagraph 4.3.5. Such controversies or Claims upon which the Architect has given notice and rendered a decision as provided in Subparagraph 4.4.4 shall be subject to arbitration upon written demand of either party. Arbitration may be commenced when 45 days have passed after a Claim has been referred to the Architect as provided in Paragraph 4.3 and no decision has been rendered.

FIGURE 11–1 (cont'd)

4.5.2 Rules and Notices for Arbitration. Claims between the Owner and Contractor not resolved under Paragraph 4.4 shall, if subject to arbitration under Subparagraph 4.5.1, be decided by arbitration in accordance with the Construction Industry Arbitration Rules of the American Arbitration Association currently in effect, unless the parties mutually agree otherwise. Notice of demand for arbitration shall be filed in writing with the other party to the Agreement between the Owner and Contractor and with the American Arbitration Association, and a copy shall be filed with the Architect.

4.5.3 Contract Performance During Arbitration. During arbitration proceedings, the Owner and Contractor shall comply with Subparagraph 4.3.4.

4.5.4 When Arbitration May Be Demanded. Demand for arbitration of any Claim may not be made until the earlier of (1) the date on which the Architect has rendered a final written decision on the Claim, (2) the tenth day after the parties have presented evidence to the Architect or have been given reasonable opportunity to do so, if the Architect has not rendered a final written decision by that date, or (3) any of the five events described in Subparagraph 4.3.2.

4.5.4.1 When a written decision of the Architect states that (1) the decision is final but subject to arbitration and (2) a demand for arbitration of a Claim covered by such decision must be made within 30 days after the date on which the party making the demand receives the final written decision, then failure to demand arbitration within said 30 days' period shall result in the Architect's decision becoming final and binding upon the Owner and Contractor. If the Architect renders a decision after arbitration proceedings have been initiated, such decision may be entered as evidence, but shall not supersede arbitration proceedings unless the decision is acceptable to all parties concerned.

4.5.4.2 A demand for arbitration shall be made within the time limits specified in Subparagraphs 4.5.1 and 4.5.4 and Clause 4.5.4.1 as applicable, and in other cases within a reasonable time after the Claim has arisen, and in no event shall it be made after the date when institution of legal or equitable proceedings based on such Claim would be barred by the applicable statute of limitations as determined pursuant to Paragraph 13.7.

4.5.5 Limitation on Consolidation or Joinder. No arbitration arising out of or relating to the Contract Documents shall include, by consolidation or joinder or in any other manner, the Architect, the Architect's employees or consultants, except by written consent containing specific reference to the Agreement and signed by the Architect, Owner, Contractor and any other person or entity sought to be joined. No arbitration shall include, by consolidation or joinder or in any other manner, parties other than the Owner, Contractor, a separate contractor as described in Article 6 and other persons substantially involved in a common question of fact or law whose presence is required if complete relief is to be accorded in arbitration. No person or entity other than the Owner, Contractor or a separate contractor as described in Article 6 shall be included as an original third party or additional third party to an arbitration whose interest or responsibility is insubstantial. Consent to arbitration involving an additional person or entity shall not constitute consent to arbitration of a dispute not described therein or with a person or entity not named or described therein. The foregoing agreement to arbitrate and other agreements to arbitrate with an additional person or entity duly consented to by parties to the Agreement shall be specifically enforceable under applicable law in any court having jurisdiction thereof.

4.5.6 Claims and Timely Assertion of Claims. A party who files a notice of demand for arbitration must assert in the demand all Claims then known to that party on which arbitration is permitted to be demanded. When a party fails to include a Claim through oversight, inadvertence or excusable neglect, or when a Claim has matured or been acquired subsequently, the arbitrator or arbitrators may permit amendment.

4.5.7 Judgment on Final Award. The award rendered by the arbitrator or arbitrators shall be final, and judgment may be entered upon it in accordance with applicable law in any court having jurisdiction thereof.

ARTICLE 5

SUBCONTRACTORS

5.1 DEFINITIONS

5.1.1 A Subcontractor is a person or entity who has a direct contract with the Contractor to perform a portion of the Work at the site. The term "Subcontractor" is referred to throughout the Contract Documents as if singular in number and means a Subcontractor or an authorized representative of the Subcontractor. The term "Subcontractor" does not include a separate contractor or subcontractors of a separate contractor.

5.1.2 A Sub-subcontractor is a person or entity who has a direct or indirect contract with a Subcontractor to perform a portion of the Work at the site. The term "Sub-subcontractor" is referred to throughout the Contract Documents as if singular in number and means a Sub-subcontractor or an authorized representative of the Sub-subcontractor.

5.2 AWARD OF SUBCONTRACTS AND OTHER CONTRACTS FOR PORTIONS OF THE WORK

5.2.1 Unless otherwise stated in the Contract Documents or the bidding requirements, the Contractor, as soon as practicable after award of the Contract, shall furnish in writing to the Owner through the Architect the names of persons or entities (including those who are to furnish materials or equipment fabricated to a special design) proposed for each principal portion of the Work. The Architect will promptly reply to the Contractor in writing stating whether or not the Owner or the Architect, after due investigation, has reasonable objection to any such proposed person or entity. Failure of the Owner or Architect to reply promptly shall constitute notice of no reasonable objection.

5.2.2 The Contractor shall not contract with a proposed person or entity to whom the Owner or Architect has made reasonable and timely objection. The Contractor shall not be required to contract with anyone to whom the Contractor has made reasonable objection.

5.2.3 If the Owner or Architect has reasonable objection to a person or entity proposed by the Contractor, the Contractor shall propose another to whom the Owner or Architect has no reasonable objection. The Contract Sum shall be increased or decreased by the difference in cost occasioned by such change and an appropriate Change Order shall be issued. However, no increase in the Contract Sum shall be allowed for such change unless the Contractor has acted promptly and responsively in submitting names as required.

5.2.4 The Contractor shall not change a Subcontractor, person or entity previously selected if the Owner or Architect makes reasonable objection to such change.

FIGURE 11-1   (cont'd)

5.3   SUBCONTRACTUAL RELATIONS

5.3.1 By appropriate agreement, written where legally required for validity, the Contractor shall require each Subcontractor, to the extent of the Work to be performed by the Subcontractor, to be bound to the Contractor by terms of the Contract Documents, and to assume toward the Contractor all the obligations and responsibilities which the Contractor, by these Documents, assumes toward the Owner and Architect. Each subcontract agreement shall preserve and protect the rights of the Owner and Architect under the Contract Documents with respect to the Work to be performed by the Subcontractor so that subcontracting thereof will not prejudice such rights, and shall allow to the Subcontractor, unless specifically provided otherwise in the subcontract agreement, the benefit of all rights, remedies and redress against the Contractor that the Contractor, by the Contract Documents, has against the Owner. Where appropriate, the Contractor shall require each Subcontractor to enter into similar agreements with Sub-sub-contractors. The Contractor shall make available to each proposed Subcontractor, prior to the execution of the subcontract agreement, copies of the Contract Documents to which the Subcontractor will be bound, and, upon written request of the Subcontractor, identify to the Subcontractor terms and conditions of the proposed subcontract agreement which may be at variance with the Contract Documents. Subcontractors shall similarly make copies of applicable portions of such documents available to their respective proposed Sub-subcontractors.

5.4   CONTINGENT ASSIGNMENT OF SUBCONTRACTS

5.4.1 Each subcontract agreement for a portion of the Work is assigned by the Contractor to the Owner provided that:

   .1 assignment is effective only after termination of the Contract by the Owner for cause pursuant to Paragraph 14.2 and only for those subcontract agreements which the Owner accepts by notifying the Subcontractor in writing; and

   .2 assignment is subject to the prior rights of the surety, if any, obligated under bond relating to the Contract.

5.4.2 If the Work has been suspended for more than 30 days, the Subcontractor's compensation shall be equitably adjusted.

ARTICLE 6

CONSTRUCTION BY OWNER OR BY SEPARATE CONTRACTORS

6.1   OWNER'S RIGHT TO PERFORM CONSTRUCTION AND TO AWARD SEPARATE CONTRACTS

6.1.1 The Owner reserves the right to perform construction or operations related to the Project with the Owner's own forces, and to award separate contracts in connection with other portions of the Project or other construction or operations on the site under Conditions of the Contract identical or substantially similar to these including those portions related to insurance and waiver of subrogation. If the Contractor claims that delay or additional cost is involved because of such action by the Owner, the Contractor shall make such Claim as provided elsewhere in the Contract Documents.

6.1.2 When separate contracts are awarded for different portions of the Project or other construction or operations on the site, the term "Contractor" in the Contract Documents in each case shall mean the Contractor who executes each separate Owner-Contractor Agreement.

6.1.3 The Owner shall provide for coordination of the activities of the Owner's own forces and of each separate contractor with the Work of the Contractor, who shall cooperate with them. The Contractor shall participate with other separate contractors and the Owner in reviewing their construction schedules when directed to do so. The Contractor shall make any revisions to the construction schedule and Contract Sum deemed necessary after a joint review and mutual agreement. The construction schedules shall then constitute the schedules to be used by the Contractor, separate contractors and the Owner until subsequently revised.

6.1.4 Unless otherwise provided in the Contract Documents, when the Owner performs construction or operations related to the Project with the Owner's own forces, the Owner shall be deemed to be subject to the same obligations and to have the same rights which apply to the Contractor under the Conditions of the Contract, including, without excluding others, those stated in Article 3, this Article 6 and Articles 10, 11 and 12.

6.2   MUTUAL RESPONSIBILITY

6.2.1 The Contractor shall afford the Owner and separate contractors reasonable opportunity for introduction and storage of their materials and equipment and performance of their activities and shall connect and coordinate the Contractor's construction and operations with theirs as required by the Contract Documents.

6.2.2 If part of the Contractor's Work depends for proper execution or results upon construction or operations by the Owner or a separate contractor, the Contractor shall, prior to proceeding with that portion of the Work, promptly report to the Architect apparent discrepancies or defects in such other construction that would render it unsuitable for such proper execution and results. Failure of the Contractor so to report shall constitute an acknowledgment that the Owner's or separate contractors' completed or partially completed construction is fit and proper to receive the Contractor's Work, except as to defects not then reasonably discoverable.

6.2.3 Costs caused by delays or by improperly timed activities or defective construction shall be borne by the party responsible therefor.

6.2.4 The Contractor shall promptly remedy damage wrongfully caused by the Contractor to completed or partially completed construction or to property of the Owner or separate contractors as provided in Subparagraph 10.2.5.

6.2.5 Claims and other disputes and matters in question between the Contractor and a separate contractor shall be subject to the provisions of Paragraph 4.3 provided the separate contractor has reciprocal obligations.

6.2.6 The Owner and each separate contractor shall have the same responsibilities for cutting and patching as are described for the Contractor in Paragraph 3.14.

6.3   OWNER'S RIGHT TO CLEAN UP

6.3.1 If a dispute arises among the Contractor, separate contractors and the Owner as to the responsibility under their respective contracts for maintaining the premises and surrounding area free from waste materials and rubbish as described in Paragraph 3.15, the Owner may clean up and allocate the cost among those responsible as the Architect determines to be just.

FIGURE 11–1 (cont'd)

ARTICLE 7

CHANGES IN THE WORK

7.1 CHANGES

7.1.1 Changes in the Work may be accomplished after execution of the Contract, and without invalidating the Contract, by Change Order, Construction Change Directive or order for a minor change in the Work, subject to the limitations stated in this Article 7 and elsewhere in the Contract Documents.

7.1.2 A Change Order shall be based upon agreement among the Owner, Contractor and Architect; a Construction Change Directive requires agreement by the Owner and Architect and may or may not be agreed to by the Contractor; an order for a minor change in the Work may be issued by the Architect alone.

7.1.3 Changes in the Work shall be performed under applicable provisions of the Contract Documents, and the Contractor shall proceed promptly, unless otherwise provided in the Change Order, Construction Change Directive or order for a minor change in the Work.

7.1.4 If unit prices are stated in the Contract Documents or subsequently agreed upon, and if quantities originally contemplated are so changed in a proposed Change Order or Construction Change Directive that application of such unit prices to quantities of Work proposed will cause substantial inequity to the Owner or Contractor, the applicable unit prices shall be equitably adjusted.

7.2 CHANGE ORDERS

7.2.1 A Change Order is a written instrument prepared by the Architect and signed by the Owner, Contractor and Architect, stating their agreement upon all of the following:

    .1 a change in the Work;

    .2 the amount of the adjustment in the Contract Sum, if any; and

    .3 the extent of the adjustment in the Contract Time, if any.

7.2.2 Methods used in determining adjustments to the Contract Sum may include those listed in Subparagraph 7.3.3.

7.3 CONSTRUCTION CHANGE DIRECTIVES

7.3.1 A Construction Change Directive is a written order prepared by the Architect and signed by the Owner and Architect, directing a change in the Work and stating a proposed basis for adjustment, if any, in the Contract Sum or Contract Time, or both. The Owner may by Construction Change Directive, without invalidating the Contract, order changes in the Work within the general scope of the Contract consisting of additions, deletions or other revisions, the Contract Sum and Contract Time being adjusted accordingly.

7.3.2 A Construction Change Directive shall be used in the absence of total agreement on the terms of a Change Order.

7.3.3 If the Construction Change Directive provides for an adjustment to the Contract Sum, the adjustment shall be based on one of the following methods:

    .1 mutual acceptance of a lump sum properly itemized and supported by sufficient substantiating data to permit evaluation;

    .2 unit prices stated in the Contract Documents or subsequently agreed upon;

    .3 cost to be determined in a manner agreed upon by the parties and a mutually acceptable fixed or percentage fee; or

    .4 as provided in Subparagraph 7.3.6.

7.3.4 Upon receipt of a Construction Change Directive, the Contractor shall promptly proceed with the change in the Work involved and advise the Architect of the Contractor's agreement or disagreement with the method, if any, provided in the Construction Change Directive for determining the proposed adjustment in the Contract Sum or Contract Time.

7.3.5 A Construction Change Directive signed by the Contractor indicates the agreement of the Contractor therewith, including adjustment in Contract Sum and Contract Time or the method for determining them. Such agreement shall be effective immediately and shall be recorded as a Change Order.

7.3.6 If the Contractor does not respond promptly or disagrees with the method for adjustment in the Contract Sum, the method and the adjustment shall be determined by the Architect on the basis of reasonable expenditures and savings of those performing the Work attributable to the change, including, in case of an increase in the Contract Sum, a reasonable allowance for overhead and profit. In such case, and also under Clause 7.3.3.3, the Contractor shall keep and present, in such form as the Architect may prescribe, an itemized accounting together with appropriate supporting data. Unless otherwise provided in the Contract Documents, costs for the purposes of this Subparagraph 7.3.6 shall be limited to the following:

    .1 costs of labor, including social security, old age and unemployment insurance, fringe benefits required by agreement or custom, and workers' or workmen's compensation insurance;

    .2 costs of materials, supplies and equipment, including cost of transportation, whether incorporated or consumed;

    .3 rental costs of machinery and equipment, exclusive of hand tools, whether rented from the Contractor or others;

    .4 costs of premiums for all bonds and insurance, permit fees, and sales, use or similar taxes related to the Work; and

    .5 additional costs of supervision and field office personnel directly attributable to the change.

7.3.7 Pending final determination of cost to the Owner, amounts not in dispute may be included in Applications for Payment. The amount of credit to be allowed by the Contractor to the Owner for a deletion or change which results in a net decrease in the Contract Sum shall be actual net cost as confirmed by the Architect. When both additions and credits covering related Work or substitutions are involved in a change, the allowance for overhead and profit shall be figured on the basis of net increase, if any, with respect to that change.

7.3.8 If the Owner and Contractor do not agree with the adjustment in Contract Time or the method for determining it, the adjustment or the method shall be referred to the Architect for determination.

7.3.9 When the Owner and Contractor agree with the determination made by the Architect concerning the adjustments in the Contract Sum and Contract Time, or otherwise reach agreement upon the adjustments, such agreement shall be effective immediately and shall be recorded by preparation and execution of an appropriate Change Order.

FIGURE 11-1 (cont'd)

7.4   MINOR CHANGES IN THE WORK

7.4.1 The Architect will have authority to order minor changes in the Work not involving adjustment in the Contract Sum or extension of the Contract Time and not inconsistent with the intent of the Contract Documents. Such changes shall be effected by written order and shall be binding on the Owner and Contractor. The Contractor shall carry out such written orders promptly.

ARTICLE 8

TIME

8.1   DEFINITIONS

8.1.1 Unless otherwise provided, Contract Time is the period of time, including authorized adjustments, allotted in the Contract Documents for Substantial Completion of the Work.

8.1.2 The date of commencement of the Work is the date established in the Agreement. The date shall not be postponed by the failure to act of the Contractor or of persons or entities for whom the Contractor is responsible.

8.1.3 The date of Substantial Completion is the date certified by the Architect in accordance with Paragraph 9.8.

8.1.4 The term "day" as used in the Contract Documents shall mean calendar day unless otherwise specifically defined.

8.2   PROGRESS AND COMPLETION

8.2.1 Time limits stated in the Contract Documents are of the essence of the Contract. By executing the Agreement the Contractor confirms that the Contract Time is a reasonable period for performing the Work.

8.2.2 The Contractor shall not knowingly, except by agreement or instruction of the Owner in writing, prematurely commence operations on the site or elsewhere prior to the effective date of insurance required by Article 11 to be furnished by the Contractor. The date of commencement of the Work shall not be changed by the effective date of such insurance. Unless the date of commencement is established by a notice to proceed given by the Owner, the Contractor shall notify the Owner in writing not less than five days or other agreed period before commencing the Work to permit the timely filing of mortgages, mechanic's liens and other security interests.

8.2.3 The Contractor shall proceed expeditiously with adequate forces and shall achieve Substantial Completion within the Contract Time.

8.3   DELAYS AND EXTENSIONS OF TIME

8.3.1 If the Contractor is delayed at any time in progress of the Work by an act or neglect of the Owner or Architect, or of an employee of either, or of a separate contractor employed by the Owner, or by changes ordered in the Work, or by labor disputes, fire, unusual delay in deliveries, unavoidable casualties or other causes beyond the Contractor's control, or by delay authorized by the Owner pending arbitration, or by other causes which the Architect determines may justify delay, then the Contract Time shall be extended by Change Order for such reasonable time as the Architect may determine.

8.3.2 Claims relating to time shall be made in accordance with applicable provisions of Paragraph 4.3.

8.3.3 This Paragraph 8.3 does not preclude recovery of damages for delay by either party under other provisions of the Contract Documents.

ARTICLE 9

PAYMENTS AND COMPLETION

9.1   CONTRACT SUM

9.1.1 The Contract Sum is stated in the Agreement and, including authorized adjustments, is the total amount payable by the Owner to the Contractor for performance of the Work under the Contract Documents.

9.2   SCHEDULE OF VALUES

9.2.1 Before the first Application for Payment, the Contractor shall submit to the Architect a schedule of values allocated to various portions of the Work, prepared in such form and supported by such data to substantiate its accuracy as the Architect may require. This schedule, unless objected to by the Architect, shall be used as a basis for reviewing the Contractor's Applications for Payment.

9.3   APPLICATIONS FOR PAYMENT

9.3.1 At least ten days before the date established for each progress payment, the Contractor shall submit to the Architect an itemized Application for Payment for operations completed in accordance with the schedule of values. Such application shall be notarized, if required, and supported by such data substantiating the Contractor's right to payment as the Owner or Architect may require, such as copies of requisitions from Subcontractors and material suppliers, and reflecting retainage if provided for elsewhere in the Contract Documents.

9.3.1.1 Such applications may include requests for payment on account of changes in the Work which have been properly authorized by Construction Change Directives but not yet included in Change Orders.

9.3.1.2 Such applications may not include requests for payment of amounts the Contractor does not intend to pay to a Subcontractor or material supplier because of a dispute or other reason.

9.3.2 Unless otherwise provided in the Contract Documents, payments shall be made on account of materials and equipment delivered and suitably stored at the site for subsequent incorporation in the Work. If approved in advance by the Owner, payment may similarly be made for materials and equipment suitably stored off the site at a location agreed upon in writing. Payment for materials and equipment stored on or off the site shall be conditioned upon compliance by the Contractor with procedures satisfactory to the Owner to establish the Owner's title to such materials and equipment or otherwise protect the Owner's interest, and shall include applicable insurance, storage and transportation to the site for such materials and equipment stored off the site.

9.3.3 The Contractor warrants that title to all Work covered by an Application for Payment will pass to the Owner no later than the time of payment. The Contractor further warrants that upon submittal of an Application for Payment all Work for which Certificates for Payment have been previously issued and payments received from the Owner shall, to the best of the Contractor's knowledge, information and belief, be free and clear of liens, claims, security interests or encumbrances in favor of the Contractor, Subcontractors, material suppliers, or other persons or entities making a claim by reason of having provided labor, materials and equipment relating to the Work.

9.4   CERTIFICATES FOR PAYMENT

9.4.1 The Architect will, within seven days after receipt of the Contractor's Application for Payment, either issue to the

AIA DOCUMENT A201 • GENERAL CONDITIONS OF THE CONTRACT FOR CONSTRUCTION • FOURTEENTH EDITION
AIA® • ©1987 THE AMERICAN INSTITUTE OF ARCHITECTS, 1735 NEW YORK AVENUE, N.W., WASHINGTON, D.C. 20006

FIGURE 11-1 (cont'd)

Owner a Certificate for Payment, with a copy to the Contractor, for such amount as the Architect determines is properly due, or notify the Contractor and Owner in writing of the Architect's reasons for withholding certification in whole or in part as provided in Subparagraph 9.5.1.

9.4.2 The issuance of a Certificate for Payment will constitute a representation by the Architect to the Owner, based on the Architect's observations at the site and the data comprising the Application for Payment, that the Work has progressed to the point indicated and that, to the best of the Architect's knowledge, information and belief, quality of the Work is in accordance with the Contract Documents. The foregoing representations are subject to an evaluation of the Work for conformance with the Contract Documents upon Substantial Completion, to results of subsequent tests and inspections, to minor deviations from the Contract Documents correctable prior to completion and to specific qualifications expressed by the Architect. The issuance of a Certificate for Payment will further constitute a representation that the Contractor is entitled to payment in the amount certified. However, the issuance of a Certificate for Payment will not be a representation that the Architect has (1) made exhaustive or continuous on-site inspections to check the quality or quantity of the Work, (2) reviewed construction means, methods, techniques, sequences or procedures, (3) reviewed copies of requisitions received from Subcontractors and material suppliers and other data requested by the Owner to substantiate the Contractor's right to payment or (4) made examination to ascertain how or for what purpose the Contractor has used money previously paid on account of the Contract Sum.

9.5   DECISIONS TO WITHHOLD CERTIFICATION

9.5.1 The Architect may decide not to certify payment and may withhold a Certificate for Payment in whole or in part, to the extent reasonably necessary to protect the Owner, if in the Architect's opinion the representations to the Owner required by Subparagraph 9.4.2 cannot be made. If the Architect is unable to certify payment in the amount of the Application, the Architect will notify the Contractor and Owner as provided in Subparagraph 9.4.1. If the Contractor and Architect cannot agree on a revised amount, the Architect will promptly issue a Certificate for Payment for the amount for which the Architect is able to make such representations to the Owner. The Architect may also decide not to certify payment or, because of subsequently discovered evidence or subsequent observations, may nullify the whole or a part of a Certificate for Payment previously issued, to such extent as may be necessary in the Architect's opinion to protect the Owner from loss because of:

.1   defective Work not remedied;

.2   third party claims filed or reasonable evidence indicating probable filing of such claims;

.3   failure of the Contractor to make payments properly to Subcontractors or for labor, materials or equipment;

.4   reasonable evidence that the Work cannot be completed for the unpaid balance of the Contract Sum;

.5   damage to the Owner or another contractor;

.6   reasonable evidence that the Work will not be completed within the Contract Time, and that the unpaid balance would not be adequate to cover actual or liquidated damages for the anticipated delay; or

.7   persistent failure to carry out the Work in accordance with the Contract Documents.

9.5.2 When the above reasons for withholding certification are removed, certification will be made for amounts previously withheld.

9.6   PROGRESS PAYMENTS

9.6.1 After the Architect has issued a Certificate for Payment, the Owner shall make payment in the manner and within the time provided in the Contract Documents, and shall so notify the Architect.

9.6.2 The Contractor shall promptly pay each Subcontractor, upon receipt of payment from the Owner, out of the amount paid to the Contractor on account of such Subcontractor's portion of the Work, the amount to which said Subcontractor is entitled, reflecting percentages actually retained from payments to the Contractor on account of such Subcontractor's portion of the Work. The Contractor shall, by appropriate agreement with each Subcontractor, require each Subcontractor to make payments to Sub-subcontractors in similar manner.

9.6.3 The Architect will, on request, furnish to a Subcontractor, if practicable, information regarding percentages of completion or amounts applied for by the Contractor and action taken thereon by the Architect and Owner on account of portions of the Work done by such Subcontractor.

9.6.4 Neither the Owner nor Architect shall have an obligation to pay or to see to the payment of money to a Subcontractor except as may otherwise be required by law.

9.6.5 Payment to material suppliers shall be treated in a manner similar to that provided in Subparagraphs 9.6.2, 9.6.3 and 9.6.4.

9.6.6 A Certificate for Payment, a progress payment, or partial or entire use or occupancy of the Project by the Owner shall not constitute acceptance of Work not in accordance with the Contract Documents.

9.7   FAILURE OF PAYMENT

9.7.1 If the Architect does not issue a Certificate for Payment, through no fault of the Contractor, within seven days after receipt of the Contractor's Application for Payment, or if the Owner does not pay the Contractor within seven days after the date established in the Contract Documents the amount certified by the Architect or awarded by arbitration, then the Contractor may, upon seven additional days' written notice to the Owner and Architect, stop the Work until payment of the amount owing has been received. The Contract Time shall be extended appropriately and the Contract Sum shall be increased by the amount of the Contractor's reasonable costs of shut-down, delay and start-up, which shall be accomplished as provided in Article 7.

9.8   SUBSTANTIAL COMPLETION

9.8.1 Substantial Completion is the stage in the progress of the Work when the Work or designated portion thereof is sufficiently complete in accordance with the Contract Documents so the Owner can occupy or utilize the Work for its intended use.

9.8.2 When the Contractor considers that the Work, or a portion thereof which the Owner agrees to accept separately, is substantially complete, the Contractor shall prepare and submit to the Architect a comprehensive list of items to be completed or corrected. The Contractor shall proceed promptly to complete and correct items on the list. Failure to include an item on such list does not alter the responsibility of the Contractor to complete all Work in accordance with the Contract Documents. Upon receipt of the Contractor's list, the Architect will make an inspection to determine whether the Work or desig-

FIGURE 11-1 (cont'd)

nated portion thereof is substantially complete. If the Architect's inspection discloses any item, whether or not included on the Contractor's list, which is not in accordance with the requirements of the Contract Documents, the Contractor shall, before issuance of the Certificate of Substantial Completion, complete or correct such item upon notification by the Architect. The Contractor shall then submit a request for another inspection by the Architect to determine Substantial Completion. When the Work or designated portion thereof is substantially complete, the Architect will prepare a Certificate of Substantial Completion which shall establish the date of Substantial Completion, shall establish responsibilities of the Owner and Contractor for security, maintenance, heat, utilities, damage to the Work and insurance, and shall fix the time within which the Contractor shall finish all items on the list accompanying the Certificate. Warranties required by the Contract Documents shall commence on the date of Substantial Completion of the Work or designated portion thereof unless otherwise provided in the Certificate of Substantial Completion. The Certificate of Substantial Completion shall be submitted to the Owner and Contractor for their written acceptance of responsibilities assigned to them in such Certificate.

9.8.3 Upon Substantial Completion of the Work or designated portion thereof and upon application by the Contractor and certification by the Architect, the Owner shall make payment, reflecting adjustment in retainage, if any, for such Work or portion thereof as provided in the Contract Documents.

9.9   PARTIAL OCCUPANCY OR USE

9.9.1 The Owner may occupy or use any completed or partially completed portion of the Work at any stage when such portion is designated by separate agreement with the Contractor, provided such occupancy or use is consented to by the insurer as required under Subparagraph 11.3.11 and authorized by public authorities having jurisdiction over the Work. Such partial occupancy or use may commence whether or not the portion is substantially complete, provided the Owner and Contractor have accepted in writing the responsibilities assigned to each of them for payments, retainage if any, security, maintenance, heat, utilities, damage to the Work and insurance, and have agreed in writing concerning the period for correction of the Work and commencement of warranties required by the Contract Documents. When the Contractor considers a portion substantially complete, the Contractor shall prepare and submit a list to the Architect as provided under Subparagraph 9.8.2. Consent of the Contractor to partial occupancy or use shall not be unreasonably withheld. The stage of the progress of the Work shall be determined by written agreement between the Owner and Contractor or, if no agreement is reached, by decision of the Architect.

9.9.2 Immediately prior to such partial occupancy or use, the Owner, Contractor and Architect shall jointly inspect the area to be occupied or portion of the Work to be used in order to determine and record the condition of the Work.

9.9.3 Unless otherwise agreed upon, partial occupancy or use of a portion or portions of the Work shall not constitute acceptance of Work not complying with the requirements of the Contract Documents.

9.10   FINAL COMPLETION AND FINAL PAYMENT

9.10.1 Upon receipt of written notice that the Work is ready for final inspection and acceptance and upon receipt of a final Application for Payment, the Architect will promptly make

such inspection and, when the Architect finds the Work acceptable under the Contract Documents and the Contract fully performed, the Architect will promptly issue a final Certificate for Payment stating that to the best of the Architect's knowledge, information and belief, and on the basis of the Architect's observations and inspections, the Work has been completed in accordance with terms and conditions of the Contract Documents and that the entire balance found to be due the Contractor and noted in said final Certificate is due and payable. The Architect's final Certificate for Payment will constitute a further representation that conditions listed in Subparagraph 9.10.2 as precedent to the Contractor's being entitled to final payment have been fulfilled.

9.10.2 Neither final payment nor any remaining retained percentage shall become due until the Contractor submits to the Architect (1) an affidavit that payrolls, bills for materials and equipment, and other indebtedness connected with the Work for which the Owner or the Owner's property might be responsible or encumbered (less amounts withheld by Owner) have been paid or otherwise satisfied, (2) a certificate evidencing that insurance required by the Contract Documents to remain in force after final payment is currently in effect and will not be cancelled or allowed to expire until at least 30 days' prior written notice has been given to the Owner, (3) a written statement that the Contractor knows of no substantial reason that the insurance will not be renewable to cover the period required by the Contract Documents, (4) consent of surety, if any, to final payment and (5), if required by the Owner, other data establishing payment or satisfaction of obligations, such as receipts, releases and waivers of liens, claims, security interests or encumbrances arising out of the Contract, to the extent and in such form as may be designated by the Owner. If a Subcontractor refuses to furnish a release or waiver required by the Owner, the Contractor may furnish a bond satisfactory to the Owner to indemnify the Owner against such lien. If such lien remains unsatisfied after payments are made, the Contractor shall refund to the Owner all money that the Owner may be compelled to pay in discharging such lien, including all costs and reasonable attorneys' fees.

9.10.3 If, after Substantial Completion of the Work, final completion thereof is materially delayed through no fault of the Contractor or by issuance of Change Orders affecting final completion, and the Architect so confirms, the Owner shall, upon application by the Contractor and certification by the Architect, and without terminating the Contract, make payment of the balance due for that portion of the Work fully completed and accepted. If the remaining balance for Work not fully completed or corrected is less than retainage stipulated in the Contract Documents, and if bonds have been furnished, the written consent of surety to payment of the balance due for that portion of the Work fully completed and accepted shall be submitted by the Contractor to the Architect prior to certification of such payment. Such payment shall be made under terms and conditions governing final payment, except that it shall not constitute a waiver of claims. The making of final payment shall constitute a waiver of claims by the Owner as provided in Subparagraph 4.3.5.

9.10.4 Acceptance of final payment by the Contractor, a Subcontractor or material supplier shall constitute a waiver of claims by that payee except those previously made in writing and identified by that payee as unsettled at the time of final Application for Payment. Such waivers shall be in addition to the waiver described in Subparagraph 4.3.5.

FIGURE 11–1 (cont'd)

ARTICLE 10

PROTECTION OF PERSONS AND PROPERTY

10.1 SAFETY PRECAUTIONS AND PROGRAMS

10.1.1 The Contractor shall be responsible for initiating, maintaining and supervising all safety precautions and programs in connection with the performance of the Contract.

10.1.2 In the event the Contractor encounters on the site material reasonably believed to be asbestos or polychlorinated biphenyl (PCB) which has not been rendered harmless, the Contractor shall immediately stop Work in the area affected and report the condition to the Owner and Architect in writing. The Work in the affected area shall not thereafter be resumed except by written agreement of the Owner and Contractor if in fact the material is asbestos or polychlorinated biphenyl (PCB) and has not been rendered harmless. The Work in the affected area shall be resumed in the absence of asbestos or polychlorinated biphenyl (PCB), or when it has been rendered harmless, by written agreement of the Owner and Contractor, or in accordance with final determination by the Architect on which arbitration has not been demanded, or by arbitration under Article 4.

10.1.3 The Contractor shall not be required pursuant to Article 7 to perform without consent any Work relating to asbestos or polychlorinated biphenyl (PCB).

10.1.4 To the fullest extent permitted by law, the Owner shall indemnify and hold harmless the Contractor, Architect, Architect's consultants and agents and employees of any of them from and against claims, damages, losses and expenses, including but not limited to attorneys' fees, arising out of or resulting from performance of the Work in the affected area if in fact the material is asbestos or polychlorinated biphenyl (PCB) and has not been rendered harmless, provided that such claim, damage, loss or expense is attributable to bodily injury, sickness, disease or death, or to injury to or destruction of tangible property (other than the Work itself) including loss of use resulting therefrom, but only to the extent caused in whole or in part by negligent acts or omissions of the Owner, anyone directly or indirectly employed by the Owner or anyone for whose acts the Owner may be liable, regardless of whether or not such claim, damage, loss or expense is caused in part by a party indemnified hereunder. Such obligation shall not be construed to negate, abridge, or reduce other rights or obligations of indemnity which would otherwise exist as to a party or person described in this Subparagraph 10.1.4.

10.2 SAFETY OF PERSONS AND PROPERTY

10.2.1 The Contractor shall take reasonable precautions for safety of, and shall provide reasonable protection to prevent damage, injury or loss to:

  .1 employees on the Work and other persons who may be affected thereby;

  .2 the Work and materials and equipment to be incorporated therein, whether in storage on or off the site, under care, custody or control of the Contractor or the Contractor's Subcontractors or Sub-subcontractors; and

  .3 other property at the site or adjacent thereto, such as trees, shrubs, lawns, walks, pavements, roadways, structures and utilities not designated for removal, relocation or replacement in the course of construction.

10.2.2 The Contractor shall give notices and comply with applicable laws, ordinances, rules, regulations and lawful orders of public authorities bearing on safety of persons or property or their protection from damage, injury or loss.

10.2.3 The Contractor shall erect and maintain, as required by existing conditions and performance of the Contract, reasonable safeguards for safety and protection, including posting danger signs and other warnings against hazards, promulgating safety regulations and notifying owners and users of adjacent sites and utilities.

10.2.4 When use or storage of explosives or other hazardous materials or equipment or unusual methods are necessary for execution of the Work, the Contractor shall exercise utmost care and carry on such activities under supervision of properly qualified personnel.

10.2.5 The Contractor shall promptly remedy damage and loss (other than damage or loss insured under property insurance required by the Contract Documents) to property referred to in Clauses 10.2.1.2 and 10.2.1.3 caused in whole or in part by the Contractor, a Subcontractor, a Sub-subcontractor, or anyone directly or indirectly employed by any of them, or by anyone for whose acts they may be liable and for which the Contractor is responsible under Clauses 10.2.1.2 and 10.2.1.3, except damage or loss attributable to acts or omissions of the Owner or Architect or anyone directly or indirectly employed by either of them, or by anyone for whose acts either of them may be liable, and not attributable to the fault or negligence of the Contractor. The foregoing obligations of the Contractor are in addition to the Contractor's obligations under Paragraph 3.18.

10.2.6 The Contractor shall designate a responsible member of the Contractor's organization at the site whose duty shall be the prevention of accidents. This person shall be the Contractor's superintendent unless otherwise designated by the Contractor in writing to the Owner and Architect.

10.2.7 The Contractor shall not load or permit any part of the construction or site to be loaded so as to endanger its safety.

10.3 EMERGENCIES

10.3.1 In an emergency affecting safety of persons or property, the Contractor shall act, at the Contractor's discretion, to prevent threatened damage, injury or loss. Additional compensation or extension of time claimed by the Contractor on account of an emergency shall be determined as provided in Paragraph 4.3 and Article 7.

ARTICLE 11

INSURANCE AND BONDS

11.1 CONTRACTOR'S LIABILITY INSURANCE

11.1.1 The Contractor shall purchase from and maintain in a company or companies lawfully authorized to do business in the jurisdiction in which the Project is located such insurance as will protect the Contractor from claims set forth below which may arise out of or result from the Contractor's operations under the Contract and for which the Contractor may be legally liable, whether such operations be by the Contractor or by a Subcontractor or by anyone directly or indirectly employed by any of them, or by anyone for whose acts any of them may be liable:

  .1 claims under workers' or workmen's compensation, disability benefit and other similar employee benefit acts which are applicable to the Work to be performed;

FIGURE 11–1 (cont'd)

.2 claims for damages because of bodily injury, occupational sickness or disease, or death of the Contractor's employees;

.3 claims for damages because of bodily injury, sickness or disease, or death of any person other than the Contractor's employees;

.4 claims for damages insured by usual personal injury liability coverage which are sustained (1) by a person as a result of an offense directly or indirectly related to employment of such person by the Contractor, or (2) by another person;

.5 claims for damages, other than to the Work itself, because of injury to or destruction of tangible property, including loss of use resulting therefrom;

.6 claims for damages because of bodily injury, death of a person or property damage arising out of ownership, maintenance or use of a motor vehicle; and

.7 claims involving contractual liability insurance applicable to the Contractor's obligations under Paragraph 3.18.

11.1.2 The insurance required by Subparagraph 11.1.1 shall be written for not less than limits of liability specified in the Contract Documents or required by law, whichever coverage is greater. Coverages, whether written on an occurrence or claims-made basis, shall be maintained without interruption from date of commencement of the Work until date of final payment and termination of any coverage required to be maintained after final payment.

11.1.3 Certificates of Insurance acceptable to the Owner shall be filed with the Owner prior to commencement of the Work. These Certificates and the insurance policies required by this Paragraph 11.1 shall contain a provision that coverages afforded under the policies will not be cancelled or allowed to expire until at least 30 days' prior written notice has been given to the Owner. If any of the foregoing insurance coverages are required to remain in force after final payment and are reasonably available, an additional certificate evidencing continuation of such coverage shall be submitted with the final Application for Payment as required by Subparagraph 9.10.2. Information concerning reduction of coverage shall be furnished by the Contractor with reasonable promptness in accordance with the Contractor's information and belief.

11.2 OWNER'S LIABILITY INSURANCE

11.2.1 The Owner shall be responsible for purchasing and maintaining the Owner's usual liability insurance. Optionally, the Owner may purchase and maintain other insurance for self-protection against claims which may arise from operations under the Contract. The Contractor shall not be responsible for purchasing and maintaining this optional Owner's liability insurance unless specifically required by the Contract Documents.

11.3 PROPERTY INSURANCE

11.3.1 Unless otherwise provided, the Owner shall purchase and maintain, in a company or companies lawfully authorized to do business in the jurisdiction in which the Project is located, property insurance in the amount of the initial Contract Sum as well as subsequent modifications thereto for the entire Work at the site on a replacement cost basis without voluntary deductibles. Such property insurance shall be maintained, unless otherwise provided in the Contract Documents or otherwise agreed in writing by all persons and entities who are beneficiaries of such insurance, until final payment has been made as provided in Paragraph 9.10 or until no person or entity

other than the Owner has an insurable interest in the property required by this Paragraph 11.3 to be covered, whichever is earlier. This insurance shall include interests of the Owner, the Contractor, Subcontractors and Sub-subcontractors in the Work.

11.3.1.1 Property insurance shall be on an all-risk policy form and shall insure against the perils of fire and extended coverage and physical loss or damage including, without duplication of coverage, theft, vandalism, malicious mischief, collapse, falsework, temporary buildings and debris removal including demolition occasioned by enforcement of any applicable legal requirements, and shall cover reasonable compensation for Architect's services and expenses required as a result of such insured loss. Coverage for other perils shall not be required unless otherwise provided in the Contract Documents.

11.3.1.2 If the Owner does not intend to purchase such property insurance required by the Contract and with all of the coverages in the amount described above, the Owner shall so inform the Contractor in writing prior to commencement of the Work. The Contractor may then effect insurance which will protect the interests of the Contractor, Subcontractors and Sub-subcontractors in the Work, and by appropriate Change Order the cost thereof shall be charged to the Owner. If the Contractor is damaged by the failure or neglect of the Owner to purchase or maintain insurance as described above, without so notifying the Contractor, then the Owner shall bear all reasonable costs properly attributable thereto.

11.3.1.3 If the property insurance requires minimum deductibles and such deductibles are identified in the Contract Documents, the Contractor shall pay costs not covered because of such deductibles. If the Owner or insurer increases the required minimum deductibles above the amounts so identified or if the Owner elects to purchase this insurance with voluntary deductible amounts, the Owner shall be responsible for payment of the additional costs not covered because of such increased or voluntary deductibles. If deductibles are not identified in the Contract Documents, the Owner shall pay costs not covered because of deductibles.

11.3.1.4 Unless otherwise provided in the Contract Documents, this property insurance shall cover portions of the Work stored off the site after written approval of the Owner at the value established in the approval, and also portions of the Work in transit.

11.3.2 Boiler and Machinery Insurance. The Owner shall purchase and maintain boiler and machinery insurance required by the Contract Documents or by law, which shall specifically cover such insured objects during installation and until final acceptance by the Owner; this insurance shall include interests of the Owner, Contractor, Subcontractors and Sub-subcontractors in the Work, and the Owner and Contractor shall be named insureds.

11.3.3 Loss of Use Insurance. The Owner, at the Owner's option, may purchase and maintain such insurance as will insure the Owner against loss of use of the Owner's property due to fire or other hazards, however caused. The Owner waives all rights of action against the Contractor for loss of use of the Owner's property, including consequential losses due to fire or other hazards however caused.

11.3.4 If the Contractor requests in writing that insurance for risks other than those described herein or for other special hazards be included in the property insurance policy, the Owner shall, if possible, include such insurance, and the cost thereof shall be charged to the Contractor by appropriate Change Order.

AIA DOCUMENT A201 • GENERAL CONDITIONS OF THE CONTRACT FOR CONSTRUCTION • FOURTEENTH EDITION
AIA® • ©1987 THE AMERICAN INSTITUTE OF ARCHITECTS, 1735 NEW YORK AVENUE, N.W., WASHINGTON, D.C. 20006

FIGURE 11–1 (cont'd)

11.3.5 If during the Project construction period the Owner insures properties, real or personal or both, adjoining or adjacent to the site by property insurance under policies separate from those insuring the Project, or if after final payment property insurance is to be provided on the completed Project through a policy or policies other than those insuring the Project during the construction period, the Owner shall waive all rights in accordance with the terms of Subparagraph 11.3.7 for damages caused by fire or other perils covered by this separate property insurance. All separate policies shall provide this waiver of subrogation by endorsement or otherwise.

11.3.6 Before an exposure to loss may occur, the Owner shall file with the Contractor a copy of each policy that includes insurance coverages required by this Paragraph 11.3. Each policy shall contain all generally applicable conditions, definitions, exclusions and endorsements related to this Project. Each policy shall contain a provision that the policy will not be cancelled or allowed to expire until at least 30 days' prior written notice has been given to the Contractor.

11.3.7 Waivers of Subrogation. The Owner and Contractor waive all rights against (1) each other and any of their subcontractors, sub-subcontractors, agents and employees, each of the other, and (2) the Architect, Architect's consultants, separate contractors described in Article 6, if any, and any of their subcontractors, sub-subcontractors, agents and employees, for damages caused by fire or other perils to the extent covered by property insurance obtained pursuant to this Paragraph 11.3 or other property insurance applicable to the Work, except such rights as they have to proceeds of such insurance held by the Owner as fiduciary. The Owner or Contractor, as appropriate, shall require of the Architect, Architect's consultants, separate contractors described in Article 6, if any, and the subcontractors, sub-subcontractors, agents and employees of any of them, by appropriate agreements, written where legally required for validity, similar waivers each in favor of other parties enumerated herein. The policies shall provide such waivers of subrogation by endorsement or otherwise. A waiver of subrogation shall be effective as to a person or entity even though that person or entity would otherwise have a duty of indemnification, contractual or otherwise, did not pay the insurance premium directly or indirectly, and whether or not the person or entity had an insurable interest in the property damaged.

11.3.8 A loss insured under Owner's property insurance shall be adjusted by the Owner as fiduciary and made payable to the Owner as fiduciary for the insureds, as their interests may appear, subject to requirements of any applicable mortgagee clause and of Subparagraph 11.3.10. The Contractor shall pay Subcontractors their just shares of insurance proceeds received by the Contractor, and by appropriate agreements, written where legally required for validity, shall require Subcontractors to make payments to their Sub-subcontractors in similar manner.

11.3.9 If required in writing by a party in interest, the Owner as fiduciary shall, upon occurrence of an insured loss, give bond for proper performance of the Owner's duties. The cost of required bonds shall be charged against proceeds received as fiduciary. The Owner shall deposit in a separate account proceeds so received, which the Owner shall distribute in accordance with such agreement as the parties in interest may reach, or in accordance with an arbitration award in which case the procedure shall be as provided in Paragraph 4.5. If after such loss no other special agreement is made, replacement of damaged property shall be covered by appropriate Change Order.

11.3.10 The Owner as fiduciary shall have power to adjust and settle a loss with insurers unless one of the parties in interest shall object in writing within five days after occurrence of loss to the Owner's exercise of this power; if such objection be made, arbitrators shall be chosen as provided in Paragraph 4.5. The Owner as fiduciary shall, in that case, make settlement with insurers in accordance with directions of such arbitrators. If distribution of insurance proceeds by arbitration is required, the arbitrators will direct such distribution.

11.3.11 Partial occupancy or use in accordance with Paragraph 9.9 shall not commence until the insurance company or companies providing property insurance have consented to such partial occupancy or use by endorsement or otherwise. The Owner and the Contractor shall take reasonable steps to obtain consent of the insurance company or companies and shall, without mutual written consent, take no action with respect to partial occupancy or use that would cause cancellation, lapse or reduction of insurance.

11.4 PERFORMANCE BOND AND PAYMENT BOND

11.4.1 The Owner shall have the right to require the Contractor to furnish bonds covering faithful performance of the Contract and payment of obligations arising thereunder as stipulated in bidding requirements or specifically required in the Contract Documents on the date of execution of the Contract.

11.4.2 Upon the request of any person or entity appearing to be a potential beneficiary of bonds covering payment of obligations arising under the Contract, the Contractor shall promptly furnish a copy of the bonds or shall permit a copy to be made.

ARTICLE 12

UNCOVERING AND CORRECTION OF WORK

12.1 UNCOVERING OF WORK

12.1.1 If a portion of the Work is covered contrary to the Architect's request or to requirements specifically expressed in the Contract Documents, it must, if required in writing by the Architect, be uncovered for the Architect's observation and be replaced at the Contractor's expense without change in the Contract Time.

12.1.2 If a portion of the Work has been covered which the Architect has not specifically requested to observe prior to its being covered, the Architect may request to see such Work and it shall be uncovered by the Contractor. If such Work is in accordance with the Contract Documents, costs of uncovering and replacement shall, by appropriate Change Order, be charged to the Owner. If such Work is not in accordance with the Contract Documents, the Contractor shall pay such costs unless the condition was caused by the Owner or a separate contractor in which event the Owner shall be responsible for payment of such costs.

12.2 CORRECTION OF WORK

12.2.1 The Contractor shall promptly correct Work rejected by the Architect or failing to conform to the requirements of the Contract Documents, whether observed before or after Substantial Completion and whether or not fabricated, installed or completed. The Contractor shall bear costs of correcting such rejected Work, including additional testing and inspections and compensation for the Architect's services and expenses made necessary thereby.

12.2.2 If, within one year after the date of Substantial Completion of the Work or designated portion thereof, or after the date

FIGURE 11-1   (cont'd)

for commencement of warranties established under Sub-paragraph 9.9.1, or by terms of an applicable special warranty required by the Contract Documents, any of the Work is found to be not in accordance with the requirements of the Contract Documents, the Contractor shall correct it promptly after receipt of written notice from the Owner to do so unless the Owner has previously given the Contractor a written acceptance of such condition. This period of one year shall be extended with respect to portions of Work first performed after Substantial Completion by the period of time between Substantial Completion and the actual performance of the Work. This obligation under this Subparagraph 12.2.2 shall survive acceptance of the Work under the Contract and termination of the Contract. The Owner shall give such notice promptly after discovery of the condition.

12.2.3 The Contractor shall remove from the site portions of the Work which are not in accordance with the requirements of the Contract Documents and are neither corrected by the Contractor nor accepted by the Owner.

12.2.4 If the Contractor fails to correct nonconforming Work within a reasonable time, the Owner may correct it in accordance with Paragraph 2.4. If the Contractor does not proceed with correction of such nonconforming Work within a reasonable time fixed by written notice from the Architect, the Owner may remove it and store the salvable materials or equipment at the Contractor's expense. If the Contractor does not pay costs of such removal and storage within ten days after written notice, the Owner may upon ten additional days' written notice sell such materials and equipment at auction or at private sale and shall account for the proceeds thereof, after deducting costs and damages that should have been borne by the Contractor, including compensation for the Architect's services and expenses made necessary thereby. If such proceeds of sale do not cover costs which the Contractor should have borne, the Contract Sum shall be reduced by the deficiency. If payments then or thereafter due the Contractor are not sufficient to cover such amount, the Contractor shall pay the difference to the Owner.

12.2.5 The Contractor shall bear the cost of correcting destroyed or damaged construction, whether completed or partially completed, of the Owner or separate contractors caused by the Contractor's correction or removal of Work which is not in accordance with the requirements of the Contract Documents.

12.2.6 Nothing contained in this Paragraph 12.2 shall be construed to establish a period of limitation with respect to other obligations which the Contractor might have under the Contract Documents. Establishment of the time period of one year as described in Subparagraph 12.2.2 relates only to the specific obligation of the Contractor to correct the Work, and has no relationship to the time within which the obligation to comply with the Contract Documents may be sought to be enforced, nor to the time within which proceedings may be commenced to establish the Contractor's liability with respect to the Contractor's obligations other than specifically to correct the Work.

12.3   ACCEPTANCE OF NONCONFORMING WORK

12.3.1 If the Owner prefers to accept Work which is not in accordance with the requirements of the Contract Documents, the Owner may do so instead of requiring its removal and correction, in which case the Contract Sum will be reduced as appropriate and equitable. Such adjustment shall be effected whether or not final payment has been made.

ARTICLE 13

MISCELLANEOUS PROVISIONS

13.1   GOVERNING LAW

13.1.1 The Contract shall be governed by the law of the place where the Project is located.

13.2   SUCCESSORS AND ASSIGNS

13.2.1 The Owner and Contractor respectively bind themselves, their partners, successors, assigns and legal representatives to the other party hereto and to partners, successors, assigns and legal representatives of such other party in respect to covenants, agreements and obligations contained in the Contract Documents. Neither party to the Contract shall assign the Contract as a whole without written consent of the other. If either party attempts to make such an assignment without such consent, that party shall nevertheless remain legally responsible for all obligations under the Contract.

13.3   WRITTEN NOTICE

13.3.1 Written notice shall be deemed to have been duly served if delivered in person to the individual or a member of the firm or entity or to an officer of the corporation for which it was intended, or if delivered at or sent by registered or certified mail to the last business address known to the party giving notice.

13.4   RIGHTS AND REMEDIES

13.4.1 Duties and obligations imposed by the Contract Documents and rights and remedies available thereunder shall be in addition to and not a limitation of duties, obligations, rights and remedies otherwise imposed or available by law.

13.4.2 No action or failure to act by the Owner, Architect or Contractor shall constitute a waiver of a right or duty afforded them under the Contract, nor shall such action or failure to act constitute approval of or acquiescence in a breach thereunder, except as may be specifically agreed in writing.

13.5   TESTS AND INSPECTIONS

13.5.1 Tests, inspections and approvals of portions of the Work required by the Contract Documents or by laws, ordinances, rules, regulations or orders of public authorities having jurisdiction shall be made at an appropriate time. Unless otherwise provided, the Contractor shall make arrangements for such tests, inspections and approvals with an independent testing laboratory or entity acceptable to the Owner, or with the appropriate public authority, and shall bear all related costs of tests, inspections and approvals. The Contractor shall give the Architect timely notice of when and where tests and inspections are to be made so the Architect may observe such procedures. The Owner shall bear costs of tests, inspections or approvals which do not become requirements until after bids are received or negotiations concluded.

13.5.2 If the Architect, Owner or public authorities having jurisdiction determine that portions of the Work require additional testing, inspection or approval not included under Subparagraph 13.5.1, the Architect will, upon written authorization from the Owner, instruct the Contractor to make arrangements for such additional testing, inspection or approval by an entity acceptable to the Owner, and the Contractor shall give timely notice to the Architect of when and where tests and inspections are to be made so the Architect may observe such procedures.

FIGURE 11–1 *(cont'd)*

The Owner shall bear such costs except as provided in Subparagraph 13.5.3.

13.5.3 If such procedures for testing, inspection or approval under Subparagraphs 13.5.1 and 13.5.2 reveal failure of the portions of the Work to comply with requirements established by the Contract Documents, the Contractor shall bear all costs made necessary by such failure including those of repeated procedures and compensation for the Architect's services and expenses.

13.5.4 Required certificates of testing, inspection or approval shall, unless otherwise required by the Contract Documents, be secured by the Contractor and promptly delivered to the Architect.

13.5.5 If the Architect is to observe tests, inspections or approvals required by the Contract Documents, the Architect will do so promptly and, where practicable, at the normal place of testing.

13.5.6 Tests or inspections conducted pursuant to the Contract Documents shall be made promptly to avoid unreasonable delay in the Work.

13.6   INTEREST

13.6.1 Payments due and unpaid under the Contract Documents shall bear interest from the date payment is due at such rate as the parties may agree upon in writing or, in the absence thereof, at the legal rate prevailing from time to time at the place where the Project is located.

**13.7   COMMENCEMENT OF STATUTORY
            LIMITATION PERIOD**

13.7.1 As between the Owner and Contractor:

   .1 Before Substantial Completion. As to acts or failures to act occurring prior to the relevant date of Substantial Completion, any applicable statute of limitations shall commence to run and any alleged cause of action shall be deemed to have accrued in any and all events not later than such date of Substantial Completion;

   .2 Between Substantial Completion and Final Certificate for Payment. As to acts or failures to act occurring subsequent to the relevant date of Substantial Completion and prior to issuance of the final Certificate for Payment, any applicable statute of limitations shall commence to run and any alleged cause of action shall be deemed to have accrued in any and all events not later than the date of issuance of the final Certificate for Payment; and

   .3 After Final Certificate for Payment. As to acts or failures to act occurring after the relevant date of issuance of the final Certificate for Payment, any applicable statute of limitations shall commence to run and any alleged cause of action shall be deemed to have accrued in any and all events not later than the date of any act or failure to act by the Contractor pursuant to any warranty provided under Paragraph 3.5, the date of any correction of the Work or failure to correct the Work by the Contractor under Paragraph 12.2, or the date of actual commission of any other act or failure to perform any duty or obligation by the Contractor or Owner, whichever occurs last.

ARTICLE 14

TERMINATION OR SUSPENSION OF THE CONTRACT

14.1   TERMINATION BY THE CONTRACTOR

14.1.1 The Contractor may terminate the Contract if the Work is stopped for a period of 30 days through no act or fault of the Contractor or a Subcontractor, Sub-subcontractor or their agents or employees or any other persons performing portions of the Work under contract with the Contractor, for any of the following reasons:

   .1 issuance of an order of a court or other public authority having jurisdiction;

   .2 an act of government, such as a declaration of national emergency, making material unavailable;

   .3 because the Architect has not issued a Certificate for Payment and has not notified the Contractor of the reason for withholding certification as provided in Subparagraph 9.4.1, or because the Owner has not made payment on a Certificate for Payment within the time stated in the Contract Documents;

   .4 if repeated suspensions, delays or interruptions by the Owner as described in Paragraph 14.3 constitute in the aggregate more than 100 percent of the total number of days scheduled for completion, or 120 days in any 365-day period, whichever is less; or

   .5 the Owner has failed to furnish to the Contractor promptly, upon the Contractor's request, reasonable evidence as required by Subparagraph 2.2.1.

14.1.2 If one of the above reasons exists, the Contractor may, upon seven additional days' written notice to the Owner and Architect, terminate the Contract and recover from the Owner payment for Work executed and for proven loss with respect to materials, equipment, tools, and construction equipment and machinery, including reasonable overhead, profit and damages.

14.1.3 If the Work is stopped for a period of 60 days through no act or fault of the Contractor or a Subcontractor or their agents or employees or any other persons performing portions of the Work under contract with the Contractor because the Owner has persistently failed to fulfill the Owner's obligations under the Contract Documents with respect to matters important to the progress of the Work, the Contractor may, upon seven additional days' written notice to the Owner and the Architect, terminate the Contract and recover from the Owner as provided in Subparagraph 14.1.2.

14.2   TERMINATION BY THE OWNER FOR CAUSE

14.2.1 The Owner may terminate the Contract if the Contractor:

   .1 persistently or repeatedly refuses or fails to supply enough properly skilled workers or proper materials;

   .2 fails to make payment to Subcontractors for materials or labor in accordance with the respective agreements between the Contractor and the Subcontractors;

   .3 persistently disregards laws, ordinances, or rules, regulations or orders of a public authority having jurisdiction; or

   .4 otherwise is guilty of substantial breach of a provision of the Contract Documents.

14.2.2 When any of the above reasons exist, the Owner, upon certification by the Architect that sufficient cause exists to jus-

FIGURE 11–1 (cont'd)

tify such action, may without prejudice to any other rights or remedies of the Owner and after giving the Contractor and the Contractor's surety, if any, seven days' written notice, terminate employment of the Contractor and may, subject to any prior rights of the surety:

.1 take possession of the site and of all materials, equipment, tools, and construction equipment and machinery thereon owned by the Contractor;

.2 accept assignment of subcontracts pursuant to Paragraph 5.4; and

.3 finish the Work by whatever reasonable method the Owner may deem expedient.

14.2.3 When the Owner terminates the Contract for one of the reasons stated in Subparagraph 14.2.1, the Contractor shall not be entitled to receive further payment until the Work is finished.

14.2.4 If the unpaid balance of the Contract Sum exceeds costs of finishing the Work, including compensation for the Architect's services and expenses made necessary thereby, such excess shall be paid to the Contractor. If such costs exceed the unpaid balance, the Contractor shall pay the difference to the Owner. The amount to be paid to the Contractor or Owner, as the case may be, shall be certified by the Architect, upon application, and this obligation for payment shall survive termination of the Contract.

14.3 SUSPENSION BY THE OWNER FOR CONVENIENCE

14.3.1 The Owner may, without cause, order the Contractor in writing to suspend, delay or interrupt the Work in whole or in part for such period of time as the Owner may determine.

14.3.2 An adjustment shall be made for increases in the cost of performance of the Contract, including profit on the increased cost of performance, caused by suspension, delay or interruption. No adjustment shall be made to the extent:

.1 that performance is, was or would have been so suspended, delayed or interrupted by another cause for which the Contractor is responsible; or

.2 that an equitable adjustment is made or denied under another provision of this Contract.

14.3.3 Adjustments made in the cost of performance may have a mutually agreed fixed or percentage fee.

FIGURE 11–2

Concrete, Forms, and Reinforcement

1. GENERAL NOTES:

   The work required under this section consists of all labor, equipment, materials necessary to furnish and install all concrete work and other related items necessary to complete the project, unless specifically excluded.

2. MATERIALS:

   Portland Cement: ASTM C 150, Type I.

   Fine Aggregate: ASTM C 33, natural sand.

   Coarse Aggregate: ASTM C 33, gravel or crushed stone. Size: ACI 613.

   Water: Drinkable quality.

   Reinforcing Bars: ASTM Specification A-615 grade 40, domestic manufacture.

   Reinforcing Mesh: ASTM Specification A-615 grade 40, domestic manufacture.

   Curing Compound: ASTM C 309.

   Porous Fill: Gravel or crushed stone evenly graded from $\frac{3}{4}$ inch to $1\frac{1}{2}$ inches. Top portion of fill from $\frac{1}{4}$ inch to $\frac{3}{4}$ inch.

   Ready Mixed Concrete: ASTM C 94.

   Forms: Clean, straight lumber or moisture resistant plywood. Use hardboard as form liner for required smooth finish on exposed work.

3. FORMS:

   Construct forms of clean, straight lumber or plywood, tight to prevent leakage of water and fine materials.

   Brace to prevent dislocation or distortion during and after concrete pouring.

   Earth sides may be used for forming footings providing that conditions are such that accurate size and shape may be obtained.

   Where form oil is used, remove excess before pouring concrete.

   Use adjustable form ties with working strength of not less than 3000 psi. Metal not permitted closer than $1\frac{1}{2}$ inches to finished surfaces. Do not use ties or spreaders that will leave hole larger than $\frac{7}{8}$ inch in exposed surfaces. Wire ties not permitted.

   Meet recommendations of "Recommended Practice for Concrete Formwork," ACI 347.

   Forms, completely assembled and erected, shall be approved before concrete pour is started.

4. REINFORCING:

   Meet requirements of ACI and CRSI for fabricating and placing reinforcing.

   Place, support, and tie reinforcing for a minimum of one day's pour, or for a fill pour between joints before concrete is ordered.

   Reinforcing steel and mesh in place, shall be approved before placing of concrete is started.

5. STRENGTH AND PROPORTIONS:

   Proportion materials to produce concrete that will have a minimum compressive strength, at 28 days, as indicated for various uses. Mini-

FIGURE 11-2 (cont'd)

mum strength for any concrete shall be 3000 psi. Exposed concrete for exterior wall, steps, etc. to be 4000 psi, air entrained.

Concrete shall contain not less than 5 sacks of cement per cubic yard.

Quantity of mixing water shall not exceed $7\frac{1}{2}$ gallons per sack of cement, including the free water contained in the aggregate.

Proportion for minimum slump of 3 inches and maximum slump of 5 inches.

6. MIXING CONCRETE:

General: Except as otherwise specified, concrete shall be ready-mixed or job-mixed at the Contractor's option, and in accordance with requirements of The American Concrete Institute Building Code 318-56, Chapter 4.

7. PLACING:

Surfaces to receive concrete shall be clean, properly prepared, and approved before concrete pour is started.

Reinforcing, sleeves, anchors, and other inserts shall be installed, secured, and approved before starting to place concrete.

Convey concrete to point of use promptly to prevent separation of ingredients or loss of water.

Use handling equipment and methods to insure a continuous flow from mixer to place of deposit. Keep equipment clean and free from partly hardened concrete.

Place concrete near its final position and avoid rehandling.

Spade, tamp, or vibrate freshly placed concrete to compact thoroughly and eliminate voids.

Wood forms shall be wetted thoroughly or oiled before concrete is poured. Earth banks or ground surfaces shall be wetted immediately before pouring concrete.

Basement floor slabs shall be not less than 4 inches thick.

Concrete entrance stairways are to be of the solid slab type resting on 6 inches of compacted gravel fill. Bottom of stairway foundation to be at or below frost line. Sweep all surfaces of exterior concrete intended for a walking surface.

8. VIBRATION:

Concrete shall be placed with the aid of mechanical vibrating equipment or hand spading. Vibration shall be applied directly to the concrete unless otherwise approved by the Owner. The intensity of vibration shall be sufficient to cause flow or settlement of the concrete into place. To secure even and dense surfaces free from aggregate pockets or honeycomb, vibration shall be supplemented by hand spading in the corners and angles of forms and along form surfaces while the concrete is plastic under the vivratory action. Caution must be exercised when using vibrators and hand spades to prevent any injury to the inside face of the forms or any movement of the reinforcement.

9. PROTECTION:

Provide for heating and protecting concrete poured in cold weather. Use of frozen or ice-covered materials not permitted.

Meet recommendations of "Recommended Practice for Winter Concreting," ACI 604.

FIGURE 11–2 *(cont'd)*

Reduce concrete temperature and prevent rapid evaporation of water in hot weather.

Meet recommendations of "Recommended Practice for Hot Weather Concreting," ACI 605.

10. CURING (exterior concrete only):

Start curing as soon as free water has left surface of concrete. Cure for a minimum of 7 days.

Cure with one of methods listed;

Moist Curing: Cover with burlap, fabric, and sand and keep continuously moist for curing period. Keep forms wet while curing. Continue curing when forms are removed.

Waterproofing Materials: Cover with waterproof paper or .004 inch polyethylene lapped, sealed, and weighted. Maintain unbroken surface during curing period.

Liquid Compound: Apply compound according to manufacturer's recommendations. Permit no traffic over compound during curing period.

11. REMOVAL OF FORMS:

Forms shall be removed in accordance with requirements of the ACI Building Code Requirements for Reinforced Concrete No. 318-63, without damage to concrete and in manner to insure complete safety of the structure. Leave shoring in place until concrete member will safely support its own weight plus any live loads that may be placed upon it.

12. CUTTING AND PATCHING:

No cutting of concrete without specific prior approval.

Cutting, when approved, shall be done by experienced workmen and shall be done to avoid damage to adjacent work.

Remove defective work to a minimum depth of one inch with slightly undercut sides. Wet surface to be patched at least 6 inches beyond edge of patch.

Brush thin grout, of equal parts cement and sand, into area to be patched.

Patch with mortar of same mix as original concrete but without coarse aggregate.

Compact patch into place to exclude voids. Leave patch slightly higher than adjacent surface. After initial set of patch, finish to match adjacent similar surface.

Use pressure gun or device to force grout into holes that pass through wall.

13. POROUS FILL UNDER SLAB:

Place thoroughly compacted gravel or crushed stone, thickness as indicated, over properly prepared sub-grade.

Place larger sizes of fill near bottom, grading to fine at top. Top of fill shall be free from material that would perforate membrane. Repair torn places and holes.

14. JOINTS:

Built-in embedded portions of expansion joints. Maintain indicated clearances in intersections of concrete with other materials, or with perpendicular surfaces.

Mark exterior concrete slabs as indicated or longitudinally not further apart than width of surface. Use marking tool to produce joint $\frac{3}{4}$ inch deep or $\frac{1}{4}$ depth of slab.

15. FINISHES:

Rubbed Finish

Build forms of plywood, using as large pieces as is practical.

Remove projections and fins. Grout and repair damaged places and honeycomb. Remove or repair form marks.

Rub with cement bricks or abrasive blocks to leave surfaces uniform in texture, smooth, and clean.

Rough Finish

Rough concrete finish shall be used for all other vertical concrete for which no other finish is indicated or specified. Concrete having a rough finish shall have honeycombing and minor defects patched.

Monolithic Finish

A standard monolithic finish shall be provided for all cement floors.

Force coarse aggregate away from surface by tamping or rolling. Screed level, or to a plane within $\frac{1}{4}$ inch in 10 feet.

Float surface carefully to avoid disturbing plastic concrete.

When concrete has hardened sufficiently, finish with a steel trowel to a smooth and even surface. Do not sprinkle with dry cement, sand or a mixture.

16. VERIFICATION OF CONCRETE STRENGTHS:

The Contractor shall keep in his file all delivery slips or other written document from the concrete mixing plant indicating the design strength of concrete delivered to each building site. These documents shall be given to the architect.

FIGURE 11–2 *(cont'd)*

QUESTIONS

11–1. Define *specifications.* _____

_____

11–2. A complete set of plans does not require specifications.
True or False

11–3. Specifications control the quality of workmanship.
True or False

11–4. *CSI* means:
   (a) Construction Services Incorporated
   (b) Contractor's steady employment
   (c) Custom Services Industry
   (d) All of the above
   (e) None of the above

11–5. How many divisions are there in the CSI specifications format?

_____

11-6. Name two CSI main divisions:
       1. _____
       2. _____

11-7. Only quality control of building material will be found in the specifi-
       cations.
       True or False

11-8. In case of a conflict between plans and specifications, which take pre-
       cedent? _____
       _____

11-9. Where does the information come from in writing specifications? __
       _____

11-10. There are both short-form and long-form specifications.
       True or False

12

Models

Introduction

Not all prospective homeowners can read a set of plans. A perspective drawing of the building will help the owner see what the building will look like, but a model is a three-dimensional scaled-down version of the actual building.

Models take many forms, from the entire outside surfaces of a building to room and furniture models of different parts of the building. Models also help test the building to be sure that the plans are buildable. The details of model building are left to the model builder.

There are many variations of models, from small solid-wood model to various life-like component-parts models. All models should be built to scale; the scale selected will depend on the size of the building. Scales vary from $\frac{1}{32}$ in. to $1'\text{-}0''$. The model scale is generally selected based on how much detail will be shown. The more detail, the more realistic the model.

Modeling Materials

Models are built from a variety of materials, from Styrofoam to balsa wood to cardboard to illustration board to clay. The material used depends mostly on the type of model to be built. If only a framework model is being built, balsa wood would be the likely choise, to show clearly the studs, joists, and rafters (Fig. 12–1). The members are held together with glue. An exterior model with sites and landscaping may be built of flat sheets of balsa wood with exterior siding imprinted on the sheets.

FIGURE 12–1   Frame/wood model (courtesy Edward J. Muller,
Architectural Drawing and Light Construction, *3/E © 1985,*
Prentice-Hall, Inc., Englewood Cliffs, N.J. Fig. 16–10 on page 457.
Reprinted with permission.).

Site models with varying contours are built up from several layers of
cardboard, and if a smooth appearance is desired, a thin coat of plaster of paris
is applied over the varying grade contours (Fig. 12–2, page 308). Scaled landscaping details can be purchased: trees, shrubs, grass, and so on. Patience and
attention to detail are the keys to success in building models.

Although ingenuity plays a great part in model making, a few basic tools
are often required:

1. Knife (razor)
2. Scale
3. Tweezers
4. Scissors
5. Small handsaw
6. Small hammer
7. Straightedge
8. Paintbrushes
9. Sandpaper
10. Masking tape
11. Pins
12. Thumbtacks

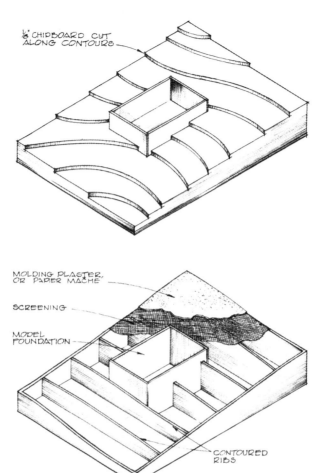

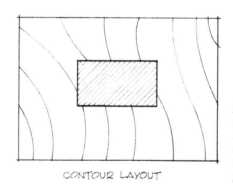

Building Models

No model of a building can be constructed unless a plan or working drawings have been completed. All dimensions and material are taken from the plans, and constant reference to the plans must be made to build the model.

A base for the model is the first step in construction. This can be $\frac{1}{4}$-in. plywood or $\frac{1}{2}$-in. hardboard (Fig. 12–3). The size of the base is determined by

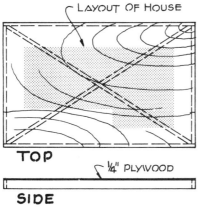

LAYOUT OF HOUSE

TOP

¼" PLYWOOD

SIDE

FIGURE 12–3 Model base (Edward J. Muller, Architectural Drawing and Light Construction, 3/E, © 1985, Prentice-Hall, Inc. Englewood Cliffs, N.J. Fig. 16–9 on p. 456. Reprinted with permission.).

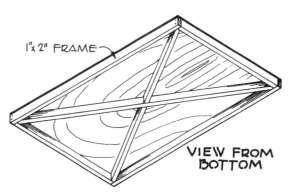

1"x 2" FRAME

VIEW FROM BOTTOM

the size and scale of the model. If the building and land are both to be shown, the base dimensions can be the property dimensions, and a little larger if the road is shown. The importance of the base size is to make it convenient to carry around.

Everything included must be built to scale. Glass can be used for water; a light tinted or painted blue color on the reverse side of the glass will make it look like real water.

The building model is constructed in sequential order much like the actual building—from the foundation up. The foundation can be built from Styrofoam of thickness equal to the foundation thickness. Stryofoam is the color of concrete.

Material for the exterior walls can be purchased, made of a flat sheet of balsa wood imprinted with the building material: stone, brick, shingles, clapboards, vertical siding, or plywood. Doors and windows can be cut out or glued over the siding with plastic-looking glass. A roof also can be purchased, resembling any selection of roof-covering material (Fig. 12–4).

FIGURE 12–4 Completed model (Edward J. Muller, Architectural Drawing and Light Construction, 3/E © 1985, Prentice-Hall, Inc. Englewood Cliffs, N.J. Fig. 16–2 on p. 450. Reprinted with permission.

QUESTIONS

12–1. Name two types of models.
    1. _____
    2. _____

12–2. Because of their size, models are difficult to build to scale.
True or False

12–3. How are landscaping and contour grades built for models? _____
_____

12–4. Name five tools generally required for building models.
    1. _____
    2. _____
    3. _____
    4. _____
    5. _____

12–5. There is no sequence in model building.
True or False

12–6. What part does a model play in architectural service? _____
_____

12–7. The scale of most architectural models is:
    (a) $\frac{1}{4}$ in.
    (b) $\frac{1}{2}$ in.
    (c) $1'' = 10'$
    (d) 2 in.

12–8. What material is used for the base of a model? _____

12–9. Foundations of models can be built of:
    (a) Plywood
    (b) Styrofoam
    (c) Balsa wood
    (d) All of the above
    (e) None of the above

12–10. Only those who specialize in model making can build a model.
True or False

Appendix

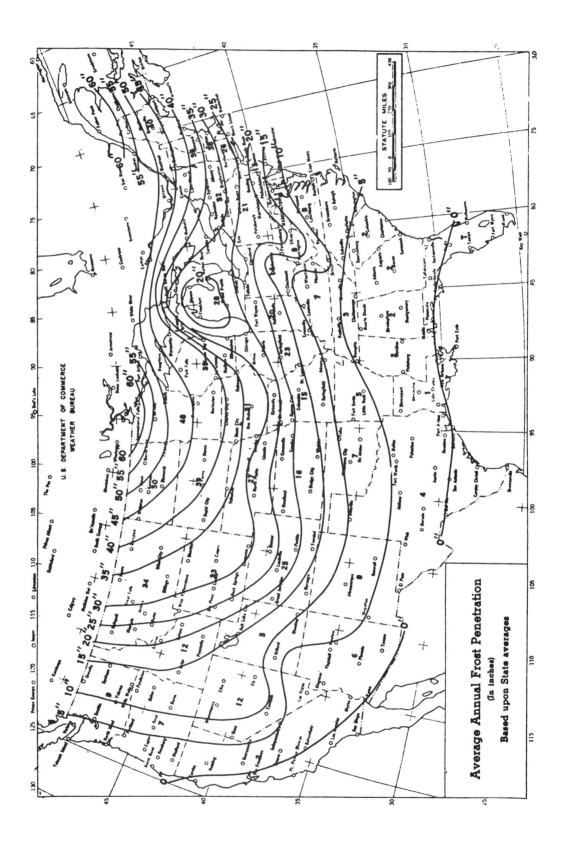

U.S. DEPARTMENT OF COMMERCE
WEATHER BUREAU

Average Annual Frost Penetration
(In inches)
Based upon State averages

STATUTE MILES

BRICK AND BLOCK COURSES

BLOCK NO. OF COURSES	BRICK NO. OF COURSES	HEIGHT OF COURSE	BLOCK NO. OF COURSES	BRICK NO. OF COURSES	HEIGHT OF COURSE
	1	0' – 2 5/8"		37	8' – 2 5/8"
	2	0' – 5 3/8"		38	8' – 5 3/8"
1	3	0' – 8"	13	39	8' – 8"
	4	0' – 10 5/8"		40	8' – 10 5/8"
	5	1' – 1 3/8"		41	9' – 1 3/8"
2	6	1' – 4"	14	42	9' – 4"
	7	1' – 6 5/8"		43	9' – 6 5/8"
	8	1' – 9 3/8"		44	9' – 9 3/8"
3	9	2' – 0"	15	45	10' – 0"
	10	2' – 2 5/8"		46	10' – 2 5/8"
	11	2' – 5 3/8"		47	10' – 5 3/8"
4	12	2' – 8"	16	48	10' – 8"
	13	2' – 10 5/8"		49	10' – 10 3/8"
	14	3' – 1 3/8"		50	11' – 1 3/8"
5	15	3' – 4"	17	51	11' – 4"
	16	3' – 6 5/8"		52	11' – 6 5/8"
	17	3' – 9 3/8"		53	11' – 9 3/8"
6	18	4' – 0"	18	54	12' – 0"
	19	4' – 2 5/8"		55	12' – 2 5/8"
	20	4' – 5 3/8"		56	12' – 5 3/8"
7	21	4' – 8"	19	57	12' – 8"
	22	4' – 10 5/8"		58	12' – 10 5/8"
	23	5' – 1 3/8"		59	13' – 1 3/8"
8	24	5' – 4"	20	60	13' – 4"
	25	5' – 6 5/8"		61	13' – 6 5/8"
	26	5' – 9 3/8"		62	13' – 9 3/8"
9	27	6' – 0"	21	63	14' – 0"
	28	6' – 2 5/8"		64	14' – 2 5/8"
	29	6' – 5 3/8"		65	14' – 5 3/8"
10	30	6' – 8"	22	66	14' – 8"
	31	6' – 10 5/8"		67	14' – 10 5/8"
	32	7' – 1 3/8"		68	15' – 1 3/8"
11	33	7' – 4"	23	69	15' – 4"
	34	7' – 6 5/8"		70	15' – 6 5/8"
	35	7' – 9 3/8"		71	15' – 9 3/8"
12	36	8' – 0"	24	72	16' – 0"

MORTAR JOINT IS 3/8"

BOARD FEET CONTENT

LENGTH IN FEET

Size in Inches	8	10	12	14	16	18	20	22	24
1 x 2	1-1/3	1-2/3	2	2-1/3	2-2/3	3	3-1/3	3-2/3	4
1 x 3	2	2-1/2	3	3-1/2	4	4-1/2	5	5-1/2	6
1 x 4	2-2/3	3-1/3	4	4-2/3	5-1/3	6	6-2/3	7-1/3	8
1 x 5	3-1/3	4-1/6	5	5-5/6	6-2/3	7-1/2	8-1/3	9-1/6	10
1 x 6	4	5	6	7	8	9	10	11	12
1 x 8	5-1/3	6-2/3	8	9-1/3	10-2/3	12	13-1/3	14-2/3	16
1 x 10	6-2/3	8-1/3	10	11-2/3	13-1/3	15	16-2/3	18-1/3	20
1 x 12	8	10	12	14	16	18	20	22	24
1 x 14	9-1/3	11-2/3	14	16-1/3	18-2/3	21	23-1/3	25-2/3	28
1 x 16	10-2/3	13-1/3	16	18-2/3	21-1/3	24	26-2/3	29-1/3	32
5/4 x 4	3-1/3	4-1/6	5	5-5/6	6-2/3	7-1/2	8-1/3	9-1/6	10
5/4 x 6	5	6-1/4	7-1/2	8-3/4	10	11-1/4	12-1/2	13-3/4	15
5/4 x 8	6-2/3	8-1/3	10	11-2/3	13-1/3	15	16-2/3	18-1/3	20
5/4 x 10	8-1/3	10-5/12	12-1/2	14-7/12	16-2/3	18-3/4	20-5/6	22-11/13	25
5/4 x 12	10	12-1/2	15	17-1/2	20	22-1/2	25	27-1/2	30
6/4 x 4	4	5	6	7	8	9	10	11	12
6/4 x 6	6	7-1/2	9	10-1/2	12	13-1/2	15	16-1/2	18
6/4 x 8	8	10	12	14	16	18	20	22	24
6/4 x 10	10	12-1/2	15	17-1/2	20	22-1/2	25	27-1/2	30
6/4 x 12	12	15	18	21	24	27	30	33	36
2 x 4	5-1/3	6-2/3	8	9-1/3	10-2/3	12	13-1/3	14-2/3	16
2 x 6	8	10	12	14	16	18	20	22	24
2 x 8	10-2/3	13-1/3	16	18-2/3	21-1/3	24	26-2/3	29-1/3	32
2 x 10	13-1/3	16-2/3	20	23-1/3	26-2/3	30	33-1/3	36-2/3	40
2 x 12	16	20	24	28	32	36	40	44	48
2 x 14	18-2/3	23-1/3	28	32-2/3	37-1/3	42	46-2/3	51-2/3	56
2 x 16	21-1/3	26-2/3	32	37-1/3	42-2/3	48	53-1/3	58-2/3	64
3 x 4	8	10	12	14	16	18	20	22	24
3 x 6	12	15	18	21	24	27	30	33	36
3 x 8	16	20	24	28	32	36	40	44	48
3 x 10	20	25	30	35	40	45	50	55	60
3 x 12	24	30	36	42	48	54	60	66	72
3 x 14	28	35	42	49	56	63	70	77	84
3 x 16	32	40	48	56	64	72	80	88	96
4 x 4	10-2/3	13-1/3	16	18-2/3	21-1/3	24	26-2/3	29-1/3	32
4 x 6	16	20	24	28	32	36	40	44	48
4 x 8	21-1/3	26-2/3	32	37-1/3	42-2/3	48	53-1/3	58-2/3	64
4 x 10	26-2/3	33-1/3	40	46-2/3	53-1/3	60	66-2/3	73-1/3	80
4 x 12	32	40	48	56	64	72	80	88	96
4 x 14	37-1/3	46-2/3	56	65-1/3	74-2/3	84	93-1/3	102-2/3	112
4 x 16	42-2/3	53-1/3	64	74-2/3	85-1/3	96	106-2/3	117-1/3	128
6 x 6	24	30	36	42	48	54	60	66	72
6 x 8	32	40	48	56	64	72	80	88	96
6 x 10	40	50	60	70	80	90	100	110	120
6 x 12	48	60	72	84	96	108	120	132	144
6 x 14	56	70	84	98	112	126	140	154	168
6 x 16	64	80	96	112	128	144	160	176	192
8 x 8	42-2/3	53-1/3	64	74-2/3	85-1/3	96	106-2/3	117-1/3	128
8 x 10	53-1/3	66-2/3	80	93-1/3	106-2/3	120	133-1/3	146-2/3	160
8 x 12	64	80	96	112	128	144	160	176	192

WEIGHTS OF BUILDING MATERIALS

MATERIAL	WEIGHT
CONCRETE	
With stone reinforced	150 pcf
With stone plain	144 pcf
With cinders, reinforced	110 pcf
Light concrete (Aerocrete)	65 pcf
(Perlite)	45 pcf
(Vermiculite)	40 pcf
METAL AND PLASTER	
Masonry mortar	116 pcf
Gypsum and sand plaster	112 pcf
BRICK AND BLOCK MASONRY (INCLUDING MORTAR)	
4" brick wall	35 psf
8" brick wall	74 psf
8" concrete block wall	100 psf
12" concrete block wall	150 psf
4" brick veneer over 4" concrete block	65 psf
WOOD CONSTRUCTION	
Frame wall, lath and plaster	20 psf
Frame wall, 1/2" gypsum board	12 psf
Floor, 1/2" subfloor + 3/4" finished	6 psf
Floor, 1/2" subfloor and ceramic tile	16 psf
Roof, joist and 1/2" sheathing	3 psf
Roof, 2" plank and beam	5 psf
Roof, built-up	7 psf

MATERIAL	WEIGHT
WOOD CONSTRUCTION (CONTINUED)	
Ceiling, joist and plaster	10 psf
Ceiling, joist and 1/2" gypsum board	7 psf
Ceiling, joist and acoustic tile	5 psf
Wood shingles	3 psf
Spanish tile	15 psf
Copper sheet	2 psf
Tar and gravel	6 psf
STONE	
Sandstone	147 pcf
Slate	175 pcf
Limestone	165 pcf
Granite	175 pcf
Marble	165 pcf
GLASS	
1/4" plate glass	3.28 psf
1/8" double strength	1.63 psf
1/8" insulating glass with air space	3.25 psf
4" block glass	20.00 psf
INSULATION	
Cork board 1" thick	.58 psf
Rigid foam insulation 2" thick	.3 psf
Blanket or bat 2" thick	.1 psf

SAFE LOADS IN LBS. PER SQUARE FOOT ON DIFFERENT TYPES OF SOIL	
MATERIAL	Safe Load Lbs. Sq. Ft.
Soft, wet clay or soft clay and wet sand mixed	2,000
Sand and clay—Firm clay or wet sand	4,000
Dry solid clay or firm dry sand	5,000
Hard clay—Firm coarse sand—Gravel	8,000
Firm coarse sand and gravel mixed	12,000
Hard Pan	20,000

SIZES AND DIMENSIONS FOR REINFORCING BARS

WEIGHT LB. PER FT.	NOMINAL DIAMETER INCHES	SIZE	NUMBER	NOMINAL CROSS SECT. AREA SQ. IN.	NOMINAL PERIMETER
.376	.375	3/8	3	.11	1.178
.668	.500	1/2	4	.20	1.571
1.043	.625	5/8	5	.31	1.963
1.502	.750	3/4	6	.44	2.356
2.044	.875	7/8	7	.60	2.749
2.670	1.000	1	8	.79	3.142
3.400	1.128	1*	9	1.00	3.544
4.303	1.270	1-1/8*	10	1.27	3.990
5.313	1.410	1-1/4*	11	1.56	4.430
7.650	1.693	1-1/2*	14	2.25	5.320
13.600	2.257	2*	18	4.00	7.090

*These sizes rolled in rounds equivalent to square cross section area.

RECOMMENDED STYLES OF WELDED WIRE FABRIC REINFORCEMENT FOR CONCRETE

TYPE OF CONSTRUCTION	RECOMMENDED STYLE	REMARKS
Barbecue Foundation Slab	6x6-8/8 to 4x4-6/6	Use heavier style fabric for heavy, massive fireplaces or barbecue pits.
Basement Floors	6x6-10/10, 6x6-8/8 or 6x6-6/6	For small areas (15-foot maximum side dimension) use 6x6-10/10. As a rule of thumb, the larger the area or the poorer the sub-soil, the heavier the gauge.
Driveways	6x6-6/6	Continuous reinforcement between 25- to 30-foot contraction joints.
Foundation Slabs (Residential only)	6x6-10/10	Use heavier gauge over poorly drained sub-soil, or when maximum dimension is greater than 15 feet.
Garage Floors	6x6-6/6	Position at midpoint of 5- or 6-inch thick slab.
Patios and Terraces	6x6-10/10	Use 6x6-8/8 if sub-soil is poorly drained.
Porch Floor a. 6-inch thick slab up to 6-foot span b. 6-inch thick slab up to 8-foot span	6x6-6/6	Position 1 inch from bottom form to resist tensile stresses.
Sidewalks	6x6-10/10 6x6-8/8	Use heavier gauge over poorly drained sub-soil. Construct 25- to 30-foot slabs as for driveways.
Steps (Free span)	6x6-6/6	Use heavier style if more than five risers. Position fabric 1 inch from bottom form.
Steps (On ground)	6x6-8/8	Use 6x6-6/6 for unstable sub-soil.

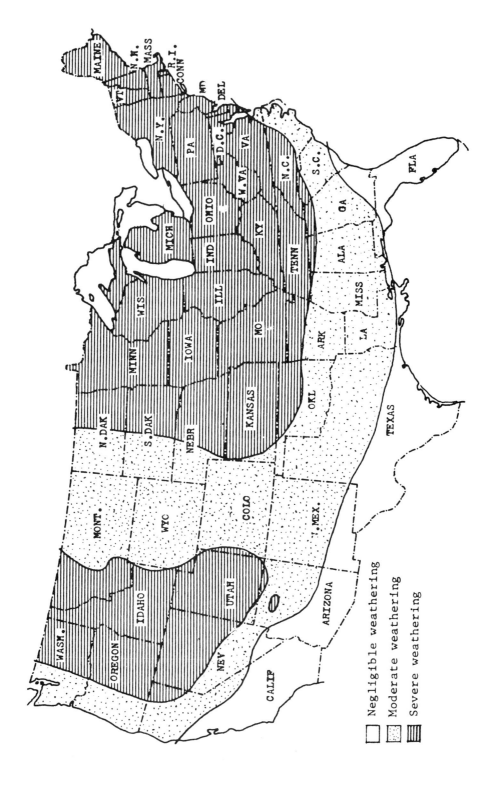

WEATHERING AREAS

☐ Negligible weathering
▨ Moderate weathering
▥ Severe weathering

317

DECIMAL EQUIVALENTS

DECIMAL OF A FOOT						DECIMAL OF AN INCH	
FRACTION	DECIMAL	FRACTION	DECIMAL	FRACTION	DECIMAL	FRACTION	DECIMAL
1/16	0.0052	4-1/16	0.3385	8-1/16	0.6719	1/64	0.015625
1/8	0.0104	4-1/8	0.3438	8-1/8	0.6771	1/32	0.03125
3/16	0.0156	4-3/16	0.3490	8-3/16	0.6823	3/64	0.046875
1/4	0.0208	4-1/4	0.3542	8-1/4	0.6875	1/16	0.0625
5/16	0.0260	4-5/16	0.3594	8-5/16	0.6927	5/64	0.078125
3/8	0.0313	4-3/8	0.3646	8-3/8	0.6979	3/32	0.09375
7/16	0.0365	4-7/16	0.3698	8-7/16	0.7031	7/64	0.109375
1/2	0.0417	4-1/2	0.3750	8-1/2	0.7083	1/8	0.125
9/16	0.0459	4-9/16	0.3802	8-9/16	0.7135	9/64	0.140625
5/8	0.0521	4-5/8	0.3854	8-5/8	0.7188	5/32	0.15625
11/16	0.0573	4-11/16	0.3906	8-11/16	0.7240	11/64	0.171875
3/4	0.0625	4-3/4	0.3958	8-3/4	0.7292	3/16	0.1875
13/16	0.0677	4-13/16	0.4010	8-13/16	0.7344	13/64	0.203125
7/8	0.0729	4-7/8	0.4063	8-7/8	0.7396	7/32	0.21875
15/16	0.0781	4-15/16	0.4115	8-15/16	0.7448	15/64	0.234375
1-	0.0833	5-	0.4167	9-	0.7500	1/4	0.250
1-1/16	0.0885	5-1/16	0.4219	9-1/16	0.7552	17/64	0.265625
1-1/8	0.0938	5-1/8	0.4271	9-1/8	0.7604	9/32	0.28125
1-3/16	0.0990	5-3/16	0.4323	9-3/16	0.7656	19/64	0.296875
1-1/4	0.1042	5-1/4	0.4375	9-1/4	0.7708	5/16	0.3125
1-5/16	0.1094	5-5/16	0.4427	9-5/16	0.7760	21/64	0.328125
1-3/8	0.1146	5-3/8	0.4479	9-3/8	0.7813	11/32	0.34375
1-7/16	0.1198	5-7/16	0.4531	9-7/16	0.7865	23/64	0.359375
1-1/2	0.1250	5-1/2	0.4583	9-1/2	0.7917	3/8	0.375
1-9/16	0.1302	5-9/16	0.4635	9-9/16	0.7969	25/64	0.390625
1-5/8	0.1354	5-5/8	0.4688	9-5/8	0.8021	13/32	0.40625
1-11/16	0.1406	5-11/16	0.4740	9-11/16	0.8073	27/64	0.421875
1-3/4	0.1458	5-3/4	0.4792	9-3/4	0.8125	7/16	0.4375
1-13/16	0.1510	5-13/16	0.4844	9-13/16	0.8177	29/64	0.453125
1-7/8	0.1563	5-7/8	0.4896	9-7/8	0.8229	15/32	0.46875
1-15/16	0.1615	5-15/16	0.4948	9-15/16	0.8281	31/64	0.484375
2-	0.1667	6-	0.5000	10-	0.8333	1/2	0.500
2-1/16	0.1719	6-1/16	0.5052	10-1/16	0.8385	33/64	0.515625
2-1/8	0.1771	6-1/8	0.5104	10-1/8	0.8438	17/32	0.53125
2-3/16	0.1823	6-3/16	0.5156	10-3/16	0.8490	35/64	0.546875
2-1/4	0.1875	6-1/4	0.5208	10-1/4	0.8542	9/16	0.5625
2-5/16	0.1927	6-5/16	0.5260	10-5/16	0.8594	37/64	0.578125
2-3/8	0.1979	6-3/8	0.5313	10-3/8	0.8646	19/32	0.59375
2-7/16	0.2031	6-7/16	0.5365	10-7/16	0.8698	39/64	0.609375
2-1/2	0.2083	6-1/2	0.5417	10-1/2	0.8750	5/8	0.625
2-9/16	0.2135	6-9/16	0.5469	10-9/16	0.8802	41/64	0.640625
2-5/8	0.2188	6-5/8	0.5521	10-5/8	0.8854	21/32	0.65625
2-11/16	0.2240	6-11/16	0.5573	10-11/16	0.8906	43/64	0.671875
2-3/4	0.2292	6-3/4	0.5625	10-3/4	0.8958	11/16	0.6875
2-13/16	0.2344	6-13/16	0.5677	10-13/16	0.9010	45/64	0.703125
2-7/8	0.2396	6-7/8	0.5729	10-7/8	0.9063	23/32	0.71875
2-15/16	0.2448	6-15/16	0.5781	10-15/16	0.9115	47/64	0.734375
3-	0.2500	7-	0.5833	11-	0.9167	3/4	0.750
3-1/16	0.2552	7-1/16	0.5885	11-1/16	0.9219	49/64	0.765625
3-1/8	0.2604	7-1/8	0.5938	11-1/8	0.9271	25/32	0.78125
3-3/16	0.2656	7-3/16	0.5990	11-3/16	0.9323	51/64	0.796875
3-1/4	0.2708	7-1/4	0.6042	11-1/4	0.9375	13/16	0.8125
3-5/16	0.2760	7-5/16	0.6094	11-5/16	0.9427	53/64	0.828125
3-3/8	0.2813	7-3/8	0.6146	11-3/8	0.9479	27/32	0.84375
3-7/16	0.2865	7-7/16	0.6198	11-7/16	0.9531	55/64	0.859375
3-1/2	0.2917	7-1/2	0.6250	11-1/2	0.9583	7/8	0.875
3-9/16	0.2969	7-9/16	0.6302	11-9/16	0.9635	57/64	0.890625
3-5/8	0.3021	7-5/8	0.6354	11-5/8	0.9688	29/32	0.90625
3-11/16	0.3073	7-11/16	0.6406	11-11/16	0.9740	59/64	0.921875
3-3/4	0.3125	7-3/4	0.6458	11-3/4	0.9792	15/16	0.9375
3-13/16	0.3177	7-13/16	0.6510	11-13/16	0.9844	61/64	0.953125
3-7/8	0.3229	7-7/8	0.6563	11-7/8	0.9896	31/32	0.96875
3-15/16	0.3281	7-15/16	0.6615	11-15/16	0.9948	63/64	0.984375
4-	0.3333	8-	0.6667	12-	1.0000	1-	1.000

Abbreviations

Acoustic	ACST
Acoustical Plaster	ACST PL
Addition	ADD
Adhesive	ADH
Aggregate	AGGR
Air Conditioning	AIR COND. OR A.C
Alternate	ALT
Alternating Current	AC
Aluminum	ALUM
American Institute of Architects	A.I.A.
American Institute of Steel Construction	A.I.S.C.
American Society of Heating, Ventilating Engineers	A.S.H.V.E.
American Society of Testing Materials	A.S.T.M.
American Wire Gauge	AWG
Amount	AMT
Ampere	AMP
Anchor Bolt	AB
Angle	L
Apartment	APT
Approval	APP
Approximate	APPROX
Architect	ARCH
Architectural Terra Cotta	ATC
Area	A
Asbestos	ASB
Asphalt	ASPH
Asphalt Tile	AT
Assemble	ASSEM
Assembly	ASSBY
Associate	ASSOC
At	@
Automatic Pressure	ATM PRESS
Automobile	AUTO
Avenue	AVE.
Average	AVG
Balcony	BLCNY
Basement	BSMT
Bathroom	B
Beam	BM
Bedroom	BR
Bench Mark	BM
Between	BET
Bevel	BEV
Blocking	BLKG
Board	BD
Board Feet	BD FT
Board Measure	BM
Book Shelves	BK SH
Bottom	BOT
Boulevard	BLVD
Bracket	BRKT
Brass	BR
British Thermal Unit	BTU
Bronze	BRZ
Broom Closet	BC
Building	BLDG
Building Line	BL
Built In	BLT IN
Bulkhead	BLKHD
Bulletin Board	BB
Buzzer	BZ
By	2"x4" (example)
Cabinet	CAB
Candlepower	CP
Carpenter	CARP
Casing	CSG
Cast Iron	CI
Catch Basin	CB
Caulking	CLKG
Ceiling	CLG
Cellar	CEL
Cement	CEM
Cement Mortar	CEMT' MR
Cement Plastic	CMT' PL
Center to Center	CC or OC or C
Ceramic Tile	CT
Cesspool	CP

Channel	C
Circuit	CIR
Circuit Breaker	CKT' BR
Cleanout	CO
Closet	CLO
Clothes Dryer	CL'D
Coefficient	COEF
Cold Water	CW
Combination	COMB
Composition	COMP
Concrete	CONC
Concrete Block	CB
Concrete Floor	CON FL
Concrete Masonry Unit	CMU
Construction	CONST
Construction Specification Institute	C.S.I.
Contractor	CONTR
Copper	CPR
Counter	CNTR
Countersunk	CSNK
Courses	C
Cover	COV
Cross Section	X SECT
Cubic	CU
Cubic Feet	CU FT
Cubic Feet Minute	CFM
Cubic Inch	CU IN
Cubic Yard	CU YD
Damper	DMPR
Dampproofing	DMPRF
Decibel	DB
Decorative	DEC
Degree Fahrenheit	0° F
Detail	DET
Diagram	DIA
Diameter	DIA. OR Ø
Dimension	DIM
Dining Room	DR
Direct Current	D. C.
Dishwasher	DW
Distance	DIST
Ditto	DO
Divide	DIV
Door	DR
Double Hung Window	DH W
Double Strength Glass Grade A	DSA
Double Strength Glass Grade B	DSB
Dowel	DWL
Down	DN
Downspout	DS
Drain	DR
Drainboard	DB
Drawing	DWG
Dressed and Matched Four Sides	D&M4S
Drinking Fountain	DF
Dryer	D
Drywall	DW
Dry Well	DW
Each	EA
East	E
Edge Grain	EG
Elbow	ELL
Electric	ELEC
Elevator	ELEV
Emergency	EMERGCY
Enclosure	ENCL
Engineer	ENG
Entrance	ENT
Equipment	EQUIP
Estimate	EST
Excavate	EXC
Expansion Joint	EX JT
Extension	EXT
Exterior	EXT
Extra Heavy	XH
Fabricate	FAB
Face to Face	F to F

Facing Tile	FT	Leader	LDR
Fahrenheit	F	Left	L
Family Room	FAM R	Length	LGTH
Federal Housing Administration	FHA	Level	LEV
Feet	FT	Library	LIB
Feet Per Minute	FPM	Light	LT
Feet Per Second	FPS	Light Weight Concrete	LWC
Figure	FIG	Limestone	LS
Finish	FIN	Lineal Feet	LF
Finish Floor	FIN FL	Linen Closet	L CL
Fire Brick	FB	Lining	LNG
Fire Extinguisher	FX	Linoleum	LINO
Fire Hose	FH	Living Room	LR
Fireproof	FP	Long	LG
Fitting	FITG	Louver	LVR
Fixture	FIXT	Lumber	LBR
Flange	FLG	Machine	MACH
Flashing	FL	Manufacturer	MFG
Floor	FL	Marble	MBL
Floor Drain	FD	Mark	MK
Fluorescent	FLUOR	Masonry Opening	MO
Foot Board Measure	FBM	Material	MAT
Footing	FTG	Maximum	MAX
Foundation	FDN	Mechanical	MECH
Frame	FR	Medicine Cabinet	MED C
Fresh Air Intake	FAI	Medium	MED
Front	FR	Metal	MET
Full Size	FS	Millemeter	m
Furred Ceiling	F CLG	Minimum	MIN
Gallon	GAL	Miscellaneous	MISC
Galvanized	GALV	Model	MOD
Gauge	GA	Modular	MOD
Glass Block	GL BL	Moulding	MLDG
Government	GOVT	National	NAT
Grade	GR	National Board of Fire Underwriters	N.B.F.U.
Granite	GR	National Electrical Code	N.E.C.
Grating	GRTG	National Lumber Manufacturers Association	N.L.M.A.
Grease Trap	GT	Nominal	NOM
Gypsum	GYP	North	N
Hall	H	Not In Contract	N.I.C.
Hardware	HDW	Number	NO. OR #
Hardwood	HDWD	Octogan	OCT
Head	HD	Office	OFF
Heater	HTR	On Center	OC
Height	HT	Opening	OPNG
Hexagon	HEX	Opposite	OPP
Hollow Metal	HM	Ornament	ORN
Horizontal	HORIZ	Ounce	OZ
Horse Power	HP	Outside Diameter	OD
Hose Bibb	HB	Overhead	OVHD
Hot Water	HW	Page	PG
Hour	HR	Painted	PTD
House	HSE	Pair	PR
Hundred	C	Panel	PNL
I Beam	I	Parallel	PAR
Inches	" OR IN	Partition	PTN
Information	INFO	Passage	PASS
Inside Diameter	ID	Pedestal	PED
Insulation	INSUL	Penny	d
Interior	INT	Percent	%
Joint	JT	Perforated	PERF
Joist	JST	Perpendicular	PERP
Kalamein	KAL	Piece	PC
Kiln Dried	KD	Plaster	PLAS
Kilowatt	KW	Plate	P
Kitchen	KIT	Plate Glass	P GL
Kitchen Cabinet	KIT CAB	Platform	PLTFM
Kitchen Sink	KIT S	Plumbing	PLMB
Knocked Down	KD	Point	P
Laboratory	LAB	Polish	POL
Ladder	LAD	Polyvinyl Chloride	PVC
Laminated	LAM	Position	POS
Landing	L	Pounds	LB OR #
Latitude	LAT	Poured Concrete	P/C
Laundry	L	Precast	PRCST
Laundry Chute	LC	Prefabricate	PREFAB
Lavatory	LAV	Property	PROP

Push Button	PB	Stock	STK
Quantity	QTY	Stone	ST
Quart	QT	Street	ST
Radiator	RAD	String	STR
Radius	R	Structural	STR
Random length and width	RL&W	Substitute	SUB
Rang	R	Supersede	SUPSD
Receptacle	RECP	Supplement	SUPP
Recessed	REC	Supply	SUP
Rectangle	RECT	Surface	SUR
Redwood	RDWD	Surface 2 Sides	S2S
Reference	REF	Surface 4 sides	S4S
Refrigerator	REFG	Suspended Ceiling	SUS CLG
Register	REG	Switch	SW
Reinforced Concrete	REINF	Symbol	SYM
Required	REQ	System	SYS
Return	RET	Tar & Gravel	T & G
Revision	REV	Technical	TECH
Revolution Per Minute	RPM	Tee	T
Right	R	Telephone	TEL
Right Hand	RH	Television	TV
Riser	R	Temperature	TEMP
Road	RD	Terra-Cotta	TC
Roof	RF	Terrazzo	TER
Roof Drain	RD	Thermostat	THERMO
Roofing	RFG	Thickness	THK
Room	RM	Thousand	M
Rough	RGH	Thread	THD
Round	RD	Tongue and Groove	T & G
Rubber	R	Tread	T
Saddle	S	Typical	TYP
Schedule	SCH	Ultimate	ULT
Screen	SCR	Unfinished	UNFIN
Second	SEC	United States Gauge	USG
Section	SECT	Urinal	UR
Self Closing	SC	Vanity	VAN
Service	SERV	Vent	V
Sewer	SEW	Vertical	VERT
Sheathing	SHTNG	Vestibule	VEST
Sheet Metal	SM	Volts	V
Shelves	SH	Volume	VOL
Shower	SH	Wall Cabinet	W/CAB
Siding	SDG	Wall Vent	WV
Sill Cock	SC	Water	W
Single Strength Grade A Glass	SAS	Water Closet	WC
Single Strength Grade B Glass	SBS	Waterproof	WP
Sink	S	Watts	W
Slop Sink	SS	Weatherstrip	WS
Socket	SOC	Weephole	WH
Soil Pipe	SP	Weight	WT
South	S	West	W
Specifications	SPEC	Wide Flange Beam	WF
Square Feet	SQ FT OR ⊡	Width	WTH
Stairs	ST	Window	WDH
Standard	STD	Wire Glass	W GL
Stand Pipe	STP	With	W/
Station	STA	Without	WO/
Steel	ST	Wood	WD
Steel Plate	SP	Wrought Iron	WI
Stirrup	STIR	Yards	YD

Zinc . . . . Z OR ZN

Index